Activating Business Ministers
© 2025-2nd Printing
Dr. Nova Dean Pack
ISBN: 979-8-218-87585-5
All Photos used by attribution;
courtesy of FreePik

All rights reserved. No part of this publication may be reproduced, distributed, or transmitted in any form or by any means, including photocopying, recording, or other electronic or mechanical methods, without the prior written permission of the publisher, except in the case of brief quotations embodied in critical reviews and certain other noncommercial uses permitted by copyright law.

For permission requests, write to the publisher, addressed "Attention: Permissions" by electronic mail to:
packnovapack@aol.com

Scriptures quotations are from the King James Version (KJV) of the bible unless otherwise stated. Emphasis on certain scripture(s) is authors own.

Activating Business Ministers

TABLE OF CONTENTS

INTRODUCTION

You will notice in reading this book that I am instructing the meaning and application of scriptures and concepts through repetition because when things are repeated continuously, they are remembered. It is similar to a Riding Instructor training someone how to ride and control a horse. It means the rider has to ride the horse over and over again, and the Riding Instructor uses kinesthetic training incrementally watching and correcting each movement the rider makes. Likewise, to learn the Bible is not reading it once or twice, but daily reading of scriptures and putting the biblical principles in action, which cause familiarity of the scriptures that transforms the soul. If you read and speak the scriptures, they are not just memorized; but they become part of your soul's vocabulary, filling your mind with God's biblical thoughts, stabilizing your emotions with godly spiritual feelings, and establishing your heart with a foundation of biblical beliefs.

You learn through continuous repetition by applying scriptural principles to life's challenges that minister God's higher thoughts, ways, truths, and wisdoms, which bring to you, as a Believer, stability and strength (Isaiah 55:8-11). Likewise, Isaiah 33:6 says, "And wisdom and knowledge shall be the stability of thy times, and strength of salvation: the fear of the LORD is his treasure."

Therefore, I will quote repetitiously many of the same scriptures in this book as references; so, those scriptures become part of your thoughts in your mind, feelings in your emotions, and beliefs in your heart which causes your soul to be transformed. Scriptures should pop up like toast at the right time as you encounter life's challenges and opportunity for you to minister God's knowledge, wisdom, and *agape* love of people, which are peaceable, gentle, easy to be intreated, full of mercy, righteous, good spiritual fruit, without partiality, and without hypocrisy. Otherwise, if you entertain the world's fallen knowledge, worldly or demonic wisdom, and hatred of people, these fallen world guidelines to life lead to your poverty, cause you to be self-focused and self-centered, make you accept sin as acceptable ideas, actions, and beliefs, discourage you from being a servant, result in you criticizing, judging, and hurting others, encourage you to offer worldly bad counsel, and lead you to reap destruction because your ideas are from the fallen world and promoted by demons (Galatians 6:7-8; James 3:13-18). God wants the foundation of your thoughts, feelings, and beliefs that are in God's word and Kingdom to be your guiding spiritual principles, morals, inspirations, and motivations.

Before you become involved deeply in the topic of this book, I want to affirm the work of the church Leaders over the last 1900 years or so with our sincere appreciation and edification. The church Leaders faithfully have been preaching repentance and remission of sins for initial salvation, have sent missionaries around the world, have recognized some ministries established outside of the church structure that fed the hungry, brought water to the thirsty, clothed the naked, prayed for the sick, visited those in prison, and have provided ministry for children. A few church leaders have spent energy helping Believers in their congregation with soul spiritual maturation after initial salvation, but most have failed to activate the rank and file Believers into the work of their individualistic ministries.

I wholeheartedly endorse much of the work of historical church leaders, but I do not endorse that they have developed religions and spent enormous amounts of money and time to construct buildings. To a large degree they failed at transforming the souls of Believers and failed to equip Believers for the work of the ministry. Also, they have failed in Christ's calling because they created a spectator Christianity instead of Jesus' pattern of true *Ekklesia* leaders that activate Believers into the work of the ministry for the edification of the body of Christ (Ephesians 4:12). Church leaders historically have failed by and large to activate Believers to take back possession of the earth for the Godhead, who is the true Owner of the earth, world, and the people who dwell within. (Psalm 24:1). Church leaders historically have done a good job of preaching the gospel of initial salvation, but it is a futuristic benefit of eternal life after death (John 3:16; Luke 24:47). Most Church leaders historically have neglected the preaching of the gospel of the kingdom (Matthew 24:14), which is preaching God's Kingdom presence and authority here on earth (Matthew 4:17; 6:10; 6:33; 28:18-20).

Finally, historical church leaders have set up an elitist group of priests, bishops, pastors, teachers, and reverends, as Nicolaitans instead of recognizing all Believers as functioning ministers, including Believer Business Owners and Believer Business Employees as ministers. Church leaders historically have failed to recognize the scholastic teaching and kinesthetic training at the business as a ministry where Believer Business Owners activate their Believer Business Employees into the work of ministry. Believer Business Owners activate their Believer Business Employees in ministry through the daily incremental problem solving at the workplace, scholastically teaching and kinesthetically training them in biblical economics, having a strong work ethic, maintaining a foundation of biblical ethics, becoming true servants of the Lord, following God's long term teleology, giving to others in need as a lifestyle mindset of consistently and proactively contributing to others, not just with money, but also with time, talent, and compassion. Believer Business Owners activate their Believer Business Employees that humility is a mature virtue, that growth comes from submitting to Believer Business Owners, managers, and each other for spiritual growth. Believer Business Owners activate their Believer Business Employees to read Bible daily, praying always with all prayer and supplication in the Spirit, and watching thereunto with all perseverance and supplication for all saints (Ephesians 6:18), seeking first God's kingdom and righteousness (Matthew 6:33), seeking to be holy as God is holy (1 Peter 1:15-16), laying aside all malice, and all guile, and hypocrisies, and envies, and all evil speakings (1 Peter 2:1), letting your conversation and actions be with faith, hope, *agape* love, grace, mercy, and truth with the motive of edification, exhortation, and comfort (1 Corinthians 14: 3; 2 John 1:3).

The work of ministry commanded in Ephesians 4:12 is not gifts, but rather Vocations for Believers. In fact, the Ephesian 4:11 functioning apostles, prophets, evangelists, pastors, and teachers are not Vocations but rather office Gifts, according to Ephesians 4:8. The spiritual Vocations that all Believers are called as the work of ministry (Ephesians 4:12) are as kings, priests (Revelation 1:6), lords (1 Timothy 6:15), ambassadors (2 Corinthians 5:20), and soldiers (2 Timothy 2:3-4). All Believers have the same Vocations, but they have different Gifts to be used in the furtherance of the work of their ministries. (1 Corinthians Chap. 12). Romans 12:6 says, "Having then gifts differing according to the grace that is given to us. . . . "

Historically, like many others, I personally had practiced being an Evangelical, so over the years I purposefully have led hundreds of unsaved people through the heartfelt confession of repentance, faith, and professing Jesus Christ as their Lord and Savior. As an Evangelical, I discovered that most things Evangelicals did were right, but they were lacking in other areas. Evangelicals were lacking important things that are the premise of this book. To their credit, Evangelicals emphasize a personal relationship with Jesus Christ, receiving a born-again spirit, where individuals acknowledge their need for salvation and accept Jesus as their Lord and Savior. Yet, initial salvation is just the beginning of every Believer's spiritual journey in God's Kingdom for the transformation of his or her soul and upon the Lord's return receiving a resurrected body. Evangelicals have a strong emphasis on evangelism that leads to initial salvation by sharing the "good news" of Jesus Christ with others, with the goal of leading unbelievers by accepting God's grace and with their faith receiving salvation, but not by works alone (Ephesians 2:8-9). Evangelicals correctly believe the Bible is the authoritative and inerrant word of God, believing it to be the foundation for their faith. Evangelicals believe that Jesus is the way, truth, and life and the only way to the Father (John 14:6). They believe that reading and studying the Bible daily is the primary way of living with God's *agape* love, grace, and God's holiness, with their faith.

To their discredit, some Evangelical Leaders do not believe that apostles or prophets are gifts that exist today because the church Leaders have canonized the word of God. While they believe that the church consists of the members of the body of Christ, they emphasize the church building as the center where they meet, where decisions are made, where most of the offerings are used to maintain, and where ministry work is coordinated from the top down. Also, to their discredit, Evangelicals rarely preach the gospel of God's Kingdom, and they do not believe that every individual Believer is a minister to do the work of the ministry, except witnessing to unbelievers and bringing them to the church building. Evangelicals are quite diverse, including the Reformed, Holiness, Baptist, Pentecostal, Charismatic, and others. Some Evangelicals do not believe that a business is a place of ministry and some do not believe that Believer Business Owners and Believer Business Employees are ministers at the workplace. Most Evangelicals believe that the seat of government for a ministry is a warehouse auditorium lecture hall paradigm structure where teaching the word of God and sermons that lead unbelievers to accept Jesus as Savior is the duty of ordained ministers while the church building is the venue of ministries.

To their credit, Evangelicals do instruct the Believer that witnessing is everywhere, but that the Believer is to bring the unsaved and the new Believer to the church building as the venue of church authority and government. Evangelicals also teach that going to the church building, sitting in a chair or pew as spectators, participating in praise and worship, listening and taking notes of sermons week after week Saturday or Sunday, paying tithes and offerings, praying for self, family, and others, and reading the Bible is the total duty and way of life that God wants them to do. On the other hand, most priests, bishops, pastors, teachers, and reverends fail to teach and activate all Believers as ministers. Also, most heads of church fail to inform Believers that the primary duty of priests, bishops, pastors, teachers, and reverends is to activate all Believers into their spiritual Vocations and spiritual Gifts and then send them out to minister.

The foregoing illuminations are all true, but there is **so much more,** which I hope this book clarifies your thoughts and ways that need to be in line with the Lord's higher thoughts and ways. Isaiah 55:7-11 says, "Let the wicked forsake his way, and the unrighteous man his thoughts: and let him return unto the LORD, and he will have mercy upon him; and to our God, for he will abundantly pardon. (8) For my thoughts are not your thoughts, neither are your ways my ways, saith the LORD. (9) For as the heavens are higher than the earth, so are my ways higher than your ways, and my thoughts than your thoughts. (10) For as the rain cometh down, and the snow from heaven, and returneth not thither, but watereth the earth, and maketh it bring forth and bud, that it may give seed to the sower, and bread to the eater: (11) So shall my word be that goeth forth out of my mouth: it shall not return unto me void, but it shall accomplish that which I please, and it shall prosper in the thing whereto I sent it."

The anemic goal that the functioning priests, bishops, pastors, teachers, and reverends is to fill the church building every Sunday and have an altar call for those that are unsaved and those who want to rededicate their lives once again to the Lord. Believers are taught Hebrews 10:25 that says, "**Not forsaking the assembling of ourselves together,** as the manner of some is but **exhorting one another**: **and so much the more**, as ye see **the day approaching**." When Believers go to the church warehouse lecture hall, they are not "exhorting one another"; they sit in a chair or pew, sing along with the praise and worship team, enjoy a solo song, and listen and sometimes take notes of the sermon; drop an offering into the plate, and then go home and repeat the religious practice week after week, year after year. "Exhorting one another" means strongly encouraging or urging other members during the "assembling of ourselves together" preserving our faith, resisting sin, and living out our Christian salvation and calling. "Exhorting one another" is about engaging in supportive and encouraging words to each other, reminding each other of their purpose and identity in Christ, and helping each other to stay strong in their walk with God in Christ Jesus, being led by the Holy Spirit, and seeking first every day the kingdom of God and His righteousness. "Exhorting one another" is not being done in the Sunday morning warehouse lecture hall church meeting. "Exhorting one another" could be done better in home fellowships, but some church leaders do not sanction home fellowships for fear of home fellowship leaders will steal their sheep. There is **"so much more"** to be done as **"the day approaching"** in the scripture is the return of Christ Jesus back here on earth to rule and reign throughout all eternity.

The church leaders often teach that one of the reasons Believers need faithfully to come together at the warehouse lecture hall church building each week is because 1 Peter 5:8 says, "Be sober, be vigilant; because your adversary the devil, as a roaring lion, walketh about, seeking whom he may devour." Church leaders quote these verses to convince Believers to come to the church building for protection and pastoral covering. Yet, church leaders do not teach that the regular member Believers are to not forsake the assembling together for the purpose of "exhorting one another" which is rarely practiced at meetings in the warehouse lecture hall church building.

A few Evangelical churches that practice home fellowship should always be a major part where Believers are activated into the work of ministry. The pastor should tell the congregation to join a community of Believers in home fellowship where they can exhort one another. "Exhorting one another" means persuading, encouraging, and urging each other to engage in the work of the ministry. It involves reminding, comforting, and strengthening one another, often with the goal of living with God's grace and the Believers' faith, encouraging each other to resist sin and the importance of inspiring one another to participate with spiritual gifts for the purpose of building up a fellowship of loving and caring Believers. To "exhort one another" also means to develop close friendship with one another, be friendly and genuinely loving, but do not make it a social event. The primary purpose is to help each other to be submissive to the Godhead living inside them, as the Godhead spiritually transforms the minds, emotions, and hearts in Believer's souls. The membership in the home fellowship should form teams to be activated to go and evangelize and use each of their spiritual gifts as witnesses with their own overcoming testimonies to those unsaved and those saved that God is present through them. As additional part of their work of the ministry, it is to exhort one another to spread the gospel of the Kingdom (Matthew 24:1) and repentance and remission of sins (Luke 24:27) to the unsaved while continuing in fellowship with other Believers throughout the week in their daily lives. When Believers leave the church building or home fellowship, they should be ready to share the gospel of Christ with the waitress at the restaurant, on Monday morning with fellow employees, and saying "The Lord bless you!" to the cashier at the store, the gas station, or on the way to work as they traverse the drive through at Starbucks. The Believer must believe he or she is the *Ekklesia*, not the building where they attended Saturday or Sunday services. Believers bring the *Ekklesia* with them because God lives inside them as Believers are His Temple (2 Corinthians 6:16), and God's Kingdom is within them (Luke 17:21).

Believers should be taught 1 John 4:4, which says, "... greater is He (God) that is in you, than he (devil) that is in the world." The whole experience at Saturday or Sunday morning warehouse church lecture hall pyramid structure by and large is a spectator experience and is not an activation of Believers for the work of the ministry outside of the church building. Every ministry outreach, whether it is providing food for the hungry, visiting those in prisons, or any other activity, although good, is required to be sanctioned by the priest, bishop, pastor, teacher, or reverend because the traditional church structure paradigm is set up like a pyramid, where all authority, ministries, and money flows to the head minister at the top. Because of this warehouse church lecture hall pyramid structure, most Believers think they can hide out in the large auditorium and will do nothing unless they are first asked by one of the leaders. They rush out of the building each Saturday or Sunday morning and into their cars to be first out of the parking lot to avoid the crowd.

It is clear that most functioning priests, bishops, pastors, teachers, and reverends have been scholastically taught biblical scriptures, church history, and doctrinal interpretation of the Bible that have fostered denominational differences. It is good that most church leaders accept the foundational beliefs of Jesus' virgin birth, death on the Roman Cross, resurrection on the third day, ascension, intercession while in heaven, His return, along with God's *agape* love, grace, mercy, and eternal life for all those who repent and call upon the name of the Lord. Yet, most all functioning priests, bishops, pastors, teachers, and reverends fail in activating the rank and file Believers to do the work of ministry, as kings, priests, lords, ambassadors, and soldiers that should be sent out and be led by the Holy Spirit.

Thus, my purpose is not to condemn the church leaders, but to shed light from scriptures, Jesus' kinesthetic training, and reveal also what the first Century functioning apostles, prophets, evangelist, pastors, and teachers did that activated all Believers at that time to preach the gospel of the Kingdom and repentance and remission of sins, with signs following (Mark 16:20). My purpose is to call the church leaders to fulfill their duties to activate all Believers for the work of the ministry for the edification of the body of Christ (Ephesians 4:11-12).

For an example of the first Century *Ekklesia* activation of Believer doing the work of the ministry, Acts 8:1,4 says, "And Saul was consenting unto his (Stephen's) death. And at that time there was a great persecution against the church (*Ekklesia* - government assembly or military assembly) which was at Jerusalem; and they were all scattered abroad throughout the regions of Judea and Samaria, except the apostles. . . (4) Therefore they that were scattered abroad went everywhere preaching the word." Here, the apostles activated every Believer in the *Ekklesia* in Jerusalem to do the work of the ministry and sent out to be preachers of the gospel of the kingdom (Matthew 24:14) and repentance and remission of sins (Luke 24:47). The apostles stayed in Jerusalem and sent out every Believer to preach the messages Jesus mandated and to have faith for signs following.

THE FOLLOWING SCRIPTURAL TEACHINGS ARE FOUNDATIONAL TRUTHS AND MUST BE TAUGHT TO THE BELIEVER BUSINESS EMPLOYEES BY THE BELIEVER BUSINESS OWNERS.

My primary emphasis in this book is to show that God has called Believer Business Owners to be functioning ministers, and their businesses are legitimate instruction centers through scholastic teaching and kinesthetic training to evangelize the lost and spiritually disciple and spiritually mature Believer Business Employees. Through scholastic teaching and kinesthetic repetitive training in applying biblical economics, instructing a good work ethic, insisting on a strong moral compass, and becoming a loving servant as unto the Lord, Believer Business Employees are equipped and activated into the work of ministry in the business while engaging in commerce in the marketplace. The Believer Business Owners are in a unique position to fulfill God's mandate in Ephesians 4:12 of activating and perfecting or maturing Believer Business Employees for the work of the ministry for the edification of the body of Christ.

Each Believer at initial salvation acquires a born again spirit as a new creature in Christ (2 Corinthians 5:17), and this born again spirit is perfect, sinless, holy, and righteous (Hebrews 12:23, 1 John 3:9, Ephesians 4:24). After initial salvation the Believer's soul must be transformed spiritually (Romans 12:2). This is done by the Godhead living inside of the Believer to protect the born again spirit and transform the soul throughout the Believer's life. God the Father prunes and removes the influence of the flesh in the soul to bear more spiritual fruit (John 15:2). God the Word cleanses the influence of the flesh and sanctifies the soul by the water of the *rhema* word of God, so the soul is without spot, wrinkle, or blemish but is holy (Ephesians 5:26-27). God the Holy Spirit mortifies the deeds of the flesh in the Believer's soul, so the Believer's soul can experience more *zoe* life (Romans 8:13).

This transformation of the soul is not for self-aggrandizement but to make the Believer humble, submissive, obedient, scholastically taught, and kinesthetically trained to be led by the Holy Spirit as a minister. When Jesus' humanity nature returns to set up His everlasting Kingdom here on earth, the Believer will receive a new resurrected body that is incorruptible, glorious, powerful, spiritual, and immortal (Revelation Chap. 21; 1 Corinthians 15:23, 42-44, 53).

When Jesus' humanity nature returns to earth, Believers are qualified to rule and reign with Christ over the entire earth, world system, and as servants of the people throughout eternity (Revelation 5:10). This is the great eternal hope that the Godhead and Christ Jesus' humanity nature gives to Believers. Eternal life is a not a work free heaven. It is the work of obediently ruling and reigning with Christ over the entire earth throughout eternity.

It is best if Believer Business Employees become activated to do the work of the ministry while being about the Father's business here on earth before they die, as there are crowns to be achieved based upon the ministry work while the Believers are still here on earth. Since God's government is a Kingdom, then crowns represent the authority given by the King. Believers can earn crowns as part of the Kingdom Age when Believers return to earth with Christ Jesus for the degree of their submissive work here on earth during their lifetimes. The Crown of life (James 1:12), the Imperishable Wreath (1 Corinthians 9:25), the Crown of Righteousness (2 Timothy 4:8), the Crown of glory (1 Peter 5:4) and the Crown of Exaltation (1 Thessalonians 2:19) are special rewards in God's Kingdom given by God for special work on behalf of Christ Jesus by Believers while alive here on earth.

The concept of Believers as kings and priests in Revelation 1:6 is spiritual, not a continuation of the Old Testament priestly system. Believers participate as Christ's royal priesthood, with Christ being the great High Priest in the order of Melchizedek (Hebrews chap. 7). 1 Peter 2:9 says, "But ye are a chosen generation, a royal priesthood, a holy nation, a peculiar people; that ye should shew forth the praises of Him who hath called you out of darkness into His marvelous light." The scriptures are clear that all Believers are appointed to do the work of ministry as God's kings, priests (Revelation 1:6), lords (1 Timothy 6:15), ambassadors (2 Corinthians 5:20), and soldiers (2 Timothy 2:3-4) in His Kingdom.

Believers as kings and priests emphasize the dual role of having authority in a kingdom and a priesthood. The royal priesthood of all Believers is a concept universally accepted by most all Protestant leaders that precludes the necessity of a ceremonial consecration. Yet, both Catholic and Protestant's priests, bishops, pastors, teachers, and reverends do not activate and perfect Believers for the work of the ministry as kings and priests, as these offices do not fit in with the warehouse auditorium lecture hall pyramid paradigm structure with one man or one woman at the top.

Why has even the Protestant denomination leaders in practice set up an elite priesthood and spectator laity system that does not consider all Believers having authority as kings and priests? Jesus said in Revelation 2: 6, "But this thou hast, that thou hatest the deeds of the Nicolaitans, which I also hate." The word Nicolaitans is formed from two words, "*Nico*" meaning hatred and "*laitans*" meaning the regular members Believers of the *Ekklesia.* Jesus said that the greatest in the kingdom were servants, not elitist rulers like the Gentiles lord over people (Matthew 23:11; Mark 10:42-45; John 13:12-15).

Jesus kinesthetically trained His disciples that true evangelism is witnessing, heralding, and proclaiming by first preaching the gospel of the Kingdom (Matthew 24:14) and by second preaching repentance and remission of sins (Luke 24:47), which are the two messages that Jesus mandated every Believer to preach as His witnesses in every part of a culture in every country in the world where people live, work, and fellowship (Acts 1:8). Jesus' two messages lead unbelievers to repent and turn away from their sinful lives, having heartfelt belief that Jesus rose from the dead, and confessing Jesus as Lord for initial salvation (Matthew 4:17; Romans 10:9; 2 Corinthians 7:10). Too often the requirement of repentance is left out in the preaching and leading unbelievers to the Lord and becoming born again. Leaving out the requirement of repentance can cause spiritual birth defects because it negates the need to repent for the continuance and ongoing transformation of the soul (Philippians 2:12-13; 1 John 1:8).

Jesus said in Luke 13:3, "I tell you, 'Nay: but, except ye repent, ye shall all likewise perish.'" Repent means turning around and no longer existing and taking into one's soul carnal stimuli from the fallen world and the lust of the flesh, lust of the eyes, and pride of life; and in turn, wholeheartedly following Christ Jesus in the Kingdom of God which is righteousness, peace, and joy in the Holy Spirit (Romans 14:17). John 2:15-17 says, "Love not the world, neither the things that are in the world. If any man love the world, the love of (God) the Father is not in him. (16) For all that is in the world, the lust of the flesh, and the lust of the eyes, and the pride of life, is not of (God) the Father, but is of the world. (17) And the world passeth away, and the lust thereof: but he that doeth the will of God abideth forever."

Preaching Jesus' two messages in Matthew 24:14 and Luke 24:47 are aimed to bring forgiveness of sins and righteousness of God (2 Corinthians 5:21), voids the curse of the law (Galatians 3:13), gives eternal life (John 3:16), grants grace (Romans 6:14-15), and instills hope (Hebrews 6:19) for the future because it is the goodness of God that leads a person to repentance (Romans 2:4). With these two gospel messages, Jesus persuaded and converted unbelievers to become born again spiritually to see the Kingdom of God (John 3:3; 1 Peter 1:23) and to receive the gift of eternal life through Him (John 4:4; John 5:24, John 6:51; John 17:3; John 10:27-28). Believers become the spiritual children of Jesus' humanity nature (Isaiah 9:6; Hebrews 2:13), and Believers become children of God the Father by adoption (Romans 8:15).

After initial salvation, Believers' continuous repentance in Believers' souls from a sinful life in the secular world by turning around and living in God's holy nation is a way to experience kingdom spiritual *zoe* life abundantly and righteousness, peace, and joy in the Holy Spirit (Romans 12:2; 1

John 1:8-9; John 10:10b; Romans 14:17). Initial salvation is based solely upon a Believer's heartfelt belief in repentance and accepting Jesus' death on the Roman Cross, His resurrection (Luke 24:47; Ephesians 2:8-9), and in confessing that Jesus is Lord (Romans 10:9). Believers are taught that Jesus took Believers' sins vicariously upon Himself (2 Corinthians 5:21), and they are taught that Jesus took away the curse of the law for Believers by hanging on the Roman Cross (Galatians 3:13). The result is giving Believers a perfect, incorruptible, sinless, righteous, and holy born again spirit as a new man and new creature in Christ (Hebrews 12:23; 1 Peter 1:23; 1 John 3:9, Ephesians 4:24; 2 Corinthians 5:17).

1 John 1:7-10 says, "But if we (Believers) walk in the light, as He is in the light, we have fellowship one with another, and the blood of Jesus Christ His Son cleanseth us (Believers) from all sin. (8) If we (Believers) say that we (Believers) have no sin (in our souls after initial salvation), we (Believers) deceive ourselves, and the truth is not in us (Believers' souls). (9) If we (Believers) confess our sins, He is faithful and just to forgive us (Believers) our sins (in Believers' souls), and to cleanse us (Believers' souls) from all unrighteousness. (10) If we (Believers) say that we have not sinned (in our souls), we (Believers) make Him a liar, and His word is not in us (Believers' souls)."

After initial salvation, Believer Business Owners with the spiritual gifts as functioning apostles, prophets, evangelists, pastors, and teachers (Ephesians 4:11) have the mandate to activate and perfect Believer Business Employees into the work of the ministry to edify the body of Christ (Ephesians 4:12). Again, the work of the ministry is laboring in Vocations as kings, priests (Revelation 1:6), lords (1 Timothy 6:15), ambassadors (2 Corinthians 5:20), and soldiers (2 Timothy 2:3-4).

Also, the Believer Business Owners as Ephesians 4:11 functioning ministers must help discern and activate Believer Business Employees with their spiritual Gifts. The spiritual Gifts of God the Father are listed in Romans 12:6-8. The spiritual Gifts of God the Word are introduced in Ephesians 4:11. The spiritual Gifts of God the Holy Spirit are enumerated in 1 Corinthians 12:8-10. Most Believer Business Owners have spiritual Gifts that are of God the Father.

Although all Believers have the same spiritual work of ministry authority, which is their spiritual Vocations, they do not have the same spiritual Gifts. The shared spiritual works of ministry are for the edification of the body of Christ. The divergent spiritual Gifts also are for the edification of the body of Christ. 1 Corinthians 12:28-30 says, "And God hath set some in the church (*Ekklesia,* which means a government assembly or military assembly, as will be discussed historically later), first apostles, secondarily prophets, thirdly teachers, after that miracles, then gifts of healings, helps, governments, diversities of tongues. (29) Are all apostles? Are all prophets? Are all teachers? Are all workers of miracles? (30) Have all the gifts of healing? Do all speak with tongues? Do all interpret?" Regarding spiritual gifts, the answers to the questions by Paul are that Believers have different spiritual Gifts, but all spiritual Gifts are for the edification of the entire body of Christ, but Paul makes it clear that all Believers have the same Vocations as spiritual kings (Revelation 1:6), spiritual priests as living stones (1 Peter 2:5), spiritual lords as stewards of the earth (1 Timothy 6:15), spiritual ambassadors of Christ (2 Corinthians 5:20), and spiritual soldiers of Jesus Christ (2 Timothy 2:3-4).

I have been told by functioning priests, bishops, pastors, teachers, and reverends over the years that it is not practical for them to meet every day with business Believers (as Jesus did with His apostles) to activate them into the work of the ministry. I agree that under the current auditorium lecture hall structure pyramid paradigm, it is not designed to make disciples through kinesthetic training. What was the method that Jesus and the first century apostles and disciples used to activate other Believers into the work of the ministry? The answer is the first century functioning apostles, prophets, evangelists, pastors, teachers, and disciples met with other Believers daily, ate meals with them, and through kinesthetic training activated the Believers into the work of the ministry in their Vocations as kings, priests, lords, ambassadors, and soldiers and was helpful to watch and determine each Believers spiritual Gifts.

Instead of tearing down the current auditorium lecture hall structure pyramid paradigm and telling people not to attend, I am suggesting that biblically-based spiritual leaders from Monday through Friday should spiritually instruct and spiritually mature Believer Business Owners by going to the place of business and instructing them how to make their businesses a ministry using scholastic teaching and kinesthetic training to activate their Believer Business Employees into the work of the ministry as kings, priests, lords, ambassadors, and soldiers and to use their spiritual Gifts for the edification of the body of Christ while working and being about God the Father's business (Luke 2:49).

Also, Believer Business Owners pay the Believer Business Employees a salary to work eight to ten hours a day, five to six days a week, and submit to instruction how to be ministers at work while using biblical economics, good work ethic, the importance of humility in servanthood that brings promotion, being guided by a moral compass that is mandated and taught from the Scriptures in the Bible, how to have a good marriage, how to raise obedient children that honor their parents, and all other biblical principles that manifests life abundantly. Believer Business Employees can participate in a one hour Bible study before normal business work begins. They together can take turns in reading a portion of five chapters of Psalms and one chapter of Proverbs each day and finish the Book of Psalms and Book of Proverbs every thirty days. Then the Believer Business Employees should start over month after month until these biblical wisdom principles transform the beliefs in Believer Business Employees' minds, emotions, and hearts of their souls. Kinesthetic training is transforming souls through repetition of spiritual truths and application of those spiritual truths daily at the workplace, so the Believer Business Employees have a habit of addressing problems with biblical principles, wisdom how to apply those principles, servanthood, and *agape* love.

Every Believer Business Employee's soul consists of thoughts in the mind, feelings in the emotions, and beliefs in the heart; and the heart is where the human will functions. Every Believer Business Employee's soul has to be spiritually transformed (Romans 12:2) by God the Father who prunes away the flesh in the soul to produce more spiritual fruit (John 15:2); by God the Word who washes away the flesh and sanctifies the soul through the *rhema* word to remove spots, or wrinkles, without blemish but is holy (Ephesians 5:26-27); and by God the Holy Spirit Who mortifies the deeds of the flesh in the soul to obtain more *zoe* life (Romans 8:13).

Believer Business Employers and Believer Business Employees will become prosperous, and the priests, bishops, pastors, teachers, or reverends should see these maturing Believer Business Employers and Believer Business Employees as leaders in the local congregation that can help activate other Believers in the work of the ministry. Thus, the Holy Spirit sees businesses also as the instruction center for His spiritual *Ekklesia* for making disciples of Christ Jesus through kinesthetic training. Both the Believer Business Owners and the Believer Business Employees must be about God the Father's business (Luke 2:49) of saving the lost and spiritually maturing the saved.

Believers must be discipled and sent to the local culture, and from there spread out to the whole world on the mission field as Christ's witnesses. Paul's mandate to Timothy is also for all Believers to be activated to preach the two gospel messages (Matthew 24:14; Luke 24:47) in every place in the culture, commerce, and ethnic groups in every country. Teaching Believer Business Employees how to be spiritually transformed in their souls while they work. 2 Timothy 2:15, 22, 24-25 says, "Study to show thyself approved unto God, a workman (in business) that needeth not to be ashamed, rightly dividing the word of truth…(22) Flee also youthful lusts: but follow righteousness, faith, charity, peace, with them that call on the Lord out of a pure heart (in their soul)… (24) And the servant of the Lord (already a born again Believer) must not strive; but be gentle unto all men, apt to teach, patient, (25) In meekness instructing those that oppose themselves; if God peradventure will give them repentance to the acknowledging of the truth."

Paul says that every Believer Servant of the Lord (not just only traditional church leaders) "… must not strive; but be gentle unto all men, apt to teach, patient, in meekness instructing those that oppose themselves." Every Believer must study the Bible, so he or she is "apt to teach" and "instructing those that oppose themselves." You cannot be a functioning scholastic teacher and functioning kinesthetic instructor unless you are mature in knowing the word of God and are activated for the work of the ministry.

Colossians 3:16-17 says, "Let the word of Christ dwell in (all of) you (Believers) richly in all wisdom; (and all of you) **teaching and admonishing one another** in psalms and hymns and spiritual songs, singing with grace in your hearts to the Lord. (17) **And whatsoever ye do in word or deed, do all in the name of the Lord Jesus, giving thanks to God and the Father by Him**." This mandate is for all Believers, so all Believers must be activated and perfected into the work of the ministry, continuously learning the wisdom derived from studying the word of God. Yet, these scriptures require all Believers to be teaching, exhorting, and admonishing one another, which means it is not just the leader's function but the mandate for every Believer. Every Believer must learn psalms, hymns, and spiritual songs to participate in group praise and worship, in which the traditional church leadership generally does a good job starting out with praise and worship. However, verse 17 says whatever you do in word or deed refers to professionals and workers in trades. It says do it all in the name of Jesus, giving thanks to the Lord. The gospel must be preached in the workplace, in media broadcasting, in film scripting, in music producing, in school instructing, in government ruling, in store shopping, and in everyplace and activity that is the *Kosmos*. The *Kosmos* is much more than in every country, or all ethnicities, but everywhere people gather to work in businesses, learn in schools, entertain by movies and music, or gather in societal fellowship.

Peter speaks to all Believers in 1 Peter 3:15, which says, "But sanctify the Lord God in your hearts: and be ready always to give an answer to every man that asketh you a reason of the hope that is in you with meekness and fear." This means wherever a Believer is, the Believer is to be a witness for Christ Jesus privately and publicly when the opportunity is provided. In the Upper Room on the Day of Pentecost when the Holy Spirit came to take jurisdictional authority of the *Ekklesia,* there were the original eleven apostles. Then, in Acts 1:26 they selected Matthias as the twelfth apostle to fill Judas' apostolic position. Out of approximately 120 men and women in the Upper Room, only ten percent were the governmental apostles appointed by Christ Jesus. The additional ninety percent, which were about 108 other people, both men and women, in the upper room also received the same power and anointing from the Holy Spirit to be Jesus' witnesses.

All those in the Upper Room had been commissioned by Jesus before His ascension and were told to stay in Jerusalem until empowered by the Holy Spirit, so they all could be His witnesses. Jesus said in Acts 1:8, "But ye (all Believers, both men and women) shall receive power, after that the Holy Ghost is come upon you: and ye shall be witnesses unto Me both in Jerusalem, and in all Judaea, and in Samaria, and unto the uttermost part of the earth." The Greek for the word "earth" in Acts 1:8 is *ge,* which means according to Strongs G1093, "Contracted from a primary word; *soil*;

by extension a *region*, or the solid part or the whole of the *terrene* globe (including the occupants in each application): - country, earth (-ly), ground, land, world." Thus, the promise land was then the whole earth, not just Israel as it is today, although Jerusalem will be the capitol of the Lord's kingdom when He returns to live in a new heaven and new earth (Revelation Chap. 21).

This book draws attention to areas where the church leaders have failed historically and continue to fail by not pursuing the mandates of Scripture that desperately need consideration and obeyance. First, the church leaders have not been preaching for the most part the gospel of the kingdom of God, which was mandated by Christ Jesus in Matthew 24:14. Second, the church has set up a warehouse auditorium lecture hall structure paradigm that has become a spectator religious gathering having singers, musicians, and a priest, bishop, pastor, teacher, or reverend giving lecture-type sermons for 45 to 60 minutes. Third, the church leaders have ushers take a monetary collection from the audience, maybe have an altar call for initial salvation, and then invite people to come to the front for prayer for problems or healing. Fourth, the congregation goes home and returns the following week as spectators of religion. Fifth, the church leaders spend hundreds of thousands and millions to construct a building that remains empty an estimated 70% of the time, which the congregation members have paid for but often are still charged to use the building for marriages and funerals. Sixth, the mandates of Ephesians 4:11-13 are not followed by church leaders, so the masses in congregations are not being activated and perfected into their spiritual Vocations, Gifts and maturity. Seventh, the church leaders have made converts with initial salvation but have not made disciples that are activated and perfected into the work of ministry.

In particular, this book introduces the idea how the Ephesians 4:11 functioning ministries of the apostle, prophet, evangelist, pastor, and teacher as Believer Business Owners by the leading of the Holy Spirit, who will disciple Believer Business Employees, instructing them through scholastic teaching and kinesthetic training to learn and use God's biblical economic principles and servanthood to activate and perfect them with spiritual Vocations as kings, priests, lords, ambassadors, and soldiers and with spiritual Gifts of God the Father (Romans 12:6-8), spiritual Gifts of God the Word (Ephesians 4:11), and spiritual Gifts of God the Holy Spirit (1 Corinthians 12:8-10).

The main passage of scripture of the topic of this book is Ephesians 4:7-16, which says, "But unto every **one of us is given grace according to the measure of the gift of Christ**. (8) Wherefore He saith, 'When He ascended up on high, He led captivity captive and gave gifts unto men. (9) (Now that He ascended, what is it but that He also descended first into the lower parts of the earth? (10) He that descended is the same also that ascended up far above all heavens, that He might fill all things.) **(11) And He gave some, apostle; and some, prophets; and some, evangelists; and some, pastors and teachers; (12) For the perfecting of the saints, for the work of the ministry, for the edifying of the Body of Christ: (13) Till we all come in the unity of the faith, and of the knowledge of the Son of God, unto a perfect man, unto the measure of the stature of the fullness of Christ:** (14) That we henceforth be no more children, tossed to and fro, and carried about with every wind of doctrine, by the sleight of men, and cunning craftiness, whereby they lie in wait to deceive; (15) But speaking the truth in love, may grow up into Him in all things, which is the head, even Christ: (16) From whom the whole body fitly joined together and compacted by that which every joint supplieth, according to the effectual working in the measure of every part, maketh increase of the body unto the edifying of itself in love."

THE WORD "CHURCH" IS INCORRECTLY INTERPRETED FROM THE WORD *EKKLESIA*

In my book, Ekklesia in Glorious Revival, on page 36, I discussed the false translation of the Greek word *Ekklesia* into English as "church." The following is a quote from that book.

"In Matthew 16:18, in the Greek, Jesus did not say He would build His *Kuriakos* (Strongs reference G2960, the Greek word for church), but rather His *Ekklesia* (Strongs G1577, military assembly). *Ekklesia* is used more than 120 times in the King James Version of the Bible. The word "church" is derived from the Greek word *Kuriakos*, (Strongs reference G2960), which is derived from the Greek word *Kurios,* (Strongs G2962). *Kurios* means "supreme in authority, that is, (as noun) controller; by implication God, meaning Lord, Master, Sir." Thus, the Greek word *Kuriakos* means belonging to one's Lord or Master as a bondservant, and this is what church means. The word came from the Teutonic word *kirk, kirch*, from where we get the word "church." The word *Kuriakos* appears only in 1 Corinthians 11:20 which modifies the Greek word for the Lord's (*Kuriakos*) supper and in Revelation 1:10 which modifies the Greek word for the Lord's (*Kuriakos*) day.

Wikipedia describes the word *kirk* "(a)s a common noun, *kirk* (meaning "church") is found in Scots, Scottish English, Ulster-Scots and some English dialects, attested as a noun from the 14th century onwards, but as an element in place names much earlier. Kirk and church are derived from the koine Greek, *kyriakondōma* meaning Lord's house, which was borrowed into the Germanic languages in late antiquity, possibly in the course of the Gothic missions. (Only a connection with the idiosyncrasies of Gothic explains how a Greek neuter noun became a Germanic feminine.) Whereas church displays Old English palatalisation, *kirk* is a loan word from Old Norse and thus has the original mainland Germanic consonants. Compare cognates: Icelandic & Faroese *kirkja*; Swedish *kyrka*; Norwegian (Nynorsk) *kyrkje*; and Danish *kirke*; German *kirche*, Dutch *kerk*; West Frisian *tsjerke*; and borrowed into non-Germanic languages: Estonian *kirik* and Finnish *kirkko*."

Thus, the English word "church" did not come from the Greek word *Ekklesia* but from the Scottish word *kirk.* In Acts 19:37 the Greek word correctly translated as "churches" is *hierosulos.* In the same discourse, in Acts 19:34-41 the word *Ekklesia* three times was translated correctly as "government assembly." Here the secular council meeting, called an *Ekklesia* in the Greek, was formed to determine what to do with Paul and his co-workers for preaching the gospel of the Kingdom in their city. The secular rulers in the city were threatened because these Believers were introducing a new Kingdom authority in their city. Also, the Roman Senate was called an *Ekklesia,* and Jesus took this Greek word *Ekklesia* and applied it to His body of Believers, either as a government assembly or an assembly of soldiers. In fact, in the Roman Empire any group of citizens who were "called out" to do a work for the government was called an *Ekklesia.*

CHURCH LEADERS ARE NOT ADEQUATELY DEALING WITH PROBLEMS THAT BELIEVERS ENCOUNTER IN THE CULTURES,THE MARKETPLACES, AND COLLEGES

Let's look at a modern day problem that the church leaders have not adequately addressed. Few church leaders never heard the term *woke* until about 2010. Prior to that time, *woke* was used often to describe people who were awakened to the injustices of racism. I do not know one Believer who promotes racial prejudice in today's polite society. Since 2010, it seems the word *woke* has been highjacked by political left activists who are socialistic in their views. These far left Socialists do not want equal justice but want outcome equity based upon race or LGBTQ, which is not the want of equal justice but want special superior rights than others, including special privileges not based upon merit.

Look where the United States and Europe have fallen away from the moral precepts in the Bible. Mature Believers are against the extreme and discriminatory abortion agenda of the left, and Believers uphold the value, dignity, and potential of every person's life, especially the innocent unborn. The left base their idea that the growing life in the womb is not human until he or she is in the third trimester or is born. Yet, they ignore science and God's truth. As soon as the egg is fertilized, God puts a soul in those fertilized cells, and the mind of the soul is what instructs the cells to grow the placenta, the umbilical cord, the blood type, the feet, hands, eyes, ears, nose, mouths, the sex, the color of skin and hair. This is not the undeveloped brain in the body that is making these decisions, nor the mother's mind in her soul or the brain in her body, but rather the mind in the soul of the baby. Thus, when abortion occurs, the mother and medical doctor intentionally murder a living soul.

Here is another area where the United States and Europe have fallen away with the moral precepts in the Bible. The radical left agenda created an entirely new vocabulary that most Believers do not use and do not want to use, but the next generation is using. This new language is a deception by the devil.

Take a look of a few of these words that created a new vocabulary. **Identity politics** is based on ethnicity, race, nationality, religion, denomination, gender, sexual orientation, social background, caste, age, disability, intelligence, and social class. There has sprung up numerous names that people use as their identity.

For example, **cisgender** (a term for people whose gender identity matches their sex assigned at birth), **androgyny** (against assigned sex at birth)**, cissexism (t**he assumption that all people are cisgender because it is deeply ingrained in our society through socialization) **transgender, cultural appropriation, intersectionality, conscious capitalism, diversity equity inclusion (DEI), agender, BIPOC, biphobia, biracial, bigender/dual gender, bisexual, gay, coming out (**that they refer to as **LGBTQ), Critical Race Theory (**the challenge to dominant ideology and centrality of experiential knowledge), **diversity** (each individual is unique and different, and all have equal rights that protect differences of race, ethnicity, gender, sexual orientation, socio- economic status, age, physical abilities, religious beliefs, political beliefs, or other ideologies), **drag queen / king** (taking on the appearance and characteristics associated of the opposite gender), **first generation** (an individual, whose parents never obtained a baccalaureate college degree), gender (what a person wants to be rather than a biological sex at birth), **gender affirming surgery** (surgical procedures associated with altering the genitals or secondary sex characteristics to be consistent with a person's gender identity that he or she chooses), **gender expression** (external manifestations of gender, expressed through a person's name, pronouns, clothing, haircut, behavior, voice, and/or body characteristics), **gender-neutral or gender-inclusive** (inclusive alternative language to describe relationships, such as **spouse and partner** instead of husband/boyfriend and wife/girlfriend, spaces that are **gender-neutral/inclusive restrooms** are for use by all genders, pronouns **they and ze are gender neutral/inclusive** pronouns among other things), and a host of other things.

The fact is that human beings are saying that they can make a boy/man into a girl/woman, and a girl/woman into a boy/man. Yet, only God is Creator. What Believers know is true, and that is God made a person with a certain sex. The sex of a human is the Creator's decision, and hard as they try, humans cannot change the sex of a human. What happens if these transgender people become converted and become Believers? They will find out they were wrong. They may realize that God loves them and has a particular purpose for each person to be born as a male or female.

These *woke* activists aggressively promote through legislation new laws and vocabulary introduced regularly; and they do not accept that God, who created all mankind, thinks that sexual deviant behavior and lifestyles are an abomination that will destroy our country.

When they continuously throw their deviant lifestyles in public, it is an outright insult towards Believers and what they know is true. These sexual deviants do not understand, or will not accept Scriptures in the Bible as reality truth. Their actions of deviancy that God calls abominations can be used by God to remove the U.S. citizens from their homeland.

Leviticus 18: 22, 24-30 says, "Thou shalt not lie with mankind, as with womankind: it is abomination. (24) Defile not ye yourselves in any of these things: for in all these the nations are defiled which I cast out before you: (25) And the land is defiled: therefore I do visit the iniquity thereof upon it, and the land itself vomiteth out her inhabitants. (26) Ye shall therefore keep My statutes and My judgments, and shall not commit any of these abominations; neither any of your own nation, nor any stranger that sojourneth among you: (27) For all these abominations have the men of the land done, which were before you, and the land is defiled; (28) That the land spue not you out also, when ye defile it, as it spued out the nations that were before you. (29) For whosoever shall commit any of these abominations, even the souls that commit them shall be cut off from among their people. (30) Therefore shall ye keep mine ordinance, that ye commit not any one of these abominable customs, which were committed before you, and that ye defile not yourselves therein: I am the LORD your God."

THE PYRAMID STRUCTURED CHURCH VERSUS THE "V" STRUCTURED *EKKLESIA*

Most *Ekklesia* leaders (including myself) all need adjustments and changes to be better to meet the challenges that are in the fallen world. James 4:7 says, "Submit yourselves therefore to God. Resist the devil, and he will flee from you." Notice the conditional priority for this resistance of the devil. First of all, submit to God by seeking first the Kingdom of God and His righteousness and have an intimate relationship with God through Christ Jesus. Second, humble yourself before the Lord. 1 Peter 5:5 says, "... Yea, all of you be subject one to another, and be clothed with humility: for God resisteth the proud, and giveth grace to the humble."

God will fight Believers' battles against the devil once you submit to Him, and then resist the devil in that order. Exodus 14:14 says, "The LORD shall fight for you, and ye shall hold your peace." Isaiah 54:17 is a covenant promise from God, "No weapon that is formed against thee shall prosper; and every tongue that shall rise against thee in judgment thou shalt condemn. This is the heritage of the servants of the LORD, and their righteousness is of me, saith the LORD."

As pertain to the problems in the fallen world that confront Believers, Romans 12:16-20 says, "Be of the same mind one toward another. Mind not high things, but condescend to men of low estate. Be not wise in your own conceits. (17) Recompense to no man evil for evil. Provide things honest in the sight of all men. (18) If it be possible, as much as lieth in you, live peaceably with all men. (19) Dearly beloved, avenge not yourselves, but rather give place unto wrath: for it is written, 'Vengeance is mine; I will repay,' saith the Lord. (20) Therefore if thine enemy hunger, feed him; if he thirst, give him drink: for in so doing thou shalt heap coals of fire on his head."

Similarly, 2 Corinthians 6:14 says, "Be ye not unequally yoked together with unbelievers: for what fellowship hath righteousness with unrighteousness? And what communion hath light with darkness?" Great differences exist between Believers and unbelievers. The principles, beliefs, truths, motivations, *agape* love, purposes, and procedures of Believers in business are incompatible with those of an unbeliever. Spiritual salvation and spiritual maturation of the soul change the character of an unbeliever. If a Believer Business Owner wants to employ a person, then lead him or her to the Lord and involve that new Believer Business Employee in a strong scholastic teaching from the Bible, along with kinesthetic training that involves application of scriptures, biblical principles of economics, importance of a good work ethic, servanthood toward others, expressing *agape* love, and a sound foundation of biblical morality. A Believer Business minister's highest motivation in business should focus on being about the Father's business (Luke 2:49) and to do all things as under the Lord that glorifies the Lord (Colossians 3:23). An unbeliever employee is, at best, indifferent to such foundational beliefs because of his or her ignorance and needs initial salvation and afterwards needs to be trained spiritually through the incremental repetitive work and customer servanthood required at the business. If a Believer's methods and goals in business are identical to the methods and goals of an unbeliever as being okay, the Believer in business needs to reevaluate seriously his/her priorities and principles of life.

A structural problem is that most church congregations are built following a warehouse lecture hall pyramid structure paradigm that is patterned after historical precedence. The warehouse lecture hall pyramid structure paradigm is built on the premise that all the authority and money flow to the top where there is a small elite of paid workers with a CEO priest, bishop, pastor, teacher, or reverend in primary control. In the large church warehouse lecture hall pyramid structure paradigm today, millions of dollars are wasted on constructing these big buildings as the scriptures call a farmer who wants to build bigger barns.

The New King James version of Luke 12:16-21 says, "Then He spoke a parable to them, saying: 'The ground of a certain rich man yielded plentifully. (17) And he thought within himself, saying, 'What shall I do, since I have no room to store my crops?' (18) So he said, 'I will do this: I will pull down my barns and build greater, and there I will store all my crops and my goods. (19) And I will say to my soul, 'Soul, you have many goods laid up for many years; take your ease; eat, drink, and be merry.' (20) But God said to him, 'Fool! This night your soul will be required of you; then whose will those things be which you have provided?' (21) So is he who lays up treasure for himself and is not rich toward God."

Jesus' admonishment in Luke 12:16-21 is directed to all Ephesians 4:11 functioning ministers, whether they work in a traditional ecclesiastical church with a building as its central place or as owners of a business which they have dedicated as a business in ministry. The focus of both should not be on bigness but rather obedience, submitting to the leading of the Holy Spirit, and focused on all work being done humbly as unto the Lord and not for self-aggrandizement.

In their defense, most church leaders today do say the true Body of Christ is the Believers, not a building. Yet, habitually, church leaders' energy financially is supporting the building and those who work in the building as employees instead of activating Believers in their spiritual Vocations and spiritual Gifts. Western European countries and Eastern European countries have majestic religious buildings, which evident the belief that the building is the center of attention instead of building Believer disciples into ministers who have spiritual Vocations and spiritual Gifts that were activated after initial salvation through work in ministry as led by the Holy Spirit (Ephesians 2:10; Ephesians 4:12; Philippians 2:12-13).

Even in the U.S., priests, bishops, pastors, teachers, or reverends refer to the building out of tradition as the church. After a while, most Believers refer to attending church as going to the church building at a given location. They mistakenly are too casual about the concept of true *Ekklesia.* The leaders have not corrected the historical mistake of not seeing that the *Ekklesia* is a spiritual Kingdom assembly of kings, priests, lords, ambassadors, and soldiers, with each Believer having distinct spiritual Gifts for the edification of the whole body of Christ. All Believers should be engaged in preaching the gospel of the Kingdom and repentance and remission of sins in the businesses, schools, homes, professions, industries, media, laboratories, scientific centers, and governments. The Godhead refuses to be trapped in the four walls of church buildings, as He is omnipresent; and His temple is the body of Believers, individually (2 Corinthians 6:16), local community (1 Corinthians 3:16), and internationally (Ephesians 2:21).

The ecclesiastical priests, bishops, pastors, teachers, or reverends of local churches and denomination headquarters have primarily built a church structure that supports them financially; so, they do not have to work in a secular business or be employed at a secular job to earn a living. The warehouse lecture hall pyramid structure paradigm concept gives them freedom during the week going to a gym, playing golf, or contacting other ministries for engagements at their church to receive an offering as a visiting functioning evangelist, pastor, or teacher. Some of these priests, bishops, pastors, teachers, or reverends, following the traditional church paradigm, have built a warehouse lecture hall auditorium structure that sits over 10,000 members, and the priests, bishops, pastors, teachers, or reverends are multi-millionaires. Yet, they are not following Scriptures because they simply teach Believers that it is okay to be just spectators. Again, they violate the mandate to activate all Believers into their ministry spiritual Vocations and spiritual Gifts.

The modern day warehouse lecture hall pyramid structure paradigm with a large auditorium was not what Jesus used to preach the gospel of the Kingdom, preach repentance and remission of sins, pray for the sick, cast out demons, and confront religious leaders. Rather, Jesus' primary focus was spending daily contact with His disciples, kinesthetically training and activating His disciples to be humble servants and humble ministers to preach the gospel of the Kingdom and repentance and remission of sins, to cast out demons, and to heal the sick outside of the then Jewish religious hierarchy.

God does not have a problem with His ministers having money, but God does not want the money to have them as their idol and primary reward for ministry. When Paul was staying in a city for a season and not on the mission field, he did not require the local *Ekklesia* to give him financial support. He worked as a tent maker in his own business. Paul said in 1 Thessalonians 2:9, "For ye remember, brethren, our labour and travail: for labouring night and day, because we would not be chargeable unto any of you, we preached unto you the gospel of God." Similarly, Paul said in 2 Thessalonians 3:8, "Neither did we eat any man's bread for nought; but wrought with labour and travail night and day, that we might not be chargeable to any of you." Paul wanted to be an example to other Believers, so Paul worked with Priscilla and Acquilla to make tents to support himself (Acts 18:2-3).

When Paul was not on the mission field traveling city to city, Paul supported himself when staying in a city for a season as a functioning apostle in business where he could freely preach the gospel, teach, instruct, and activate other Believers in the work of the ministry without appearing to be motivated by financial gain or seeking monetary support from the local *Ekklesia.*

Paul also spoke against lazy people who refused to work. Paul said in 2 Thessalonians 3:10, "For even when we were with you, this we commanded you, that if any would not work, neither should he eat." If the functioning apostle Paul worked in a business, even though he started the local *Ekkle-*

sia, but did not ask for financial support, then why do the church leaders believe they cannot work in a business or job part time instead of taking from the donations for their personal support. In a small church (under 300), when the church leader has little to do during the week, he or she should have part-time employment or a business that earns money regularly.

On the other hand, Jesus used a "V" shaped *Ekklesia* structure (defined as a government assembly and/or military assembly), where all Believers were to be activated as ministers for the work of the ministry and where the greatest ministers were the servants of all (Matthew 23:11; Mark 10:42-45; John 13:1-15).

PURIFYING THE MINISTRIES BY SHARING THE TITHE AND OFFERINGS

Here is another historical practice that needs to be changed. This concerns the sharing of the donations with other Ephesians 4:11 functioning ministers. In the Old Testament, the duties of the Levitical priesthood included: **1)**. the teaching of the Law to the people (Leviticus 10:11); **2)**. handling the people's offering in the sacrificial system (Leviticus chapter 9); **3)**. maintaining the Tabernacle and the Temple (Numbers 18:3); **4)**. officiating in the Holy Place (Exodus 30:7-10); **5)**. inspecting ceremonially unclean persons, (Leviticus chapters 13 and 14); and **6)**. adjudicating disputes (Deuteronomy 17:8-13).

The tithe was paid to and shared with all the Levite priests who educated the people concerning the Temple and offerings, etc., not just to one of them. Numbers 18:21 says, "And, behold, I have given the children of Levi all the tenth (tithe) in Israel for an inheritance, for their service which they serve, even the service of the tabernacle of the congregation." Then the Lord commanded the Levites to tithe to Him a tenth of their tithed they received, but then give that ten percent to the Aaron Priests (Numbers 18:28).

Initially, God had selected the entire nation of Israel to be His kings and priests, according to Exodus 19:5-6. However, after the nation resisted to be His kings and priests, in Exodus 32:7-10 the Levites and Aarons, who supported Moses in Exodus chapters 26-28, were selected as God's priests, Numbers 3:5-9.

The Ephesians 4:11 functioning apostles, prophets, evangelists, pastors, and teachers have similar responsibilities by analogy and similar to the Levite priesthood of old, which is to teach and equip the Believers to do the work of the Ministry for the edification of the whole Body of Christ. They are to teach Believers seeking of the kingdom of God, continuing to repentance of sins in their souls, staying humble and submissive, practicing grace toward others, ministering mercy to people, receiving the Believers' tithes and offerings that are cheerfully given, and maintaining the Tabernacle or Temple, which in the New Testament *Ekklesia* is the bodies of all Believers.

The *Ekklesia* was not designed by the Godhead and Christ Jesus' humanity nature to be a onefold ministry headed up by one priest, bishop, pastor, teacher, or reverend; but it was designed to be a functioning fivefold local leadership of apostles, prophets, evangelists, pastors, and teachers, who would activate Believers through kinesthetic training and scholastic teaching to do the work of the ministry through their spiritual Vocations and with their spiritual Gifts for the maturation and edification of the Body of Christ.

The local congregations need to be activated in the work of ministry by all the Ephesians 4:11

functioning ministers because each of the functioning apostles, prophets, evangelists, pastors, and teachers bring a spiritual dynamic that is designed to activate Believers differently than the other four Ephesians 4:11 functioning ministers. All the functioning fivefold local leadership of the functioning apostles, prophets, evangelists, pastors, and teachers should have authority, should be given part of the tithe, and should be ministering regularly at local congregations, especially when there is a multiplicity of home fellowships. Thus, to a large degree, the leaders at the traditional warehouse lecture hall pyramid structure paradigm do not want to share authority and money with any of the other fivefold ministers of Ephesians 4:11, even if the Ephesians 4:11 functioning ministers are in the same local congregation. The reason is the modern warehouse lecture hall pyramid paradigm is structured as a pyramid with one man or one woman at the top where all authority is and where all the money flows.

Again, in Ephesians 4:12 all the functioning apostles, prophets, evangelists, pastors, and teachers are to be involved in the local *Ekklesia* community in activating Believers into their ministries of spiritual Vocations as kings, priests (Revelation 1:6), lords (1Timothy 6:15), ambassadors (2 Corinthians 5:20), and soldiers (2 Timothy 2:3-4). Again, all spiritual Gifts differ, but all Believers have the same spiritual Vocations. All Believers are commanded to be witnesses of Christ Jesus after being empowered by the Holy Spirit (Acts 1:8) and are anointed by God with the Holy Spirit and with power. 2 Corinthians 1:21-22 says, "Now He who establishes us with you in Christ **and has anointed (every one of) us (as Believers) is God**, who also has sealed us and given us the earnest of the Spirit in our hearts."

This failure in the local warehouse lecture hall pyramid structure paradigm is one of the primary reasons the Holy Spirit is establishing the *Ekklesia* in the local businesses ministers that have Ephesians 4:11 Believer Business Owners who will activate Believer Business Employees in their ministry spiritual Vocations and spiritual Gifts.

GET RID OF CULTIST SYMBOLS

The Obelisk which was put in Vatican City came from Egypt at Heliopolis, which was the cult center of the Egyptian sun-god Ra (Greek Helios). If you travel to Rome, Italy, and go to Vatican City (as I have done), you will see an erected Egyptian Obelisk that was transported to Rome by the Roman Emperor Caligula, where it was placed in the Circus of Nero, which was later moved at the order of the then Pope to St. Peter's Square, Vatican City. The Pope tried to make it a Christian Symbol by putting a Cross at the top.

During the Renaissance period the Catholic Church leadership wanted to consider the classical era as worthy of reverence and setting the stage for acceptance of Christianity. To make the Catholic Church acceptable, they reinterpreted elements of classical Greek philosophy (especially Platonism) as Christian. The Catholic Church leadership allowed the art of the Greeks and Romans to be part of Christian culture in the church buildings or cathedrals. Alongside the rediscovery of classical Greek and Roman art, it became commonplace to mix pagan art with Christian art.

You can see this example with the Sibyls that are depicted together with prophetesses in the ceiling of the Sistine Chapel, which Pope Julius II commissioned Michelangelo Buonarroti to do the fresco. The Sibyls, despite originating in paganism, were considered by accepted Renaissance Christian theological practice to be true prophetesses, whom God had given the ability to even reveal the coming of Christ. Yet, the mixture of paganism art with Christian art would not have happened if the church buildings were not considered the "church." Even today, the Protestant church leaders consider the statues in Catholic Church buildings a form of idol worship, but the Protestant church leaders center their ministry primarily around the church building like the Catholic leaders do. Is the warehouse lecture hall pyramid structure paradigm an idol? Of course, most church leaders would deny this.

JESUS DID NOT SANCTION THE WAREHOUSE PYRAMID LECTURE HALL PARADIGM MINISTRY SYSTEM

Jesus never told His disciples, "Peter, Andrew, James, and John, I have rented a building; and as a Carpenter I, and My half-brothers, have already built a stage, along with benches. So, here is what I want all of you young apostles to do. Invite and bring as many people as possible to this building and refer to the building as the church. Three services will be at 8:00 a.m., 10:00 a.m., and 12:00 noon. We will have evening services at 6:00 p.m. on Thursdays and Saturday evenings. This building holds about 1,000 people at a time. We can have three or four services a day and bring in multitudes. We can request and receive tithes and offerings, so I can put you guys on salary. I want the women that we have following Me to be greeters, and some of you apostles can be ushers to help people sit on the benches until deacons are appointed or others. Tell the people they can stand during praise and worship, but they must sit and be quiet while I am teaching and ministering. I do not want any spiritual gifts to be exercised while I am teaching and ministering. I will teach beatitudes, parables, the kingdom of God, and the sinners' need for repentance. I will have an altar call for those who want to be saved and accept me as Lord after, in the future, I die on a Roman Cross. I will have a second call for those who are sick to come forward where I will lay hands-on them, and many will recover or be instantly healed."

Jesus did not sanction the warehouse lecture hall pyramid structure paradigm ministry system; otherwise, He would have used it and instructed His apostles to hold services with the same structure. Yet, this is the two thousand year old warehouse lecture hall pyramid structure paradigm the church leaders have been using primarily, both Catholic and later Protestants.

Personally, I prefer home fellowships where there is genuine loving community with twenty people or less that are motivated by *agape* love of each other during the week, and where the Believers' spiritual Vocations and spiritual Gifts are operational in the meeting, where testimonies of activities during the week of each Believer are encouraged, and where each Believer is heartened to make contact over lunch or coffee during the week with other Believers. These home fellowships can grow and multiply, so long as the Believers maintain righteousness, peace, and joy in the Holy Spirit. Prayer that invites the Holy Spirit with His anointing is the key that unlocks the Kingdom of God. Home fellowships will multiply as all Ephesians 4:11 functioning ministers will be invited, and every Believer can be activated for the work of the Ministry, including how ministry is God's business. Believers can exercise their spiritual Vocations and spiritual Gifts in the community of Believers during the home fellowships and while working in the business or job during the week as servants who practice the loving, spiritual, and gratuitous work in Matthew 25:34-45.

The truth is that Jesus did not instruct His functioning apostles to own or rent buildings to conduct services in a priesthood/laity structure for His disciples to attend their entire lives. Since every Believer has the spiritual Vocation as a king, priest, lord, ambassador, and soldier; then, this is what the Ephesians 4:11 functioning apostles, prophets, evangelists, pastors, and teachers are supposed to activate in Believers those spiritual Vocations and help them discover with the Holy Spirit their spiritual Gifts.

MOST OF JESUS' MINISTRY WAS OUTSIDE OF A BUILDING.

In Matthew 4:18-21 Jesus called His Believer Business Owner functioning apostles along the shore of Galilee. In Matthew 13:13, Jesus was baptized at the Jordan River. Neither was His baptism done in a religious building.

Jesus taught in the Synagogue in Nazareth in Luke 4:18-23, and the people tried to throw Him off a cliff but He escaped. He then moved to Galilee. At first in Galilee, Jesus taught in the Synagogues (Matthew 4:23). In Luke 4: 31-36 Jesus casted out a demon in a Synagogue in Capernaum. Later, most all of Jesus' ministry was outside the Synagogue building as He was not always well received.

In Matthew 4: 24-25, it says, "And His fame went throughout all Syria: and they brought unto Him all sick people that were taken with divers diseases and torments, and those which were possessed with devils, and those which were lunatick, and those that had the palsy; and He healed them. (25) And there followed Him great multitudes of people from Galilee, and from Decapolis, and from Jerusalem, and from Judaea, and from beyond Jordan." Then Matthew 5:1-12 says, "And seeing the multitudes, He went up into a mountain: and when He was set, His disciples came unto Him: (2) And He opened His mouth, and taught them, saying, (3) 'Blessed are the poor in spirit: for theirs is the kingdom of heaven. (4) Blessed are they that mourn: for they shall be comforted. (5) Blessed are the meek: for they shall inherit the earth. (6) Blessed are they which do hunger and thirst after righteousness: for they shall be filled. (7) Blessed are the merciful: for they shall obtain mercy. (8) Blessed are the pure in heart: for they shall see God. (9) Blessed are the peacemakers: for they shall be called the children of God. (10) Blessed are they which are persecuted for righteousness' sake: for theirs is the kingdom of heaven. (11) Blessed are ye, when men shall revile you, and persecute you, and shall say all manner of evil against you falsely, for my sake. (12) Rejoice, and be exceeding glad: for great is your reward in heaven: for so persecuted they the prophets which were before you.'" Jesus continued sitting on the side of a mountain teaching people beatitudes, which was the greatest teaching that Jesus did. Wherever Jesus was He was the *Ekklesia*, which was and is not a religious building.

In Luke 8: 26-32 Jesus sailed to a country called Gadarenes, where Jesus cast out legions of demons existing in a man, who was living in a graveyard. Jesus allowed the demons to enter a herd of pigs and the pigs ran off a cliff to drown in the sea.

Coming down from the Mountain after Jesus' transfiguration, in Mark 9:17-29, Matthew 17:14-21, and Luke 9:40-44, outside of the religious building, Jesus came to His disciples. His disciples could not cast out an unclean spirit that caused a boy not to hear or speak and would throw the boy into the fire. Jesus casted out the deaf and dumb demon in the boy. Upon inquiry by Jesus' disciples why they could not cast out this demon, Jesus told them this demon only came out after their prayer and fasting. This is a good example how Jesus instructed with kinesthetic training of His disciples.

Jesus conducted miracles of changing elements outside the Synagogue or Temple. In John 2:7-9 Jesus attended a wedding in Cana, and He turned water into wine. This was a miracle of changing one element into another element outside of a religious building. In Matthew 14:13–21, Mark 6:31–44, Luke 9:12–17, and John 6:1–14, Jesus went to a desert place and taught five thousand men and their families; and Jesus fed them by multiplying five loaves of bread and two fish. In Matthew 15:32–39 and Mark 8:1–9, Jesus used seven loaves of bread and a few small fish to feed a crowd of four thousand.

Jesus addressed disciples of John the Baptist in Matthew 11:2-5, "Now when John had heard in the prison the works of Christ, he sent two of his disciples, (3) And said unto Him, 'Art thou He (Messiah) that should come, or do we look for another?' (4)Jesus answered and said unto them, 'Go and shew John again those things which ye do hear and see: (5) The blind receive their sight, and the lame walk, the lepers are cleansed, and the deaf hear, the dead are raised up, and the poor have the gospel preached to them.'"

In Luke 17:11-19 while traveling along the road while heading toward Jerusalem, Jesus healed ten lepers. In John 11:1-11 in Jerusalem near the Temple, Jesus encountered a blind man on the street, who was blind from birth. Jesus healed the blind man by spitting into the dirt to make mud, smearing the mud on his eyes, and then commanding the blind man to go and wash his eyes in the Pool of Siloam.

Most of the miracles of healings were outside of a religious building. In Luke 8:40-48, while Jesus was walking through a crowd He healed a woman in the streets. The woman merely touched the hem of Jesus' garment, and she was healed. In Luke 4:38-39, Jesus healed Simon Peter's mother who had a fever in Peter's house.

Miracles of healing outside of the religious building by one's faith for another person's healing was honored by Jesus. In Matthew 15:21-28 Jesus was requested by a Canaanite woman for Him to heal her daughter of sickness, and she was persistent. Jesus said, "O woman, great is thy faith," and immediately her daughter was healed. In Matthew 8:5-13 and Luke 7:1-9 when Jesus walked into Capernaum, a Roman Centurion approached Him and requested Jesus to heal his servant who was paralyzed in bed in the Centurion's house. Jesus agreed to come to the Gentile home even though under the law it was forbidden for a Jew to enter a Gentile home. The Centurion told Jesus that it was not necessary to come into his Gentile home because he was a Soldier under authority and an Officer who had authority, and his soldiers would obey him. The Centurion said he recognized that Jesus was a man of authority and that His word was sufficient to heal his servant. Jesus said in Matthew 8:10, 13 "... I have not found so great faith, no, not in Israel . . . (13) And Jesus said unto the centurion, 'Go thy way; and as thou hast believed, so be it done unto thee.' And his servant was healed in the selfsame hour."

RAISING THE DEAD BY GOD'S BUSINESS SERVANTS IN THE OLD TESTAMENT

Referencing the history of God's people, the writer to the Hebrews wrote about the Old Testament looking forward to the Messiah and their resurrection in Hebrews 11:35, "Women received their dead raised to life again: and others were tortured, not accepting deliverance; that they might obtain a better resurrection." The women mentioned here are most likely the two Old Testament mourning mothers who called upon the functioning prophets Elijah and Elisha with their strong anointed spiritual gifts.

Elijah's name in Hebrew is "Eliyah," which combines two Hebrew words – *Elohim* (God as Creator) and *Yahweh* (Jehovah as covenant God). 1 Kings 17:1 indicates Elijah was born in Tishbeh of Naphtali and resided in Gilead of Gad, which was a farming territory and a place where shepherds of sheep and herdsman of animals lived. In can be surmised that Elijah lived in the wilderness in the Northern Kingdom called Israel in the farming area and where he lived with his flock or herd at the time of King Ahab and his wife, Jezebel. Although what Elijah's work was before he stepped out and functioned as a great prophet of God is not revealed in the Bible, but his appearance was dressed like someone living outdoors in the sun and was a rough looking man, who wore a leather belt around his waist and was not dressed as those in the King Ahab and Queen Jezebel's court. 2 Kings 1:8 says, "And they answered him, 'He was an hairy man, and girt with a girdle of leather about his loins.' And he said, 'It is Elijah the Tishbite.'" Elijah looked like John the Baptist or vice versa. So, when God called Elijah to ministry he was living in the wilderness, and this fact further supports that he had his own business caring for his animals as a shepherd or herdsman. However, it is significant that Elijah had great stature as one of God's functioning prophets, as Elijah's prominence is further confirmed in Matthew 17:3, where Elijah was used by God to appear with Jesus on the Mount of Transfiguration as the representative for all the prophets along with Moses who represented the law.

Also, Malachi 4:4-6 says, "Remember ye the law of Moses my servant, which I commanded unto him in Horeb for all Israel, with the statutes and judgments. (5) Behold, I will send you Elijah the prophet before the coming of the great and dreadful day of the LORD: (6) And he shall turn the heart of the fathers to the children, and the hearts of the children to their fathers, lest I come and smite the earth with a curse."

Like Elijah, John the Baptist lived in the wilderness and was rough, but Jesus said in Matthew11:7-14, "And as they departed, Jesus began to say unto the multitudes concerning John, **What went ye out into the wilderness to see? A reed shaken with the wind?** (a fragile man) (8) **But what went ye out for to see? A man clothed in soft raiment? behold, they that wear soft clothing are in kings' houses**. (9) But what went ye out for to see? **A prophet? yea, I say unto you, and more than a prophet.** (10) For this is he, of whom it is written, '**Behold, I send my messenger before thy face, which shall prepare thy way before thee**.' (11) **Verily I say unto you, 'Among them that are born of women there hath not risen a greater than John the Baptist:** notwithstanding he that is least in the kingdom of heaven is greater than he. (12) And from the days of John the Baptist until now the kingdom of heaven suffereth violence, and the violent take it by force. (13) For all the prophets and the law prophesied until John. (14) And if ye will receive it, this is Elias (same spirit as Elijah), which was for to come.'"

Thus, John the Baptist was neither a weak person like a reed that bends with the wind nor like a king in is fine and soft dress. John the Baptist wore rough camel hair and ate locust and honey and lived in the wilderness outdoors in the sun. He was like Elijah the prophet, a man use to roughing it outdoors. This is what God likes in His prophets, not how they are dressed but tough enough to speak God's truths against idolatry.

The reference in Hebrew 11:35 was that Elijah lay his body upon the body of the widow's son at Zarephath three times and prayed for his life to return. The man was raised from the dead and life came back into him (1 Kings 17:17-24).

1 Kings 18:20-40 details the confrontation on Mount Carmel where Elijah proposes a public contest with the prophets of Baal before the Israelites to determine which god is the true God. Elijah had the prepare bullocks as sacrifices, and covered the altar with wood, laying the bullocks selected to be sacrificed. When it was Elijah's turn to call down fire, he dosed the altar, sacrificed animals, all the wood and even the dirt soaked with extra amounts of water. Elijah then prayed to the Hebrew true God, and God sent His holy, cleansing fire and consumed everything even the sacrifice, wood, stones, and even the dirt. 1 Kings 18:38-40 says, "Then the fire of the LORD fell, and consumed the

burnt sacrifice, and the wood, and the stones, and the dust, and licked up the water that was in the trench. (39) And when all the people saw it, they fell on their faces: and they said, 'The LORD, He is the God; the LORD, He is the God.' (40) And Elijah said unto them, 'Take the prophets of Baal; let not one of them escape.' And they took them: and Elijah brought them down to the brook Kishon, and slew them there.'" Elijah's battle against idolatry was similar when Moses came down the mountain and "the golden calf" was totally consumed. Speaking against idolatry and false religions in the world, and against religiosity instead of a intimacy with the Lord and the entire Godhead, is what God expects functioning prophets must do as leaders of God's people.

In some respects most Believer Business Owners functioning as prophets are tough and will come up against idolatry and falsehoods in the marketplace. Believer Business Owners functioning as prophets lay down the solid concrete for the business and establish the business on the sound foundation where real life that manifest by our Creator and the Lord Jesus Christ. John 8:31-32 says, ". . . If ye continue in my word, then are ye My disciples indeed; (32) And ye shall know the truth, and the truth shall make you free."

1 Kings 19:19 says, "So he (Elijah) departed thence, and found Elisha the son of Shaphat, who was plowing with twelve yokes of oxen before him, and he with the twelfth: and Elijah passed by him and cast his mantle upon him." Twenty-four oxen (each of the 12 yokes having two oxen) show that Elisha was a farmer, working in his family's successful farming business. After Elijah threw his mantle on Elisha, Elisha requested him permission to go and give his mother and father a goodbye kiss.

Continuing, 1 King 19:21, it says, "And he (Elisha) returned back from him (Elijah), and took a yoke of oxen, and slew them, and boiled their flesh with the instruments of the oxen, and gave unto the people, and they did eat. Then he arose, and went after Elijah, and ministered unto him (with food)." Having twelve yokes of oxen (each yoke having two oxen), meaning twenty-four oxen, showed Elisha being about His father's business, had authority as an owner to kill one yoke of oxen (meaning two oxen) and provide food for the people related to the family business. This action showed Elisha cared for people like a benevolent feudal lord and would be submissive to his new spiritual father, Elijah. Also, Elisha did not dishonor his parents, which was an indication that Elisha would honor Elijah as his spiritual father and carry the elder functioning prophet's bags.

Thereafter, for several years Elisha was kinesthetically trained by Elijah how to minister as a functioning prophet. In the end Elisha asked Elijah for his mantle received the double anointing upon Elijah taken up in God's chariot. The twelve yoke of oxen is liturgical as the twenty-four oxen that were in service of Elisha could be the reference to the twelve tribes of Israel on the one side of the yokes and with Jesus' twelve apostles on the other side of the yokes. This is the Old Testament and New Testament linked together under the anointing of two prophets. Elisha's twenty-four oxen also could be a liturgical model of priesthood since oxen are "servants", so they pictured the priesthood, men who humble themselves before God and serve in His household. Here we have Elisha, a business farmer, is called as a functioning prophet "employee" under training of another business elder functioning prophet, Elijah. In the Old Testament the priesthood was supposed to be all of Israel's children, who were called as a Kingdom of priest and holy nation (Exodus 19:6), while under 1 Peter 2:9, all New Testament Believers of Christ Jesus are also called as royal priests (kingdom of priests) and a holy nation.

Being a functioning prophet had great esteem in the Old Testament, as functioning prophets had spiritual authority as they spoke with the commanding prophetic word from God. Prophets interpreted dreams, appointed and counseled kings and individuals, exhorted Israelites to follow Commandments and Laws of the true God. Prophets pronounced judgment against unfaithful servants (Gehazi- 2 Kings 5:23, 27), and judgment of self-absorbed and proud kings not recognizing God's provision and favor (Nebuchadnezzar II went crazy for a season because his prideful belief that he built Babylon without gratitude for God's blessing, so he did not listen to the prophet Daniel, went crazy, ate grass with the animals, but then came to his senses and praised God of Israel- Daniel 4:31-37). Prophets reveal the sins of kings (David's sin with Bathsheba and his sin of killing her husband, Uriah, as a cover-up, David was rebuked by the functioning prophet, Nathan, with the consequence of Bathsheba and David's first baby died, but David's repentance and God's forgiveness caused Solomon to be born-2 Samuel 12:1-24). Prophets were sometimes able to see angels (Elisha by the leading of the Lord opens the eyes of his servant to see a heavenly host of angels- 2 Kings 6:17). Prophets performed miracles (Moses, a sheep herder employee of his father-in-law, Jethro, of the prior 40 years when he returned to Egypt at age 80 as a functioning prophet and deliverer, and through the leading of the Lord caused ten plagues to fall on Egypt to convince Pharaoh to let the Children of Israel leave Egypt- Exodus chap. 7 and on the way to the Promise Land caused the Red Sea to part allowing the Children of Israel to walk on dry land and when the wall of water felled back, the Egyptian soldiers drowned-Exodus Chap. 14). Prophets by the leading of the Holy Spirit can prophesy about future events (Isaiah prophesied the coming of the suffering Messiah-Isaiah chap. 53).

Although Old Testament, functioning prophets by and large were highly respected, their ministry was also a perilous one. If they spoke against the king's wishes their lives could be in danger, as Daniel was thrown into the lion's den (Daniel 6:10-23), or if they misspoke what was meant by the King's vision or if the prophetic word did not come to past, they could be stoned. Luke 13:34 says, "O Jerusalem, Jerusalem, which killest the prophets, and stonest them that are sent unto thee; how often would I have gathered thy children together, as a hen doth gather her brood under her wings, and ye would not!"

Elisha was trained by one of the most important figures in the history of Israel, who was Elijah. For a while after he began to follow Elijah, there is little mentioned of Elisha until at the time of Elijah's departure. Elisha merely must have been observing and watching, learning through kinesthetic training by spending time with Elijah. Elisha was like Elijah's employee in spiritual training. This is how a Believer Business Owner is to scholastically teach and kinesthetically train a Believer Business Employee. Later, when Elijah was taken up by God in a chariot, Elisha picked up Elijah's mantle and received a double portion of Elijah's anointing (2 Kings 2:9). Elisha's ministry was anointed by the power of God, and he performed double the miracles of Elijah and more miracles than any other individual in the Bible except for Jesus.

At the unction and anointing of God, Elisha ministered by lying on top of a dead Shunammite boy, and the Shunammite woman's son was raised from the dead (2 Kings 4:18-37). Elisha's prophetic anointing was still in his bones; and even after he died, a dead man's body was thrown into Elisha's sepulcher. When the dead man's body touched the bones of Elisha, and the man rose from the dead and regained his life (2 Kings 13:20-21).

Jesus had His Sermon on the Mount of Beatitudes (Matthew chap. 5), and with parables He taught those, bound in Jewish religion, who could not understand the more sophisticated spiritual truths that the Messiah was present and pronounced that the Kingdom of God had come to earth. On the other hand, Jesus spent most of His time instructing His apostles using kinesthetic training how to heal the sick, cast out demons, and preach both the gospel of the kingdom along with repentance and remission of sins (Matthew 10:7-8; 24:14; Luke 24:27). Jesus was training His disciples through kinesthetic hands on instruction to be His witnesses throughout the world after He ascended to heaven (Acts 1:8).

In continuing the discussion His functioning apostles needed kinesthetic training and with scholastic teaching of the Bible are both needed; but kinesthetic training activates better Believer Business Employees to become ministers, especially using the business as a biblical scholastic teaching and kinesthetic training center for ministers in business. Jesus taught His disciples mostly with kinesthetic training, as that was the method that His step-father kinesthetically trained Him to become a journeyman carpenter and stonemason. Jesus was trained as a builder in the natural, and He continued building Believers to be His ministers in God's kingdom.

JESUS WAS A BUSINESS CARPENTER AND STONEMASON MESSIAH AND HE RAISED THE DEAD AS THE ONLY BEGOTTEN SON OF GOD

Jesus raised the dead outside of religious buildings. In Mark 5:22 and Luke 8:49-56, Jairus, who was one of the a rulers of a local synagogue, had a daughter who died. At the behest of Jairus, Jesus went to his home and raised his daughter from the dead. In Luke 7:11–17 Jesus came to a village of Nain and encountered a funeral procession, and Jesus stopped the procession and raised a widow's only son from the dead. In John 11:38-44, in Bethany near Jerusalem, Jesus went to the sepulcher and called out to Lazarus to "come forth" and thereby raised Lazarus from the dead. Each of these three people were raised from the dead for the purpose of demonstrating that Jesus had the authority and power from God over death in any place, not a particular fellowship building. As the carpenter and stonemason Messiah, in John 11:25-26, "Jesus said unto her (Lazarus' sister, Martha), I am the resurrection, and the life: he that believeth in Me, though he were dead, yet shall he live: (26) And whosoever liveth and believeth in Me shall never die. Believest thou this?"

This most miraculous of signs continued, of course, through Jesus Christ. Resurrection life was on His agenda. Witnessing Jesus raising the dead, showing His Ephesians 4:11 functioning ministers how to do it, Jesus commissioned the twelve functioning apostles to do the same, saying in Matthew 10:7-8, "And as ye go, preach, saying, 'The kingdom of heaven is at hand.' (8) Heal the sick, cleanse the lepers, **raise the dead,** cast out devils: freely ye have received, freely give." And His functioning apostles did raise the dead. The Gospels record that Jesus' functioning apostles were "healing people everywhere" (Luke 9:6). Over the crucifixion weekend, not only did Jesus arise Himself from the dead (John 2:19), but also there was a mysterious resurrection of many "...bodies of the saints which slept arose, and came out of the graves after His resurrection, and went into the holy city, and appeared unto many" (Matthew 27:52-53).

While raising the dead is not specifically included among the "Great Commission" list of miracles to follow the word preached in Mark 16:15-20, it is clear that the early *Ekklesia* Believers continued to raise people from the dead. Jesus promised in John 14:12, "Verily, verily, I say unto you, He that believeth on Me, the works that I do shall he do also; and greater works than these shall he do; because I go unto my Father." In fulfillment of Jesus' promise, Peter brings Tabitha back from the dead (Acts 9:36-42). Replicating Elijah's method of raising the dead, Paul placed himself around the body of Eutychus, who fell asleep and fell from a window; and God through Paul raised him from the dead (Acts 20:7-10). Paul, while preaching at Lystra was stoned by the angry Jews, and most believed he was dead, having no signs of life; but as the Believers surrounded Paul and prayed, Paul was revived and apparently rose from the dead (Acts 14:19-20). Later, in 2 Corinthians 12:2-4, Paul remembered the stoning and said, "I knew a man in Christ above fourteen years ago, (whether in the body, I cannot tell; or whether out of the body, I cannot tell: God knoweth;) such an one caught up to the third heaven. (3) And I knew such a man, (whether in the body, or out of the body, I cannot tell: God knoweth;) (4) How that he was caught up into paradise, and heard unspeakable words, which it is not lawful for a man to utter."

SMITH WIGGLESWORTH WAS A BUSINESS PLUMBER AND AS A MODERN DAY FUNCTIONING EVANGELIST RAISED 14 PEOPLE FROM THE DEAD

Wikipedia says, "Smith Wigglesworth was born on 10 June 1859 in Menston, Yorkshire, England, to an impoverished family. As a small child, he worked in the fields pulling turnips alongside his mother; he also worked in factories to help provide for his family. He was illiterate as a child, being unschooled because of his labours.

Wigglesworth married Mary Jane 'Polly' Featherstone on 4 December 1882 at St Peter's church, Bradford. At the time of their marriage, she was a preacher with the Salvation Army and had come to the attention of General William Booth. They had one daughter, Alice, and four sons, Seth, Harold, Ernest and George. Polly died in 1913. Their grandson, Leslie Wigglesworth, after more than 20 years as a missionary in the Congo, served as the president of the Elim Pentecostal Church.

Wigglesworth learned to read after he married Polly; she taught him to read the Bible. He often stated that it was the only book he ever read, and did not permit newspapers in his home, preferring the Bible to be their only reading material.

Wigglesworth worked as a plumber, but he abandoned this trade because he was too busy for it after he started preaching. In 1907, Wigglesworth visited Alexander Boddy during the Sunderland Revival, and following a laying-on of hands from Alexander's wife, Mary Boddy, he experienced Baptism with the Holy Spirit and spoke in tongues. He spoke at some of the Assemblies of God events in Great Britain. He also received ministerial credentials with the Assemblies of God in the United States, where he evangelized from 1924 to 1929.

He continued to minister until the time of his death on March 12, 1947.

Christianity.com says, "Various miracles were reported during Wigglesworth's ministry—including raising 14 people from the dead."

THE REVELATION THAT JESUS WAS THE CHRIST WAS DONE OUTSIDE OF A RELIGIOUS BUILDING.

The revelation that Jesus was the Christ was done outside of a religious building. In John 4: 1-26 Jesus first announced to the woman at the well outside a religious building in Samaria that He was the prophesied Messiah.

Matthew 16:13-19 reveals Jesus walking with His disciples to preach in the villages near Caesarea Philippi where there was a mixed city of Greeks, Romans, and Jews. These villages were located at the crossroads of a major road, about 40 miles north of the Sea of Galilee. This area was associated with pagan worship. While walking, Jesus asked His disciples who did men say He was? At that time, many Jews believed in rebirth through resurrection, although they did not believe in reincarnation like the Hindus. For example, Luke 1:17 says that John the Baptist would come "in the spirit and power of Elijah," which means he would mirror Elijah's ministry. Matthew 16:14 says, "And they said, 'Some say that thou art John the Baptist: some, Elias (Elijah); and others, Jeremias (Jeremiah), or one of the prophets.'" In response to Jesus' question as to who they thought He was, Peter said in Matthew 16:16 "… 'Thou art the Christ, the Son of the living God.'" This revelation of Christ was not done in a religious building but while walking along a road.

Here is another great revelation that was spoken outside of a religious building. In John 11:23-27 Jesus was speaking to Martha after her brother Lazarus had died and was in the tomb. "Jesus saith unto her, 'Thy brother shall rise again.' (24) Martha saith unto him, 'I know that he shall rise again in the resurrection at the last day.' (25) Jesus said unto her, 'I am the resurrection, and the life: he that believeth in Me, though he were dead, yet shall he live: (26) And whosoever liveth and believeth in Me shall never die. Believest thou this?' (27) She saith unto Him, 'Yea, Lord: I believe that thou art the Christ, the Son of God, which should come into the world.'" After this conversation, Jesus rose Lazarus from the dead who was in a tomb where people were buried.

Perhaps, the greatest foundational truth stated by Jesus was outside of the religious building in John 3:1-21. When it was dark, the Pharisee Nicodemus came to Jesus where He was staying, and John 3:2-6, memorializes this great conversation "… 'Rabbi, we know that thou art a teacher come from God: for no man can do these miracles that thou doest, except God be with Him.' (3) Jesus answered and said unto him, 'Verily, verily, I say unto thee, Except a man be born again, he cannot see the kingdom of God.' (4) Nicodemus saith unto Him, 'How can a man be born when he is old? Can he enter the second time into his mother's womb, and be born?' (5) Jesus answered, Verily, verily, I say unto thee, 'Except a man be born of water and *of* the Spirit, he cannot enter into the kingdom of God. (6) That which is born of the flesh is flesh; and that which is born of the Spirit is spirit.'" Then at the same night outside of a religious building, Jesus said to Nicodemus in John 3:16, "For God so loved the world, that he gave his only begotten Son, that whosoever believeth in him should not perish, but have everlasting life."

Jesus taught His disciples, especially His apostles, that their ministry assignments were in every place where there is a need for spiritual intervention to bring a spiritual change, blessings, and eternal life in people's lives. That means ministry is in the street corners, in the homes, in businesses, in schools, in media, in movies, in governments, and in everywhere and to everyone who has faith to accept Christ Jesus as Lord and Savior.

CHURCH HISTORY REVEALS THE EKKLESIA STRUGGLED IN ITS BEGINNING FOUNDATION

Historically, around 313 A.D., the Roman Emperor, Maximian, had persecuted the Believers. General Constantine, with his superior army, was in war against Maximian. Maximian knew he would be dethroned, and Maximian knew that Constantine was a converted Christian and was supportive of those of the Christian faith. Before Maximian lost power, he issued a decree in an unsuccessful attempt to gain Constantine's favor and peace by decreeing that Believers in all the Western part of the Roman Empire could build the *Ekklesia* as a building and call it the "house of God." Thus, from that day forward, the "house of God," or building, started being referred to as the church. Since then, for approximately 1800 years, the church has been referred to as the building, cathedral, or the warehouse lecture hall paradigm system, which continues as a great mistake that Jesus did not mandate.

Instead of sticking with the functioning apostles' doctrines of the first Century *Ekklesia*, the church leadership allowed politics to come into the church and engage in arguments over the issues as whether Jesus was just all human, or was He all God, or was He both. Some church leaders developed inaccurate arguments, false concepts, and aberrant theology. These debates and arguments went on for centuries.

For example, Thomas Aquinas lived from 1225 to 1274. He became a Catholic Italian Dominican Friar and Priest, and he was considered one of the foremost scholastic thinkers in Catholic Church history. Aquinas became one of the most influential philosophers and theologians in the Western church tradition. Yet, Aquinas postulated that faith should consider rational thought and practical application as well as belief in God's grace and *agape* love. Aquinas suggested that many church scholars focused on pointless questions rather than important matters of faith. Aquinas said, "Therefore, I say that this proposition, 'God exists', of itself is self-evident, for the predicate is the same as the subject ... Now because we do not know the essence of God, the proposition is not self-evident to us; but needs to be demonstrated by things that are more known to us, though less known in their nature—namely, by effects." (Thomas Aquinas. The Existence of God (Prima Pars, Q. 2). *Summa Theologica* – via newadvent.org.)

The arguments and actions in church history regarding the canonized word and printed scriptures reveal debates by religious elitists as opposed to prophetic utterances. The Council of Nicaea called by the Emperor Constantine met in 325 C.E., and Constantine's mandate was for the religious leaders to establish a unified Catholic Church throughout the known world as a state-sanctioned religion. The problem was that the religious leaders did not have unity of agreement on universally sanctioned scriptures that constituted a canonized Bible. There were many writings of letters, such as the gospel of Thomas and others; so, the leaders had to decide what writings would be contained in one sanctioned canonized New Testament Bible. Also, what language would the Bible be written- Latin, French, German, or English?

Various church leaders and officials were using different Greek texts and different letters and gospels for translation into Latin for the scriptures to be included in the canonized Bible. For this primary reason, in 393 C.E. the Council of Hippo sanctioned 27 books for the New Testament written in Latin. Still not universally accepted, so in 397 C.E. the Council of Cartage confirmed the same 27 books as the authorized version and authoritative canonized scriptures for the State church.

At that time, after church leaders spent much work and time in eliminating all other writings that were competing gospels and scriptures, you would think that leaders would want all Believers to read and study these 27 books of the New Testament for their edification, right? That did not happen.

The Catholic State Church discouraged the rank and file Believers in the Catholic pyramid structure headed by a Pope from reading the Bible on their own, and this policy was intensified throughout the Middle Ages. Also, the Catholic Church forbade the printing of the Bible in other languages, such as in English, French, German, or any other native tongues.

The *Decree of the Council of Toulouse* of 1229 C.E. stated: "We prohibit also that the laity should be permitted to have the books of the Old or New Testament; but we most strictly forbid their having any translation of these books." Similarly, the Ruling of the Council of Tarragona of 1234 C.E. states: "No one may possess the books of the Old and New Testaments in the Romance language, and if anyone possesses them, he must turn them over to the local bishop within eight days after promulgation of this decree, so that they may be burned..."

The *Proclamations at the Ecumenical Council of Constance* in 1415 C.E. stated that the English

Oxford professor, and theologian John Wycliffe, was the first (1380 C.E.) to translate the New Testament into English for the purpose to "...helpeth Christian men to study the Gospel in that tongue in which they know best Christ's sentence." For this pronounced heresy Wycliffe was posthumously condemned by Arundel, the archbishop of Canterbury. By the Council's decree "Wycliffe's bones were exhumed and publicly burned, and the ashes were thrown into the Swift River."

One of the best Bibles translated into English was that of William Tyndale. According to Tyndale, the Catholic Church at that time still forbade owning or reading any unauthorized Bible. The underlying purpose was so the Catholic Priests and Catholic ecclesiastical hierarchy could control and restrict the teachings by the laity to enhance the Catholic church leaders' own power, riches, and prestige.

The Catholic ecclesiastical hierarchy was set up in an anemic and false dichotomy of priesthood and laity. The Catholic ecclesiastical hierarchy set as church edict that the laity could never be ministers. Again, speaking to the church in Ephesus, Jesus said in Revelation 2:6, "But this thou hast, that thou hatest the deeds of the Nicolaitans, which I also hate." *Nico* means hatred, and *laitans* means the ordinary people or laity. So, the Catholic ecclesiastical hierarchy hated and did not want the laity to be activated as Believer ministers, although all Believers are to be activated as ministers pursuant to the mandate in Ephesians 4:12. Jesus hated the deeds of those who established an elitest church who kept the working class Believers in spiritual darkness not to know the truth that sets them free from the bondage of ignorance about the things of God.

Tyndale was a student at Magdalen Hall, Oxford, and believed that everyone should be able to read the Bible in their own language. Tyndale left England in 1524 to translate the Catholic Church's Latin Bible into English, which the Catholic Church was totally against its translation and totally against its printing and distribution. Tyndale had a German Printer publish his translation of the Bible in English because he wanted the common Believer to be able to read and study the Bible. Tyndale's Bible was smuggled into England. Tyndale's translations were used in later English Bibles, including the King James Version. For his "crime" of publishing an English Bible, the Catholic authorities in Antwerp, Belgium arrested Tyndale, convicted him of heresy, sentenced him to death by burning at the stake; but Tyndale was strangled before his body was set on fire and burned at the stake in 1536. So, what was the fate of William Tyndale in 1536 C.E. for simply translating the Bible from Latin to English? He was martyred.

SCOFIELD'S MISUSE OF THE CANONIZED SCRIPTURES

There are those who foster the idea that ever since the church produced the canonize word and the functioning apostles and prophets were done away and no longer part of the Ephesians 4:11 functioning ministers, functioning apostles and prophets are not here today. None of the Ephesians 4:11-13 ministers have been abolished or deemed not applicable to the *Ekklesia* today. So, according to scripture, the functioning apostles and prophets have equal mandates to activate the Believers for the work of their spiritual Vocations and spiritual Gifts for the edification of the Body of Christ (Ephesians 4:12).

Thus, the exclusion of functioning apostles and prophets on the ground that the Bible was canonized is flawed. Why? After the canonized word was printed in Latin, a dead language that only religious scholars at that time could read, how many Believers lived and died without ever reading the Bible in their native tongue during the middle ages because they were forbidden to do so by the Catholic Church ecclesiastical hierarchy. In truth, the laity are ministers in the true "V" shape *Ekklesia* structure, but at that time the church was structured as a pyramid shape as the Catholic Hierarchy, where all authority and power were in the office of "Pope." God wanted the Bible in every language to allow all Believers to read the Bible in their own language to mature and activate them into ministry. When God spoke to any Believer in the world during those years, God spoke in that Believer's language, not just Latin

These are false teachings primarily promoted by Cyrus Ingerson Scofield. His teachings have caused disunity in the body of Christ for his misuse of canonize scriptures to bolster his viewpoints of not believing spiritual gifts or apostles or prophets are for today. What would be Scofield's underlying motive or proclivity to start this disunity. Let's look at his personal life. Scofield was born in Michigan but grew up in Tennessee. He fought for the Confederacy during the Civil War, studied law in Saint Louis, Missouri, and then he entered the Kansas State Bar and moved to Kansas in 1869. He served there as a state legislator and U.S. district attorney but experienced serious drinking and marital problems. He returned to St. Louis to practice law. However, this period was marked by heavy drinking alcohol and financial troubles, causing his legal practice and marriage to suffer. He returned to St. Louis, Missouri and between 1874 to 1879 practiced law there. In 1879 Scofield converted to Christianity and immediately stopped practicing law. He became a YMCA worker but later pastored Congregational churches in Texas and Massachusetts. In 1883, He was ordained as a congregational minister. He published the Scofield Reference Bible in 1909, which significantly influenced fundamentalist Christianity, particularly in the United States; and the theology promoted within its notes was dispensational, as he accepted Darby's teachings on dispensationalism, among other new ideas of Darby.

How did Scofield's alcoholic addiction affect his ministry after sobriety. Although not all psychologists would promote the idea that alcoholic personality traits are permanent, research and clinical observation support the proposition that traits like self-centeredness, mood swings, anger, and grandiosity can persist after the alcoholic's sobriety. These psychological disorder behaviors that persist are sometimes called "dry drunk syndrome," as used by Alcoholic Anonymous. These psychological personality traits are well-documented in addiction recovery studies too numerous to mention here. You can attend any Alcoholics Anonymous meeting where every speaker begins by saying, "My name is John Smith, and I am an alcoholic."

To his credit Scofield was first an American lawyer, so He was an intelligent man, who was born in 1843 and died in 1921. Yet, like Thomas Jefferson, Scofield did not believe in healings, miracles, spiritual gifts, or functioning apostles or prophets. He used his legal skills to argue away healings, miracles, spiritual gifts, or that functioning apostles or prophets are not for today because of the canonized word. Yet, lawyers are trained to argue alternative ideas, but taking scriptures out of the Bible can be a violation of having God's truth alone.

He promoted dispensational premillennialism, particularly through his widely influential Scofield Reference Bible in 1909, used the King James Version, but wrote extensive notes explaining his theological views. His Bible notes have been used to spread dispensational premillennialism in America, especially his ideas on the rapture of the church. His core beliefs, outlined in his Bible's extensive notes, included the idea of seven distinct eras (dispensations) in God's dealings with humanity and a strong emphasis on a future literal return of Christ and a special status for Israel, which significantly shaped American fundamentalist theology and Christian Zionism. Again these ideas were introduced by John Nelson Darby.

One of his most popular doctrines was to promote with headings in his Bible the rapture theology.

Theological dispensationalism, including the new doctrine of rapture, was developed by John Nelson Darby, However, Scofield put his notes directly beside scriptures, and stated the word rapture as a heading. His Scofield Bible made the complex theological system of dispensationalism, including the new doctrine of rapture with explanation notes and cross-references created a detailed guide for interpreting the entire Bible through a dispensationalist lens. He made with his notes much easier to understand theological dispensationalism. The Bible was a huge commercial success amongst Believers and sold more than two million copies in its first few decades. The sales of Scofield Bible kept its publisher, Oxford University Press, to survive the Great Depression. Scofield's orderly system offered readers a clear and organized timeline for understanding biblical prophecy, which was very appealing during a period of heightened interest in eschatology. This framework provided a structure for later popular works, such as Hal Lindsey's *The Late Great Planet Earth.* Also, the *Left Behind series* was published by Tyndale House Publishers, written by Tim LaHaye and Jerry B. Jenkins, and it promoted Scofield's theological dispensationalism, with an emphasis in promoting the rapture as the great escape.

Concerning the rapture theology, it fit in with Darby and Scofield's theological dispensationalism. The early 20th century provided fertile ground for the rapture theology. Scofield's Bible appeared in 1909 just a few years before World War I. World War I caused depression and fear, but Scofield's Bible caused widespread optimism in the U.S. Darby and Scofield's premillennial theology predicted the world was rapidly heading towards Christ's return. However, to avoid all God's Judgment initial salvation and the rapture theology offered escape, which resonated with Believers just prior to World War I.

The theology of rapture started in 1830 when a teenage functioning prophetess named Margaret Macdonald, associated with the Irvingite movement in Scotland, reportedly received a prophetic vision of a **pre-tribulation rapture**. John Nelson Darby was a prominent figure in the Plymouth Brethren movement, especially in England, and the idea of a pre-tribulation rapture was used and adapted into his broader theological system of dispensationalism. Darby spread his thoughts that the present Church Age was a separate period in God's plan for Israel, culminating in a secret return of Christ to rapture Believers before the Great Tribulation and the rise of the Son of Perdition (perdition meaning ruin, destruction, and eternal damnation) or better known as the Antichrist. Darby taught that the idea of a pre-tribulation rapture also is a period of the great "falling away" of Believers, indicating that soon the Antichrist will bring doom and destruction. Darby taught that the Antichrist exalts himself over all others, takes his place in the Temple in Jerusalem, and by possessing and controlling the Antichrist, Satan is worshiped in the Jerusalem Temple instead of the God of the Bible. Darby said those who worship Satan will be punished with Satan to God's infernal Lake of fire. Furthermore, Darby interpreted scripture that after a certain amount of time, Jesus Christ returns in the brightness of His glory and the Beast, Antichrist, and Satan, the fallen angels, demons, hell, death, and all those humans whose names are not written in the Book of Life are thrown into the Lake of Fire in Revelation 20:10-15.

After rapture theology started from a teenage prophetess, Margaret Macdonald, the rapture theology became very popular in the U.S. by the teaching Darby taught. Since the rapture theology was written with predominance in the Scofield Bible, his Bible commentary made Scofield very popular and made him and his family a continuous flow of money, especially during the Great Depression.

Since Scofield did not believe that functioning apostles and prophets are for today, why would Scofield base his rapture theology on a teenager's "prophetic word" in 1830?

Personally, I think it will be nice if the rapture theology is true, but I also understand that the rapture theology is not widely accepted globally. Also, for the first 1900 years, no recognized Christian scholar spoke about rapture. The rapture theology has a rather recent acceptance since 1830, but especially in the 1900's or twentieth century. The rapture theology has been promulgated in the U.S. for a Century by the Scofield Bible, Hal Lindsey's *The Late Great Planet Earth,* and Tim LaHaye and Jerry B. Jenkins' *Left Behind series* along with the Jesus movement. Although like some others, I acknowledged but did not promote the rapture theology. I will merely mention some scriptures that I question concerning the rapture theology, without accepting or rejecting the rapture theology.

Although I am not endorsing their book, Dr. Harold R. Eberle and Dr. Martin Trench's book, titled *Victorious Eschatology: A Partial Preterist View*, Second Edition, 2007, Second Printing, World Publishing, P.O. Box 10653, Yakima, WA 989909, www.worldcastministries.com, (509) 248-5837 has made critical arguments against the rapture theology. They see the primary discussion of Jesus in Matthew 24 is about the destruction of the Temple that indeed happened in 70 A.D. They also believe that according to scriptures used by rapture promoters is really about the Second Coming of Jesus back to earth in Revelation Chap 21

I am not revealing all discussions and ideas in their book, but their arguments did make it clear that Matthew 24 was about the destruction of the Temple in A.D. 70. Jesus was at the Temple and spoke judgment to the Pharisees concerning the Temple in Matthew 23:33-38, "Ye serpents, ye generation of vipers, how can ye escape the damnation of hell? (34)Wherefore, behold, I send unto you prophets, and wise men, and scribes: and some of them ye shall kill and crucify; and some of them shall ye scourge in your synagogues, and persecute them from city to city: (35) That upon you may come all the righteous blood shed upon the earth, from the blood of righteous Abel unto the blood of Zacharias son of Barachias, whom ye slew between the temple and the altar. (36) **Verily I say unto you, All these things shall come upon this generation.** (37) O Jerusalem, Jerusalem, thou that killest the prophets, and stonest them which are sent unto thee, how often would I have gathered thy children together, even as a hen gathereth her chickens under her wings, and ye would not! (38) **Behold, your house is left unto you desolate."**

Dr. Harold R. Eberle and Dr. Martin Trench stated on page 10, "Typically, we understand a generation to be about 40 years in length, e.g., the Hebrew people wandered in the wilderness for 40 years until a generation passed away." So, Jesus' words would have to come true while those He was addressing were still alive, not over 2000 years or more in the future. Then Jesus concluded in Matthew 23:38, "Behold, your house (Temple) is left unto you desolate." Now coming to Matthew chapter 24, the issue that is discussed is the destruction of the Temple within the next 40 years, which, again, happened in A.D. 70, not 2000 years in the future of a worldwide rapture.

Regardless, the Authors make it clear that in Matthew 24 the topic is the destruction of the Temple, as Jesus made this clear in Matthew 24. Thus, they argue that His discourse cannot be supportive of the rapture theology as it pertains to Roman Soldiers coming to destroy Jerusalem and its Temple in A.D. 70, where Matthew 24:1-3 says, "And Jesus went out, and departed from the Temple: and His disciples came to Him for to shew Him the buildings of the Temple. (2) And Jesus said unto them, 'See ye not all these things? Verily I say unto you, "There shall not be left here one stone upon another, that shall not be thrown down." (3) And as He sat upon the mount of Olives, the disciples came unto Him privately, saying, 'Tell us, when shall these things be? and what *shall be* the sign of thy coming, and of the end of the world?'" The Greek here for "world" is *aion,* (meaning age), which in context means someone's predominant life's "world." It is like someone says, "My world in business is over!" Another example would be, "The Great Industrial Age is over!" Without the Temple, Jesus' disciples said that it will be the end of the Jewish world of religious customs in Israel, so this is clear that the reference was regarding the destruction of the Jewish Temple, not the end of the entire world including the Gentile nations at that time or in the future.

On page 7-8 of their book, Dr. Harold R. Eberle and Dr. Martin Trench wrote there were three questions that were answered in Matthew 24: "Question #1: 'When will these things happen?' Question #2: 'What will be the sign of your coming?' Question #3: 'What about the end of the age?' ... We will see how our Lord first answered question one in Matthew 24:4-28. Then He answered the second question in Matthew 24:29-35. Finally, He answered the question about the end of the age in Matthew 24:36-25:46."

The Authors went on to say on pages 11-12, "Jesus declared this while standing in the Temple in Jerusalem. He cried out to the scribes and Pharisees saying that the destruction would come upon them, their city, and their Temple. Did the words of Jesus come true? Historically, did anything happen? Yes, in AD 70 Jerusalem was destroyed. Within 40 years after Jesus' judgment, 20,000 Roman soldiers surrounded the city and cut off all supplies of food so the people would starve. Then the soldiers, under the command of General Titus, came into the city and mercilessly killed more than one million Jews. The soldiers set the Temple on fire and led away 97,000 Jews as captives." [citing Flavius Josephus, *Josephus: The Complete Works*. Translated by William Whiston (Nashville, TN: Thomas Nelson Publishers, 1998) *The Wars of the Jews*, VI.ix.iii.]

Further, Dr. Harold R. Eberle and Dr. Martin Trench continuing quoted *Josephus, Wars*, 1998,VI. Viii,v., "When they [the Roman soldiers] were come to the houses to plunder them, they found in them entire families of dead men . . . that is of such as died by the famine; they then stood in a horror at this sight, and went out without touching anything. But although they had this commiseration for such as were destroyed in that manner, yet had they not the same for those that were still alive, but they ran every one through whom they met with, and obstructed the very lanes with their bodies, and made the whole city (Jerusalem) run with blood, to such a degree indeed that the fire of many of the houses was quenched with these men blood."

The Authors discussed Matthew 24:15-16, which says, "When ye therefore shall see the abomination of desolation (destruction of the temple), spoken of by Daniel the prophet, stand in the holy place, (whoso readeth, let him understand:) (16) Then **let them which be in Judea flee into the mountains**."

The Authors state that Matthew 24:15 describes the "abomination of desolation" as an event where something profane or idolatrous stands in the "holy place," which refers to the Jewish Temple by referencing what was spoken by the functioning prophet, Daniel, which means Daniel 9:27, Daniel 11:31, and Daniel 12:11. These prophecies refer to the historical desecration of the Temple by Antiochus IV Epiphanes and also applies to the destruction of the Temple in Jerusalem by the Romans. Yet, verse 15 brings relevance again to the destruction of the Temple in Jerusalem in 70 A.D., not some end time Temple.

The Authors direct that Jesus' talk to His disciples refers to Daniel 9:27, which describes a future event involving the desecration of the Jewish Temple in Jerusalem that occurred in AD 70. Jesus also referred to Daniel 11:31, which mentions forces (Roman military) setting up something that will bring desolation and profanation in the Temple. Finally, the Authors reveal that Daniel 12:11 speaks of the abomination that causes desolation and the halting of sacrifices in the Temple, and this happened in A.D. 70. These prophesies were fulfilled in A.D. 70 upon the destruction of the Temple by the Roman military and surrounded Jerusalem and starved the Jews and eventually totally destroyed every stone of the Temple.

The Authors also mentioned that Matthew 24:16 refers to a local event as Jesus said that Jews that are in Judea should flee to the mountains, so this is not a worldwide event. Judea was a specific place at the time of Jesus. Judea is specifically in Israel, not the whole world, so Jesus' prophecy was for the people who were living then in Judea, not the whole world. Thus, Matthew 24 is not supportive of the new rapture theology that was never preached as truth during the entire Church Age until the first one-third of the 1800's and did not gain popularity until the 20th Century.

The Authors argue the very important statement when Jesus continues in Matthew 24:34, "Verily I say unto you, 'This generation shall not pass, till all these things be fulfilled.'" The generation at that time saw the Temple as their life and religion. Again, Matthew 24:34 speaks about the destruction of the Temple during that current generation, not a worldwide rapture at the end of the days at the time of a future generation.

Dr. Harold R. Eberle and Dr. Martin Trench also address 1 Thessalonians 4:14-17, which says, "For if we believe that Jesus died and rose again, even so them also which sleep in Jesus will God bring with Him. (15) For this we say unto you by the word of the Lord, that we which are alive and remain unto the coming of the Lord shall not prevent them which are asleep. (16) For the Lord himself shall descend from heaven with a shout, with the voice of the archangel, and with the trump of God: and the dead in Christ shall rise first: (17) Then we which are alive and remain shall be caught up together with them in the clouds, to meet the Lord in the air: and so shall we ever be with the Lord."

Dr. Harold R. Eberle and Dr. Martin Trench bring forth the following criticisms of the rapture theology. **First of all**, 1 Thessalonians 4:14 says, "For if we believe that Jesus died and rose again, even so them also which sleep in Jesus will God bring with Him." Why would God require Believers who are already dead come to earth to pick up other live Believers and then turn around and take them back to heaven? It makes more sense that when Jesus returns, He will bring the spirits and souls of Believers already in heaven to return as the New Jerusalem as stated in Revelation chap. 21 to reign with Christ Jesus for all eternity (Revelations 5:10). Thus, this is a passage regarding Jesus' Second Coming, not a rapture. He is coming to earth to start His eternal rule with the saints (Revelation 5:10).

Second of all, 1 Thessalonians 4:16 says, "For the Lord himself shall descend from heaven with a shout, with the voice of the archangel, and with the trump of God: and the dead in Christ shall rise first."

Paul, as the same author who wrote 1 Thessalonians 4:16, also wrote 1 Corinthians 15:23, 42-44, 52 and 2 Corinthians 5:8. Consequently, when verse 16 says that the dead in Christ shall rise (bodily resurrection) this means that Darby and Scofield argue that Believers' bodies are resurrected and changed in a twinkling of an eye and Believers' bodies are taken to heaven to unite with their spirits and souls in heaven? This is contrary to other scriptures written by Paul (1 Corinthians 15:23, 42-44, 52), where the resurrection of the dead bodies will happen upon Jesus' Second Coming back here on earth to rule and reign with Believers throughout eternity. Believers' bodies never go to heaven, but only their born again spirits and souls. Thus, Paul's statement in 1 Thessalonians 4:16 refers to Jesus' Second Coming, not a pretribulation rapture.

Hebrews 11:13 says that the Old Testament saints who believed in the coming Messiah "all died in faith," which means their spirits and souls entered Abraham's Bosom after death, and their bodies decayed away in the grave. Yet, these Old Testament Saints in Abraham's Bosom went to heaven following Jesus' resurrection and ascension (Ephesians 4:8). Jesus said in John 3:13, "And no man (including Enoch or Elijah) hath ascended up to heaven, but He that came down from heaven, even the Son of man which is in heaven."

The only resurrected body allowed to ascend to heaven is that of Christ Jesus, as His body and His blood are the two most precious things in heaven. Jesus' body is the only body that was and is sinless. No where in 1 Thessalonians 4:14-17 does it say that Jesus leads Believers back to heaven, so the proponents of the rapture theology ignore that resurrection of Believers' bodies occur when the spirits and souls entered into those resurrected bodies upon Jesus' Second Coming. The term "dead in Christ shall rise first" is a statement of resurrection of dead Believers' bodies reuniting with their spirits and souls that had already died and went and entered heaven. This is nothing but an assumption by the proponents of the rapture theology that dead bodies come alive, unite with their spirits and souls in the air and then go back to heaven. In fact, 1 Thessalonians 4:14-17 does not say they go back to heaven.

Most Believers who live globally follow scriptures and have faith that the spirits and souls of Believers who have died are currently with God and Christ Jesus, but their bodies will be resurrected and glorified at Christ's Second Coming, not resurrected at the time of pretribulation rapture. At Jesus' Second Coming, all believers will have new, resurrected bodies like Jesus' body and will be with Him to rule and reign eternally with Him here in the new heaven and new earth (1 Corinthians 15:23, 42-44; Revelation 5:10; Revelation Chap. 21).

Thus, it is the truth that those Believers who die before Jesus' Second Coming do not take their bodies to heaven, as the bodies of Believers are mortal and decay away, waiting for when the Lord returns where they obtain resurrected glorious, powerful, incorruptible, immortal, spiritual bodies (1 Corinthians 15:23, 42-44). To give scripture support, 2 Corinthians 5:8 says, "We are confident, I say, and willing rather to be absent from the body, and to be present with the Lord." Thus, it is only the born again spirits and souls of Believers that go to heaven immediately upon death, and Believers' dead bodies are buried and decay away, waiting to have resurrected glorious, powerful, incorruptible, immortal, and spiritual bodies when the Lord returns to earth with the New Jerusalem to rule and reign with the Believers throughout eternity.

The Lord Jesus Christ's Second Coming is stated in Revelation 21:1-3, 9-10, which says, "And I saw a new heaven and a new earth: for the first heaven and the first earth were passed away; and there was no more sea. (2) And I John saw the holy city, new Jerusalem, coming down from God out of heaven, prepared as a bride adorned for her husband. (3) And I heard a great voice out of heaven saying, Behold, the tabernacle of God is with men, and he will dwell with them, and they shall be his people, and God himself shall be with them, and be their God. . . (9) And there came unto me one of the seven angels which had the seven vials full of the seven last plagues, and talked with me, saying, 'Come hither, I will shew thee the Bride, the Lamb's Wife. (10) And he carried me away in the spirit to a great and high mountain, and shewed me that great city, the holy Jerusalem, descending out of heaven from God."

In 1 Corinthians 15:23,42-44, God changes atoms that make up the mortal, dead bodies into new resurrected bodies, which again are glorious, powerful, incorruptible, immortal, and spiritual; and these resurrected bodies are reunited with their immortal, holy, righteous, sinless, and perfect born again spirits and souls. When those who died are Believers, only their immortal souls and born again spirits go to heaven, not their mortal bodies. Yet, when the souls and born again spirits reenter their resurrected bodies in the new heaven and new earth, then that is the fulfillment of their eternal hope. Again, these completed transformed resurrected Believers will rule and reign with Christ for all eternity (Revelation 5:10).

Also, Philippians 3:20-21 says, "For our conversation (citizenship) is in heaven; from whence also we look for the Saviour, the Lord Jesus Christ: (21) Who shall change our vile body, that it may be fashioned like unto His glorious body, according to the working whereby He is able even to subdue all things (back here on earth) unto Himself." This scripture refers to Jesus' Second Coming, not a rapture. Paul writes when Jesus returns to the earth God will put all things under Jesus' feet (Ephesians 1:22). Paul stated in 1 Corinthians 15:27, "For He hath put all things under His feet..." Paul would not contradict himself in 1 Thessalonians 4:16, as the reference is of Jesus return to earth when He subdue all things on earth.

Third of all, 1 Thessalonians 4:17 says, "Then we which are alive and remain shall be caught up together with them in the clouds, to meet the Lord in the air: and so shall we ever be with the Lord." Another interpretation for 1 Thessalonians 4: 17 would be that Jesus comes back in the clouds and then He sets up His eternal reign with the saints of the Lord (Revelation 5:10). The phrase "... so shall we ever be with the Lord" means here on earth, not in heaven. Our eternal life is living throughout internally here on earth with Christ Jesus, as heaven is not our eternal destination. Jesus' humanity nature does not live all eternity in heaven. He returns to the earth, and Believers' final destination is back here on earth, we do not live eternally in heaven.

What is Believers' eternal hope? It is not going to heaven but living here in a new heaven and new earth throughout eternity with Christ Jesus as our King and Lord. Romans 8:17 says, "And if children, then heirs; heirs of God, and joint-heirs with Christ; if so be that we suffer with Him, that we may be also glorified together... (24) For we are saved by hope: but hope that is seen is not hope: for what a man seeth, why doth he yet hope for?" Believers' hope is to live back here in the new heaven and new earth with our resurrected bodies, born again spirits, and spiritually transformed souls.

As heirs, Believers are not inheriting heaven but inheriting earth jointly with Christ Jesus' humanity nature. Ephesians 1:18-23 says, **"**The eyes of your understanding being enlightened; that ye may know what is the hope of His calling, and what the riches of the glory of His inheritance in the saints, (19) And what *is* the exceeding greatness of His power to us-ward who believe, according to the working of His mighty power, (20) Which He wrought in Christ, when He raised Him from the dead, and set Him at His own right hand in the heavenly places, (21) Far above all principality, and power, and might, and dominion, and every name that is named, **not only in this world, but also in that which is to come**: (22) And hath put all things under His feet (on earth), and gave Him to be the Head over all things to the church, (23) Which is His body, the fulness of Him that filleth all in all."

Daniel 7:22, 27 reveals the future, "Until the Ancient of days came, and judgment was given to the saints of the most High; and the time came that the saints possessed the kingdom... (27) And the kingdom and dominion, and the greatness of the kingdom under the whole heaven, shall be given to the people of the saints of the most High, whose kingdom is an everlasting kingdom, and all dominions shall serve and obey Him."

To be sure, the Believers' ultimate hope and heirship is back here on earth living with immortality ruling with Christ Jesus over the entire earth as servants for all those living here on earth throughout eternity. There still will be people being born, so there will be babies, teenagers, and adults living here on earth that will need to accept Jesus as Lord and Savior.

Obviously, Paul was thinking about the prophecy of Daniel 7:13-14, 22, 27 where Daniel said, "I saw in the night visions, and, behold, one like the Son of Man (Jesus, the only begotten Son of God) came with the clouds of heaven, and came to the Ancient of days (Father God), and they brought Him near before Him. (14) And there was given Him dominion, and glory, and a kingdom, that all people, nations, and languages, should serve Him: His dominion is an everlasting dominion, which shall not pass away, and His kingdom that which shall not be destroyed. . . (22) Until the Ancient of days came, and judgment was given to the saints of the most High; and the time came that the saints possessed the kingdom… (27) And the kingdom and dominion, and the greatness of the kingdom under the whole heaven, shall be given to the people of the saints of the most High, whose kingdom is an everlasting kingdom, and all dominions shall serve and obey Him."

The phrase "to meet the Lord in the air" does not mean to be "caught away" and does not mean going to heaven. The Greek word for "meet" is *apantesis.* Paul used the same word in Acts 28:15-16, which says, "And from thence, when the brethren heard of us, they came to meet (*apantesis*) us as far as Appii forum, and the three taverns: whom when Paul saw, he thanked God, and took courage. (16) And when we came to Rome, the centurion delivered the prisoners to the captain of the guard: but Paul was suffered to dwell by himself with a soldier that kept him." Here, Paul met the disciples, but Paul did not reverse his directions and go away from Rome.

Daniel 7:13 says the same statement that Jesus is returning to earth in the clouds of heaven. Likewise, Acts 1:9-11 says, "And when he had spoken these things, while they beheld, he was taken up; and a cloud received Him out of their sight. (10) And while they looked steadfastly toward heaven as he went up, behold, two men (angels) stood by them in white apparel; (11) Which also said, 'Ye men of Galilee, why stand ye gazing up into heaven? this same Jesus, which is taken up from you into heaven, shall so come in like manner as ye have seen him go into heaven." The message was that Jesus is coming back to earth the same way He was ascended in the clouds. The message was not that Jesus was coming back to pick up Believers and head back to heaven with those Believers.

Daniel 7:13 also refers to the Ancient of days, which is God the Father, that already is here on earth, presumably because He created a new heaven and a new earth to live here on earth (Revelation 21:1-2). So, when the Son of Man comes in the clouds, He is coming to meet with the Ancient of days, and the Ancient of Days is granting Jesus with all authority, along with the saints to have "dominion, and glory, and a kingdom, that all people, nations, and languages, should serve Him" (Daniel 7:14) and "the kingdom and dominion, and the greatness of the kingdom under the whole heaven, shall be given to the people of the saints of the most High, whose kingdom is an everlasting kingdom, and all dominions shall serve and obey Him" (Daniel 7:27).

The "Ancient of days" is God the Father who just created a new heaven and new earth (Revelation 21:1-2). The Son of man, Jesus Christ shall receive dominion over the entire earth where He will reign with the saints throughout eternity (Revelation 5:10).

It is a proper interpretation that Daniel 7:27 is fulfilled in Revelation 5:10, which says, "And hast made us unto our God kings and priests: and we shall reign on the earth." Believers reigning with Christ Jesus is back here in the new heaven and new earth, not heaven. Believers were made to live on earth and fulfill God's mandate through Christ Jesus as stated in Genesis 1:28.

Thus, Dr. Harold R. Eberle and Dr. Martin Trench argue that Scofield and his followers failed to consider all the scriptures and misinterpreted the scriptures. Paul often threw different metaphors together, expecting that Believers would understand what he means, having ministered these ideas before he wrote his letters to the various churches.

Finally, Jesus said in John 14:1-4, "Let not your heart be troubled: ye believe in God, believe also in Me. (2) In my Father's house are many mansions: if *it were* not *so,* I would have told you. I go to prepare a place for you. (3) And if I go and prepare a place for you, I will come again, and receive you unto Myself; that where I am, *there* ye may be also. (4) And whither I go ye know, and the way ye know."

First, the primary purpose of the passage is Jesus' continued "Farewell Discourse" (John chapters 13-17), which was aimed at comforting His functioning apostles who were experiencing sadness about His statements of imminent physical departure from the earth. In this passage Jesus said that He would have continuing relationship with His functioning apostles because the Holy Spirit (John 14:17, along with God the Father and God the Word (John 14:23)) would reside with them after they are born again and after His death on the Roman Cross and after His resurrection and ascension. This was not a specific end-times timeline or an early evacuation plan prior to the tribulation.

Additionally, John 14:1-4 does not explicitly mention the key "rapture" elements described elsewhere in the New Testament (like 1 Thessalonians 4), such as a trumpet call, a shout, resurrection of the dead, or meeting in the air, and the Greek rapture word *harpazo* is not used by Jesus in John 14:3.

Matthew 18: 20 says, " For where two or three are gathered together in my name, there am I in the midst of them." Matthew 28:20 says, "… and, lo, I am with you alway, even unto the end of the world (Greek aion - age)." Thus, through Jesus' divine nature, God the Word, Jesus is always with us.

Second, Jesus said in John 14:2 in "My Father's house there are many mansions" is not a reference to a physical house in heaven, but the Father's house is in a multiplicity of individuals Believers. In fact, the word "mansion" is the Greek "*mone*" in John 14:23, which says the mansion will be inside Believers. Therefore, the Greek *mone* suggests a spiritual dwelling of the Father and Son in the hearts of believers through the Holy Spirit, which can be experienced here on Earth, rather than a physical structure in heaven.

The New Testament in many places points to one return of Christ Jesus at the end of the age, which is called the "Second Coming," where the souls whose names are not in the Book of Life will face judgment at the White Throne (Revelation 20). Interpreting John 14:2-3 as a pretribulation return by Christ (rapture) is unfounded, and this interpretation requires a two-stage model of Christ's return that is not explicitly taught in this text.

The time for Jesus' return is in scripture in Revelation 21:1-3 where the biblical narrative culminates in a new heaven and a new earth where God dwells inside His adopted children. This also suggests then that the "eternal dwelling" is a restored creation of a new heaven and a new earth, not a permanent residence in a heavenly mansion away from the earth.

Furthermore, the phrase "I will come again" could refer to various reunions between Jesus and His functioning apostles, including His post-resurrection appearances before His ascension, or the final Second Coming in Revelation 21:1. Jesus did not explicitly define His return as a rapture event.

Regardless, I still hope the rapture theology is true because I would love to have the Lord come and take me away. Unfortunately, I cannot come to the same conclusions as Scofield, but I am open for both arguments. Notwithstanding, I am not waiting for the rapture to come, as I want to serve the Lord with my whole heart while I am alive here on earth. I am continuously in submission to the Godhead as the Godhead works to transform my soul by me submitting to God the Father to prune the flesh out of my soul to bear more spiritual fruit (John 15:2), God the Word to continue washing away the influence of my flesh out of my soul and sanctifying my soul to be part of the *Ekklesis*, that does not have spot, or wrinkle, or any such thing; but that it should be holy and without blemish" (Ephesians 5:26-27), and God the Holy Spirit to continue mortifying the deeds of my flesh influencing my soul so I can enjoy more *zoe* life (Romans 8:13).

Scofield also had a disdain for the current operation of spiritual gifts, and Scofield did not believe that functioning apostles and prophets exist today.

Scofield critics says he misinterpreted scripture to deny that spiritual gifts were for today because we now have the canonized scriptures. 1 Corinthians 13:8-10 says, "Charity (*agape* love) never faileth: but whether there be prophecies, they shall fail; whether there be tongues, they shall cease; whether there be knowledge, it shall vanish away. (9) For we know in part, and we prophesy in part. (10) But when that which is perfect is come, then that which is in part shall be done away."

Here, Scofield wrongly concludes that the phrase "perfect is come" is the reference to the coming of the canonized word. Critics of Scofield say their core criticisms against the Scofield argument are that the word "perfect" in 1 Corinthians 13:10 does not refer to the canonized Bible; but instead the word "perfect" refers to Christ's return to earth.

Many critics of Scofield also argue that the word "perfect" refers to Ephesians 5:27 and Revelations 19:6-8 and 21:9 concerning the Lord's wife having her soul **spiritually perfected** like the born again spirit. Ephesians 5:27 says, "That he might present it to Himself a glorious church, **not having spot, or wrinkle, or any such thing; but that it should be holy and without blemish."** Since the **born again spirit is already perfect** (Hebrews 12:23), does not sin (1 John 3:9), and is holy and righteous (Ephesians 4:24), it refers to when the born again spirit is joined with the soul of Believers as the ongoing transformed and perfected *Ekklesia.* Revelation 19:7-8 says, "Let us be glad and rejoice, and give honour to Him: for the marriage of the Lamb is come, and **His Wife hath made Herself ready.** (8) And to Her was granted that She should be arrayed in fine linen, clean and white: for the fine linen is the righteousness of saints." Revelation 21:9 says, "And there came unto me one of the seven angels which had the seven vials full of the seven last plagues, and talked with me, saying, **'Come hither, I will shew thee the Bride, the Lamb's Wife.'**"

Furthermore, Scofield argued that when the perfect canonized word came, 1 Corinthians 13:8 gifts of tongues and prophecies fail. However, his misinterpretation is obvious when you see what he does not mention in his commentaries regarding 1 Corinthians 13:8, which again says, "Charity (*agape* love) never faileth: but whether there be prophecies, they shall fail; whether there be tongues, they shall cease; **whether there be knowledge, it shall vanish away."**

Scofield's argument only addresses tongues and prophecies that failed with the coming of the canonized word. However, he fails to advance a strong argument that knowledge vanished away as well. Scofield basically argues that only his interpretation of scriptures is proper interpretation. If Scofield's interpretation that knowledge has vanished away, then the *Ekklesia* no longer needs teachers like Scofield and those who share his views that are his commentaries in the Scofield Bible.

Scofield taught his students that the canonized word likewise replaced the need for apostles and prophets. Contrary to what Scofield's commentaries say, what does the scriptures say whether apostles and prophets are needed for today or not needed for today?

Ephesians 4:11-16 says, "And He (Jesus' divine nature, God the Word and Jesus humanity nature) gave some, apostles; and some, prophets; and some, evangelists; and some, Pastors and Teachers; (12) For the perfecting of the saints, for the work of the ministry, for the edifying of the Body of Christ: (13) **Till we all come in the unity of the faith, and of the knowledge of the Son of God, unto a perfect man, unto the measure of the stature of the fulness of Christ:** (14) That we henceforth be no more children, tossed to and fro, and carried about with every wind of doctrine, by the sleight of men, and cunning craftiness, whereby they lie in wait to deceive; (15) But speaking the truth in love, may grow up into Him (Christ Jesus' divine nature and humanity nature) in all things, which is the Head, even Christ: (16) From Whom (Christ Jesus' divine nature and humanity nature) the whole body fitly joined together and compacted by that which every joint supplieth, according to the effectual working (spiritual vocations, spiritual gifts, by matured transformed souls) in the measure (of given grace according to the measure of the gift of Christ- Ephesians 4:7) of every part, maketh increase of the body unto the edifying of itself in (*agape*) love."

In analyzing Ephesians 4:11-16 above, it is clear that verse 13 suggests the "timing" as to how long the *Ekklesia* will have functioning apostles and prophets, including the whole fivefold ministers. Ephesians 4:13 says, "Till (or Until) we all come ("we all" means all Believers come) in the unity of the faith, and of the knowledge of the Son of God, unto a perfect man, unto the measure of the stature of the fulness of Christ." This is the timing as to how long all the Ephesians 4:11 ministers is still valid.

No one can convince me, or any true scholar in Christendom, that Believers in any given generation became spiritually matured to the point that all Believers have the (1) unity of the faith, (2) and the knowledge of the Son of God, (3) unto a perfect man, (4) unto the measure of the stature of the fulness of Christ. Therefore, until these conditions are met, the ministries of the functioning apostles and prophets are needed for each generation.

Again, another major problem is that extremely few of the functioning apostles, prophets, evangelists, pastors, and teachers are fulfilling the mandate in Ephesians 4:12 of activating all Believers in their spiritual Vocation work as kings, priests, lords, ambassadors, and soldiers in the *Ekklesia,* which is God's kingdom government assembly and kingdom soldier assembly.

Additionally, Scofield, and his followers, misinterpreted scriptures to conclude there are no more healings by God today, even though the canonize word still mentioned that healings are still happening today.

1 Peter 2:24-25 says, "Who His own self bare our sins in His own body on the tree, that we, being dead to sins, should live unto righteousness: by whose stripes ye were healed. (25) For ye were as sheep going astray; but are now returned unto the Shepherd and Bishop of your souls."

Scofield denies that Peter's statement in 1 Peter 2:24-25 is a reference to Isaiah 53:4-6, which says, "Surely He hath borne our griefs, and carried our sorrows: yet we did esteem Him stricken, smitten of God, and afflicted. (5) But He was wounded for our transgressions, He was bruised for our iniquities: the chastisement of our peace was upon Him; and with His stripes we are healed. (6) All we like sheep have gone astray; we have turned everyone to his own way; and the LORD hath laid on Him the iniquity of us all." Scofield has poor scholarship, to conclude, that denies the Lord's blessing of healing that is for today.

It was unscholarly for Scofield, and those who agree with him, that physical or soulish healing is no longer for today. It is obvious that Peter was the first to accept Jesus as the Messiah that was prophesied by the functioning prophet, Isaiah, about the Messiah.

Scofield and his followers also argue that healing is not for today because Jesus fulfilled the scriptures during His healing ministry here on earth. They use as their source Matthew 11:4-6, which says, "Jesus answered and said unto them, 'Go and shew John again those things which ye do hear and see: (5) The blind receive their sight, and the lame walk, the lepers are cleansed, and the deaf hear, the dead are raised up, and the poor have the gospel preached to them. (6) And blessed is he, whosoever shall not be offended in Me." Also, they use as their argument to deny that healings are for today in Matthew 8:16-17, which says, "When the even was come, they brought unto Him many that were possessed with devils: and He cast out the spirits with His word, and healed all that were sick: (17) **That it might be fulfilled which was spoken by Esaias (Isaiah) the prophet**, saying, 'Himself took our infirmities, and bare our sicknesses.'"

Scofield and his followers argue incorrectly that the word "fulfilled" means no more healings were to be done afterwards. What the scriptures mean in Matthew 11: 4-6 is that Jesus performing the healing of the blind, lame, and deaf as signs that fulfill the prophecy in Isaiah, which proves He was the Messiah. Similarly, Matthew 8:16-17 proved that Jesus' healing of people fulfilled Isaiah's prophecy that Jesus would carry our sicknesses and diseases.

The Word "fulfilled" does not mean that all the healings that Jesus was going to do was not those He had done on this one day and no more healings would be done by Him thereafter because no more healings were needed to "fulfill" Isaiah 53:4.

Instead of the Word "fulfilled" being interpreted by the Scofield and his followers to mean that the prophecy by Isaiah referred to the healings only on one particular day, a better interpretation is that it was fulfilled to confirm that the Divine Healer, Himself, was present as evident by the healings done by Him that day.

Were there other "healings" done by Jesus later which also were a continuous fulfillment of Isaiah 53:4? Yes! Does Jesus still heal people today in fulfillment of Isaiah 53:4? Yes! Perhaps the Word "fulfilled" means the commencement of the fulfillment of this prophetic scripture, with all the activities being declared as mature and perfect in their results because the Perfect One (the Messiah) has arrived.

A similar use of the word "fulfilled" is in the discourse by Jesus in Luke 4:18-21, when He said, "The Spirit of the Lord is upon Me, because He hath anointed Me to preach the gospel to the poor; He hath sent Me to heal the brokenhearted, to preach deliverance to the captives, and recovering of sight to the blind, to set at liberty them that are bruised, (19) To preach the acceptable year of the Lord. (20) And He closed the book, and He gave it again to the minister, and sat down. And the eyes of all them that were in the synagogue were fastened on Him. (21) And He began to say unto them, 'This day is this scripture fulfilled in your ears.'"

In Luke 4:21, Dr. Luke made it very clear that Jesus was merely defining His ministry and declaring the presence of the Messiah. Jesus later passed the same preaching of the gospel to the poor, healing, casting out demons, and proclaiming ministries on to His disciples that He manifested and said during His walk here on earth (Matthew 10:1; Luke 9:1-2).

The Greek Word for "fulfilled" in both Matthew 8:17 and Luke 4:21 is "*pleroo*" that has as an important meaning of "to satisfy or execute an office." The same Greek Word is used in both Scriptures. The same Greek Word "*pleroo*" also is used in Matthew 13:13-15, which says, "Therefore I speak to them in parables, because seeing they do not see, and hearing they do not hear, nor do they understand. And in them the prophecy of Isaiah is fulfilled (*pleroo*), which says: 'Hearing you will hear and shall not understand and seeing you will see and not perceive; for the hearts of this people have grown dull. Their ears are hard of hearing, and their eyes they have closed, lest they should see with their eyes and hear with their ears, lest they should understand with their hearts and turn, so that I should heal them.'"

The Greek word *pleroo* means fully done with perfection by the Messiah. *Pleroo* means that Jesus is the fulfillment of Old Testament scripture, not an abrogation of it. It means done with perfection. It confirmed Jesus as the Messiah.

Therefore, Scofield and his followers' use of the word "fulfilled" in these scriptures was misinterpreted and incorrectly applied by Scofield to foster the belief that there are no spiritual gifts functioning today. The problem is Scofield does not cancel out teaching or preaching the gospel to the poor, and he only believes in functioning evangelists, pastors, and teachers, but not functioning apostles and prophets.

Without functioning apostles and prophets, the Ekklesia is without a solid foundation. Psalms 11:3 says, "If the foundations be destroyed, what can the righteous do?"

PURITY OF ALTAR HAS TO BE IN THE BUSINESS WORK AND IN THE HEARTS OF THE BELIEVER BUSINESS OWNERS AND BELIEVER BUSINESS EMPLOYEES.

In God's Holy Nation, God wants the altars where offerings are given to have purity and holiness. In God's businesses with Believer Business Owners and Believer Business Employees, there can be God's altar where contributions are made for good causes in the community, such as helping people delineated in Matthew 25:35-49, or joining others to purchase a new police car for local municipality. When these donations are made, you are doing it unto the Lord. God will reward the business by bringing new and repeated customers or clients to purchase products or services from God's Believer Business Owners and Believer Business Employees who are professing, working, and living out God's economic principles, wisdom, *agape* love, holiness, and righteousness as their moral compass. Therefore, God is quoted in 1 Peter 1:16, as saying, "… 'Be ye holy; for I am holy.'" Customers and clients of Believer Business Owners come to be blessed by the Believer Business Employees being about the Father's business (Luke 2:49).

Jesus spoke about the necessity of the purity of the altar that brings blessings to those who are giving to a ministry, even a business as ministry established by Ephesian 4:11 Business Owners. In Matthew 23:15-23 Jesus said, "If the altar is impure, will your offering bring to you a blessing?

(16) Woe unto you, ye blind guides, which say, 'Whosoever shall swear by the temple, it is nothing; but whosoever shall swear by the gold of the temple, he is a debtor!' (17) Ye fools and blind: for whether is greater, the gold, or the temple that sanctifieth the gold? (18) And, Whosoever shall swear by the altar, it is nothing; but whosoever sweareth by the gift that is upon it, he is guilty. (19) Ye fools and blind: for whether is greater, the gift, or the altar that sanctifieth the gift? (20) Whoso therefore shall swear by the altar, sweareth by it, and by all things thereon. (21) And whoso shall swear by the temple, sweareth by it, and by Him that dwelleth therein. (22) And he that shall swear by heaven, sweareth by the throne of God, and by Him that sitteth thereon. (23) Woe unto you, scribes and Pharisees, hypocrites! For ye pay tithe of mint and anise and cummin, and have omitted the weightier matters of the law, judgment, mercy, and faith: these ought ye to have done, and not to leave the other undone."

Although I have positives thoughts for the historical *Ekklesia*, I want to encourage the leaders to cooperate with the Holy Spirit when revival comes where Believer Business Owners all over the world are activated as Ephesians 4:11 functioning apostles, prophets, evangelists, pastor, and teachers hiring Believer Business Employees, who will receive kinesthetic on the job training in biblical economics, biblical morality, biblical work ethic, biblical servanthood, biblical humility and biblical submissiveness as disciples of Christ.

The Believer Business Employees will be paid to be spiritually instructed through kinesthetic training as well as scholastic teaching by studying of the Bible. This will be the most efficient way for Believer Business Owners to teach and train Believer Business Employees in fulfilling the mandate of Ephesians 4:12. Scholastically educating and kinesthetically training Believers to serve God by seeking first the Kingdom of God and His righteousness and in speech and deed do them as unto the Lord (Colossians 3:17). Again, this was the methods how Jesus taught and trained His apostles and disciples.

Today's priests, bishops, pastors, teachers, or reverends, under their warehouse church lecture hall pyramid structure, often means these leaders cannot commune together daily during weekdays with each member of the congregation or even with small home groups. However, a Believer Business Owner, functioning as an Ephesians 4:11 apostle, prophet, evangelist, pastor, and/or teacher, can be with his or her Believer Business Employees eight to ten hours a day, five to six days a week, with ongoing physical on the job experience using kinesthetic training, coaching, and tutoring to mature his or her Believer Business Employees into biblitarian servants of Christ Jesus as they learn that work is a holy calling to fulfill God's kingdom purposes. 2 Timothy 1:9 says, "Who hath saved us, and called us with a holy calling, not according to our (self-centered) works, but according to His own purpose and grace, which was given us in Christ Jesus before the world began."

Biblitarian Servant Business Employees will work bringing prosperity to biblitarian Servant Ephesians 4:11 Business Owners that results in economic gain and greater goodwill in the business. The reason is that clients and customers will be pleased that the biblitarian Believer Business Owners and biblitarian Believer Business Employees are sincerely honest, caring, fair, and hard working servants to meet the needs of the clients and customers.

On the other hand, in the pyramid-structured warehouse church paradigm, the Ephesians 4:11 functioning ministers in that structure deliver sermons to so-called lay Believers, along with leading any programs involved in the church building or hierarchy. Non-believers wanting to be saved and being accepted in the fellowship of Believers, so they attend lecture halls or historic cathedrals, where they are told to continue to come every week to sing along with the choir and take notes of sermons about denominational precepts by priests, bishops, pastors, teachers, or reverends. These traditions are effective to teach religious traditions but are not the pattern that Jesus instructed and trained His apostles to follow as mature servant Ephesians 4:11 functioning ministers in Mark 10:44-45. At the end of each sermon at the warehouse church lecture hall pyramid structure, the student pays tuition for the teaching but is never activated in the work of the ministry. The church going Believer never graduates from the priests, bishops, pastors, teachers, or reverends lifetime scholastic teachings of sermons.

The warehouse or cathedral lecture hall pyramid paradigm structure commenced with the Catholic Church hierarchy, and the warehouse or cathedral lecture hall pyramid paradigm structure has been the pattern taught to follow in both the Catholic and Protestant churches. The warehouse or cathedral lecture hall pyramid paradigm structure is built where all the authority (and money) balloons to the top where the head priest, bishop, pastor, teacher, or reverend has most all authority. All ministry flows downward only with the permission of the priest, bishop, pastor, teacher, or reverend. Unfortunately, they fail in God's mind because the warehouse or cathedral lecture hall pyramid paradigm structure is not designed to fulfill God's purpose as stated in Ephesians 4:12 to perfect every Believer into the work of the ministry for the edification of the body of Christ.

Again, Believer Business Owners have the obligations to equip Believer Business Employees into their spiritual Vocations as kings, priests, lords, ambassadors, and soldiers, and helping them find their spiritual Gifts. Instead, the priest, bishop, pastor, teacher, or reverend largely makes followers of themselves or the warehouse or cathedral lecture hall pyramid paradigm structure. The *Ekklesia* cannot take back possession of the world for God to submit and operate under the authority of His Kingdom and righteousness.

The biblical truth is that Jesus structured the *Ekklesia* as a "V" where all Believers are to be activated as leaders in their spiritual Vocations and spiritual Gifts to bring the Kingdom of God and God's will to be done in the culture and society where people are dying in their sins without the true Shepherd of their souls. The *Ekklesia* cannot saturate the culture with God's Kingdom and God's will here in earth as it is in heaven under the current traditions of the warehouse or cathedral lecture hall pyramid paradigm structure, with all decisions and money flowing to the top.

The current church structure is set up more like a corporation with a CEO and Board of Directors (and most smaller churches do not have directors or board of elders with decision-making authority), and all decisions are made by the top, not the rank and file Believers. At least in a business corporation, the Shareholders, Board of Directors, President, Secretary, Chief Financial Officer, and Employees daily working the business get paid. Surely, the men and women of God are good people who love the Lord, but they are told that the warehouse or cathedral lecture hall pyramid paradigm structure is the teaching center or lecture hall that stays empty during the week except for one night during the work week and Sunday or Saturday, whatever day they follow as the Sabbath.

Many Believers are tired of paying donations every week to build these large church buildings, when after they are built have to continue contributing toward paying the monthly mortgages, insurance, utilities, and maintenance expenses of the building. Believers are disappointed when they are charged additionally for using the building for their wedding or memorial when they or their family members get married or die. Believers would rather give offerings to fulfill Matthew 25:35-40 and Acts 1:8. When a new Believer arrives at the warehouse auditorium where the church service is conducted, all that he or she sees are pews or chairs, a stage, greeters, ushers, talented musical performers on stage, and the priest, bishop, pastor, teacher, or reverend giving a sermon and sometimes an altar call for unsaved people to become new Believers with the condition that they will join as members to the warehouse or cathedral lecture hall pyramid paradigm structure and attend there until death when they depart to heaven. The reality of this warehouse or cathedral lecture hall pyramid paradigm structure of the church practice is that the same number of people coming through the front door are the same or less number going out the back door.

If the priest, bishop, pastor, teacher, or reverend opened a business and through kinesthetic methods trained disciples at the workplace, and the local church used 70% home fellowship structure with 30% at the warehouse or cathedral lecture hall pyramid paradigm structure, Believer Business Employees would attend, bring their families with them, and the home fellowship congregation would multiply the *Ekklesia* more rapidly because at the home fellowship structure spiritual Vocations and spiritual Gifts by all attendees are encouraged and allowed. Then, the Ephesians 4:11 Believer Business Owner, as a leader in the home fellowship, will practice the same principles of *agape* love, caring, and fellowship at the business as he is at the *Ekklesia* congregation home fellowship. When Believers sit in pews and are made to remain silent, this is not a kinesthetic training center that fulfills the purpose mandated in Ephesians 4:12.

Believers do not know what happens during the week when most of the auditorium or building is not opened; or if opened, the Believers are not allowed in the auditorium or building but can only go to the bookstore to buy books, recorded sermons, Christian music, and religious gifts they can send to friends and relatives. Believers are admonished to attend the warehouse or cathedral lecture hall pyramid paradigm structure every week and are admonished to pay their tithes and offerings to be blessed by God. The tithes and offerings pay the salaries of a small elite of priest, bishop, pastor, teacher, or reverend, along with the expenses of the warehouse or cathedral lecture hall pyramid paradigm structure. After twenty years, many Believers are tired of the same messages they hear repeatedly, and they are tired of never being activated as ministers themselves. After taking sermon notes for ten, twenty, or thirty years, what is the pew-sitting disciple supposed to do with all these classroom-type notes of teachings and sermons?

Very few Believers are activated into their ministry spiritual Vocations as kings, priests (Revelation 1:6), lords (1 Timothy 6:15), ambassadors (2 Corinthians 5:20), and soldiers (2 Timothy 2:3-4). Believers are not told that the priest, bishop, pastor, teacher, or reverend has committed malpractice by not activating the Believers in his or her congregation into their spiritual Vocations and spiritual Gifts, so they too can be about God the Father's business (Luke 2:49).

Most Believers think that if they do not contribute to the financial needs of the priests, bishops, pastors, teachers, or reverends, and if they do not contribute to pay the expenses of the warehouse or cathedral lecture hall pyramid paradigm structure, they may backslide and lose their headship "covering" of the priests, bishops, pastors, teachers, or reverends. This is part of the Believer's compulsive attendance based upon fear promulgated by the religious structure instead of the goodness of God that leads one to repentance (Romans 2:4).

The best message to bring to the culture and society is the goodness, grace, *agape* love, and eternal life given by our faithful God to those who accept Jesus Christ as Lord and Savior and who has chosen and predestinated Believers to become the ministering children of Father God by way of adoption and to be joint heirs with Christ (Romans 8:15-17) and intimately to be involved in seeking first the Kingdom of God and His righteousness.

Again, Believers have expressed to me for years of being tired of giving tithes, offerings, and donations for mortgage and rent payments of a building instead of spreading the gospel messages of Christ Jesus throughout the world as mandated by Jesus in Acts 1:8. These same Believers are tired they do not use or have any say of the use of the warehouse or cathedral lecture hall pyramid paradigm structures that are vacant most of the time. Believers surmise that only the priest, bishop, pastor, teacher, or reverend, along with a group of advisors in the inner circle, decide the agenda and direction of the church. The priest, bishop, pastor, teacher, or reverend and the inner elites usually make decisions without any input by the silent majority in the congregation, even though the silent majority in the congregation are paying the expenses and salaries and are told they are not mere customers but are part of the fellowship and family of God.

I estimate that upwards of twenty-five percent of these very costly warehouse or cathedral lecture hall pyramid paradigm structures are used for Believers to sit in pews or chairs once or twice a week to engage in praise and worship and listen to sermons. The rest of the time these extremely expensive auditoriums and cathedrals are built by offerings of Believers, but these buildings are most of the time left empty and remain empty until filled with soul sleeping inactivated Believers trying to find their ministry calling in God's kingdom. The rank and file Believers sing praise and worship songs they do not choose, and they listen to sermons by the priests, bishops, pastors, teachers, or reverends that they have heard before. Also, most of the time the sermons preached are directed often only to the unsaved, which is good, but not that interesting for those Believers who received initial salvation ten to forty years ago.

A better scholastic sermon would be the privilege and calling of every Believer into the work of ministry in the world marketplace. A better sermon is for perfecting and activating Believers for the work of the ministry as spiritual kings, priests (Revelation 1:6), lords (1 Timothy 6:15), ambassadors (2 Corinthians 5:20), and soldiers (2 Timothy 2:3-4) and how to conduct themselves in those positions of authority in the business, marketplace, school place, professional offices, media, and every place that each Believer knows that the Lord Jesus and the Godhead, living inside them is leading them. Then set up leaders to perfect and active Believers through hands on scholastic teaching and kinesthetically training to fulfill the work in ministry assignments to bring the gospel of the kingdom and repentance and remission of sins, along with establish God's kingdom which can only be done *en masse* all together in all places in the world where people live, work, have family gatherings, and even in government. Most of the best sermons is to teach how to lovingly teach ignorant non-believer and immature Believers how to think as principled biblitarians, submitting to God, being humble, and learning to seek first the Kingdom of God and His righteousness in every area of life. This would include learning how to be a submissive employee, learning proper dating ethics, learning how to be a good and loving mother and wife and a good and loving father and husband. Believer Business Owners who know how to set up a biblitarian business can scholastically teach and kinesthetically train Believers in a home fellowship for the work of the ministry by starting their own business and the wisdom needed to carry on successful business ideas and principles that are taught in this book (and my other books and podcasts).

Believers read Ephesians 4:11-13, and they know they are not being activated or perfected into their spiritual Vocations and spiritual Gifts and how they fit in with this warehouse or cathedral lecture hall pyramid paradigm structure where there are only a few ministers at the top. Some Believers decide to leave the warehouse or cathedral lecture hall pyramid paradigm structure and start a new ministry elsewhere if they want to be activated into ministry, or they may feed the hungry or set up programs to help people with drug or alcohol addictions. Other Believers realize they have invested years of tithes and offerings in the current warehouse or cathedral lecture hall pyramid paradigm structure, and many conclude they will never receive a return on their spiritual donative investment and cannot use their anemic spiritual training to start a ministry. Finally, Believers see that the only pattern in ministry is to build or rent out a building and conduct ministry with the pattern of the warehouse or cathedral lecture hall pyramid paradigm structures.

Most Believers want to see that the *Ekklesia* members make a difference in their society and their culture, but they do not see *Ekklesia* leadership having but little influence with game-changers in society or politicians, except during an election year. Believers in the U.S. are trapped in a country that has a national debt over thirty-seven trillion dollars (at the time of this writing) because of a socialist agenda and constant military activity in other countries by politicians. Believers see the national debt, and they fear for their posterity and following generations because politicians wrongfully foster globalism through financial aid when the U.S. is the largest debtor nation in the world. Believer Business Owners want to do something, but they believe they have no authoritative voice as they are the silent spiritual majority where Humanists are ignoring God's word.

CHAPTER ONE

PERSONAL TESTIMONIES OF BECOMING BUSINESS DISCIPLES OF CHRIST

MY PERSONAL SPIRITUAL TESTIMONY

My own relevant testimony is this. Although I was a in full time practice of law, I also was the Senior pastor/teacher of a local congregation in Redlands, California for over five years between 1993 through 1998, where I kinesthetically trained and activated men and women for the work of their spiritual Vocations and spiritual Gifts. Additionally, I ministered at other churches on Monday nights for one year activating a team of their Believer Business Owners how to kinesthetically instruct and train their Believer Business Employees with biblical economic principles, servanthood, sturdy work ethic, and an ethical foundation of morality. Upon request, I visited some of the Believer Business Owners businesses to resolve problems using biblitarian principles, which I did regularly.

I scheduled a meeting with their employees, where the employees started with prayer and then reading a chapter of Proverbs and a chapter of Psalms, although later they were instructed to read one chapter of Proverbs and five chapters of Psalms each morning before work began. Then I used live situations of me being a client coming to the business with a complaint and allowing the employee to converse with me as the customer. I showed employees examples of being a servant, being able to see if another employee is getting frustrated in performing a task and how the helping employee is to give a quick guiding hand. Also, I went to the break room to examine if it was clean or if employees left soiled coffee cups in the sink or left them on the table and how disrespectful and discourteous it was to other employees. Also, I taught every employee to put work papers, parts, or tools on their desk in an orderly manner before leaving the business building every day; so, when they return the next morning, their minds would not be overwhelmed by the clutter.

Little things can change business morale and production. I taught them that part of *agape* love was to make sure everyone's birthday is calendared and celebrated. I instructed the employees to pray for fellow employees to help them with their faith, be kind to them, express *agape* love always, and give other employees a welcome hug when they return to work after vacation or sickness.

There are many adjustments that can cause a business to become a ministry and a spiritual workplace. I instructed how Jesus taught if two employees were arguing, and one of them meets a customer, the employee's attitude will be bad for business. Employees were instructed that forgiveness was Jesus' way of bringing harmony, so one employee should quickly forgive another employee who trespassed. I instructed the employees to honor each other at the workplace, which would carry over to honoring family members at home and every interaction with others. Finally, I taught the employees that saying "please" and "thank you," and a smile should be on every employee's lips. Of course, I instructed the Believer Business Owners I taught in seminars to set an example on how to treat employees with kindness, respect, and *agape* love.

Some of those business biblical principles that I taught and instructed with kinesthetic methods to Believer Business Owners and Believer Business Managers were: **1)**. God's Business Servants must be Kingdom seeking (Matthew 6:33), faith believing (Hebrews 11:6), and covenant keeping with God for the wealth He brings to fulfill the covenants He has given to the forefathers of faith (Deuteronomy 8:18; Proverbs 13:22); **2)**. Doing your work assignments wholeheartedly, as unto the Lord, and not unto men (Colossians 3:23); **3)**. Letting your primary motive in all things to be *agape* love (John 13:34-35; 1 John 4:16); **4)**. All problems are usually resolved by those who are closest to the problem (Proverbs 16:3); **5)**. Building God's businesses according to God's pattern and not the world's pattern (Hebrews 8:5); **6)**. Making money should not be the primary goal and motivation (Matthew 6:20); **7)**. Making money will only be a derivative of faithful work if the business is built by obeying God (Proverbs 3:1-2); **8)**. Authority and power are designed by God to come through the covenantal process of working in obedience with God in the stewardship of God's creation (Genesis 1:28); **9)**. Godly kingdom relationships will bring righteousness, peace, and joy in the Holy Spirit (Romans 14:17); **10)**. Believers are not here on earth for God to serve them but for them to serve God and the Lord Jesus Christ as Head of the *Ekklesia* (Mark 10:45; Romans 12:1; Ephesians 1:21-22; Colossians 1:18); **11)**. Work is a holy calling after initial salvation (2 Timothy 1:9; Ephesians 2:10; Philippians 2:12-13); **12)**. Believer Business Owners and Believer Business Employees are God's ministers being about God the Father's business (Luke 2:49); **13)**. Business promotion comes through skill of tasks done, being teachable, showing leadership qualities, practices *agape* love, being submissive and humble to authority (Psalms 113:7-8; James 4:10); **14)**. The Believer Business Owner is required to spiritually transform the souls of Believer Business Employees, teaching business principle, servanthood, biblical morality, and through kinesthetic training through incremental tasks at the business (John 15:2; Ephesians 5:26; Romans 8:13); **15)**. Requiring honesty, integrity, a good work ethic, a strong moral compass as foundational in business (Proverbs 11:1); **16)**. God reveals His plans and the steps how to accomplish those plans (Proverbs 16:3, 9); **17)**. God practices teleology, and He wants His Business Owners to do the same, which is looking ahead at the result desired and planning how to accomplish what is necessary to obtain God's desired outcome (Colossians 1:16); **18)**. Spiritual maturation comes by successfully handling the daily incremental business work using biblical economic principles with humility as servants (John 3:30; Galatians 2:20; 2 Peter 3:18; 1 Timothy 4:7-8); **19)**. Strategic planning means assessment of assets, procurement of assets, allocation of assets, and deployment of assets (Proverbs 24:3-7); **20)**. The Principle of Incremental Successful Growth is that all complicated things are built upon basic things incrementally constructed according to the Creator's pattern (2 Peter 1:5-8); **21)**. Strategic thinking means holding to the business plan while you are undergoing spiritual pressures, temptations, or tribulations (1 Corinthians 10:13); **22)**. Knowing the strategies of the enemy and the wisdom from God how to resist the enemy (Philippians 4:6; James 4:7); **23)**. As God speaks His *rhema* word, faith is believing in and exercising the Holy Spirit anointing, power, and authority in Christ as the Holy Spirit leads to bring about a covenantal promise to fulfill God's Kingdom business purpose (Romans 10:17; 2 Corinthians 1:21-22; Galatians 5:16); **24)**. God is a work assignor (1 Corinthians 7:17-24), a work pattern builder (Ephesians 2:10; Colossians 1:16-17), a continuous worker (John 15:17), a rest participator (Genesis 2:3), and a guardian of His creation (Genesis 1:1-31); **25)**. Building your business first before you buy a house (Proverbs 24:27), increasing work skills and have a strong work ethic (Ecclesiastes 9:10; Proverbs 14:23), fulfilling God's purpose of spiritually maturing Believer Business Employees (Ephesians 4:11-13; 2 Peter 3:18), building the business by capturing a market share for the next generation (Proverbs 13:23), spending on research and development, and setting aside money in savings for future expenditures to avoid debt (Luke 14:25-33); **26)**. Righteous labor and business practices lead to life and wealth, while wealth and riches gained by dishonesty will be diminished (Proverbs 13:11; Mark 4:19); **27)**. Enduring sufferings to obtain good character traits (Romans 5:3-5), thinking on things that are honorable, just, pure, loving, commendable, excellent in all your work (Philippians 4:8), maintaining management in all business transactions (2 Peter 1:5-7), recognizing and developing your natural gifts, strengths, and limitations, knowing and practicing your spiritual gifts, having a moral compass as a servant to others (Colossians 3:12-14), developing leadership management skills (Luke 16:2), maintaining good stewardship of God's assets (Matthew 25:14-30), and keeping good accounting so nothing is lost (Proverbs 27:23-27; John 6:12); **28)**. Performing good work yourself as the owner as an example, and in your teaching and kinesthetically training of employees show integrity, dignity, and sound speech to avoid shame (Titus 2:7-8); **29)**. Counting business ups and downs with joy, as these trials of various kinds strengthen your faith and produce steadfastness, which brings maturity and completeness, lacking in nothing (James 1:2-4); **30)**. God's wisdom and knowledge shall be the stability of your times and strength of salvation (Isaiah 33:6); **31)**. Avoiding bad company that corrupts good morals (1 Corinthians 15:33); **32)**. Being not unequally yoked together with unbelievers because they are unprincipled and biblically ignorant as they may influence you to have bad thoughts and actions (2 Corinthians 6:14-17); **33)**. Present your body as a living sacrifice, holy, acceptable unto God (Romans 12:1); **34)**. You are free to make your own choices but are not free to choose the consequences (Galatians 6:7-10); **35)**. Set not your mind on the uncertainty of riches, but on God (1 Timothy 6:17); **37)**. Trust in the Lord in all your ways and lean not on your own understanding (Proverbs 3:5-6), **38)**. The avarice of money is a root of all kinds of evil (Ecclesiastes 5:10; 1 Timothy 6:10); **39)**. Avoiding single generation consumption and single generation planning, instead of God's plan which is multi-generational, as He is the God of Abraham, Isaac, and Jacob. This means God's plans are for at least three generations, and righteous parents leave an inheritance to their children and grandchildren (Matthew 22:32; Proverbs 13:22); and **40)**. Avoiding debt by setting aside savings for future expenditures and maintaining a strict business budget (Proverbs 22:7).

As God's Kingdom Believer Business Owner minister in my law practice, I personally instructed and trained my law clerks and legal secretaries with a complete system of calendaring, how to interview clients, timely letters to be sent, scheduling Statutes of Limitation dates, filing of Complaints, Answers, Motions, Discovery Requests, calendaring court dates, and all aspects of the legal practice.

I had a small law firm where I employed three to five Believer Business Employees. For scholastic teaching, each morning during the week before business started at my law office, I and my Believer Business Employees read scriptures, including five chapters of Psalms and One chapter of Proverbs. Sometimes, I would teach a fifteen minute teaching. For kinesthetic training my employees were instructed through practice how to pray for clients who were injured in car accidents if the clients indeed requested prayer. For a season my secretary typed out my sermons and teachings that I used in scholastic teaching to my *Ekklesia* congregation, which also increased her biblical knowledge through kinesthetic training by typing and proofing my teachings and sermons. (My secretary would take a copy home with her of each sermon or teaching for her further reading.) She eventually taught me how to use the computer, so I could type my own sermons and teachings, but she continued retrieving the sermon or lesson. Physically typing my sermons and teachings also trained me how to write the books that I publish. Writing books has both scholastic teaching and kinesthetic training at the same time. If you personally type your teachings, sermons, or an employee manual or handbook, you will remember what you wrote because the best memory comes from kinesthetic instruction and hands on training.

History is a subject that requires knowing many, many facts, names, dates, and events. When I was studying in college, living in the dorms at Cal State University Long Beach, I purchased little plastic ships, soldiers on horses, marching army soldiers with guns, and ladies and gentlemen figures to use in kinesthetic study of history. I would study and then move the pieces that represented a particular historical event like a discovery or war. For example, I took a little plastic sailing ship, and I physically moved the ship from Spain to the Caribbean Island. While physically moving the little ship across the Atlantic Ocean on the map I stretched out on my desk, I said, "Columbus sailed the ocean blue in 1492."

Also, I would hold up a stately looking man and say something like, "Abraham Lincoln delivered the Gettysburg Address on November 19, 1863, during the dedication ceremony of the Civil War Soldiers' National Cemetery at Gettysburg, Pennsylvania." Once I went through this routine, historical facts were imbedded in my mind, which I could regurgitate on the college exams.

When I attended Pepperdine University School of Law, I read and briefed numerous judicial cases, not only read outlines on the law of each subject, but wrote out on yellow tablets my own outlines, plugging in the case law I briefed. To a law student outlining was a verb, not a noun. Physical writing, instead of just reading, my notes on paper were kinesthetic training. I was able to remember vast volumes of law, and what facts as life examples generated the law for resolution, and I thereby passed the law school test of each class, along with the California State Bar Exam in 1974 in the first sitting. In church, I always took notes of the sermons of the functioning pastor or functioning teacher. It was and still is a good habit.

After becoming a civil litigation lawyer, I wrote out many motions, trial briefs, and testimonies of witnesses, along with my opening statement and closing argument at trial. Once I wrote it down, my memory was very strong, and I could focus on my delivery of questions and arguments in the presence of the trier of fact.

Later I established a church building, as I thought this was the expectation of ministers. As a functioning scholastic teacher and kinesthetic trainer, I focused activating both men and women to minister the word of God with examples in their sermons. I insisted each of them stand behind the pulpit and teach or preach their sermons to the congregation. I instructed them through kinesthetic training on how to pray for people, the rudiments of overseeing a church, how to counsel, and every aspect of the ministry that I knew at that time. We had outreaches, *agape* feasts and inviting the community to join, and had a special children's ministry. At the same time, I had daily radio ministry, and taught in other congregations, some of which were in central America. I attended pastoral conferences. I also had weekly home fellowship meetings and regular meetings with business owners.

I also was the Overseer of a ministry called "Roses of Sharon" in Rancho Cucamonga, California, where we instructed, trained, activated, and ordained over one hundred women and men ministers, and some of them became missionaries where they continue to live in other countries.

The problem was that God did not grow the local *Ekklesia* for me to lead because I established a building as the place of worship and teaching the local congregation, where we attended Wednesday nights, Sunday mornings, and Sunday nights. I was following traditional church practices, although by the leading of the Holy Spirit, I did things differently. My focus was on activating Believers in their assigned work of ministry. At first, I ministered through scholastic teaching the word of God, but the Holy Spirit guided me to activate other ministers, especially women in the local congregations, and even to preach or teach behind the pulpit, which I obeyed. We also had home fellowships where I encouraged all Believers present to participate in sharing a testimonial of spiritually engaging with someone outside the church building since the last home fellowship, practice exercising their spiritual gifts, along with sharing a meal together, and having a very spiritual and loving fellowship in the church building and home fellowships. When the Holy Spirit led, I would teach them how to lay hands on the sick and pray for someone, how to prophesy, and how to use other gifts. Finally, I would encourage each Believer to have fellowship with other Believers present outside of the home fellowship meeting, such as inviting another Believer over for dinner, having lunch together, shopping together, watching children play and exercise in the park, coming over for coffee after children are in school, seeing a good film together, or traveling on a holiday together. This allowed each member of the *Ekklesia* family to experience community fellowship in real life interactions. I also instructed people to be wary of tricksters, and I brought my law experience into my imparted wisdom without charge.

Since I had my law practice where I continued to work, I did not take any money from the offerings at the *Ekklesia* for my family's financial benefit, but used all the donations for the ministry, such as food for the hungry, for *agape* feasts, for helping someone in need, using my own money paying the shortfall on the rent and utilities each month, and paying for improvements of the church building. I personally used my own money to purchase the podium and the sound equipment and other equipment.

The last sermon that I ministered in the church building was titled, "What Constitutes a Good Local Fellowship of Believers." While I was teaching this sermon, the Holy Spirit said to me, "Today, this is the last teaching I want you to teach in this building. I have other plans for you." Being obedient, I informed the congregation to take the sermon I had just taught and use it to find another congregation because the Holy Spirit has just closed the doors to this building. Afterwards, all the congregation hugged each other but confirmed that what I said was the leading of the Holy Spirit. Most members of the *Ekklesia* there that day went with their friends and together joined another congregation. I had two years left on the lease of the building, and I paid the monthly lease payments; but I advertised for another ministry to take over the lease, and God provided another ministry.

BEING ACTIVATED TO PHYSICALLY HEAL PEOPLE

In 1990, before I had my own church building and congregation, I went on a missionary trip to Mexico with a minister named Dr. Richard Maiden (now deceased, who I highly loved and honored in the Lord), where we ministered in the barrios near Acapulco, Mexico. It was outside, with public concrete bleachers and a concrete stage which we rented for the service. There were about 250 to 350 people that showed up on a Saturday during early evening.

There was a short teaching by Dr. Maiden. He presented an altar call for new salvations, and there were a few that accepted or rededicated their lives back to Jesus as their Lord and Savior. Then under the unction of the Holy Spirit, Dr. Maiden said that God wanted to heal people; and he invited all that needed a healing to come forward on stage and that he and his team would pray for their healing. There were over one hundred people that came on stage and lined up to be the recipients of prayer and laying hands on them for healing.

Dr. Maiden started praying and laying hands on people, and they were being healed. It was great to watch. He saw me standing near him watching and extending my hand toward the people, as I was thinking, "Well, Dr. Maiden is the one with the gift; and I am here merely to support his ministry." He looked at me, grabbed my hand, and said, "What are you doing? We have many people to pray for. Go lay hands on the people over there and pray for their healing." I was obedient, but quite frankly I did not think I was qualified. I was not ordained. I thought my praying for healing was a disservice to the people wanting God to heal them because of the stripes Jesus obtained by the cruel beatings He suffered. Yet, I obeyed.

The first person I prayed for was a man with lockjaw, and I laid my hand on his face, prayed, and I felt his jaw move. The man was moving his mouth, and the lady who was my Interpreter said he was saying in Spanish, "Thank you, I am healed." I thought, "Well, my friend, your healing did not come from me but God. I cannot heal a bent wing on a fly." Seeing the healing, a woman stepped forward, and my Interpreter said, "She has a large tumor in her abdomen areas, which is badly swollen." I asked the Interpreter to lay her hand on the woman's abdomen, and I laid my hand on the Interpreter's hand and prayed. People around witnessed that her abdomen started going back to normal, and she was excited that her pain had left. Her modest dress now looked too big for her since the swollen abdomen was gone. I was shocked like the onlookers were. The people were getting very excited in witnessing healing being done by God through His servants. These people were very poor, and they were grateful for someone helping them with their serious physical healing needs.

Next, my Interpreter asked me to pray for her father. He was a medical doctor, and many of these local people were his patients. Yet, the medical doctor opened his mouth to show me that his gums in his mouth were infected badly, and the gums were very red, swollen, and the odor was bad. He had lost most of his teeth, and those remaining teeth were brown with rot. The Interpreter said the medical doctor was scheduled to go for a dentist appointment that coming week to pull the remainder of his teeth and fit him with false teeth. I said, "Okay, I will pray for you." I thought this was going to be my empty hands touching an infected mouth with only about four or five rotten teeth, but I obeyed. This is hard even to this day for me to believe, but he suddenly had a mouth full of brand new white teeth, and his gums were beautifully pink. He started yelling and jumping and going around showing people as he smiled with beautiful white teeth. He said in Spanish, "Look what God just did." His daughter, the Interpreter, started crying because this was an undeniable miracle from God. I just kept pointing upward and saying, "Dios el Espíritu Santo". It certainly was not a miracle that I did.

Surprisingly, I was surrounded by people wanting me to pray for them. In my mind, I was thinking, "I am in big trouble because the healings seemed to be more profound, and more than Dr. Maiden was seeing happen. I thought, "Dr. Maiden is the leader; he is the one who has the experience, but these healings are making me like I am the main minister. I want God to receive the credit, not me. I want God to have all the glory. I am not a healer; God is." The miraculous healings meant that God showed up at this crusade and healing was what the people needed. These healings enhanced the belief that God is with us and loves His children.

Yet, after the healing ministry part of the celebration being with God had subsided, at the insistence of the Interpreter, Dr. Maiden invited the medical doctor to the platform to give his testimony of healing. The people in the bleachers, some of whom knew him, stood, clapped, raised their hands in praising the Lord. I was relieved that they gave the proper credit to the Lord and not me.

I knew that the traditional church rule was that the minister at the top was supposed to have the superior anointing and greater signs and wonders, and Dr. Maiden was known for having healings in his crusades. All of these healings that night in the barrios outside of Acapulco that I participated in were never mentioned by Dr. Maiden or anyone on his team thereafter.

Years later, after I had my own congregation in Redlands, California, I was requested by my friend functioning evangelist Sondra Berry Young (now deceased) to be one of the ministers at a meeting in San Bernardino, California. About 350 Believers showed up. Towards the end of the service, there was a call for whomever was sick to come forward. I, along with two to three other ministers, were asked to pray for those suffering from illnesses, injuries, or sicknesses, which we did. There were about 75 Believers who came forward for spiritual healing. Since there was a time restraint, we laid hands on the Believers, saying a quick prayer, thanking Jesus and the Holy Spirit for their healing, and went to the next person.

About five weeks later, a local functioning pastor was having a conference meeting with several speakers, and I was invited to attend. While sitting waiting for the service to begin, a young lady in her early thirties came up to me to thank me because she said her back was healed at the San Bernardino Sondra Berry Young meeting after I had laid hands on her and prayed that the Lord and the Holy Spirit heal her.

I had seen in the past that many people who had back problems were healed, so I said, "Well thank the Lord and the Holy Spirit that They touch you and healed you." She said, "No, you do not understand, my back received a major miracle. Will you be here tomorrow?" I responded, "Yes." She said smiling and excited, "Good, I will bring the x-rays to show you."

The next day, I was at the same meeting, and again she came to me before the meeting started. She opened two large x-ray packages, and she held up two x-rays into the lights. I and others sitting with me looked at the x-rays and her pointing to the dates they were taken. The first one dated years ago, and the second one dated about three weeks ago. The first one showed a steel rod in her back where she had back surgery after removing the vertebras. She turned around and raised her blouse a little and showed all of us her large scar. Then she showed us the second, more recent x-ray. There was no more steel rod but had totally functioning new vertebras. I asked, "Was your doctor surprised?" She said, "Well the doctor called me into his office after receiving the new x-ray, and he confronted me and asked me if I had a twin sister that went with me and took the new x-ray. I told him, 'No. I had to show my I.D. when I went to have the x-ray done, so the x-ray was of my back.' He looked at me and showed me the new x-ray and then compared it with the old post-surgery x-ray. He said, 'Both of these x-rays are your back, and you still have the scar from my surgery. I do not know what to say. I have never seen this before.' I told him about you praying for me. He said, 'This is very hard for me to believe, but the x-rays cannot lie. Your healing was a miracle from God. You know what, I am going to order another x-ray, and I am going to give you a complete set of x-rays proving your miracle because you need to show this miracle of God that you received.'" She concluded, "He gave me these two x-rays. I called the 700 Club, and they asked me to come and give my testimony, but as yet, they have not scheduled a date." I was very pleased, as it encouraged me to continue to pray for people because God is still a miracle-making God, and He loves His children.

I am obliged to let everyone know that most people that I have prayed for here in the States were not healed, and I do not know why. Yet, having seen God's miracles make me continue to pray for people for the healing of their bodies. God is sovereign, and by virtue of Jesus' stripes we are healed; but God chooses whom He wants to miraculously heal. God loves Believers, and He is a covenant making and covenant keeping God. God is not an egalitarian. He chooses whom He wants to heal. I know that God loves certain Believers because they love Him more than others. David was a man after God's own heart (Acts 13:22), and He decides to bring them to heaven earlier to have a closer relationship with them. God could be seeing something happening in their future that might affect their eternal salvation if He waits until they die of old age. Thus, taking them home early is a sign of God's mercy. I am just God's obedient servant. I am not embarrassed when people are not healed, nor do I affirm my ministry calling by healings. I just believe in healing and that God loves people, and I believe the scriptures and that by Jesus' stripes God does heal.

All Believers are destined to die sometime in the future; so, the healing of the body is merely a temporary matter. What is more important is that Believers will receive new resurrected bodies when the Lord returns, and those new bodies are honorable, glorious, powerful, immortal, and incorruptible (1 Corinthians 15: 23, 42-44). This is our eternal hope that we add to the immortality of our spirits and soul immortal bodies. Scripture says the functioning apostle Paul went to heaven early as a martyr, and he said in 2 Corinthians 5:8, "We are confident, I say, and willing rather to be absent from the body, and to be present with the Lord."

Several decades ago, I went to Guatemala to minister, and I was invited in several large congregations. One *Ekklesia* had several separate congregations throughout what we would call about four counties. There were five minister overseers that had oversight, and each would go to a different church congregation each Sunday, and there was leadership in each congregation. There were several thousands of Believers, but what I found interesting was that these five minister overseers all had several businesses; they were financially secure, and neither took a salary from the offerings given by the *Ekklesia* members. They believed God had blessed them financially enough through their businesses, and they left all the offerings to support the church congregations. Of course, these five minister overseers gave abundantly into the offerings. These five minister overseers insisted that every Ephesians 4:11 functioning minister has an independent business or employment, so only a few of the leadership were paid. The congregations kept growing and expanding. These five minister overseers would announce that a new congregation was being opened in another area, and they need to plant seeds of Believers who live near that new area and start going to this new location. This method of expanding the *Ekklesia* still goes on in their country. There was never a financial scandal, and the Believers knew that the leaders had pure hearts. Perhaps this example could be used in the churches in the United States, Europe, and throughout the world.

Another example of a man I personally knew a couple of years between 1989 through 1991, was Dr. Bill Bright, founder of Campus Crusade for Christ. In 1991, Campus Crusade moved to Orlando, Florida. While Campus Crusade was in San Bernardino, Dr. Bright and I would sit together at monthly Minister meetings, where the local Ministers were trying to unite the local church leadership. Dr. Bright really enjoyed my perspective that my law practice was a ministry. Dr. Bright started listening to my radio program called "Business in Ministry" every Saturday where it broadcasted on a local radio station in San Bernardino, California called KLFE ("K-LIFE"). Dr. Bright personally revealed to me how he lived his life. Campus Crusade was a worldwide ministry that received donations in millions of dollars annually. Dr. Bright and his wife raised their personal support each year just like all Campus Crusade staff for a modest income by any measurement. He had a few businessmen and businesswomen who supported him and his wife. While at Campus Crusade, Dr. Bright never owned a car or any real estate. Once, Dr. Bright won the million-dollar Templeton Award for Progress in Religion in 1996; and instead of putting the money in his personal bank account, he donated the money toward developing a Campus Crusade new ministry initiative. Like all Campus Crusade staff, he paid into a modest retirement fund, but he eventually liquidated most of his retirement fund to start a new training center in Moscow, Russia. He and his wife had no savings account and never accepted any speaking fees personally. All offerings he brought back from a speaking engagement were deposited into the Campus Crusade bank account. When Dr. Bright died in 2003, he left behind few worldly goods. God provided for him and his wife sufficiently throughout their lives. God's spiritual riches were bestowed upon them in heaven and throughout eternity in the New Heaven and New Earth (Revelation 21:1). May we all learn from their way of life totally dedicated to the Lord and His Crusade on the student campuses of the world.

OTHER BUSINESS MINISTERS OUTSIDE THE TRADITIONAL CHURCH

Believers should study the work of Franklin Graham's "Samaritan's Purse" who swoops in at most every disaster with food, shelter, clothing, electrical generators, and communications. Also, "World Vision International" started as an ecumenical Christian humanitarian aid, development, and advocacy. It was founded in 1950 by Robert Pierce as a service organization to provide care for children in South Korea. In 1975, emergency and advocacy work were added to World Vision's objectives. Mother Teresa's organization is called the "Missionaries of Charity," dedicated to serving the poor and whose primary mission was to love and care for those persons nobody was prepared to look after. I like all these ministries.

One type of ministry that I believe should be in every city is to be like "Feed My Sheep." They have gone into the community and built relationships with Believer Business Owners in the Columbus, Ohio area to help provide for the low-income and homeless. They partner with local church leaders to expand their reach in the community, while spreading the gospel of the Kingdom and repentance and remission of sins, as Jesus taught His disciples. They also see that Believers in the local community can give support to keep providing food, clothing, and hygiene essentials to the low-income and homeless.

There was a time when I moved with my family to Colorado Springs, Colorado. I had a fellow attorney friend who lived in Evergreen, Colorado, who wanted me to come to the Denver, Colorado, area to meet a great woman of God, who's named was Dr. Rebecca Hager of Mount Beth-El Ministries. Dr. Hagar and I had communicated with each other beforehand while I was living in California, and she really enjoyed my written teachings which I sent her. When we met, I asked her to tell me her story how she started her television ministry in Ukraine, and I will reveal her story as she told it to me.

Dr. Hagar was a little retired grandma in the greater Denver, Colorado, area that had a great story of how God used her to bring the gospel to a whole country. Dr. Hagar had worked in business her entire adult life, retired with a modest pension, was collecting Social Security, had her modest home mortgage paid off, and was out of debt except for living expenses. She loved Ukraine and had traveled there on several missionary trips over the years during her vacation times off from work in business. Dr. Hager was very intelligent, loved studying the word of God, and she was a woman of faith when it came to praying for the sick. Yet, she was not an Ephesians 4:11 functioning minister of a local church, and she did very little teaching here in the U.S. After retirement Dr. Hagar said she prayed to God to keep her healthy and allow her to travel at least one last trip to Ukraine before she became disabled and died. God granted her prayer in a big way.

Dr. Hagar, along with a missionary team had a history of a relationship with a local *Ekklesia* in Ukraine, where they were invited to minister before. While there at this particular time, a Believer nurse in the local *Ekklesia* asked Dr. Hagar if she would go to the hospital where the nurse worked and asked Dr. Hagar to pray for the sick. Dr. Hagar agreed, and when she and the nurse arrived at the hospital, she started praying for the sick in the regular beds. Several patients confessed they were healed. Then, Dr. Hagar was asked to go to the basement to pray for the terminally ill, which she agreed. She noticed professional media people with their television insignia with their T.V. cameras following her and televising her activity. When she reached the basement, she began praying for the terminally ill, and some patients were miraculously healed. The cameras kept running. The hospital staff and patients were excited and clapped their hands and praised the Lord. All of this was televised and broadcasted on Ukraine's nationwide television.

After Dr. Hagar was done praying, the camera crew people took her to the side and told her they were from Ukraine's national television, such as the U.S.'s ABC, NBC, or CBS. The camera crew then asked her if she would help them obtain newer camera equipment from the U.S. and ship it to them? In return, the television crew said they were given permission to offer her two one-half hours a week on nationwide television in Ukraine to teach the Bible, seek new salvations, and to pray for people. She accepted their offer and agreed to do her best to obtain the equipment for them.

When Dr. Hager returned to the Denver, Colorado area, she went to a local television News broadcast station and inquired if they had any used television equipment that they could donate to her ministry to be sent to Ukraine, and she would write them a donation receipt. Dr. Hagar was informed that the Denver News Station had just bought new equipment, and it had the used, but still in excellent shape, television cameras and equipment for a whole studio in storage. The Newscasts workers called her and said the station agreed to donate all their used, but working very well equipment that was in storage. Dr. Hagar wrote out a ministry receipt, and she had some local church members help her bring the equipment to her garage. They all worked, packing the equipment securely in wooden containers with lots of stuffing. She had the money in savings to pay for the shipping costs and communicated and faxed her Ukraine News broadcast station the broadcast equipment was being shipped by plane to Ukraine. They delivered the boxed equipment to the airport and had it shipped, along with every legal document required, such as a destination, commercial invoice, bill of lading, packing list, certificate of origin, and potentially export/import licenses and customs declarations. Afterwards, being very grateful, the television company lived up to their agreement in allowing her a one-half hour ministry program each week .

Dr. Hager built a studio room off her garage, where she would teach the word of God from Genesis through Revelation and giving a salvation call and prayer for healing. In her small room, she had a desk, plastic flowers, wonderful colors, and wore a blond wig. She had a young lady friend who used a VCR camera and recorded on VHS Cassettes her teaching the Bible and praying for people in Ukraine. The Ukraine television station transcribed the VHS Cassettes to the Phase Alternating Line, known as the PAL system. The Ukraine television station hired an interpreter who did subtitles in the Ukraine language at the bottom of her spoken teaching. Dr. Hagar started her weekly T.V. ministry in her late 60s to the whole country of Ukraine with very little cost. She used her pension and Social Security payments to pay for the VHS Cassettes recording and mailing to Ukraine. Dr. Hagar's show became popular in Ukraine. People in Ukraine thought she must be a very popular television evangelist in America. The Ukraine television broadcasts were reaching millions of people every week with Dr. Hagar's teachings and the invitation of repentance and remission of sins unto salvation.

When I met her in 1990, Dr. Hagar was in her 80s and has by now passed and went home to Jesus. This one elderly lady's teaching through the Bible, leading people to the Lord, and praying for the sick and the people's need through her weekly broadcast took a nation for the Lord. The cost of her production to reach a nation was minuscule compared to broadcast costs here in the United States. Like Moses, God mightily used this elderly woman to bring His gospel of repentance and remission of sins to a whole nation at a time when most people in America would think about retiring and relaxing in comfort.

There are other ministries outside the Ekklesia structure too numerous to list in America, Europe,

Africa, China, and many other countries that are properly fulfilling the mandates of Mark 16:15 and Matthew 25:35-45. These ministers were not satisfied of just being converts. They wanted to be disciples of Christ in His *Ekklesia,* as is the primary mandate of Christ and the whole Godhead. (See Mark 16:15; Matthew 28:19, Ephesians 4:12, Matthew 5:19, 2 Timothy 2: 2,15, 3:16-17, and 1 Timothy 4:7-8).

All Christian denomination leaders, who desire to be in the perfect will of God should read my book titled, The Great Bride Awakening and stop the discrimination of women, like Dr. Hagar and many others, from being Ephesian 4:11 functioning ministers in the local *Ekklesia* congregation.

To cure another wrongful practice, the traditional church leaders should stop establishing the church based upon skin color, such as white, black, brown, red, or yellow predominately congregations or based exclusively on cultures, as this is building the *Ekklesia* based upon the flesh and not the Spirit. We still have *Ekklesia* congregations and denominations that are 80%-90% of a particular race, ethnicity, or culture, and this causes division and leads to elitism in the *Ekklesia.*

CHAPTER TWO

KINESTHETIC TRAINING OF BUSINESS DISCIPLES OF CHRIST

DIFFERENCE BETWEEN A TEACHER AND AN INSTRUCTOR

A functioning teacher is someone who provides scholastic teachings to students, typically in a classroom setting. A functioning teacher of high school or college has the focus of imparting book knowledge, fostering understanding, and promoting critical thinking. Functioning teachers require students to study books, write term papers, and give feedback to the functioning teacher during the classroom lectures. Today's church Leaders are normally functioning pastors or functioning teachers of the Bible.

On the other hand, a functioning instructor focuses on training specific skills, techniques, or procedures, and in providing instruction, demonstrating techniques, offering feedback, and ensuring trainees meet specific learning objectives. Functioning instructors use primarily kinesthetic training, such as a hair stylist functioning instructor, an animal care functioning instructor, a car mechanic functioning instructor, a carpenter functioning instructor, an electrician functioning instructor, a plumber functioning instructor, a planting, cultivating, and harvesting of crops functioning instructor, a driving functioning instructor, a fitness functioning instructor, a cooking functioning instructor, a software training functioning instructor, and a business functioning instructor. Jesus and His apostles were functioning instructors that demonstrated the anointing and power of the Holy Spirit and took disciples with them on missionary journeys.

Paul was a functioning teacher in a Jewish University for two years, teaching the gospel of the Kingdom and revealing that Jesus was and is the prophesized Jewish Messiah of the Old Testament (Acts 19:8-10), Yet, Paul also taught, trained, and activated disciples of Christ Jesus, such as Timothy, Luke, Silas, Silvanus, Titus, Aristarchus, Priscilla, Aquila, Lidia, and Onesimus, and many others.

FROM THE BEGINNING GOD HAS EXPECTED MANKIND TO WORSHIP GOD IN THE WORKPLACE

Genesis 2:8 says, "And the LORD God planted a Garden eastward in Eden; and there He put the man whom he had formed." Thus, the first man, Adam, was created by God on the sixth day (Genesis 1:26, 31) before the Garden eastward of Eden was created by God. God created the earth and the Garden east of Eden, and the first time God mandated Man to do something was in Genesis 2:15, which says, "And the LORD God took the man, and put him into the garden of Eden to dress it and to keep it."

God's purpose is clear. God created Mankind, both men and women, to replenish and subdue the earth and take dominion over all living creatures, and to govern every aspect of Planet Earth pursuant to God's instructions. God mandated Mankind, both men and women, to govern his and her own life, to marry, give birth and raise children, work to acquire an occupation, start and run a business, train employees about God the Father's business, along with establishing the governments to run towns, cities, counties, states, and countries in boundaries selected by God. Acts 17:26-27 says, "And hath made of one blood all nations of men for to dwell on all the face of the earth, and hath determined the times before appointed, and the bounds of their habitation; (27) that they should seek the Lord, if haply they might feel after Him, and find Him, though He be not far from every one of us."

The original mandate of God to Adam and Eve, and their posterity, was stated in Genesis 1:28: "And God blessed them, and God said unto them, 'Be fruitful, and multiply, and replenish the earth, and subdue it: and have dominion over the fish of the sea, and over the fowl of the air, and over every living thing that moveth upon the earth.'"

Genesis 1:28 is still the foundational dominion mandate that all Believers are commanded to fulfill. The Hebrew word for "dominion" in Genesis 1:26, 28 is *mamlaka,* (Strongs H4467), from the primitive root words *malak* (Strongs H4427), *melek* (Strongs H4428), or *mashal* (Strongs H4910), which are the same or similar Hebrew words that elsewhere in the Bible are translated into English as "kingdom" (Exodus 19:6), "reign" (Exodus 15:18), "King" (Genesis 14:8), "rule" (Judges 8:22), and "realm" (2 Chronicles 20:30). Yet, all these Hebrew words are related to the Kingdom of Heaven becoming the Kingdom of God here on earth, as earth is a colony of heaven where God's Kingdom Throne is.

The point is that Adam and Eve's mission from God as *Elohim* Creator was to establish the Kingdom of God here on earth as it is in Heaven. To have citizens of Heaven to be citizens of God's Kingdom here on earth, Adam and Eve's dominion mandate was to be God's under rulers and as God's servant kings, priests (Revelation 1:6), lords (1 Timothy 6:15), ambassadors (2 Corinthians 5:20), and soldiers (2 Timothy 2:3-4). Being spiritual priests and spiritual soldiers had to be added after Adam and Eve's fall because priests were needed to reconcile fallen men and women, boys and girls to be saved, and also spiritual soldiers were needed because God's possessory dominion mandate was stolen by Satan from Adam and Eve, which caused mankind to have the proclivity to sin with lust of the flesh, lust of the eyes, and pride of life in the souls of fallen mankind.

Now, I direct your attention back to Genesis 2:15, which again says that God put Man in the Garden east of Eden "to dress it and to keep it." The Hebrew word for "dress" is *abad* which means "to work, labor, serve, and worship" (Strongs H5647). *Abad* is often used in Scripture meaning to "serve" and "worship" God in all that you do. This mandate to serve and worship is like Colossians 3:17, which says, "And whatsoever ye do in word or deed, do all in the name of the Lord Jesus, giving thanks to God and the Father by Him." Adam obeyed and started serving God to take care of God's garden by all that he did in word or deed, giving thanks to His Creator. This means God created a garden from where Adam, and later his helper, Eve, would work as servants to care for the animals and all living things and vegetation created by God, while at the same time the mandate of worshipping God at the workplace. From the beginning, God always intended for man and woman to worship Him at the workplace, as mankind was created to take care of God's special planet, Earth, where His only begotten Son would find His multi-membered Bride, and both would eventually live throughout eternity.

The Hebrew word *abad* is regularly used in the Old Testament in referenced to serving the Lord God and not any other gods. Joshua 24:14 says, "Now therefore fear the LORD, and serve *(abad)* Him in sincerity and in truth: and put away the gods which your fathers served *(abad)* on the other side of the flood, and in Egypt; and serve (*abad)* ye the LORD." Thus, God's mandate in Genesis 2:15 to "dress" which is translated from *abad* has a spiritual reference of Believers after initial salvation and becoming born again as Believer Business Owners and Believer Business Employees doing work unto the Lord at the business or workplace where working is a form of serving and worshipping (*abad)* the Lord. There should be no separation of *Ekklesia* and workplace or separation of *Ekklesia* and being about the Father's Business (Luke 2:49).

Colossians 3:23-24 says, "And whatsoever ye do, do it heartily, as to the Lord, and not unto men; (24) Knowing that of the Lord ye shall receive the reward of the inheritance: for ye serve the Lord Christ." These verses mandate that Believer Business Owners and Believer Business Employees are to work with dedication, enthusiasm, and God's purpose because they are working for the Lord as functioning ministers in His business. When they focus on the Lord while they are working, then the Lord will reward them with experiencing righteousness, peace, and joy in the Holy Spirit along with health and prosperity as their souls prosper through spiritual transformation (Romans 14:17; 3 John 2).

In Genesis 2:15, the Hebrew word for "keep" is *shamar*, which means "to guard, protect, or observe" (Strongs H8104). *Shamar* is often used in Scripture to mean to be circumspect, beware of harm all around you because you are working in a fallen world. It means taking heed, and observing, in the sense of keeping yourself in the ways of the Lord, and it means while laboring in business doing in word and deed the Lord's way and not the fallen world's way. At your memorial, if you have been obedient, submissive, and faithful to your business as your ministry calling, someone could say or sing, "For what is a man, what has he got? If not the Lord, then he has naught. I said the prayers as one who kneels. And the record shows I took the blows and did it God's way!"

Shamar in Strongs H8104 says, "a primitive root; properly, to hedge about (as with thorns), i.e., guard; generally, to protect, attend to, etc.: KJV - beware, be circumspect, take heed (to self), keep (-er, self), mark, look narrowly, observe, preserve, regard, reserve, save (self), sure, (that lay) wait (for), watch (-man)."

Deuteronomy 5:1 says, "And Moses called all Israel, and said unto them, 'Hear, O Israel, the statutes and judgments which I speak in your ears this day, that ye may learn them, and keep (*shamar*), and do them.'"

Speaking of the mandates of the Ten Commandments, Moses said in Deuteronomy 6:12-13, "Then beware (*shamar*) lest thou forget the LORD, which brought thee forth out of the land of Egypt, from the house of bondage. (13) Thou shalt fear the LORD thy God, and serve (*abad*) Him, and shalt swear by His name." It is significant that with Moses addressing the children of Israel the Ten Commandments, he used both *abad* and *shamar,* so this is the significance of reading *abad* and *shamar* in Genesis 2:15 about worshipping God while at work doing labor unto the Lord.

PRACTICAL KINESTHETIC METHODS OF BUSINESS DISCIPLESHIP TRAINING

The purpose of this chapter is to focus now on presenting a deeper understanding of what Jesus used in scholastically teaching and kinesthetically training His Ephesians 4:11 functioning ministers, who then had the assignment to scholastically teach and kinesthetically train other born again Believers into their spiritual Vocations and spiritual Gifts. Jesus preferred using kinesthetic training instead of mere scholastic teaching as the Rabbis did to His Ephesians 4:11 functioning ministers, as Jesus used the journeyman training like His step-father, Joseph, used to kinesthetically train Jesus as a carpenter and stonemason.

Jesus worked in business from about the age of ten until He was thirty years old just to have a ministry that lasted three and one-half years here on earth before He was crucified on the Roman cross. Yet, it was the most effective work that has ever been accomplished since the creation of Adam and Eve. Jesus sacrificed Himself to redeem fallen mankind and reconcile mankind back to God (2 Corinthians 5:21) and died on the Roman Cross to relieve Believers from the curse of the law. Jesus lived with His apostles twenty-four hours a day, seven days a week for three and one-half years that culminated with His death on the Roman Cross, His resurrection on the third day, and His ascension to heaven.

The Holy Spirit is expanding the venue of discipleship training of Believers, not only to a degree in the warehouse lecture hall buildings, but more importantly at businesses where Believer Business Owners who are Ephesians 4:11 functioning apostles, prophets, evangelists, pastors, and teachers can kinesthetically train their Believer Business Employees to become biblitarians with spiritual Vocations and spiritual Gifts. These Ephesians 4:11 Believer Business Owners will instruct with kinesthetic training their Believer Business Employees disciples, along with non-believers who become Believers, with direct firsthand supervisory kinesthetic training oversight five to six days a week, eight to ten hours a day at the business workplace. These Ephesians 4:11 Business Owners will be mandated to train their Believer Business Employees to use God's biblical economic principles, especially with a strong work ethic, with biblical morality, and with servanthood, and *agape* love in their Vocations as kings, priests (Revelation 1:6), lords (1Timothy 6:15), ambassadors (2 Corinthians 5:20), and soldiers (2 Timothy 2:3-4), along with the training to seek first the Kingdom of God and His righteousness with the goal of transforming the Believer Business Employees' souls unto spiritual maturity. Hands-on spiritual training five to six days a week, eight to ten hours a day of these Believer Business Employees should be done through kinesthetic training methodologies more than just scholastic teaching in a classroom setting.

In business, the Believer Business Owner must use Kinesthetic training of the Believer Business Employees through daily repetition of the same tasks, with follow up examination of work in progress, with time restraints for completion of steps, and with examining the product after assembled or fabricated before it is sold to a customer or client. Eventually, the Believer Business Employees do not need such scrutiny and checking for completion. This oversight training in business is called management, which is the work of making the Believer Business Employee become of mature age in his or her work assignments and responsibilities. Even at the business the Believer Business Owner can use Kinesthetic instruction of the Believer Business Employees to train them how to lead an unbeliever to the Lord, apply the principles of biblical economics, practice the moral lessons of the Bible, submit as an obedient employee with a strong work ethic, maintain self-control, be kind, while seeking first the Kingdom of God and His righteousness (Matthew 6:33). Discipleship training is not done by just going to a church building once a week and listening to sermons week after week, year after year. Again, making disciples is bringing the disciples into the work of the ministry in a practical way exercising servanthood in their Vocations as Kingdom kings, priests, lords, ambassadors, and soldiers, along with discerning and activating the Believer Business Employees with their spiritual Gifts.

The pertinency is that journeyman ministry training is done primarily by hands-on kinesthetic physically doing the work of the ministry of the spiritual Vocations, where trainee Believer Business Employees learn best by physically engaging with the material world through movement, touching, and building, whether the business is engaged in producing and selling a product to customers or performing a service to clients.

As the Believer Business Employees become spiritually-mature at work, they will be financial supporters of their local *Ekklesia* community and contributors as mature servant ministers themselves. Because these Believer Business Employees see their place of ministry as in the business venue, they will not try to steal the flock of another separate traditional *Ekklesia* warehouse lecture hall ministry that sometimes takes away the "flock" from the Senior Pastor. *Ekklesia* splits often are the quickest way to have *Ekklesia* expansion with a new Ephesians 4:11 minister, who starts a new *Ekklesia* because the old Senior minister would not endorse the new minister's Ephesians 4:11 functioning ministry. Mature Believer Business Employees will be true blessings to the local priest, bishop, pastor, teacher, or reverend, especially those who establish home fellowships, where there is freedom to use spiritual Vocations and spiritual Gifts that can be expressed by all present where the Lord's commandment to *agape* love one another is fulfilled (John 13:34-35).

Believer Business Employers are mandated to disciple Believer Business Employees working in the business. God's purpose and goal after initial salvation is to mature the souls of Believer Business Employees with the way, truth, and life during their working hours eight to ten hours a day, five to six days a week through continuous repetitious tasks while following God's principles of economics, work ethic, moral values, trustworthiness, *agape* love, grace, and caring servanthood toward others, including fellow Believer Business Employees, customers, and clients. God wants to activate Believer Business Employees as ministers. He does this by maturing Believer Business Employees into Believer Business Manager ministers through the daily incremental work assignments they encounter in business. During the daily work assignments in business, God wants Believer Business Employees to use and apply God's biblical principles in performing business labor to touch lives, convert hearts, and submit to the work of the Godhead in soul maturation as the Believer Business Employer and Believer Business Employees both daily seek first the kingdom of God and His righteousness, believing God's promise that all things for life will be added to them (Mathew 6:33).

In His ministry, Jesus was totally obedient to God the Father, as He only did and said what God the Father did and said (John 5:19, 12:49-50). Starting at age thirty, Jesus lived with His functioning apostles generally twenty-four hours a day, seven days a week for three and one-half years, kinesthetically training them with the way, truth, and life through practical hands-on guidance, supervision, and tutelage. However, what did Jesus do for twenty years before He started His ministry?

During New Testament biblical times, at about age ten usually young Jewish boys started their apprenticeship of a trade, and Luke 2:49 reveals that Jesus was knowledgeable about business at age twelve.

Even at twelve years old, Jesus knew the fundamentals of God the Father's business here on earth. **1).** Jesus spent time learning God's gift to be presented to unbelievers (eternal life and adoption into God's family), **2).** learning the recipient's method of acceptance of the gift (repentance, accepting Jesus as Lord, and being born again into the Kingdom of God), **3).** learning His competition (Satan and religious hierarchy), **4).** learning and engaging His market focus (first the Jews, then the Gentiles), and **5).** learning His business territory (Jerusalem, Judea, Samaria, and the uttermost parts of the world).

When Jesus started His journeyman training as a carpenter and stonemason at about age ten to age thirty when Jesus started His ministry was about twenty years. Jesus learned carpentry and stonemasonry through kinesthetic instruction and training. After His Stepfather Joseph passed, Jesus continued to supervise and used kinesthetic training of His half-brothers to become carpenters and stonemasons.

Jesus' humanity nature as a young boy, then as a teenager, and into manhood, was kinesthetically trained as a journeyman and worked in business for about twenty years to have a ministry where He trained apostles using similar journeyman training methods for three and one-half years. During those twenty years as a carpenter and stonemason, Jesus engaged customers and learned about people's wrongful attachment to money to fulfill their needs, learned about God's biblical principles of economics and servanthood, and learned how to mature His younger half-brothers to become journeymen carpenter and stonemason specialists through kinesthetic hands-on daily training like His step-father, Joseph, and God the Father trained Jesus' humanity nature. Jesus used journeyman kinesthetic training with daily Instructor/Student relationships to disciple His functioning apostles and disciples by using the same methods He first learned in business. In the four gospels, Jesus often spoke about finances and not to serve money (Matthew 6:24). Hebrews 5:8 says, "Though He was a Son, yet learned He obedience by the things which He suffered."

Most Believers are taught to be spectators in everything they do except in their work at their job or business, and it is at the job or business that they are touching peoples' lives as servants and are making a difference, but far less during their times of entertainment and rest. It is during business hours that Believers work as servants at a business during the weekdays, and during the weekends they often want to rest, including on Sunday. So, when is it that the *Ekklesia* leaders in the warehouse lecture hall pyramid paradigm structure kinesthetically train Believers in the congregation to work as ministers? All they could do is to be trained to do religious practices on Sundays or Saturdays (Seventh Day Adventists). When does the functioning priest, bishop, pastor, teacher, or reverend supposed to kinesthetically train and activate the Believers for the work of ministry as kings, priests, lords, ambassadors, and soldiers? The weekend is the worse time to activate Believers because it is Believers' day off from work. This is why Jesus lived with His apostles in training twenty four hours a day, seven days a week. Jesus kinesthetically trained His functioning apostles and disciples for the work of the ministry when everyone else was working, which was from Sunday through Friday; but He often was accused of breaking Jewish religious Sabbath laws on Saturday by healing someone. If current church priests, bishops, pastors, teachers, and reverends work only on Saturday preparing a sermon and on the Sunday delivering that sermon instead of during the weekdays, they cannot take time training disciples a few hours on the weekend to fulfill their obligations commended in Ephesians 4:12. This is one of the strong reasons current church leaders are not activating Believers as ministers because the religious tradition and hierarchy is not set up to do it. The First Century Ekklesia met every day of the week, and this is how Believers spent time with the apostles and leaders for scholastic teaching and kinesthetic training because their fellowship was daily. Then, God wants to change the venue and the days and times to kinesthetically train His ministers. This is why the Holy Spirit is ordaining Believer Business Owners with the important ministry of activating Believer Business Employees at the business venue eight to ten hours a day, five to six days a week.

Mark 10:42-44 says, "But Jesus called them to Him, and saith unto them, 'Ye know that they which are accounted to rule over the Gentiles exercise lordship over them; and their great ones exercise authority upon them. (43) But so shall it not be among you: but whosoever will be great among you, shall be your minister: (44) and whosoever of you will be the chiefest, shall be servant of all.'" Again, Jesus' admonition connotes the "V" shaped structure in the *Ekklesia* that He built and trained His functioning apostles and disciples to accept, as they were young men in their late teens and twenties seeking authority in Jesus' Kingdom structure. Yet, Jesus said that the one with the most authority were humble servants, who would train others using kinesthetic methods throughout the *Ekklesia* Age to be humble servants.

The purpose of the Ephesians 4:11 functioning apostles, prophets, evangelists, pastors, and teachers are commanded to activate all Believers into their spiritual Vocations and spiritual Gifts. Again, every Believer has the same Vocations but different Gifts. All Believers' spiritual Vocations are under the authority of Christ, with His dual natures, and are activated by the leading of the Holy Spirit, which are: **1)** as a spiritual king that rules over the world commerce system in the venue that God places him or her (Revelation 1:6); **2)** as a spiritual priest reconciling unsaved people to God through evangelism (Romans 10:9; 15:16; 2 Corinthians 5:19), **3**); as a spiritual lord (1 Timothy 6:15), who is faithful over that portion of God's earth that the Believer is assigned where he or she can prophesy over the earth, "O earth, earth, earth, hear the word of the LORD" (Jeremiah 22:29); **4)** as a spiritual ambassador that represents God's Holy, heavenly kingdom and will here on earth (Matthew 6:10; 2 Corinthians 5:20; Philippians 3:20); and **5)** as a good spiritual soldier who resists the devil and the evil in this fallen world while pulling down strongholds and tearing down imaginations and every high thing that exalts itself against the knowledge of God, and bringing into captivity every thought to the obedience of Christ (2 Timothy 2:3-4; 2 Corinthians 10:4-5; Ephesians 6:10-18; James 4:7).

Believers should not neglect the study of the scriptures daily, praying always, maintaining humility and submission to the leading of the Holy Spirit, having continuous servanthood and fellowship expressing *agape* love with other Believers, and being about God the Father's business of reconciling fallen mankind back to God by accepting Jesus Christ as Lord and Savior. The question is, how does one apply the scriptures into ministry practical kinesthetic training? Believers need to be activated into the work of ministry through both scholastic teaching and kinesthetic training, but it has to be done daily as Jesus did His disciples.

EXAMPLES OF KINESTHETIC DISCIPLESHIP TRAINING

Ekklesia discipleship experience should be more like kinesthetic training in driving a car. Think about how you were trained to drive the car. You could not just read a book to learn how to drive the car. You had to get into the car, have a trainer who pointed out the safety precaution of wearing the seat belt, where the turning signals are, how to turn on the windshield wipers in case of rain, how to insert the key to start the engine, and then let go of the key to disengage the starter after the engine is running, how to adjust the rear view mirror and the side mirrors before driving, how to do proper signaling, how to back up and park the car, how to enter the freeway with caution by speeding up to safely merge into traffic, the meaning of traffic signs, the significance of colors on curbs, the basic speed law that changes with the weather conditions, to travel under the speed limit as conditions dictate, and all this is in addition to studying the Motor Vehicle laws to pass a written test. The kinesthetic training is through repetition driving to pass a physical driving test to obtain your driver's license. Instruction and training through hands-on practicing driving are primarily repetitive motions that become almost automatic because of physical memory. You can develop good driving habits or bad driving habits. Eventually, the bad driving habits will result in a traffic ticket issued by a police officer, or the bad driving habits will cause you to have an accident, where property damages and personal injury damages are involved. Good driving habits, such as defensive driving, mean no tickets, no accidents, no debilitating injuries, and lower insurance rates.

I never received financial help from my natural father for expenses to pay for my college education, as he had a heart attack in his mid-forties and was medically disabled. So, I always had to find a job on the side during the school year, along with full-time employment during spring break and summer and save my money to pay for my living needs going to college. I found odd jobs to do, and my training always involved book studying and personal hands-on kinesthetic training.

Here is my personal example of the value of kinesthetic instructing and training to make money, which can be applied to making disciples in ministry. While attending college in 1969, I purchased a 1967 Volkswagen Beetle. The maintenance was critical, but I did not know how to do the maintenance. I had to do a tune-up and adjust the valves every 3,000 miles to ensure optimal engine performance and to avoid potential damage from valves becoming too tight due to wear and tear, destroying the engine. Adjusting the valves was a crucial maintenance requirement for all air-cooled Volkswagen Beetle engines.

I bought a book written by John Muir, titled, How to Keep Your Volkswagen Alive: A Manual of Step-by-Step Procedures for the Compleat Idiot. Publisher: Rick Steves ; ISBN: 9781566913102. The author covered diagnostic, maintenance, and repair procedures in simple, illustrated detail. Since I was in college, I thought I easily could learn anything by reading a book. I read the manual and looked at the diagrams several times, but I still did not have the knowledge through experience to tune up my Volkswagen Beetle.

I took my manual, opened it up on the relevant page, crawled underneath the rear of my Volkswagen Beetle, and saw the bottom part of the engine. I found the valve covers, which were held in place by a very tight bale, which I was warned not to bend out of shape, as that could cause an oil leak around the valve cover. The point to be made is that I really did not know how to do a Volkswagen Beetle tune up, including the critical valve adjustment, until I gained the experience of physically doing the tune up and valve adjustment a few times.

Many college and post graduate students owned a Volkswagen Beetle in the 1960s and the early 1970s because students had little money and needed a fuel efficient vehicle. There were lots of potential customers. I discovered there were other smart book-learning educated but practically uninformed like me that knew nothing about the critical maintenance of their Volkswagen Beetles, although some of them had been told that without a valve adjustment every 3,000 miles that the valves could break and go through the pistons, destroying the engine. Now that I had at that time become an experienced mechanic for Volkswagen Beetle tune-ups, and since the students needed a cheap mechanic, I became a parttime mechanic that made cash flow for me during my college and law school years. I charged $55-$75 per tune up, which included parts and labor. I replaced spark plugs, replaced the distributor cap, rotor, points, and condenser if needed, cleaned and adjusted the carburetor, replaced the air filter if needed, checked the timing, and adjusted the valves. Parts were cheap in those days. I was profiting about $25-$30, which I could pay my existing expenses from 1969 through 1974 as a student. I regularly had one customer per week by referral. That extra $100-$200 a month helped me to be financially sound during my college and law school years. Sometimes, the Volkswagen Beetle owners had other problems with their cars, which they paid me to fix at a quoted price.

Living expenses were a lot lower in those days. In 1970, the average cost of a gallon of gas was about $0.36. A loaf of bread was approximately $0.25, and a dozen eggs averaged $0.61. A Big Mac, fries, and a coke at McDonald's cost less than $1.00, and an apple pie for desert cost $0.20. I rented a dormitory room at Cal State University Long Beach for my Junior year. I discovered that I could do better financially by having my own place and cooking my own food. So, in 1970, I rented a small apartment above a garage in Long Beach, California and paid $75 per month, with all utilities paid, during my senior year in college. During my first year of law school in 1971, I lived in an $85 per month rental, with all utilities paid, in an older duplex in Garden Grove, California. So, young people during the early 1970s can see I did not need much money to live.

Also, in college I had other business work. Because I learned how to type with an old fashioned non-electric, ribbon typewriter, I purchased a typewriter at a used typewriter store and was paid to help students write their term papers, which I charged $50 per term paper, which was more work than repairing Volkswagen Beetles. Additionally, I went around Long Beach and painted street numbers on curbs in residential neighborhoods, but there was never repeat business with the same customers. So, new territories kept getting farther away from the dormitory or my apartment that cost me time and fuel. I eventually did not find that job profitable as it took a lot of work for $5 (although sometimes I received a tip, so my average was $7) to contact the homeowners and sell them on my services. I assured them I would do an excellent job, and they would be helping me go through college. I bought cans of black paint, and I cut out the hard back cover of notebooks for the stencil numbers. Generally, the sales pitch always worked because it was true, and it worked because I had the customer walk outside and examine my work before I left. I did not request to be paid until after I did the work where they were satisfied. No customer cheated on me. If the customer did not like my work, I used paint thinner, which is a solvent used to adjust the viscosity of oil-based paints, stains, and varnishes to remove the numbers painted. It removed the paint, and I started over, but I never once had to return the money.

The point is that when I used kinesthetic learning, people paid me to take care of their needs, especially those whose knowledge was simply book learning, although that is important as well. Again, the problem is, how does one take the book learning and apply it practically to be a servant to others? That is the reason why Jesus' method of discipleship training is best. The repetition of doing the physical labor for my Volkswagen Beetle tune up business made me good at it. I became very good at writing term papers, finding that my writing skills increased through repetition.

Perhaps the largest hands-on repetitive kinesthetic training of employees involves the manufacturer of automobiles, and the Germans were and are good at making automobiles. The first Volkswagen Beetle was imported to the U.S. on January 17, 1949 (just four days before I was born), but was initially a slow seller, with only two sold in 1949. However, the Volkswagen Beetle's popular acceptance by Americans grew steadily; and by 1960, over one-half million Volkswagen Beetles were sold in the U.S. For a whole generation, the Volkswagen Beetle was accepted as a non-pretentious affordable fuel efficient car that was an alternative to the larger gas-hog cars at that time built by Ford, Chrysler, and General Motors, but Ford, Chrysler, and General Motors sold the most cars in America in the 1960s. The Volkswagen Beetle was sold to consumers in the U.S. basically from 1949 to 1979. The new Volkswagen Beetle era was from 1998 to 2011, and the last Volkswagen Beetle generation was from 2012 to 2019. Thus, the last Volkswagen Beetle was sold in 2019.

Historically, in the 1950s and 1960s, Japanese manufacturers had an inferior reputation of making substandard products, and the slogan "Made in Japan" was a derogation of any product being imported from Japan to the U.S. and other countries. A lot of this Japanese business with substandard products was due the economic struggles Japan was having because of losing WWII.

Japan finally overcame its bad products manufacturing reputation. For example, in 1970 onward, the Japanese were very successful in manufacturing hands-on high quality sound systems that included those produced by Pioneer, Technics, Yamaha, Sansui, Kenwood, Sony, and JVC. Japan made the most excellent built quality receivers, turntables, and speakers during that season. The excellency in manufacturing sound equipment helped changed consumers' minds about Japanese import products.

In 1957, Japanese Toyota established Toyota Motor Sales, U.S.A. in Hollywood, California and sold its first Toyota Toyopet Crown sedan in 1958. Toyota was not that successful in its beginning. In 1961, Toyota's Toyopet Crown sedan and Land Cruiser were discontinued due to criticism of their prices and lack of power. In 1964 Toyota's Stout pickup truck was introduced successfully in the U.S. market, as the price to pay was reasonable and had power. Toyota's high quality vehicles continued year after year. In 1975, Toyota became the top importer of vehicles in the U.S. In 1986, Toyota manufactured and produced its first vehicle in the U.S., the Corolla FX16. Finally, in 2003, Toyota sold its thirty millionth vehicle in the U.S.

Similarly, in 1969, Honda introduced its N600 car in Hawaii, and in 1970 the Honda N600 car was first sold in the Mainland of the U.S. In 1973, the Honda Civic was introduced in the U.S., and in 1976 the Honda Accord started selling in the U.S. The sale of these Honda vehicles was highly successful. In 1982, Honda became the first Japanese manufacturer to produce vehicles in North America, when it began producing the Honda Accord at its Marysville, Ohio plant.

Today, people trust the Japanese made Honda and Toyota brand cars, as these cars had engines that were of high quality and lasted longer than the old Volkswagen Beetle and other American made cars. Japan started a revolution throughout the world of small economic cars whose engines lasted longer and had better gas mileage. The success of these Japanese cars was caused by the Japanese putting the design, engineering, and marketing joined together, teaching their employees with kinesthetic hands-on training.

Kinesthetic instruction and training are seen in the movie "The Karate Kid." Mr. Miyagi used kinesthetic karate instruction and training by having Daniel repetitive washing and waxing Mr. Miyagi's antique cars using a circular motion for "wax on" and the opposite circular motion for "wax off." Mr. Miyagi also had Daniel using sandpaper on wooden walkways and painting fences. All these physical tasks were done with specific motions that were later revealed to be foundational defensive karate techniques, even though Daniel initially perceived them as mundane work activities. Daniel became frustrated and insisted that Mr. Miyagi teach him karate moves and stop all these meaningless chores that Daniel thought was payment for Mr. Miyagi's karate training, without knowing that the chores were Daniel's defensive karate training. Mr. Miyagi stood in front of Daniel, threw a punch, and said, "wax on." Then Mr. Miyagi threw an opposite punch and said, "wax off." Each time Daniel used as a defense the "wax on" and "wax off" circular movements that he learned, and the other karate defensive technique moves that he learned by the physical chores, he blocked Mr. Miyagi's punches. The reason is Daniel was trained through Kinesthetic repetition to make the right movements with his hands and arms by doing mundane manual labor. Kinesthetic method of learning trains through the simple, repetitive movements, as the exercises prepared by Mr. Miyagi were the best training for Daniel learning and using karate defensive moves faster than being trained at a Japanese dojo or listening to a video or lecture.

A practical economic law in business is to scholastically teach and kinesthetically train Believer Business Employees for their maturity by assigning Believer Business Employees to small problems until the small problems are solved and perfected before more complex problems are assigned to the Believer Business Employees. When small incremental work is completed correctly, these small completed incremental steps can be put together with other small completed incremental steps, and the result will be to make complex products or services that buyers will purchase. Because the Moon was a movable target, the way the space craft went to the Moon was incremental adjustments of the rocket trajectory as they traveled to the moon.

One of the best examples of kinesthetic instructing, training, and learning was back in 1778 during the U.S. Revolutionary War. Baron Friedrich Wilhelm von Steuben was a Prussian Nobleman Officer assigned by General George Washington to be Inspector Major General of the American Continental Army in charge of kinesthetically training the American infantry soldiers, who were being killed because of too much time that it took to reload their muskets to fight the British Army. As a Christian man, Major General Von Steuben knew the number 120 was a very special number because it was the number of the Believers in the upper room on the Day of Pentecost when the apostles and disciples of Christ were empowered by the Holy Spirit and charged to be Jesus' witnesses in Jerusalem, and in Judaea, in Samaria, and unto the uttermost parts of the earth (Acts 1:8).

The weapons of both American and British infantry soldiers during the Revolutionary War were the smooth-bore, muzzle-loading, flintlock musket. British infantry soldiers were faster in reloading their muskets. Major General Von Steuben's goal was to make American infantry soldiers to load their muskets and refire their muskets quicker than the British infantry soldiers did. Major General Von Steuben's manual shows he studied and came up with standardized 18 separate motions that were designed for American infantry soldiers to quickly prime, load, and fire their muskets through kinesthetic repetitive practice training. The 120 infantry soldiers through kinesthetic training by continuous repetition perfected the priming, loading, and firing their muskets faster than the British infantry soldiers were doing.

Major General Von Steuben then had these 120 first infantry soldiers, now trained to perfection, sent throughout the Continental Army as Kinesthetic Instructors. These 120 highly trained kinesthetic Instructors retrained other infantry soldiers 120 at a time, training them incrementally the quickest way to reprime, reload, and refire their muskets. All the troops were retrained during the winter months when most of the battles were not being fought because of the weather. American well-trained infantry soldiers practiced and practiced in priming, loading, and refiring fifteen rounds in three and three-quarters minutes, or prime, load, and fire at a rate of one shot every fifteen seconds. This retraining through kinesthetic instruction of the priming, loading, and refiring the musket was a major factor in winning the Revolutionary War. Baron Friedrich Wilhelm von Steuben's kinesthetic training methods that were a great help in winning the Revolutionary War are still mentioned in the U.S. Army Blue Book.

The hands-on training methodology in a business is primarily kinesthetic repetitive training by Believer Business Employers and learning by Believer Business Employees. Using Jesus' Kinesthetic discipleship training, the Believer Business Owner instructs his or her Believer Business Employees by hands on training through continuous repetition, fellowship, interaction, and correction. Through these daily repetitiously performed incremental tasks correctly done lead to perfection in producing a product or performing a service that results in bringing goodwill to the business and repeating purchases by customers or retaining by clients for services.

Before they had machines, pens, and ink that detected counterfeit money, Bank Tellers kinesthetically were trained how to spot a counterfeit currency by repetitive looking at only the authentic one dollar bill, five dollar bill, ten dollar bill, twenty dollar bill, fifty dollar bill, and one hundred dollar bill. The Bank Tellers were never given examples of counterfeit currency to examine as a way of learning. In other words, by looking at what is true and authentic in life, you will spot the counterfeit concerning every opportunity or issue. This is a great, wise truth in business that can be used as life's wisdom.

Here are other examples of kinesthetic training. A Dentist and a Medical Surgeon must learn through a combination of both book scholastic teaching and Kinesthetic firsthand training doing repeated physical tasks.

Surgeons receive both book learning, scholastic lectures, but more importantly receive kinesthetic training in their medical schools by repeating surgical simulations and cadaver dissection. The medical students who are to be surgeons are trained to physically replicate and refine their movements in using surgical instruments, which causes their bodies to build muscle memory. By kinesthetic training Surgeons understand different organs and different tissue manipulation, along with training through observance of surgery done by mature medical Surgeons before surgery on actual patients.

Similarly, Dentists primarily learn through kinesthetic training by engaging in extensive hands-on practice with dental models and eventually real patients, allowing them to develop muscle memory in using various instruments to refine their motor skills through repeated practice procedures, such as tooth preparation, filling placement, extractions, root canals, and implants, all of which start with observation and assisting experienced other Dentist practitioners before taking on full responsibility with a patient.

Kinesthetic discipleship training should be the primary tool used to develop Believer Business Employees to be activated and matured as ministers. It is through kinesthetic training alongside an experienced Believer Business minister that ministry skills are learned, and this training is by observing the mature Believer Business ministers' methods and assisting them afterwards in praying for people who request prayer and physically helping others in their needs. For example, a great ministry for younger Believers on their off day from work would be to help elderly Believers, especially widows and widowers, who are on a limited fixed income, to maintain their yards. Also, kinesthetic training requires spending time during the week, having lunch, and having fellowship and hands-on training along with repetition of the Believer Business Employees' tasks along with continuous feedback from the mature Believer Business Manager minister is all important. This is how Jesus' Ephesians 4:11 functioning ministers made disciples of all nations after Jesus' ascension into heaven in the first Century *Ekklesia.* More things in the ministry are caught rather than taught through kinesthetic training rather than from teaching by a professor or functioning minister in a lecture hall.

In the first Century *Ekklesia*, there was a focus on the masses of Believers who were sent out to preach the gospel of the Kingdom (Matthew 24:14) and repentance and remission of sins (Luke 24:47). Acts 8:1,4 says, "And Saul was consenting unto his (Stephen's) death. And at that time there was a great persecution against the church which was at Jerusalem; and they were all scattered abroad throughout the regions of Judaea and Samaria, **except the apostles. . .** (4) **Therefore they that were scattered abroad went everywhere preaching the word."** Here, the scriptures say that the apostles stayed in Jerusalem, while the rank and file Believers who were trained by the Ephesians 4:11 functioning ministers by activating them into their spiritual Vocations and Gifts and sent them out to all regions in Judea and Samaria. What did these rank and file functioning ministers do when they were sent out from the local *Ekklesia* in Jerusalem? They went everywhere and preached the gospel of the Kingdom and preached repentance and remission of sins, along with laying hands on the sick to see them recover, casting out demons, raising the dead, and exhibiting other spiritual gifts, such as prophecy, speaking in tongues, words of wisdom, and words of knowledge.

Paul told Timothy in 2 Timothy 2:2, "And the things that thou hast heard of me among many witnesses, the same commit thou to faithful men, who shall be able to teach others also." If the Body of Christ is going to grow in numbers and in soulish spiritual maturity, then every minister who is mature should through kinesthetic training and activating other Believers for the work of the ministry, even those who have the Ephesian 4:11 office functioning ministries. The functioning apostles, prophets, evangelists, pastors, and teachers are very important gifts. These Ephesians 4:11 functioning ministers' main purpose is to activate and perfect Believers through hands-on kinesthetic training for the work of ministry with their spiritual Vocations as kings, priests (Revelation 1:6), lords (1 Timothy 6:15), ambassadors (2 Corinthians 5:20), and solders (2 Timothy 2:3-4), along with spiritual Gifts of God the Father (Romans 12:6-8), gifts of God the Word and Jesus' humanity nature (Ephesians 4:11-13), and gifts of the Holy Spirit, (1 Corinthians 12:8-10).

As previously discussed in the Introduction, there are some denominational minister leaders who believe and teach that Ephesian 4:11 functioning apostles and prophets are not valid ministries for today, and they believe certain spiritual gifts are not for today since Believers have the canonized word of God, the Bible. Although they are entitled to their teachings, according to Scriptures and history their conclusions are anemic at best and wrong at worst. What if the so-called laity Believers did not have the canonize word to read? What if most people before the canonize word could not read? What if the leaders in the priesthood/laity false dichotomy warehouse or cathedral spectator pyramid structure church decreed there would be no reading of the canonized Bible and that the canonized scriptures cannot be translated in languages other than Latin that was basically a dead language at that time except those who were the educated elite could read and speak Latin? This is what happened historically. The Catholic priesthood hierarchy would perform the Mass in Latin, and their Bible was written in Latin. The purpose of all Latin was so those who could not speak Latin would not be activated into Ministry as kings, priests, lords, ambassadors, and soldiers and the purpose not to train all Believers in their spiritual Gifts.

KINESTHETICALLY TRAINING IS EQUALLY IMPORTANT AS SCHOLASTIC TEACHING IN ACTIVATING AND PERFECTING BELIEVERS FOR THE WORK OF THE MINISTRY

Jesus used kinesthetic training His functioning apostles after He cast out a certain dumb and deaf spirit in a young man who did not speak or hear because of demonic possession. Mark 9:17, 18, 22-29 says, "And one of the multitude answered and said, 'Master, I have brought unto Thee my son, which hath a dumb spirit; (18) And wheresoever he taketh him, he teareth him: and he foameth, and gnasheth with his teeth, and pineth away: and I spake to Thy disciples that they should cast him out; and they could not… (22) And ofttimes it hath cast him into the fire, and into the waters, to destroy him: but if thou canst do anything, have compassion on us, and help us.' (23) Jesus said unto him, 'If thou canst believe, all things *are* possible to him that believeth.' (24) And straightway the father of the child cried out, and said with tears, 'Lord, I believe; help Thou mine unbelief.' (25) When Jesus saw that the people came running together, He rebuked the foul spirit, saying unto him, 'Thou dumb and deaf spirit, I charge thee, come out of him, and enter no more into him.' (26) And the spirit cried, and rent him sore, and came out of him: and he was as one dead; insomuch that many said, 'He is dead.' (27) But Jesus took him by the hand, and lifted him up; and he arose. (28) And when he was come into the house, His disciples asked Him privately, 'Why could not we cast him out?' (29) And He said unto them, 'This kind can come forth by nothing, but by prayer and fasting.'"

The point here made is that true professional training, as it is in medicine, dentistry, law, business, means that training functioning ministers is through both book scholastic learning and most importantly applying the book learning practically through kinesthetic hands-on training by repeating and applying scripture, actually preaching the gospel, teaching the methods of healing, and demonstrating how to cast out demons. Kinesthetic training activates the disciple into ministry, while book scholastic learning is important but does not activate and train the disciple how to apply the teaching he or she has been taught from reading the Bible or listening to a sermon. Students temporarily learn enough from books read to pass a written test, but often the information is forgotten once he or she receives a passing grade by spewing back on the test the knowledge gained in class or a book. Even a college graduate is worthless in business if he or she does not know how to apply the knowledge learned in college.

Also, if Believers are called and gifted to function as an apostle, prophet, evangelist, pastor, or teacher, continuous repetition causes maturity, but the mature Ephesians 4:11 functioning ministers must have as their primary focus of their functioning ministries is not just showing their Ephesian 4:11 office gifts before an audience, but rather to activate young Believers by watching them give a sermon, cast out a demon, lay hands on the sick and pray, lead an unsaved person to the Lord, visit someone and take care of their physical needs. Then, after the young Believers are spiritually skilled and matured, then the elder Ephesians 4:11 functioning minister should counsel and affirm him or her as a functioning minister to others. Thus, the profession of the Ephesians 4:11 functioning minister is not to do the work alone, and have people to pay him or her for doing the work, but rather perform the task of "… perfecting of the saints, for the work of the ministry, for the edifying of the Body of Christ - till we all come in the unity of the faith, and of the knowledge of the Son of God, unto a perfect man, unto the measure of the stature of the fulness of Christ" (Ephesians 4:12-13).

If you are an Ephesians 4:11 functioning evangelist, for example, take a bunch of untrained Believers into the highways and byways, near a shopping center, or other places where people are gathered. Instruct the untrained Believers how to lead someone to the Lord. Then tell them, "Now it is your turn to lead someone to the Lord, like I did; and remember, you can use the Roman Road, or John 3:16 and Romans 10:9 or Romans 10:13, depending on how much time the person with whom you are talking gives you to witness to him or her." Then let the Believer who just experienced kinesthetic training, who just had an experience of leading someone to the Lord, give opportunity for him or her to testify of the experience. You will see excitement by the Believer of being activated into his or her spiritual Vocation and spiritual Gifts. If the functioning evangelist is working with a local functioning pastor, have the local pastor bring these now excited Believers up front and let them testify of their kinesthetic training experience, so the rest of the congregation can see the excitement and want to be kinesthetically trained to go to the streets or where people are conducting commerce to evangelize.

The same with the other Ephesians 4:11 functioning apostles, prophets, pastors, and teachers who under the authority of the Holy Spirit can through kinesthetic training activate Believers into the work of ministry of their spiritual Vocations and their spiritual Gifts. For example, through the Holy Spirit, a functioning prophet can release a spirit of prophecy where others in his or her presence can be temporarily activated with that prophetic gift anointing and prophesy to others in the room.

Even though the Believer Business Employers and Believer Business Employees may have their minds full of knowledge, when the knowledge is activated through kinesthetic training, it comes into the Believer's heart and changes from mere knowledge into foundational beliefs. The primary use of kinesthetic training is to activate the Believer Business Employees' souls in their spiritual Vocations as kings, priests, lords, ambassadors, and soldiers. Why is this important?

The Believer Business Employers and Believer Business Employees must believe they have dominion kingdom authority from the Godhead and the Lord Jesus Christ's humanity nature to engage **1)**. as kings that have dominion authority in the world to rule over the world professions, trades, commercial enterprises; **2)**. as priests that have authority to lead people to Jesus and reconcile them to God; **3)**. as lords that have dominion authority over a piece of the earth that is the Believers' place of doing business and the place of the Believers' functioning ministry; **4)**. as ambassadors of the Kingdom of God that have dominion authority to speak Kingdom absolutes of Jesus' way, truth, life, *agape* love, grace, and mercy to those involved in sins and abominations in the land, and **5)** as soldiers that have dominion authority as Believers to spiritually fight evil spirits and tear down the gates of hell in people's lives to set the captives free from the oppression of the devil.

The truth is that without kinesthetic training of disciples of Christ Jesus, as an Ephesian 4:11 Believer Business Owner you will not be fulfilling your God-engifted work responsibility towards your Believer Business Employees that is mandated in Ephesians 4:12-13. Kinesthetic training of Believer Business Employees has to be of equal importance as classroom scholastic teaching as a method of learning in making disciple. 1 Corinthians 8:1 says, "... we know that we all have knowledge. Knowledge puffeth up, but charity (*agape* love) edifieth." Sharing *agape* love matures the soul better than just reading scriptures about Jesus' mandate to *agapao* loving one another (John 13:34-35).

Believer Business Employee discipleship scholastic education and kinesthetic training do require continuous daily Bible study (Joshua 1:8; Psalm 119; 2 Timothy 3:16) and continuous daily personal prayer (1 Thessalonians 5:17) for the Believer's soul transformation and maturation. The activation of a Believer Business Employee is applying and taking that scholastic biblical knowledge and applying it to kinesthetically training by physically feeding and leading unsaved people to the Lord while addressing their needs with wisdom, faith, and *agape* love to resolve problems of sicknesses, finances, and family relationship difficulties.

There are post college graduate law schools, medical schools, dental schools, and nursing schools, but all these schools have strict book scholastic studying along with kinesthetic training. You never learn all you need to know in a professional school or trade school. Ongoing kinesthetic repetition through hands-on training at the workplace after professionals graduate from trade schools or professional schools is mandated. God's school of kinesthetic hands-on training continues during each Believer's entire lifetime, so all Believers are mandated to learn scriptures but also trained how to apply their scriptural knowledge through kinesthetic repetitive training. This means training how to lead an unbeliever to the Lord by doing it, praying for the sick by doing it, casting out a demon by doing it, preaching the gospel of the kingdom and repentance and remission of sins by doing it, and acquiring and applying God's practical wisdom, knowledge, and understanding by doing it. Isaiah 33:6 says, "And wisdom and knowledge shall be the stability of thy times, and strength of salvation: the fear of the LORD is his treasure."

Matthew 28:19-20 is the mandate to Jesus' functioning apostles and disciples just before He ascended. As Believer Business Owners and Believer Business Employees, your time on earth is to make disciples of the Lord Jesus Christ of all racial groups, baptizing them in the name of the Father, Jesus (with His divine nature as God the Word and His humanity nature as the Only Begotten Son of God and Son of Man), and the Holy Spirit, and teaching less mature Believers all things that the Lord commands.

This mandate from the Lord Jesus Christ includes leading unbelievers to the Lord for salvation (Romans 10:9,15; Acts 1:8), seeking first the kingdom of God and His righteousness (Matthew 6:33), taking dominion over the earth with the Vocation as Lord over a particular place on the earth that the

Holy Spirit assigns (Genesis 1:26-28; Ephesians 1:22), being about God the Father's business (Luke 2:49), humbling yourself by entering the crucifixion of Christ and daily allowing Christ's divine nature and Jesus humanity nature to live His life in you and through you (Galatians 2:20), submitting to being led by the Holy Spirit (Romans 8:14; Galatians 5:18), and obeying the Lord's command to *agape* love other Believers by doing loving deeds as well as heartfelt caring (Matthew 25: 42-45; John 13:34-35).

God the Word, God the Father, and God the Holy Spirit did not leave Believers to fend for themselves, but the Godhead lives inside Believers (John 14:16;23), as Believers' bodies are the temple of the Godhead individually (2 Corinthians 6:16) in local community (1 Corinthians 3:16) and universally in all nations (Ephesians 2:21). Believers are guided by the entire Godhead, along with Jesus's humanity nature. Jesus' humanity nature, still attached to His divine nature, God the Word, receives the report of what all that Believers do here on earth through Jesus' divine nature, while Believers' born again spirits are seated with Jesus humanity nature in heavenly places because Believers' born again spirits are joined with Jesus' resurrected humanity spirit as one spirit (Ephesians 2:6; 1 Corinthians 6:17). The Godhead will be with Believers even unto the end of the age (Matthew 28:20) as Believers go through life's defeats and life's victories. Regardless, the Godhead is always there to edify, comfort, and exhort Believers that victory through soul spiritual transformation and spiritual maturation are promised.

MORE EXAMPLES OF KINESTHETIC DISCIPLESHIP TRAINING

Here is another example of kinesthetic training. As a lawyer I was trained by every law school professor to never speak in class unless I was standing. This kinesthetic training in the classroom was good to learn to think and speak while standing soliciting testimony from a witness or addressing a judge or jury. As a lawyer, you must be trained to think "on your feet." So, every time I, and other students, were called to brief a case, we were told to stand. In law school, we also had mock jury trials. Yes, we learned the law, but we did not learn all the rudiments of practicing law. Law school did not teach us how to prepare contracts, trusts, wills, form corporations, or prepare litigation complaints, an answer to a litigation complaint, litigation motions, litigation discovery, how to take litigation depositions, how to conduct civil trials, or how to handle a criminal case. These had to be learned by going with an experienced lawyer to a deposition, to a motion hearing, to a trial, being shown how to prepare a unlimited variety of contracts, form a corporation or limited liability company, prepare operating agreements, bylaws, shareholder agreements, minutes, and issuing stock, etc., or preparing estate planning documents, such as Trusts, Wills, Powers of Attorney, and then how to fund the Trust. Afterwards, as a young lawyer you were on your own. You had to work out your kinesthetic legal training with fear and trembling through repetition and constant perfection through doing the work. Like other professions, law practice is a hard career, and for most lawyers it is not that financially rewarding. You work long hours, always must be available, must follow very strict rules of ethics, can be sued for malpractice, and sometimes you must appear in court without being paid if you are subpoenaed as a witness regarding a legal matter that pertains to your prior client. This is why a lawyer talks about his or her legal "practice" because the law is constantly changing based upon social norms. In your law practice, the attorney is always learning through both book learning and kinesthetic training in the application of the laws and legal procedures through repetition of that legal knowledge, legal procedures, and legal writings.

Doctors also have medical practices for the same reason because you are always learning, and new drugs are being invented. There are Nurse Practitioners now that have their own practice. Dentists have dental practices. Accountants have accounting practices. Everyone continues to learn and apply that knowledge kinetically in the practice of their business or profession. This is the application of both book learning and kinesthetic application of the knowledge. When the knowledge comes from kinesthetic application, then that is when you are paid for your services or products. This is why every profession refers to practicing that profession because you are always updating your knowledge and applying that knowledge and experience to better serve your clients or patients.

So, the obvious question is, "Why is there 95% book learning and only 5% kinesthetic application training in the church and in ministry?" On the other hand, the good news is that Believer Business Employees are being trained kinesthetically in business, applying biblical principles, learning to be humble servants, doing things that spiritually mature their souls, while being paid a salary. Business experience is based upon applied knowledge, not just theoretical scholastic knowledge. Business as a place of ministry training is not a new subject because Jesus used this kinesthetic training method for His disciples, but it has not been used, except by a few, in the church world today. This is one of the reasons why the Holy Spirit is activating Believer Business Owners and Believer Business Employees to become functioning ministers at the business location eight to ten hours a day, five to six days a week that is the best way to perfect Believer Business Employees for the work of the ministry for the edifying of the body of Christ Jesus.

Thus, since Believer Business Owners use primarily scholastic teaching and kinesthetic training methods for their Believer Business Employees, God wants to use Believer Business Owners in the daily spiritual transformation and maturation of His children while engaging in business practices. Jesus said in Luke 2:49, "… Wist ye not that I must be about my Father's business?"

At twelve years old God the Father already was training His Only Begotten Son, Jesus's humanity nature, in the business of salvation, preaching the gospel of the Kingdom and preaching repentance and remission of sins and speaking the spiritual kingdom truths. Jesus was anointed by the Holy Spirit and with *dumanis* power to do good and heal people, confronting the oppressing devil who is doing evil in the world, revealing the idol of money, unmasking the religious Jewish ministers who were seeking positions of importance, training Believers to seek first the Kingdom of God and His righteousness, and commanding Believers to *agapao* love one another as Jesus first *agapao* loved them.

Before Jesus started His ministry at age 30, Jesus was fully trained to do God the Father's business and to tell people to repent for the kingdom of God was near (Matthew 4:17) and that all are mandated to do the will of God the Father on earth as it is in heaven (Matthew 6:10). Maturity comes by doing ministry as servants to others and being about God the Father's business, not just being a spectator watching others ministering. Again, Jesus was taught how to be a carpenter and stonemason by his stepfather, Joseph by Joseph kinesthetically training Jesus through the steps how to build a table, how to lay stone, or how to build scaffolding to work on the side of a building.

When you teach someone how to do a task by showing them how it's done by way of kinesthetic hands on training and then have them do it while you watch and listen, they will not forget what they have learned, as they have trained their bodies to do the physical work. Jesus employed as functioning apostles those who already were kinesthetic learners, including fishermen like Peter, Andrew, James, John, Thomas, Nathaneal, and other disciples (John 21:2). Scripture reveals that Peter, Andrew, James, and John had full time fishermen employees, who were kinesthetically trained all about the fishing business by physically doing the work as fishermen. Sometimes, they fished, and other times they had to mend their nets and do maintenance on their boats.

Evangelism is the same thing. Sometimes you fish for new disciples, while other times you are mending the disciples who have fractures in their soul. This is why Jesus told the fishermen, "Come follow Me, and I will make you fishers of men" (Matthew 4:19). Matthew was a Publican or Tax Collector that quit his profession to follow Jesus, and he constantly took notes as to what Jesus did and said (Matthew 9:9-13).

Most of Jesus' functioning apostles worked with their hands like Jesus did for about twenty years as a carpenter and stonemason. These men of labor learned their trades through kinesthetic hands-on training, valued practical information over theoretical concepts, and retained information more effectively while interacting with their physical environments. Jesus continuously demonstrated the steps involved to guide His functioning apostles how to minister. Jesus learned from His natural step-father, Joseph, and was totally obedient to His spiritual heavenly Father the same way, for twenty years to train Him how to raise up journeyman using kinesthetic training to become mature functioning apostles and disciples. Jesus taught His functioning disciples and apostles how to engage in the spiritual environments like they had done in their physical environments and trades.

Discipleship training is not just having Believers continuously listening to lecture hall sermons, but by engaging them as disciples into a fellowship that brings spiritual maturity of the soul that manifests in lifestyle changes. God is focusing His attention on the *Ekklesia* becoming strong in the marketplace by using Believer Business Owners who are willing to give their businesses to God for His will to be done here in earth as it is in heaven (Matthew 6:10). The business activity will have a central point in fostering God's economic principles with a biblitarian moral compass. Also, God's business plan He wants done is the saving of the lost to receive a born again spirit and maturing the souls of Believer Business Employees after initial salvation by the incremental problem solving in using biblical principles of the holy calling of the work ethic, the loving expression of servanthood when engaging with fellow employees, clients, and customers, and following the leading and movement of the Holy Spirit in in a particular season, time, and way.

WHY IS GOD CHOOSING BELIEVER BUSINESS OWNERS TO DISCIPLE BELIEVER BUSINESS EMPLOYEES WITH BIBLICAL ECONOMIC PRINCIPLES AND SERVANTHOOD WITH A MORAL COMPASS THROUGH KINESTHETIC TRAINING?

The Holy Spirit is moving the *Ekklesia* also into businesses to manifest His Holy Nation in every country (1 Peter 2:9). Obedient Believer Business Owners, led by the Holy Spirit in small Believer family-owned businesses, with each business having a small number of Believer Business Employees (under fifty employees), is a good model to follow to make the business a place of ministry training and activating Believer Business Employees for the work of the ministry. These smaller, Believer family-owned businesses will do better in spiritually maturing the Believer Business Employees in their spiritual Vocations and spiritual Gifts. When this happens, Believer Business Employees will have a much better opportunity of fulfilling God's spiritual purposes in their lives. Romans 8:28 says, "And we know that all things work together for good to them that love God, to them who are the called according to His purpose."

Why is God choosing Believer Business Owners to disciple Believer Business Employees with biblical economic principles, servanthood with moral compasses, and motivated with *agape* love? Because the Believer Business Owners have gifts as Ephesians 4:11 functioning apostles, prophets, evangelists, pastors, or teachers that can have his or her Believer Business Employees under his or her scholastic tutelage and kinesthetically train them eight to ten hours a day, five to six days a with the goal of making them soulishly transformed as mature Believer Business managers and Believer

Business ministers. Also, the Believer Business Owner has the Believer Business Employees' undivided attention because the Believer Business Owner is paying the Believer Business Employees to work in the business using biblical economic principles and submitting to being matured through the daily incremental problem solving work in the business. God knows that the Believer Business Employees submitting to the kinesthetic training of the Believer Business Owner is the quickest way for the Believer Business Employees skill enhancement and servanthood becoming a part of the Believer Business Employees spiritually transformed personalities.

For example, how does a Believer Business Employee that is kinesthetically trained respond to an angry customer who believes that she was sold a product that did not make her face lift or cause her body to lose weight. This has an easy answer. The Believer Business Employee is kinesthetically trained to smile and tell the customer the business stands behind its products or services; so, the Believer Business Employee tells the customer to return the balance of the product not used, immediately refund the money to the customer, and then thank the customer for their business and share with her any other products the business sells that might attain the results the customer desires. The customer now knows if the product does not work, she simply returns the product and is refunded the purchase price without argument.

You cannot learn football, soccer, rugby, baseball, basketball, tennis, swimming, gymnastics, running, or any other sport just by observance while sitting in the bleachers. You are not paid as a spectator. You are paid by working or by being an athlete engaged in the game of the sport. You buy a ticket to sit in the bleachers to watch a ball game, but the ball player is paid millions to continuously keep in shape, practice each day, and learn to follow the coach's playbook.

Likewise, the purpose of the Ephesians 4:11 functioning ministers of the functioning apostle, prophet, evangelist, pastor, and teacher are not to create followers to their own ministry but instead "For the perfecting of the saints, for the work of the ministry, for the edifying of the Body of Christ" (Ephesians 4:12).

Having the same spiritual Vocations as kings, priests, lords, ambassadors, and soldiers, every Believer Business Owner and every Believer Business Employee must know how to lead an unsaved person to the Lord for initial salvation. Every mature Believer Business Owner and every mature Believer Business Employee must illuminate to younger Believers the distinction between the initial salvation that gives the new Believer a born again spirit and eternal life with after the initial salvation where the young Believer must submit to the Godhead for his or her ongoing spiritual transformation of his or her soul by the God the Father's pruning the flesh from the soul to bear more spiritual fruit (John 15:2), God the Word washing away the flesh and sanctifying the soul to have a Ekklesia without spot, wrinkle, but is holy (Ephesians 5:26), and God the Holy Spirit mortifying the deeds of the flesh that is in the soul to experience more *zoe* life (Romans 8:13).

Every Believer Business Employer and every Believer Business Employee must take time each day to read and study the Bible. Every Believer Business Employer and every Believer Business Employee must deal with his or her own sins and repent and seek forgiveness. Every Believer Business Employer and every Believer Business Employee daily must seek first the Kingdom of God and His righteousness. Every Believer Business Employer and every Believer Business Employee must have faith in God because He is a covenant-making and a covenant-keeping God. Every Believer Business Employer and every Believer Business Employee must have other Believers as close friends, with whom they fellowship together weekly. Every Believer Business Employer and every Believer Business Employee should continuously give cheerfully into the *Ekklesia* community they attend and ministries outside the local *Ekklesia*.

Believers come to an auditorium lecture hall and sit in church pews for ten to forty years, or longer, and are never activated as ministers to do the work of their activated spiritual Vocation callings and use their activated spiritual Gifts. Jesus said for everyone to go and make disciples (not just converts) of all ethnic groups in the venue of everyone's influence in society, baptizing them in the name of God the Father, Jesus' divine nature, God the Word and Jesus' humanity nature as the sacrificial the Lamb of God, and God the Holy Spirit, and teaching them all that Jesus commanded (Matthew 28:19-20). Instead, Believers are invited to gather in a building, called "the church," sit in pews or chairs, take part in or just listen to praise and worship, be attentive during a 45-60 minute sermon, pay their tithes and offerings or "tuition" for the teaching, and then go back home and work to repeat the religious practice week after week until they pass and go to heaven. This religious cyclical practice week after week is not the dynamic Christian lifestyle that Jesus promised, instructed, and commanded. John 10:10b says, "…I (Jesus) am come that they might have *(zoe)* life, and that they might have it more abundantly." Sitting in a pew for ten to forty years is not living *zoe* life abundantly.

Again, I am not saying the above *Ekklesia* practice is all bad; I am saying it is anemic because the rank and file Believers are not being activated into ministry through kinesthetic instruction and training, so they can obtain the most out of God's *zoe* life here on earth. The warehouse auditorium lecture hall church paradigm structure is not all bad, but Believers simply are not receiving the mandates of the Ephesians 4:11 functioning apostle, prophet, evangelist, pastor, and teacher, whose primary purpose is stated in Ephesians 4:12-13, which are to activate all Believers for the work of ministry in each of their spiritual Vocations and in using their spiritual Gifts, "Till we all come in the unity of the faith, and of the knowledge of the Son of God, unto a perfect man, unto the measure of the stature of the fulness of Christ."

The populace in the U.S., and most other countries, are like Sailors traveling in a ship waiting to die, but they are on ships without a rudder, tossed about by the waves of daily existence, because most Believers are spectators and not activated working minister Sailors in the *Ekklesia*. To experience life abundantly, Believers must become responsible Sailors submitted to the Captain of the ship, Jesus. A Believer cannot be a good minister Sailor without being kinesthetically trained through the incremental repetition of tying knots for ropes, learn basic sailing terms like "port" and "starboard", understand the different parts of the boat like the "bow" and "boom", learn how to handle sails, navigate using wind and tides, read weather forecasts, practice basic safety procedures, and be proficient in essential maneuvers like tacking and jibing. Yet, most Believers come on board the ship just to be passengers, not Sailors, without realizing the Titanic will sink after hitting an iceberg, killing most of the people on board because there were insufficient numbers of lifeboats. Yet, the passengers buying their tickets and boarding passes were not instructed there was an insufficient number of lifeboats to carry the passengers to safety if the ship began to sink. Although Jesus is our lifeboat that takes Believers to heaven when we die, Jesus wants Believers to enjoy life abundantly while they are living here on earth. He wants Believers to seek first the Kingdom of God and His righteousness first (Matthew 6:33) every day and throughout the day to experience righteousness, peace, and joy in the Holy Spirit (Romans 14:17).

THE HOLY SPIRIT IS MOVING THE BODY OF CHRIST'S VENUE INTO BUSINESSES AND ANOINTING BUSINESS MINISTERS WITH FAITH

The Holy Spirit is anointing and engifting Believer Business Owners as functioning apostles, prophets, evangelists, pastors, and teachers because they are with the Believer Business Employees eight to ten hours per day, five to six days a week where and when they can disciple them face to face, one on one, or in small groups to mature them in the ways of the Kingdom with God's purpose to make the Believer Business Employees' souls spiritually transformed and matured as leaders in the Body of Christ.

God gives His children ministers a pattern to follow because in following the pattern and instruction, the spiritual task involved, whether healing, casting out demons, preaching the gospel of the Kingdom or preaching repentance and remission of sins, or even making the physical world obey God's commands that He tells you to say. God's pattern is learned through repetitious training of the work of ministry of Believers' spiritual Vocations and spiritual Gifts perfected at the business workplace. Jesus said in John 5:19, "Verily, verily, I say unto you, 'The Son can do nothing of Himself, but what He seeth the Father do: for what things soever He doeth, these also doeth the Son likewise."

2 Corinthians 1:21-22 says, "Now He who establishes us with you in Christ and has anointed us is God, who also has sealed us and given us the earnest of the Spirit in our hearts." Ephesians 5:18 says, "… but be filled with the Spirit." This means the Believer is being refilled with the Holy Spirit and His anointing repeatedly. There is a yoke of oppression by the devil that must be broken with the anointing. Isaiah 10:27 states "...the yoke (of oppression) shall be destroyed because of the anointing."

Jesus cursed a fig tree for not having fruit when He wanted figs to eat (Matthew 21:19). Jesus said in Matthew 21:21-22, "Verily I say unto you, 'If ye have faith, and doubt not, ye shall not only do this which is done to the fig tree, but also if ye shall say unto this mountain, 'Be thou removed,' and be thou cast into the sea; it shall be done. (22) And all things, whatsoever ye shall ask in prayer, believing, ye shall receive." With the fig tree, Jesus used a hyperbolic analogy to illustrate that faith comes when you hear the *rhema* word from God (Romans 10:17), and this faith instilled by God in your soul can overcome insurmountable difficulties. Mountains symbolize obstacles or momentous challenges, and the acceptance of faith from God's *rhema* word that has the *dunamis* power that can alter physical reality that transforms negative circumstances into blessings from God. Believing in God's *dunamis* power upon hearing God's *rhema* words is how faith comes to Believers, and this faith accepts the biblical principle that nothing that is good is impossible with God (Luke 1:37).

Faith also means a Believer cannot do the impossible that is good without God. Read what Jesus said. John 5:19 says, "Then answered Jesus and said unto them, 'Verily, verily, I say unto you, "The Son can do nothing of Himself, but what He seeth the Father do: for what things soever he doeth, these also doeth the Son likewise."'" Jesus said in John 12: 49-50, "For I have not spoken of myself; but the Father which sent Me, He gave Me a commandment, what I should say, and what I should speak. (50) And I know that His commandment is life everlasting: whatsoever I speak therefore, even as the Father said unto Me, so I speak."

Thus, Jesus was exercising faith as He obeyed the *rhema* word from God the Father to walk on the water (Matthew 14:22-23, Mark 6:45-52, John 6:16-21). Although it is not revealed in scripture, as a carpenter and stonemason, perhaps Jesus' humanity nature may not learn to be a top swimmer like the fishermen were; so maybe Father God told Jesus to walk with Him on the water. There is no scripture saying that Jesus ever went swimming. Not only did Jesus walk on water, John 6:21 says, the moment He got into the ship where the functioning apostles were, "… immediately the ship was at the land whither they went." John 6:21 records and chronicles that Jesus and His apostles were immediately transported to their destination, demonstrating not only Jesus' *dunamis* power over nature (Acts 10:30) but also the covenant assurance through faith of overcoming circumstances for a swift and secure arrival at their desired journey's end.

Also, in another passage, Jesus was exercising faith because He heard the *rhema* word from God the Father to rebuke the storm that was threatening to sink the ship Jesus and the functioning apostles were in. Mark 4:37-41 says, "And there arose a great storm of wind, and the waves beat into the ship, so that it was now full. (38) And He (Jesus) was in the hinder part of the ship, asleep on a pillow: and they awake Him, and say unto Him, 'Master, carest thou not that we perish?' (39) And He arose, and rebuked the wind, and said unto the sea, 'Peace, be still.' And the wind ceased, and there was a great calm. (40) And He said unto them, 'Why are ye so fearful? How is it that ye have no faith?' (41) And they feared exceedingly, and said one to another, 'What manner of man is this, that even the wind and the sea obey Him?'"

Faith is connected directly with hearing God's *rhema* word. The greatest sign of transformation and maturity of the Believer Business Servants' souls are developing an ear to hear the *rhema* word of God. Jesus said in John 8:47, "He that is of God heareth God's (*rhema*) words: ye therefore hear them not, because ye are not of God." Similarly, John the Baptist said in John 3:34, "For he whom God hath sent speaketh the (*rhema*) words of God: for God giveth not the Spirit by measure unto him."

Rhema never contradicts the *logos* of God, but may contradict tradition that is not in line with the word of God. Romans 10:17 says, "So then faith cometh by hearing, and hearing by the (*rhema*) word of God." Hebrews 11:6 says, "But without faith it is impossible to please Him: for he that cometh to God must believe that He is, and that He is a rewarder of them that diligently seek Him (in business)." Jesus said in Matthew 4:4 says, "... Man shall not live by bread alone, but by every (*rhema*) word that proceedeth out of the mouth of God." The *rhema* word is required for the Believer Business Servants to obtain the Bread of Life. Jesus said in John 6:63, "It is the spirit that quickeneth; the flesh profiteth nothing: the (*rhema*) words that I speak unto you, they are spirit, and they are life."

The *rhema* word in business is very important, and without the *rhema* word, the Believer Business Servant cannot prosper because the Believer Business Servant is not doing God's full or perfect Will in the business because God's *rhema* word must be followed. According to 3 John 2, Believer Business Servants can only prosper in business and be in health in God's kingdom equal to the measure that the Believer Business Servants' souls are prospering.

Soul prosperity comes by hearing God's *rhema* words and not listening to the carnal words, images, and ideas by the Believer Business Servants' souls. The Believer Business Servants' souls have to be cleansed and sanctified from the influence of the flesh. Ephesians 5:26 says, "That He might sanctify and cleanse it (the soul) with the washing of water by the (*rhema*) word." Finally, God adds the letter "s" that begins the word, "word" as His word that begins with an "s" spells sword, so Believers can use His *rhema* word to do battle against Satan's evil realm. Ephesians 6:17 says, "And take . . . the sword of the Spirit, which is the (*rhema*) word of God." In John 15:7, Jesus said every Believer Business Servant must accept His *rhema* words. "If ye abide in Me, and My (*rhema*) words abide in you, ye shall ask what ye will, and it shall be done unto you." God speaks a *rhema* word, and when Believer Business Servants hear that *rhema* word, it will engender faith, and with that faith the Believer Business Servants can remove any obstacles that hinder the business progress, as that is the Will of God.

In fact, the whole creation was formed by the *rhema* world of God. Hebrew 1:3 says, "Who being the brightness of His glory, and the express image of his person, and upholding all things by the (*rhema*) word of His power, when He had by Himself purged our sins, sat down on the right hand of the Majesty on high." Hebrews 11:3 says, "Through faith we understand that the worlds were framed by the (*rhema*) word of God, so that things which are seen were not made of things which do appear." 1 Peter 1:25 says, "But the (*rhema*) word of the Lord endureth forever. And this is the word which by the gospel is preached unto you."

THE EPHESIANS 4:11 FUNCTIONING MINISTERS IN BUSINESS

The soulish maturity level of Believer Business Servants is evident when God's business purpose is the goal of all in the business. God does not need real property, minerals, energy, food, water, or any natural things. God's measure of spiritual prosperity is not the accumulation of things; it is the acquiring of sons and daughters that multiplies His family and citizens of His Kingdom. God's primary purpose of spiritual discipleship in business is to make mature Believer Manager ministers who have faith because they hear the *rhema* word of God which lines up with the *logos* word of God. The word "manage" is really two words, "man" and "age," which means to make the Believer Business Servants to come of age and be spiritually matured and activated into his or her spiritual Vocation and spiritual Gifts. Money as profit is merely a result of following the pattern that God gives Believer Business Servants to transform their souls. When Believer Business Owners are faithful by instilling management skills in the souls of Believer Business Employees, the less management oversight the Ephesians 4:11 Believer Business Owner must manage personally.

To a degree, the leaders in present day church ministry, who have followed the warehouse auditorium building lecture hall paradigm structure, have failed in their leadership duties and mandates by making a pyramid-type, very expensive edifice, with only a few ministers at the top, instead of Jesus' focus and mandate that the chiefest disciple is the servant of all (Mark 10:44-45) and are found at the bottom of a "V" type *Ekklesia* fellowship where all Believers function in their ministry Vocations. Today's leaders have made and are still making followers instead of a ground-swell of kings, priests, lords, ambassadors, and soldiers.

If a natural secular government Army Officer who graduates from West Point, who is trained to create a winning battle strategy, consists of only Captains, Majors, Colonels, and Generals, then we will never win the spiritual battle skirmishes against the devil and his evil realm. Why? Because the rank and file Believers are not activated in their spiritual Vocation as soldiers (2 Timothy 2:3-4) to be trained in how to fight spiritual battles. Hebrews 11:34 admonishes, "Quenched the violence of fire, escaped the edge of the sword, out of weakness were made strong, waxed valiant in fight, turned to flight the armies of the aliens."

Again, the upper room on the day of Pentecost had approximately 120 Believers, so Jesus' twelve apostles were only ten percent of the people in the upper room. Jesus mandated every Believer in Acts 1:8 to be empowered by the Holy Spirit and to be activated by using his or her spiritual Vocations and spiritual Gifts to be His witness fifty percent of their efforts and times in Jerusalem (local), and then fifty percent of their efforts and times in Judea (regional), Samaria (state and federal), and the uttermost parts of the world (international).

Please consider the ideas in this chapter as applied to each of the Ephesians 4:11 functioning ministers. As I will walk you through the Ephesians 4:11 engiftment functions of the apostle, prophet, evangelist, pastor, and teacher for your edification; but remember, these are office gifts, not titles, but rather functions; and their assignments are to activate, perfect, and equip the Believers to work in the Believers' spiritual Vocations as spiritual kings, priests, lords, ambassadors, and soldiers and activate them in their spiritual Gifts.

Ephesians 4:11 functioning ministers' assignments are to be hands-on kinesthetically practicing their gifts in the marketplace, home fellowships, school places, and everywhere people congregate. God's business is about people coming to the Lord, living a submitted life in His kingdom unto soul maturation, and experiencing righteousness, peace, and joy in the Holy Spirit while they do business in the marketplace as a witness to others that come to the business location from the fallen world.

Christian schools for children are preferable than secular schools, but Christian schools that are only "religious" may not have the kinesthetic training where you send your children to be activated and perfected in the work of ministry while they graduate and work in a business. Send your children where students can freely express their Christian beliefs, be activated and practice their spiritual Vocations, and after graduation are taught to seek businesses where the Believer Business Owner is an Ephesian 4:11 minister who sees his or her business as the venue of God's kingdom school of minister training, using kinesthetic hands-on teaching and learning primarily for activation into ministry wherever they go in life.

Every Believer Business Owner's workplace should be a house of prayer, a place where the word of God every morning is read before the work day begins, a place where hospitality is practiced, a place where exhibiting *agape* love and caring in both a spiritual and practical way towards others, a place where gratuitous servanthood is the highest virtue and life history for leadership, a place where work is a holy calling of God unto maturation, a place where integrity and truthfulness are paramount, a place where seeking first the Kingdom of God and His righteousness is the narrow pathway, and a place where learning submission by entering into the crucifixion of Christ and letting Him do the living daily for you and through you to touch others as Jesus is the Way, Truth, and Life (Galatians 2:20; John 14:6).

CHAPTER THREE

CONSTITUTION, LEGISLATION, AND JUDICIAL LAW PROTECTING BUSINESS MINISTERS IN THE U.S.

FIRST AMENDMENT RELIGIOUS RIGHTS AGAINST GOVERNMENT INTRUSION

It is good that we in the U.S. have freedom of religion as enshrined in the Bill of Rights in the First Amendment restricting the Federal government and with the Fourteenth Amendment restricting the States and local governments from infringement of freedom of religion, prohibiting the government of forming a state religion, freedom of speech, freedom of press, freedom of assembly, and freedom to petition the government of our grievances. In the U.S., American citizens and persons living here legally enjoy the rights and freedoms guaranteed in the First Amendment, which is really a commandment to restrict the Politicians and Bureaucracies in Federal, State, and Local governments from taking away our God-given freedoms and rights guaranteed in our U.S. Constitution. In furtherance of the topic of this book, the protective rights to establish a church or ministry and exercise freedom of practice of faith has foundational constitutional authority in the U.S., but this protection is not in every country.

The First Amendment of the U.S. Constitution says, "Congress shall make no law respecting an establishment of religion or prohibiting the free exercise thereof; or abridging the freedom of speech, or of the press; or the right of the people peaceably to assemble, and to petition the Government for a redress of grievances."

After the Civil War in 1868 the Fourteenth Amendment was enacted and added to the U.S. Constitution, and it forbade States and local governments from depriving any person of "life, liberty, or property without due process of law." The U.S. Supreme Court has gradually used the due process clause of the Fourteenth Amendment to find substantive rights and freedoms for citizens and persons that are legally here in the U.S. Thus, case law through the Fourteenth Amendment adjudicated restrictions on State governments in addition to those mentioned in the Bill of Rights but favorably includes the First Amendment rights of establishment of religion and the free exercise thereof.

Chicago, Burlington & Quincy Railroad Co. v. City of Chicago (1897)**:** This case marked the first time the U.S. Supreme Court applied the Fifth Amendment of the Bill of Rights through the Fourteenth Amendment, incorporating the Fifth Amendment's guarantee of just compensation for the taking of property.

Gitlow v. New York (1925): The U.S. Supreme Court held that through the Fourteenth Amendment the states were bound to protect freedom of speech, and the Court applied the First Amendment's Free Speech Clause restricting the states.

Cantwell v. Connecticut (1940): The U.S. Supreme Court held that through the Fourteenth Amendment the states were bound to protect the First Amendment's "free exercise clause", protecting freedom of religion from state interference.

Everson v. Board of Education (1947): The U.S. Supreme Court held that the Fourteenth Amendment incorporated the First Amendment's "establishment clause" regarding religion, and the school district providing bus transportation for children going to parochial school is constitutional.

Westside Community Schools v. Mergers, (1990): The U.S. Supreme Court held that the Fourteenth Amendment incorporated the First Amendment's "free exercise clause" regarding religion. Public schools may not prohibit student religious groups from meeting on school grounds after hours. The Court held that The Equal Access Act was passed by Congress to ensure that any school receiving federal funds could not prevent religious and other groups from using school property after hours. The Supreme Court upheld the Equal Access Act, saying that "neutrality" and no "hostility" to religion is all that is required by the First Amendment so as not to be a violation of the "establishment clause."

Good News Club v. Milford Central School (2001): The U.S. Supreme Court case held that the Fourteenth Amendment forbade schools from excluding religious clubs from meeting on school property after hours if the school allowed other secular groups to use the facilities. The Court ruled that barring the club based on its religious viewpoint was a violation of free speech under the First Amendment.

Thus, from the 1920s to the 1940s the Supreme Court applied all the clauses of the First Amendment to the states. Thus, the First Amendment and Fourteenth Amendment protect citizens and legal "persons" from abusive actions by government employees in the federal, state, and local governments. Similarly, the First Amendment and the Fourteenth Amendment apply to all branches of government, including executives, legislators, courts, schools, bureaucracies, and agencies. Thus, Presidents, Governors, Legislators, Judges, Justices, Bureaucrats, Agency Personnel, every Leader in public universities and colleges, and every Administrators and Teachers in primary to public high schools and junior high schools, and grade schools in the U.S. cannot totally prohibit citizens, students, and legal "persons" from exercising their rights guaranteed in the Bill of Rights and Fourteenth Amendments, with some restrictions on gathering on public property, parking restrictions, and regulating some speech and activity that may cause violence on school and other government property.

For example, freedom of speech does not give a right to defame another person with an untrue statement, whether oral or written, that causes the victim damages of reputation, nor can your speech cause a riot or cause people to be injured. Supreme Court Justice Oliver Wendell Holmes Jr. said, "You cannot yell fire in a crowded theater" to illustrate that free speech is not absolute and does not protect speech that creates a "clear and present danger". While the case established this widely-quoted analogy, the ruling and its "clear and present danger" test were later refined in *Brandenburg v. Ohio (1969).* This case modified the standard for unprotected speech, replacing the "clear and present danger" test with one that requires speech to be "likely to incite or produce imminent lawless action."

Walz v. Tax Commission (1970): The U.S. Supreme Court held that the State had not singled out one particular church or religious group as such; rather, it had granted real property tax exemptions to all houses of religious worship within a broad class of property owned by nonprofit, quasi-public corporations which also included hospitals, libraries, playgrounds, scientific, etc. The Court held that property tax exemption for religious properties used solely for religious purposes did not violate the Establishment Clause of the First Amendment by the local government since the *Ekklesia* or religious groups were just one of many real property tax exemptions allowed. The Court held that the purpose of the exemptions was to neither advance nor inhibit religion; no one church or religious group had been singled out to receive a tax exempt status.

Hobbie v. Unemployment Appeals Commission of Florida et al. (1987): The U.S. Supreme Court found in favor of an employee named Paula Hobbie, who was employed for two and one-half years by Lawton and Company, a Florida jewelry shop. After the date of employment, Hobbie joined the Seventh-day Adventist church and informed her employer that she could not work from sundown on Friday to sundown on Saturday since it was her new church's Sabbath day. The Supreme Court reversed the State of Florida Unemployment Appeals Commission's refusal to provide unemployment benefits. Her employer refused, so Hobbie quit her employment. Lawton and Company needed an employee who could work the entire weekend, because the weekend had more customers coming to their business than during the weekdays. Hobbie filed an application for unemployment benefits, which the state denied because Hobbie intentionally quit her job as opposed to termination. Hobbie then appealed her denial on First Amendment grounds. In deciding the case, the Supreme Court Justices followed its previous ruling in both *Sherbert v. Verne*r and *Thomas v. Review Board* where the Court held that a state's refusal to provide benefits because of conduct mandated by a religious belief puts pressure on an adherent to modify his or her behavior, and the refusal could be justified and valid only by a compelling State government interest. The State of Florida argued that Hobbie's termination was appropriate because it was unfair for her to adopt new religious beliefs inconsistent with her existing employment. The State of Florida contended that the employee's refusal to work on her new Sabbath amounted to misconduct. The Court rejected the State of Florida's assertion, finding that the Free Exercise Clause of the First Amendment and the Fourteenth Amendment prevent a State from discriminating against an employee who through religious conversion was after the date of employment compared to an employee whose religious conversion belief preceded her date of employment. The Supreme Court found no State compelling interest that justified the state of Florida's denial of unemployment benefits, so Hobbie received her Unemployment Benefits. However, can every employee have the money for legal fees and legal costs to fight for their freedom of religion? In Hobbie's case the attorney fees and legal costs were paid by the Legal Department of the General Conference of Seventh-day Adventists. This was the first church-backed case argued in the United States Supreme Court.

Cutter v. Wilkinson (2005). The U.S. Supreme Court held that a federal statute protecting prisoners' religious exercise did not exceed the limits of permissible government accommodation of religious practices.

Corp. of Presiding Bishop of the church of Jesus Christ of Latter-Day Saints v. Amos (1987): The U.S. Supreme Court held that religious organizations could be exempted from secular activities to avoid federal law prohibiting employment discrimination was a permissible accommodation consistent with the prohibition of the government pursuant to the First Amendment Religious Establishment Clause. The Court held in *Wisconsin v. Yoder*, 406 U.S. 205, 234 n.22 (1972) that exempting the Amish from the state's compulsory education rules was a permissible accommodation consistent with the state not violating the First Amendment Establishment Clause.

Selective Draft Law Cases (1918): The Supreme Court held that "The constitutionality of the Selective Draft Law also is upheld (allowing conscientious objectors for religion reasons) against the following objections (that the law violated the First Amendment Establishment Clause): . . . (3) that, by exempting ministers of religion and theological students under certain conditions and by relieving from strictly military service members of certain religious sects whose tenets deny the moral right to engage in war, it is repugnant to the First Amendment, as establishing or interfering with religion;

the unsoundness of Free Exercise and Establishment Clause challenges to an exemption from the draft for conscientious objectors was apparent to excuse the conscientious objectors from the draft." Thus, exemption from the draft based upon being a conscientious objector was upheld as not the government trying to establish a state-sponsored religion.

Burwell v. Hobby Lobby Stores, Inc. (2014): The Supreme Court's decision held that the Religious Freedom Restoration Act of 1993 is a federal law forbidding governments from burdening a person's religious beliefs without proving a compelling governmental interest to do so, and the government is required to use the least restrictive methods of implementing the law and its agency regulations. The Court considered the Department of Health and Human Services (HHS) regulations implementing the 2010 "Patient Protection and Affordable Care Act" (ACA) that mandated employers' group health plans that furnish preventive care and screenings for women without cost sharing requirements for 20 FDA-approved contraceptive methods, including four that may have the effect of preventing a fertilized egg from developing. HHS exempted religious nonprofit organizations, but a Health Insurance Company were to exclude contraceptive coverage from religious nonprofit organizations employer's plan, they must provide participants with separate payments for contraceptive services.

Hobby Lobby Stores, Inc., which is a closely held for-profit corporation, known for the owners' religious beliefs, sought an injunction under the 1993 Religious Freedom Restoration Act (RFRA), which prohibits the government from substantially burdening a person's exercise of religion even by a rule of general applicability unless it demonstrates that imposing the burden is the least restrictive means of furthering a compelling governmental interest. As amended by the Religious Land Use and Institutionalized Persons Act of 2000 (RLUIPA), RFRA covers "any exercise of religion, whether or not compelled by, or central to, a system of religious belief." The Third Circuit held that a for-profit corporation could not "engage in religious exercise" under RFRA and that the mandate imposed no requirements on corporate owners in their personal capacity. The Tenth Circuit held that the businesses are "persons" under RFRA; that the contraceptive mandate substantially burdened the corporate owners' religious freedom as they were totally against any contraception that killed the unborn, including four drugs that prevented an already fertilized egg from developing any further by inhibiting its attachment to the uterus; and the court held that HHS had not demonstrated that the mandate was the "least restrictive means" of furthering a compelling governmental interest.

The *Hobby Lobby* owners sincerely believe that at the instance that an egg is fertilized that a living soul enters the fertilized egg. The truth is that it is not the mind of the mother's soul or the brain of the mother's body that instructs the baby in her womb to grow; it is the mind of the baby's soul. The mind of the soul of the baby instructs the cells to grow a placenta and an umbilical cord that attaches to the mother's uterus wall to obtain nourishment to feed the baby. At that point there is no brain in the cells of the baby that is directing the growth of the baby. Thus, the baby's mind in the baby's soul continues to instruct the cells to grow organs, eyes, nose, mouth, ears, arms, fingers, legs, feet, toes, and develop its own blood supply, which blood type may be different than the mother's blood type. Eventually, the baby's mind in his or her soul begins to start the growth of the baby's physical brain. After the baby is born, the physical brain in the body of the baby continues to develop. So, the brain is not involved in the growth of the baby in the womb; it is the baby's mind in the baby's soul that instructs and regulates the growth of the baby's body in the mother's womb. Thus, aborting or killing a fertilized egg is killing a living soul and is deemed murder in God's eyes, so Believers in business have a right to not participate in any medical insurance that covers the killing of the unborn.

The relevant main point of the *Hobby Lobby* Court ruling is that Believer Business Owners of closely-held Corporations, Limited Liability Companies, and/or Fictitious Business Entities do not lose their religious freedoms when they open and operate a family business based upon the 1993 Religious Freedom Restoration Act, although the Justices did not address the rights afforded in the U.S. Constitution First Amendment Establishment Clause or the Free Exercise of Religion Clause. So, in the event the 1993 Religious Freedom Restoration Act is abolished in the future by a future Congress and President, then the owners of a family owned closely held business may not be afforded the rights of religious freedom. In the event the 1993 Religious Freedom Restoration Act is appealed, and a small business owner is ordered to hire someone whose lifestyle is considered an abomination in the Bible, then the issue of the First Amendment rights of religious freedom must be defended and appealed before the U.S. Supreme Court. This is an area where small business owners together should start putting aside litigation savings to be used to help the defendant in the case to pay attorney fees and litigation costs, which could be over a million dollars.

Axon Enterprise, Inc. v. Federal Trade Commission (2023): The U.S. Supreme Court held that cases like this have opened the door for individuals and businesses to challenge bureaucratic agency actions that they believe infringe upon their constitutional rights. The Supreme Court held that individuals as citizens and entity businesses, as "persons," can challenge the constitutionality of bureaucratic agency structures, such as the *Federal Trade Commission* and the *Security Exchange Commission*, directly in Federal District Court, without first going through the bureaucratic agency's procedures rather than waiting for the bureaucratic agency to act and then challenging the action in a higher court.

When government bureaucracies promulgate regulations that trespass U.S. Constitution, when the rights of citizens or persons, then the regulations can be and should be challenged as unconstitutional government overreach. Although there isn't one single Supreme Court case that explicitly grants citizens and "persons" the right to challenge bureaucratic regulations, there are multiple cases confirming the principle that government laws and bureaucratic regulations can be challenged as unconstitutional overreach. This principle is rooted in the notion that the government's power is limited by the Constitution, and that individuals have rights under the Bill of Rights that cannot be infringed upon by overly broad or unjustified regulations. The Constitution's Bill of Rights (First through Tenth Amendments) protects fundamental rights such as freedom of speech, religion, assembly, and the press, right not to be violated by warrantless search and seizure, right against self-incrimination, right to be represented an attorney if criminally arrested, right to speedy criminal trial, right of criminal trial by jury by your peers, and right to due process of law.

IRC 501(C)(3) VERSUS IRC 508(C)(1)(A) RELIGIOUS PUBLIC CHARITIES

Most functioning pastors or ministers in the U.S. waive their Constitutional rights instead of standing up for and enforcing those rights. Defendants in criminal cases waive their rights for a speedy trial, trial by jury, against warrantless search and seizures, and to be represented by an attorney before a police interview and throughout the litigation. This is also true regarding the waiving of First Amendment rights to freedom of establishment of religion and the free exercise thereof. Why? church Leaders waive their rights when they request the non-profit status under IRC 501(c)(3) by submitting the IRC Form 1023 to the Internal Revenue Service to obtain a Letter of Determination approving the church or Ministry as a non-profit religious charity. However, under IRC 508(c)(1)(A), a church, an interchurch organization of local units of a church, a convention or association of churches, an integrated auxiliary of a church, or an exclusively religious activity of any religious order entity are exempt from having to file an application with the IRS to be a non-profit religious entity and income tax exempt.

In fact, on the first page of the "Department of Treasury, Internal Revenue Service's Instructions for filling out Form 1023, Application for Recognition of Exemption Under Section 501(c)(3) of the *Internal Revenue Code*, specifically states, "The following types of organizations may be considered tax exempt under section 501(c)(3) even if they don't file Form 1023. Churches, including synagogues, temples, and mosques. Integrated auxiliaries of churches and conventions or associations of churches (or an exclusively religious activity of any religious order entity)."

Under IRC 501(c)(3), to obtain an IRS Letter of Determination, the functioning pastor or minister of a church or ministry must waive some of their rights or freedoms under the First Amendment. For example, one of the quoted IRS instructions in Form 1023 says on pages 5 & 6 that a religious public charity organization and its leaders under IRC 501(c)(3) waives some of its rights of privacy. Here is a quote from those IRS instructions in filling out IRS Form 1023:

"Information Available For Public Inspection. If we (IRS grants) exempt status under Section 501(c)(3), the following information will be open to public inspection:
▪ Your complete Form 1023 and any supporting documents.
▪ All correspondence between you and the IRS concerning Form 1023....
▪ The Letter we (IRS) issue approving your exemption. . .
The public may also request inspection of the information or a copy of the information directly from the [IRC 501(c)(3) minister and ministry or church.]"

Under IRC 508(c)(1)(A) exemption the *Ekklesia* functioning ministers do not waive their rights of privacy and are not required to give any public member all their personal information, nor required to make public the names and personal information of the *Ekklesia* members who donated money to the *Ekklesia*. Under IRC 508(c)(1)(A) exemption, churches and its ministers do not waive their rights of privacy or their freedoms.

Regarding ministries or churches established under The Johnson Amendment by filing under IRC 501(c)(3): This provision, enacted by Congress in 1954, prohibits IRC 501(c)(3) non-profit organizations [which include churches and ministers if they file under IRC 501(c)(3)] from endorsing or opposing political candidates. Violating this rule can jeopardize the non-profit tax-exempt status.

President Trump's Action: In 2017, President Trump signed an executive order "to defend the freedom of religion and speech" that directed the U.S. Treasury not to take adverse action against religious organizations who are exempt under IRC 501(c)(3) when the church minister engages in political speech, as long as such speech is consistent with the law's interpretation of political campaign intervention. This order was intended to ease enforcement of the Johnson Amendment without formally repealing it.

In a Court Filing on July 7th, 2025, the IRS responded to a lawsuit from the *National Religious Broadcasters Association,* an evangelical media group, and two IRC 501(c)(3) Texas churches sought to argue that the 1954 Johnson Amendment infringed on their freedom of speech and religion. Rather than defending the lawsuit and the Johnson Amendment as passed by Congress in 1954, the IRS entered into a Consent Agreement with the plaintiffs that permitted the churches to announce to their congregations and communicate which candidates they endorse and urge their congregations and audiences to vote accordingly, but under IRS' specific conditions. The IRS agrees that when the endorsement of candidates through customary channels of communication, endorsements would not be considered as participation or intervention in political campaigns. By weaponizing freedom of religion to create a go-around for the Johnson Amendment, the IRS effectively allowed functioning pastors and ministers to utilize their tax-exempt status to support candidates for office. The IRS, under President Trump's administration, stated that the Johnson Amendment's ban on endorsing a candidate does not apply to churches when "a house of worship in good faith speaks to its congregation, through its customary channels of communication on matters of faith in connection with religious services, concerning electoral politics viewed through the lens of religious faith." The IRS said this was like a mere "family discussion" and therefore agreed it would not constitute participation or intervention in a political campaign. Yet, this is a win for IRC 501(c)(3) functioning pastors and ministers. Yet, if the IRC 501(c)(3) functioning pastors and ministers allow a candidate to come to the church building and speak to the congregation, then the IRC 501(c)(3) functioning pastors and ministers must invite the opposing candidate. On the other hand, there still are serious other IRS restrictions that violate the freedom of religion that still exist that are not restrictive under the IRC 508(c)(1)(A) exemption because the functioning pastor or minister did not agree to those restrictions in the IRS 1023 form.

A functioning pastor or minister has the personal freedom to endorse or oppose a candidate running for political office, but if the functioning pastor or minister advertises to promote a particular candidate, the requirement still is that the functioning pastor or minister must pay out of his or her own pocket for any advertisement or printed material for such endorsement or opposition to any political candidate. The functioning pastor or minister cannot use funds from the church, an interchurch organization of local units of a church, a convention association of churches, an integrated auxiliary of a church, or an exclusively religious activity of any religious order for those politically related expenditures. Thus, an IRC 508(c)(1)(A) church or ministry is far better, but you do not receive a letter of determination from the IRS. On the other hand, you were not called into ministry by the IRS, right? So, you should not choose to be endorsed by the IRS.

In addition, the July 7, 2025, IRS Consent Agreement with the *National Religious Broadcasters Association,* and the two IRC 501(c)(3) Texas churches, was a very narrow stipulation, and the IRS may take the position that this Consent Agreement was just with the parties in the lawsuit, not a regulatory change for all churches and ministries. Also, under IRC 501(c)(3) foundation rules that the functioning pastor, minister, or church is accepting, all your books still are open for public and the IRS inspection. Similarly, under IRC 501(c)(3) the church entity must form a non-profit corporation with the Secretary of State, register with regulating income tax authority as non-profit, and in most states register with the Department of State Attorney General Office with its Public Charities division and file financial statements every year. With an IRC 508(c)(1)(A) church or ministry, there is no requirement for you to be a non-profit corporation. You can be a sole proprietor or partner under IRC 508(c)(1)(A) and avoid all of this intrusion and oversight. Again, you can waive your freedoms under the First Amendment of the U.S. Constitution if you decide to establish and operate your church or ministry under IRC 501(c)(3).

In order for a IRC 501(c)(3) functioning pastor or minister to speak about any political issue, such as abortion or children given hormone blockers by school personnel, "What I am about to say is the truth of God; it is not my opinion but what God says in the Bible; and I am simply His Ambassador here on earth of the Kingdom of heaven." In these days of much sin, ministers need to be wise, so there are ways to exercise freedom of speech and freedom of religion. The functioning pastor or minister personally can preach the word of God that calls homosexuality, or killing unborn babies, abominations under Leviticus 18: 21,23,30 by pointing out that these abominations are written in scripture what the King of the Kingdom of God thinks about these issues.

THE COURAGEOUS FUNCTIONING PASTORS WHO STOOD UP AGAINST THE GOVERNMENT SHUTTING DOWN THE CHURCH BUILDINGS DUE TO COVID-19

Although there is a problem with the *Ekklesia* established as a spectator religious theater and not a dynamic articulate moral compass for society because the government knows where the house of worship is and can lock its doors in government-declared emergencies. There are very few functioning pastors or ministers who will take on the legal battles against the State or Federal Government when there is an abuse of the rights or freedom to establish a body of Believers and their free exercise of their faith. Except for a small few, most church functioning pastors and ministers succumbed to closing the church buildings during the Covid-19 pandemic, while liquor stores, fuel stations, grocery stores, and pharmacies were allowed to remain open.

I consider Rodney Howard Browne a hero of the faith for standing strong to protect religious liberty. Tampa, Florida functioning senior pastor Dr. Rodney Howard Browne said he was "arrested on trumped-up charges for conducting a church service on Sunday, March 29 (2020), which Sheriff Chad Chronister claimed, in a press conference, allegedly violated the Hillsborough County Executive Order that went into effect last Friday, March 27, at 10 p.m. The two charges are second-degree misdemeanors that carry a maximum penalty of two months in jail and $500 fine…The State of Florida's Executive Order exempts churches, as does the (Florida) Orange County Executive Order, and many other county orders." In a live video stream on Facebook, Rodney Howard Browne said, "I'm not caving. I have to do this to protect the congregation, not from the virus, but from the tyrannical government." In rebuttal, Hillsborough County Sheriff Chad Chronister said at a news conference "His (Pastor Browne's) reckless disregard for human life put hundreds of people in his congregation at risk, as well as put thousands of residents who may interact with them in danger." (By Daniel Burke, CNN Religion Editor, March 30, 2020)

Governor Ron DeSantis issued a new Executive Order that stated, "Religious services conducted in churches, synagogues, and houses of worship are 'essential activities.' Surely, Hillsborough County could follow their lead and not violate the Constitution. There are other means available to achieve the interest that we all share to protect human life." "The arrest of Dr. Rodney Howard-Browne was politically motivated. Neither the pastor nor The River at Tampa Bay church did anything wrong," Liberty Counsel founder Mat Staver said, in part, in a press release announcing the charges were dropped, "We are pleased that all the charges have been dropped. It is now time to move forward with healing and restoration."

Another hero of the faith is functioning "Senior Pastor Ché Ahn of Harvest Rock church of Pasadena, California, who sued the State of California and Governor Gavin Newsom for its injunctions of closing the church building during Covid-19. A California District Court entered an order approving Liberty Counsel's settlement of the lawsuit on behalf of Pasadena's Harvest Rock Church and Harvest International Ministry against the California Governor. A settlement reached by a California church and Gov. Gavin Newsom allowed an injunction against COVID-19 restrictions on churches. The stipulated Court Order stated that the State of California may no longer impose discriminatory restrictions upon any 'houses of worship.' It's the first statewide permanent injunction in the country against COVID restrictions on church buildings and places of worship. The State of California was ordered to pay Liberty Counsel $1,350,000 in reimbursement of attorney's fees and costs. Liberty Counsel Founder and Chairman Mat Staver said, 'Pastor Ahn's leadership and courage have toppled the tyranny and freed every Pastor and church in California. Governor Gavin Newsom has now been permanently quarantined and may not violate the First Amendment rights of churches and places of worship again.'" (By Michael Gryboski, Editor, May 20, 2021, The Christian Post) Notwithstanding, what was not addressed was the "houses of worship" is not the church building, but "houses of worship" or "temples of God" are the Believers (2 Corinthians 6:16; 1 Corinthians 3:16; Ephesians 2:21), not the physical buildings.

BECAUSE OF THE FIRST AND FOURTEENTH AMENDMENTS OF THE U.S. CONSTITUTION, THE U.S. IS A CHOSEN PLACE TO ACTIVATE BUSINESS MINISTERS

My personal confidence is that because of our religious freedoms guaranteed in the First and Fourteenth Amendments of the U.S. Constitution, the U.S. is a special place that God has chosen for Believer Business Owners and Believer Business Employees to establish a venue to practice religious beliefs outside of the traditional warehouse or cathedral lecture hall church pyramid paradigm structure.

God is restoring Ephesians 4:11 business ministers into every aspect of our society, culture, and commerce; so, the fivefold functioning business ministers in Ephesians 4:11 are being especially called forth from and into the business community because Believer Business Owners can pay Believer Business Employees to be trained in biblical economics with biblical moral ethics, and activated in their spiritual Vocations and spiritual Gifts, eight to ten hours a day for five to six days a week where the traditional priest, bishop, pastor, teacher, or reverend does not have the time, business acumen, nor proclivity to do it.

The *Ekklesia* does not have to be a non-profit organization to be a place where Believers enforce their rights to exercise and practice their faith in God without Legislative, Executive, or Judicial tyranny. Believers can exercise their freedoms to have Bible studies, prayer times, and genuine *agape* love in the profit making and while activating business ministers. Believers must choose if they truly want to be disciples of Christ and be about God the Father's business. There are eternal rewards in obediently doing God's spiritual business at the workplace while alive here on earth. Hebrews 11:6 promises God's rewards, "But without faith it is impossible to please Him: for he that cometh to God must believe that He is, and that He is a rewarder of them that diligently seek Him." The Greek for "rewarder" here is *misthapodotēs.* This Greek word is a business word, which means God's remuneration for work done, resulting in higher profits for Believer Business Owners and higher wages for Believer Business Employees, (Luke 10:7, 1 Timothy 5:18, Matthew 20:8, John 4:36, Acts 1:18, 2 Peter 2:13, 15, Jude 11). The Greek word *misthapodotēs* means God as Rewarder blesses the Believer with recognition for the Believer's moral excellence of action, for the Believer's recompense, or for God's affirmation of the Believer's laudable conduct [Matthew 5:12, 46 (rewards obtained for those who deal kindly and justly with all people not just those who love them); Matthew 6:1, 2, 5, 16; 10:42; Mark 9:41; Luke 6:23, 35 (reward of eternal life); Romans 4:4; 1 Corinthians 3:8, 14, 9:17; 2 John 8 (rewards are based upon what we have done for the edification of the body of Christ); and Revelation 11:18 (God gives rewards unto His servants the prophets, and to the saints, and them that fear God's name)].

Hebrews 11:1 says that faith itself is a gift or reward from God. God rewards Believers with eternal life (John 3:16; Romans 6:23). A relationship with God, Himself, is a reward because He will be the Believer's best friend, provider, and protector (John 15:15; Matthew 6:33; James 2:23; Romans 8:37-39). God's reward for your faith is His divine *agape* love, wisdom, knowledge, guidance, and protection (Psalm 25:4-5; Psalm 91; Proverbs 3:5-6; James 1:5; Romans 8:37-39). God's rewards are both physical and spiritual blessings of grace and life (Matthew 6:20; John 10:10b; 2 Corinthians

9:8; 2 Peter 1:3). God's word came to Abraham in a vision in Genesis 15:1, "…Fear not, Abram: I am thy shield, and thy exceeding great reward."

God's triune nature is omnipresent. Wherever the Godhead inside Believers is, His kingdom, *agape* love, blessings as God's adoptive children, *zoe* life, righteousness, peace, joy, grace, mercy, authority, power, purpose, spiritual inheritance and blessings in Christ, wisdom, knowledge, understanding, and His Will for our thankfulness is a present blessing (Luke 17:21; 1 John 4:8, 16; Romans 8:15; 1 John 1:1-2; 2 Peter 1:3; Isaiah 55:8-9; Romans 14:17; Hebrews 4:16; Luke 24:9; 1 John 1:20, 27; 2 Corinthians 1:21-22; Romans 8:17; Ephesians 1:3, 11; Luke 10:19; Colossians 2:13-15; Isaiah 33:6; James 1:5; Colossians 1:9; 1 Thessalonians 5:18).

I think that it has been well settled that the warehouse or cathedral lecture hall church pyramid paradigm structure is not where the Godhead lives. Isaiah 66:1-2 says, "Thus saith the LORD, 'The heaven is my throne, and the earth is my footstool: where is the house that ye build unto me? And where is the place of my rest? (2) For all those things hath Mine hand made, and all those things have been, saith the LORD: but to this man will I look, even to him that is poor and of a contrite spirit, and trembleth at My word.'"

Acts 17:24 says, "God that made the world and all things therein, seeing that He is Lord of heaven and earth, dwelleth not in temples made with hands." God's lives in each Believer, a local community of Believers, and international Believers in all nations as God's temple here on earth (2 Corinthians 6:16; 1 Corinthians 3:16; Ephesians 2:21), and when the Believers leave the warehouse building, God leaves with them. When the warehouse building is empty, God's focus is not there; it is not His temple. Thus, the warehouse or cathedral lecture hall church pyramid paradigm structure is not the *Ekklesia.* So, Believers need to stop calling the warehouse building the "church."

God does not see or confine His *Ekklesia* within the four walls of a building. Again, the Godhead's temple is your body, and the Godhead lives inside Believers, individually, corporately, and universally, with Believers' born again spirits (2 Corinthians 6:16; 1 Corinthians 3:17; Ephesians 2:21). God's Kingdom is within you (Luke 17:21). Thus, God the Father, God the Word, and God the Holy Spirit, as One God, is within Believers and intimately involved with soul transformation (John 14: 16, 23; John 15:2; Ephesians 5:26; Romans 8:13; 12:2).

God sees His *Ekklesia* impacting and bringing His Kingdom sovereignty, principles, knowledge, wisdom, righteousness, peace, joy, truth, grace, faith, hope, *agape* love, *zoe* life, and glory to every aspect of human endeavors. God's *Ekklesia* is inside Believer Business Owners and Believer Business Employees, so His anointed Ephesians 4:11 functioning Believer Business Owners have the mandated to activate Believer Business Employees how and in what circumstances they use their spiritual Vocations and spiritual Gifts.

CHAPTER FOUR

TIMES OF REFRESHING, RESTITUTION, AND RESTORATION OF GOD'S EKKLESIA IN BUSINESS

Acts 3:19-21 says, "Repent ye therefore, and be converted, that your sins may be blotted out, when the times of refreshing shall come from the presence of the Lord; (20) And He shall send Jesus Christ, which before was preached unto you: (21) Whom the heaven must receive until the times of restitution of all things, which God hath spoken by the mouth of all his holy prophets since the world began."

Acts 3:19 says the "times of refreshing" and Acts 3:21 says the "times of restitution of all things." If we accept the fact that the end times are coming upon us, then we must believe that "the times of refreshing" are being manifested right now and "times of restitution of all things" are soon to come before God creates a new heaven and new earth (Revelation 21:1).

Hebrews 6: 5 says, "And have tasted the good word of God, and the powers of the world to come." God will grant Believer Business Owners and Believer Business Employees a taste of "the times of refreshing" in Acts 3:19 and the "times of restitution of all things" in Acts 3:21 that will come in its fulness when the Lord returns to live in a new heaven and new earth (Revelation 21:1).

The good news is there is a future state and future hope when Believers will live in a new heaven and new earth joined together, which is a new eternal life after this life when this old earth is totally renovated (Revelation 21:1). In the meantime, if Believer Business Owners and Believer Business Employees will submit, accept, and become spiritually mature in their spiritual Vocations as kings, priests, lords, ambassadors, and soldiers in business, the Holy Spirit will give them a mere taste (but not the whole meal) of those times of refreshing and times of restitution of all things in this life (Hebrews 6:5). When the ultimate times of complete refreshing and times of thorough restitution of all things come in the future, they will come with the presence of the Lord Jesus Christ and the entire Godhead living with us here on earth, and Believers will reign with Christ Jesus over the entire new heaven and new earth for all eternity (Revelation 5:10; 11:15).

Again, the hope is that the future coming and presence of the Lord will fully manifest "times of restitution of all things" as stated in Acts 3:21, which will be the new renovated heavens and the new earth. This restitution will manifest the dissolution of all old things and the immediate renovation of the whole new creation (Revelation 21:1). In the meantime, the earth is alive but groans and travails in pain to be renewed, as it presently is burdened because of the sin of fallen mankind. Romans 8:22-25 says, "For we know that the whole creation groaneth and travaileth in pain together until now. (23) And not only they, but ourselves also, which have the firstfruits of the Spirit, even we ourselves groan within ourselves, waiting for the adoption, to wit, the redemption of our body. (24) For we are saved by hope: but hope that is seen is not hope: for what a man seeth, why doth he yet hope for? (25) But if we hope for that we see not, then do we with patience wait for it?"

Currently, Believer Business Owners and Believer Business Employees can enter into "times of refreshing" because Jesus promises them rest. Matthew 11:28-30 says, "Come unto Me, all ye that labour and are heavy laden, and I will give you rest. (29) Take My yoke upon you, and learn of Me;

for I am meek and lowly in heart: and ye shall find rest unto your souls. (30) For My yoke is easy, and My burden is light."

There is a futuristic time when we all can rest from our labors because the burden of sin is gone. Hebrews 4: 3-11 says "For we which have believed do enter into rest, as He said, 'As I have sworn in My wrath, if they shall enter into My rest: although the works were finished from the foundation of the world.' (4) For He spake in a certain place of the seventh day on this wise, 'And God did rest the seventh day from all His works.' (5) And in this place again, 'If they shall enter into My rest.' (6) Seeing therefore it remaineth that some must enter therein, and they to whom it was first preached entered not in because of unbelief: (7) Again, He limiteth a certain day, saying in David, 'Today, after so long a time; as it is said, Today if ye will hear his voice, harden not your hearts.' (8) For if Jesus had given them rest, then would He not afterward have spoken of another (future) day (of rest). (9) There remaineth therefore a (future) rest to the people of God. (10) For he that is entered into His rest, he also hath ceased from his own works, as God did from His. (11) Let us labour therefore to enter into that rest, lest any man fall after the same example of unbelief."

Even though there is a strong work ethic in the Bible, there also is a strong rest ethic in the Bible. This does not mean to "party hardy" every weekend. It means entering into a continuous Sabbath rest with the Lord every day.

RESTITUTION AND RESTORATION OF THE EKKLESIA AND CONVERTING THE OLD CHURCH STRUCTURE

Consider the restitution and restoration of an old antique piece of furniture. The first thing that happens is you remove the old cover-up paint or varnish and expose the wood underneath. The old church order Leaders must renew their focus and see that the Holy Spirit is anointing and empowering Believer Business Owners to use their spiritual Vocations and spiritual Gifts at their businesses as a kinesthetic training center to activate Believer Business Employees where the business activity is applying biblical economic principles, biblical work ethic, biblical moral ethics, and biblical servanthood, and their spiritual Vocations, and spiritual Gifts. The incremental work assignments are maturing the souls of Believer Business Employees to become Manager Servants with humble hearts to do all work as unto the Lord (Colossians 3:17, 3:23). The Believer Business Employees are to be led by the Holy Spirit as they are witnesses of Christ to the business customers and clients. God wants to open the spiritual eyes and hearts of Believer Business Owners and Believer Business Employees to discover God's will, and experience God's *agape* love, through spiritual fellowship with each other throughout the workweek and receive Jesus' promise of life abundantly in Him. God wants the traditional functioning priests, bishops, pastors, teachers, and reverends in the old church structure to participate and be a part of the new movement of the Holy Spirit in the business where the Believer Business Owners and Believer Business Employees attend with the local Ekklesia community fellowship. The more Believer Business Owners attend the local *Ekklesia* community fellowship that are recognized and honored as Business functioning ministers who employ Believer Business Employees that also attend the local *Ekklesia* community fellowship, then the more compliance in fulfilling the mandate of Ephesians 4:12 in activating Believer Business Employees for the work of the ministry will occur. The spiritual maturity level in the local *Ekklesia* community fellowship will grow steadily when Believer Business Owners and Believer Business Employees are activated in ministry. This is how the interaction and closer relationship between the old church order Leaders and the Believer Business Owners and Believer Business Employees can cause the Holy Spirit to create new wineskins to pour in the new wine of revival.

The New Testament *Ekklesia* is over 2000 years old, but for the last 1800 years or more, the true *Ekklesia* was converted to a church warehouse building or an expensive cathedral building throughout the world that today would cost over $500 million to rebuild. For example, the cost to rebuild Notre Dame Cathedral to repair the damage caused by the fire on April 15, 2019, was $928 million. That was the cost of a single cathedral building, and Notre Dame Cathedral is not the *Ekklesia.*

Some of the *Ekklesia* hierarchy have relegated Believer Business Owners and Believer Business Employees as having little spiritual contribution, except their money given as tithes and offerings in the *Ekklesia;* and they do not see there are Believer Business Owners who are functioning as apostles, prophets, evangelists, pastors, and teachers, whose commission is to equip Believer Business Employees to become Kingdom biblitarians.

Again, to restore a piece of antique furniture, the restitution and restoration process often requires the use of very toxic varnish remover and usually rough scraping and special but delicate workings to totally uncover the beautiful artistic creation beneath the toxic coverup.

Restitution and restoration of the *Ekklesia* remnant going and expressing the presence of the Holy Spirit in business involves exposure and removal of years of traditions and coverup paints of religiosity.

There is a blessing that only follows exposure leading to removal of religious traditions unto perfect restitution and restoration of the true *Ekklesia*, engifted by the Godhead and anointed with power by the Holy Spirit (Romans 12:6-8; Ephesians 4:11; 1 Corinthians 12:8-10; Acts 10:38).

AFTER THE APPLICATION OF THE REFINER'S FIRE AND SCRUBBING OF THE FULLERS' SOAP THERE IS RESTITUTION AND RESTORATION BLESSINGS GIVEN TO THE EKKLESIA IN BUSINESS

John the Baptist said in_Matthew 3:11-12, "I indeed baptize you with water unto repentance: but He (Jesus) that cometh after me is mightier than I, whose shoes I am not worthy to bear: He (Jesus) shall baptize you with the Holy Ghost, and with fire: (12) Whose fan is in his hand, and He will thoroughly purge His floor, and gather His wheat into the garner; but He will burn up the chaff with unquenchable fire."

1 Corinthians 3:11-15 says, "For other foundation can no man lay than that is laid, which is Jesus Christ. (12) Now if any man build upon this foundation gold, silver, precious stones, wood, hay, stubble; (13) Every man's work shall be made manifest: for the day shall declare it, because it shall be revealed by fire; and the fire shall try every man's work of what sort it is. (14) If any man's work abide which he hath built thereupon, he shall receive a reward. (15) If any man's work shall be burned, he shall suffer loss: but he himself shall be saved; yet so as by fire."

Hebrews 12:29 proclaims, "For our God is a consuming fire." A consuming fire devours and purifies all three parts of the soul, consisting of the mind, where your thoughts are, your emotions, where your feelings are, and your heart where your beliefs and will are. Fire burns out the briars and brambles, which represent the carnal nature in the soul. Similarly, God said in Malichi 3:2, "But who may abide the day of His coming? And who shall stand when He appeareth? For He is like a refiner's fire, and like fullers' soap." The refiner's fire takes out the impurities to produce fine metal, such as gold or silver. When the wool is removed in shearing from sheep, it is not very clean. The sheep wool collects dirt and crud, so the sheared wool must go to the Fuller, who then scrubs the wool with fullers' soap to clean, bleach, and untangle the wool so it can be made into yarn for making cloth. Fullers' soap had an alkaline mixture that served to bleach cloth and other materials as much as clean them. In early American history, fullers' soap would be akin to lye soap as both are harsh, but effective means of bleaching and cleaning cloth or sheep wool.

The above scriptures pertain to God using fire or harsh fullers' soap primarily to purify a Believer Business Owner's soul or a Believer Business Employee's soul. When everything is going well with Believers in business, with no health or financial problems, Believer Business Owners and Believer Business Employees often stop their spiritual soulish transformation unto spiritual maturation. Then, when trouble comes, Believer Business Owners and Believer Business Employees look up to God for help. They start searching for scriptures to remind God of His covenant promises, grace, and *agape* love, such as Philippians 4:19 for financial needs and 1 Peter 2:24 for healing.

However, in reply, God often speaks another Scripture to Believer Business Owners and Believer Business Employees, such as 3 John 2, "Beloved, I wish above all things that thou mayest prosper and be in health, even as thy soul prospereth." What does "even " mean? It is a comparative leveling measure, so Believers' prosperity and health will be equal to the spiritual transformation and maturation of the Believers' souls. Soul prosperity comes with the application of fiery circumstances or harsh circumstances that require the application of harsh fullers' soap for cleansing and bleaching away the dirt in the lives of Believer Business Owners and Believer Business Employees.

Acts 3:26 says, "Unto you first God, having raised up his Son Jesus, sent Him to bless you, in turning away every one of you from his iniquities." Take notice of the last part of the verse, "...in turning away every one of you from his iniquities" was the blessing that Jesus brought to earth in His ministry and sacrifice as the Lamb of God on the Roman Cross (Isaiah 53:5, 11; Galatians 3:13; Hebrews 10:17).

How do the blessings come to the *Ekklesia* in business? These blessings come by submission of Believer Business Owners and the Believer Business Employees experiencing exposure of their belief systems to the refiner's hot fire and the fullers' harsh soap, or both; so, the Believer Business Owners and the Believer Business Employees can see what unclean iniquities they must turn away from to spiritually transform the thoughts in their minds, feelings in their emotions, and beliefs in their hearts where their wills reside.

The degree of restitution and restoration needed in the *Ekklesia* in business will determine the degree of exposure of iniquity, disobedience, and sins of the flesh in the souls of the Believer Business Owners and Believer Business Employees while interacting with customers, clients, and people in the fallen world's marketplace while consummating commercial transactions.

Exposure to the refiner's fire and harsh fullers' soap used by the Godhead for purification is always done in degrees and multiple scrubbings. The heat is not turned up all at once, and the scrubbing is done in stages. This careful method of cleansing avoids fractures in the souls of the Body of Christ as Believers constituting the *Ekklesia* in business. Eventually, the temperature of the refiner's fire will rise to the point that it will be uncomfortable for the Believer Business Owners and Believer Business Employees to continue to allow the natural stimuli of the flesh to rule over their souls. Likewise, the harsh fullers' soap will cause the flesh to be red from the scrubbing, but it is clean indeed.

Also, the Holy Spirit will make the Believer Business Owners and Believer Business Employees uncomfortable to accept the practices of religious traditions that make void the commandments of God (Matthew 15:6). Romans 12:1 says, "I beseech you therefore, brethren, by the mercies of God, that ye present your bodies a living sacrifice, holy, acceptable unto God, which is your reasonable service." One major problem is that some Believers want to crawl off the hot altar before the purification and removal of the flesh out the soul is finished because baptism of fire burns away the sinful habits in their souls. Likewise, some Believers want to get out of the washing machine with the fullers' soap being used before the cycle is done.

After the refiner's fire and the fullers' soap cleansing, when customers and clients come to purchase a product from, or retain the professional services of, the Believer Business Owner's business dedicated to God, the Believer Business Employees may pray a blessing for the money that the customer or client is paying to the business. When the Believer Business Owners and Believer Business Employees see the business as an altar to bring blessings to customers and clients, they will discern and accept the necessity of restoration of the purity of the altar in business. Believer Business Owner and the Believer Business Employees will be blessed financially and spiritually when the business altar is restored with purity of motives, so heartfelt *agape* love and prayer toward others become the meaningful norm.

Most Believer Business Owners and Believer Business Employees function with God the Father's engiftments in Romans 12: 6-8, which says, "Having then gifts differing according to the grace that is given to us, whether prophecy, let us prophesy according to the proportion of faith; (7) Or ministry, let us wait on our ministering: or he that teacheth, on teaching; (8) Or he that exhorteth, on exhortation: he that giveth, let him do it with simplicity (Greek- *haplotes,* meaning without covetousness, greed, or avarice, but with a pure heart); he that ruleth, with diligence; he that sheweth mercy, with cheerfulness."

How does God remove the covetousness, greed, or avarice from the souls of the Believer Business Owners and the Believer Business Employees? This is where the baptism of refiner's fire of the Lord will burn away the dross and the fullers' soap washes away the dirt; thus, purifying their souls. When there is no covetousness, greed, or avarice in the souls of the Believer Business Owners and the Believer Business Employees, then God sees them as purified, trustworthy funnels where He can pour wealth into the business because Believer Business Owners and the Believer Business Employees hearts have been transformed to give to the needs of community and other non-profit ministries (Luke 6:38), and to leave an inheritance for their children and children's children (Proverbs 13:22).

The calling forth of the Ephesians 4:11 Believer Business ministers is the genesis of the Holy Spirit bringing revival into Believers working in businesses and in the marketplace. Restoration always occurs from the outside impacting the inside of the *Ekklesia.*

Every religious restoration movement historically required the visionary leaders to step out of the traditional religious ecclesiastical structure and speak clearly about the reformation needed in religion and society. Even in comparative religions, this was often the case. Buddha was a prince in government, not a Hindu priest, but he brought needed reforms to Hinduism. Confucius developed an ideological system of thought with earthly wisdom that would become the norm for the Chinese society, as Confucius was a prominent teacher and philosopher, but was an unsuccessful politician who knew little about business or how to be a government ruler. Mohammad was a camel trader who after his parents died lived from age six with Bedouins who lived an isolated culture as nomadic herders in the harsh Arabian desert, and he brought forth a new religion called Islam.

THERE IS A RESTORATION OF BUSINESS FUNCTIONING MINISTERS IN THE *EKKLESIA*

Jesus was a carpenter and stonemason Business minister, Who was about His heavenly Father's business here on earth (Luke 2:49). Mark 6:3 says, "Is not this the carpenter, the son of Mary, the brother of James, and Joses, and of Juda, and Simon? and are not His sisters here with us? And they were offended at Him."

Jesus was not part of the ecclesiastical Hebrew religious hierarchy at the time He walked on earth, even though He was the only begotten Son of God. Jesus belonged to God's Kingdom as God's Only Begotten Son. God the Father sent Jesus, with His divine nature, God the Word and with His humanity nature as the Only Begotten Son of God to bring reconciliation with fallen mankind and to bring the Kingdom to earth as it is in heaven. Jesus was sent by God to say in John 14:6, "… I am the way, the truth, and the life: no man cometh unto the Father, but by Me."

Although Christians believe that neither Buddha, Confucius, nor Mohammad can give eternal life to their religious believers or devotees, it is interesting that the new ideas and religions came from outside of the religious hierarchy of their culture to bring change even in manmade religion.

After Jesus was kinesthetically trained by His step-father, Joseph, as a carpenter and stonemason journeyman, and worked in that trade for about twenty years, He used the same kinesthetic methods to train His apostles and disciples. He did not just sit them down and scholastically teach them beatitudes, parables, or the Old Testament scriptures day after day. Jesus showed His twelve apostles and disciples that ministry was a hands on activity where you meet people who were seeking God for help and who were lost in their sins. Jesus trained and watched His twelve apostles and disciples minister before He sent them out two by two to minister without His presence. Luke 9:1-2 says, "Then He (Jesus) called His twelve disciples together, and gave them power and authority over all devils, and to cure diseases. (2) And He sent them to preach the kingdom of God, and to heal the sick." Then in Luke 10:1-12 Jesus also had other disciples that He used kinesthetic training to activate them into their ministries. This second time Jesus sent 72 disciples two by two with the same mission as He had previously sent the twelve "And heal the sick that are therein, and say unto them, 'The kingdom of God is come nigh unto you.'" (Luke 10:9). Jesus' primary purpose for sending His trained 72 disciples was stated in Luke 10:1, "After these things the Lord appointed other seventy (seventy-two) also, and sent them two and two before his face into every city and place, whither He Himself would come." The three primary messages that Jesus kinesthetically trained His apostles and disciples were to preach the kingdom of God, heal the sick, and cast out demons. Later in Matthew 24:14, before Jesus was crucified and was resurrected, Jesus said, "And this gospel of the kingdom shall be preached in all the world for a witness unto all nations; and then shall the end come." After His resurrection, Jesus said in Luke 24:47, "And that repentance and remission of sins should be preached in His name among all nations (including Gentiles), beginning at Jerusalem." Why do Believers today rarely hear the preaching of the gospel of the kingdom of God? There were some ministers who did and do preach as a priority the gospel of the Kingdom, such as the late, great Myles Munroe.

Jesus gave the pattern for His Ephesians 4:11 functioning ministers how to equip and train other Believer ministers, including the preaching the gospel of the kingdom, preaching repentance and remission of sins, healing the sick, and casting out demons. Jesus trained His apostles through methods by watching them do the same things repetitively He did before He sent them out on their own. This is how the Ephesian 4:11 functioning apostles, prophets, evangelists, pastors, and teachers were trained by Jesus. They were revealed that Jesus' divine nature is God the Word, who took on a humanity nature in the flesh and dwelt amongst men (John 1:14). They knew that Jesus, the Only Begotten Son of God, would sacrificed His own mortal body and life to give all men salvation and eternal life (Mark 10:45). Jesus specifically engifted them to use kinesthetic training to activate other Believers into their spiritual Vocations, spiritual Gifts, and spiritual Ministries.

Later, in 1 Corinthians 2:1-4 Paul said, "And I, brethren, when I came to you, came not with excellency of speech or of wisdom, declaring unto you the testimony of God. (2) For I determined not to know anything among you, save Jesus Christ, and Him crucified. (3) And I was with you in weakness, and in fear, and in much trembling. (4) And my speech and my preaching was not with enticing words of man's wisdom, but in demonstration of the Spirit and of power."

Each of these Ephesian 4:11 functioning apostles, prophets, evangelists, pastors, and teachers exposed the iniquity in the religious traditions being practiced at the time in their culture. When pious men codify their religious traditions, then they take on natural comfort with the way things are. Yet, the Holy Spirit is the true Comforter, and He is active, moving, and brings change in the souls of Believers. The Holy Spirit is not stagnating but is moving, teaching, comforting, and edifying to activate Believers to follow Him. In the natural, religious Believers often do not like change in their religious practices, as the traditional ways of conducting ministry services are trusted and comfortable. The Holy Spirit's new dynamic, convicting, and presence is often not trusted by the traditional religious denominations. Throughout history of revivals, the Holy Spirit and His spiritual gifts are generally rejected by the traditional religious hierarchy because the religious traditional leaders do not want to rethink the foundations of their belief system and do not want anyone to start questioning the sacredness of their denominational practices. It is true that most Christian leaders agree on the fundamentals, but they divide on the variance of their religious practices.

JESUS CHOSE BUSINESS SERVANTS AND OTHERS OUTSIDE THE TRADITIONAL RELIGIOUS HEBREW RELIGIOUS HIERARCHY TO BRING RESTITUTION AND REFRESHING OF HIS TRUE *EKKLESIA*

Jesus' functioning apostles, Peter, Andrew, James, John, Thomas, Nathanael, and others (John 21:2), who were business fishermen, fulfilled their ministries as fishers of men to multiply God's Kingdom population. After Jesus' ascension, most of Jesus' functioning apostles had some kind of businesses or family estates that they worked periodically for support, especially when the offerings from people were low, although the functioning apostles were supported by offerings when they traveled on missionary trips.

Functioning apostle Paul had his own tent-making business (Acts 18:3), and he also recognized and used business functioning ministers (such as Priscilla, Acquila, Dr. Luke, and Lydia) as functioning co-ministers. Dr. Luke was an Ephesians 4:11 Medical Doctor functioning minister and authored the gospel of Luke and the book of Acts. While traveling and ministering with functioning apostle Paul, Dr. Luke, as an Ephesians 4:11 Business functioning minister, continued practicing medicine. Furthermore, the functioning apostle Paul worked with Priscilla and Aquila in their tent-making business (Acts 18:3), and they were Ephesians 4:11 functioning ministers who accompanied functioning apostle Paul on a missionary journey (Acts 18:18). Lydia was a businesswoman who made and sold purple fabric, and she received the gospel of the Kingdom from functioning apostle Paul in Philippi (Acts 16:13-15). Lydia was the first European Believer that received salvation by the preaching of the gospel of the Kingdom and repentance and remission of sins, and she was an Ephesians 4:11 business functioning minister. As an Ephesians 4:11 business functioning minister, Lydia, set up a home fellowship and established the first *Ekklesia* for Europe that brought Christianity to the whole western world.

During more modern times, in America from 1825 to 1872, Charles Finney was a Lawyer and an Ephesians 4:11 business functioning evangelist who brought forth the practice of coming forward to the altar to give a public profession of faith while repenting and proclaiming Jesus as Lord to receive salvation. He was a revivalist preacher, theologian, and social reformer.

RG LeTourneau was an Ephesians 4:11 business functioning minister and was one of the most inspiring Christian inventors, businessmen, and entrepreneurs the world has ever seen. A sixth-grade dropout, Robert Gilmore "RG" LeTourneau went on to become the leading earth moving machinery manufacturer of his day with plants on four continents. His contribution to the advancement of the gospel of the Kingdom ranks him among the great Ephesian 4:11 business functioning ministers for his generation in America. He was famous for living on 10% of his income and giving 90% to the spread of the gospel of the Kingdom and repentance and remission of sins. In 1935, RG LeTourneau overcame a lifelong fear of public speaking and gave his first testimony and affirmation at the opening of his newest manufacturing plant, to which he urged his fellow Believer business functioning ministers in the room to do more for the Lord while working in businesses. In attendance at the presentation also were several area functioning pastors, who immediately requested he speak to their congregations about Christianity and business functioning ministers. This was the beginning of LeTourneau's lifelong commitment to speaking on Christians being Believer Business Owners and functioning ministers in the marketplace.

Dwight L. Moody worked as a shoe salesman but left his business to become an Ephesians 4:11 business functioning evangelist. He later established a successful Christian publishing company. He founded three Christian Schools, started a successful Christian Conference Center, and activated thousands of other Ephesians 4:11 business functioning ministers to preach the gospel of the Kingdom and the repentance and remission of sins. In his forty years as a business functioning minister, Moody won over a million new converts to the Lord.

There are many other examples of Believer Business Owner functioning ministers, both men and women, who have used their businesses as places to activate and kinesthetically train Believer Business Employees to enter their spiritual Vocations as kings, priests, lords, ambassadors, and soldiers and exercise their spiritual Gifts to promote Christ Jesus and to be Christ Jesus' humble and submissive servants in the business, in their families, and in their Christian local community fellowships.

THE HOLY SPIRIT IS RESTORING THE EKKLESIA INTO BELIEVER BUSINESS OWNERS AND BELIEVER BUSINESS EMPLOYEES

The days of the Holy Spirit raising up one-man ministries in large congregation warehouse lecture halls with a pyramid paradigm structure is shifting. God wants Believers to see the spiritual fruit by Believer Business Owners where they can become Believer Business Employees in that business to be kinesthetically trained to be business functioning ministers. They will minister to people where they work eight to ten hours a day, five to six days a week, and transact life issues daily as they engage as servants of customers and clients. This is the kinesthetic training that Jesus used to activate His functioning apostles and disciples to do the work of the ministry.

I pray that in the next forty years of this movement of the Holy Spirit, we will see the refreshing, restitution, and restoration of the Body of Christ in its fullness, with the Ephesians 4:11 business functioning ministers in every aspect of society and commerce as Believer Business Owners exercising spiritual leadership in activating through scholastic teaching and kinesthetically training Believer Business Employees as biblitarian functioning ministers that are spiritually mature and actively submitting and pursuing the will of God and the Lord Jesus Christ's humanity nature.

The past movements of the Holy Spirit have now become denominations and are set in their traditions and practices that make the Believer attendees comfortable and feel safe. What the Holy Spirit did yesterday He might not do today when He brings revival. Believer Business Owners and Believer Business Employees must stand ready to experience the Holy Spirit's visitation into their souls that affects the way to conduct their business. The Holy Spirit wants to manifest the reality of the Kingdom of God in the daily business work and interactions with customers and clients. The Holy Spirit wants to bring His righteousness, peace, joy, glory, love, principles, and presence in the business as the Great Teacher, so God's will be done on earth as it is in heaven (Matthew 6:33; 6:10; Romans 14:17).

Lamentations 3:22-23 are the promises of the Lord sustaining us Believers. "It is of the LORD'S mercies that we are not consumed, because His compassions fail not. (23) They are new every morning: great is thy faithfulness."

In 2 Corinthians 4:16-18, functioning apostle Paul speaks comfort and focus, "For which cause we faint not; but though our outward man (body) perish, yet the inward man (soul) is renewed day by day. (17) For our light affliction, which is but for a moment, worketh for us a far more exceeding and eternal weight of glory; (18)While we look not at the things which are seen, but at the things which are not seen: for the things which are seen are temporal; but the things which are not seen are eternal."

THE HOLY SPIRIT DOES NOT WANT BUSINESS MINISTERS TO PLACE A MAN-MADE NAME ON HIS SPIRITUAL REVIVAL MOVEMENT

This restoration, refreshing, and restitution movement of the Holy Spirit into the souls of Believer Business Owners and Believer Business Employees is not to become a sectarian or a denominational religion after the Holy Spirit's restoration, renewal, and revival matures and finishes its course.

Believer Business Owners and Believer Business Employees must avoid the temptation of putting a name on the Holy Spirit's revival movement into the souls of the *Ekklesia* who are functioning business ministers. Some Believer leaders, historically, put a name on the Holy Spirit's movement, thinking by doing so, it would make Believers not forget the revival was started and sustained by the Holy Spirit, not them. All the Holy Spirit wants to do is not just transplant the *Ekklesia* into businesses and the marketplace, although it is a very important part of the spiritual movement. The Holy Spirit has much more He wants to do in bringing forth God's Kingdom and Holy Nation in the U.S. and every country in the world. The Holy Spirit is omnipresent, and He wants to manifest His kingdom presence in every place in society, including the community gathering of Believers in home fellowships, in the family gatherings at the homeplace, while people are doing business in the marketplace, during the students' time at the school place, while doctors and nurses meet at the medical hospitals and clinic place, when lawyers and clients meet at the law office place, when carpenters, electricians, air conditioning installers, and plumbers meet and the construction place, while broadcasters and writers share ideas at the media place, and during times politicians and bureaucrats in the government place are seeking solutions for constituent problems.

Twentieth Century revivals declined when the church leaders put a name they chose on the Holy Spirit revival movement. For example, the decline of the revival at Azusa street in Los Angeles, California began when the leaders of the church called it the "Azusa Street Revival", which canonize the movement. Historical Twentieth Century revivals functioning ministers consistently put names on revivals, such as "Pentecostalism," "Charismatic Movement," "Latter Rain," "Jesus Movement," "Third Wave," "Fifth Wave," to describe movements of the Holy Spirit. People started identifying themselves as part of that movement. "I am a Pentecostal." "I am a Charismatic."

Even before the Twentieth Century revival movements, there was the Evangelical Movement. The modern Evangelical Movement began in the 18th century with the name they called the "First Great Awakening," driven by revivalist preachers like George Whitefield, Jonathan Edwards, and John Wesley. It emerged from earlier revival movements like 17th-century German Pietism and English Puritanism and is characterized by a focus on personal conversion and studying the Bible. Now, Believer call themselves, "I am an Evangelical."

Believer Business Owners and Believer Business Employees must learn about the inner working of the Holy Spirit, and how He goes about to release the Body of Christ without an earthbound name tag upon the revival that often causes division instead of unity. The name that should be lifted and exalted during the revival is Jesus. Every Believer must accept and promote the name of Jesus because God the Father gave Jesus the name that is above every other name (Philippians 2:9-11). Names that describe a movement of the Holy Spirit morph into the names of denominations that become religious traditions that lose the dynamic of being led daily and spontaneously by the Holy Spirit. Religious traditions try to replace the King, replace the Kingdom of God, and make the word of God of no effect by religious tradition. Jesus said in Mark 7:13, "Making the word of God of none effect through your (religious) tradition, which ye have delivered: and many such like things do ye." There is only One Name that should be lifted and praised for all to hear, and that is Jesus Christ.

TRUE *AGAPE* LOVE AMONGST BELIEVERS

The primary motivation is *agape* love, and *agape* love will bring the manifestation of true *Ekklesia.* A Believer may secretly think, "How does Jesus' mandate to *agapao* love one another in John 13:34-35 apply to me? Yes, I love my family, but why do I have to love my boss or fellow workers at the workplace? Personally, I would like someone to think I am worthy enough to participate in ministry amongst this large 10,000 member congregation. I am a businessman. My leadership qualities are good for my business. Why would a church want me to bring my spiritual business skills and spiritually train Believers to be workers for Jesus? I have trained kinesthetically a lot of employees over the fifty plus years practicing law. I know how to manage people. I think the church leadership likes me only because I am a faithful tither, but they do not want my spiritual wisdom that I have learned in business to help administrate other Believers."

Many Believers lack true *agape* love in their hearts, and truth to be told, most of the old church hierarchy leadership is not structured for Believers to receive any *agape* love through personal fellowship with the leaders. In fact, some leaders do not foster home fellowships because they believe that is a place where church splits start. 1 John 4:16 says that the very nature of God is *agape* love, but Believers complain they do not experience *agape* love in the warehouse or cathedral lecture hall church building from other Believers. There are a few church ministers who do see the benefits of home fellowship.

Believers are better off having their needs for *agape* love through close intimate *koinonia* by attending the week evenings at home fellowship before and after the large gathering with other Believers. Home fellowship gatherings are an absolute must with any *Ekklesia.* Yet, receiving *agape* love in fellowship is not the same as being activated into ministry under the commandment of Ephesians 4:12. Home fellowship should be restored as a foundation to duplicate the spiritual practice of the First Century Body of Christ in the *Ekklesia.*

God is going to bring forth Believers with their Vocations as His spiritual Kingdom of kings, priests, lords, ambassadors, and soldiers within a local business, which will expand into a holy nation of Believers within a country, and they will be loving, humble Believers within the Body of Believers in Christ. These will become the spiritually mature, humble, but soulishly transformed and loving overcomers (1 John 5:4).

CHAPTER FIVE

REMOVING UNRIGHTEOUS COMPETITIVENESS IN THE BUSINESS *EKKLESIA*

RAY KROC'S ACQUISTION OF MCDONALD'S CORPORATE FRANCHISES

Ray Kroc purchased the corporation owning the McDonald brothers' fast food franchises, except for the original restaurant land and building in San Bernardino, California. Kroc became the owner of the McDonald's corporation and its small number of franchises in 1955. McDonald's corporation owned the business name. Kroc is attributed with the quote: "If any of my competitors were drowning, I'd stick a hose in their mouth and turn on the water." This quote reflects Kroc's extremely competitive nature and his belief that business was a form of commercial combat. Apparently, Kroc meant what he said. As the saying goes, "Actions speak louder than words." Kroc was cold-blooded in business when he took over the McDonald's corporation. Kroc purchased the McDonald's corporation along with the land and thereafter built and owned each McDonald's land and restaurant building, so the real property ownership was the hidden wealth of the McDonald's corporation. Kroc had the McDonald's corporation enter into agreements with franchisees, who had to agree totally to follow the McDonald's corporate rules, including the purchase of food, machines, and business practices. Kroc standardized all procedure operations, ensuring every burger would taste the same in every McDonald's restaurant. He set strict rules for franchisees on how the food was to be made, portion sizes, cooking methods and times, and packaging. His business decisions in controlling and expanding the McDonald's franchise exhibited a ruthless competitive mindset in his soul, and he especially wanted to sever any connection with the McDonald brothers.

Kroc bought out the McDonald brothers but allowed them to keep their original restaurant establishment. However, Kroc required the McDonald brothers to change the name of their original "McDonald's" to the "Big M" as the McDonald brothers mistakenly failed to retain their original name for their restaurant. Kroc also opened a McDonald's restaurant across the street to compete with the McDonald brothers' "Big M" restaurant for what appeared to be the purpose of running them out of business.

Kroc also pushed an aggressive expansion through McDonald's franchising, often at the expense of established fair business practices or agreements. Some worldly businesspersons may conclude that Kroc's actions simply constituted sound and aggressive business practices, and he deserves credit for the great McDonald's restaurant empire he built.

By the time of Kroc's death in 1984, McDonald's corporation and McDonald's USA, LLC had 7,500 franchise outlets in the United States and in 31 other countries and territories, earning at that time in gross Systemwide sales of approximately $600 million. At time of his death Kroc's personal estate was worth approximately $660 million. Along with McDonald's USA, LLC, McDonald's corporation, today there are over 40,031franchisees worldwide in over 119 countries (as of 2021), and the worldwide system retail sales of McDonald's franchise restaurants were more than $8 billion in 1983. In 2024, McDonald's global Systemwide sales exceeded $130 billion. McDonald's has become the largest restaurant chain in the world. To the world, the McDonald's fast food restaurant franchise chain has been a total success. Yet, the McDonald's fast food franchise chain was not designed and operated using God's Kingdom principles.

What would Jesus say as our business Messiah about Kroc's kind of business practice? Did Kroc's business accomplishments earn any rewards in heaven? I would hope Kroc eventually accepted Jesus as Lord and Savior. I do not know the temerity of Kroc's heart. Yet, research shows that Kroc did become a philanthropist who supported various charitable causes, including funding medical research through the Kroc Foundation (specifically for diabetes, arthritis, and multiple sclerosis), supporting the Ronald McDonald House Charities, and did encourage local McDonald's franchisees to engage in community service. His wife, Joan Kroc, continued and expanded upon his philanthropic work after his death.

THE ETERNAL REWARDS OF FAITHFUL BELIEVER BUSINESS MINISTERS

On the other hand, good works alone do NOT get people into heaven (Ephesians 2:8-9) but being submissive, humble, and doing God's works here on earth after initial salvation does earn Believers special eternal rewards. God wants Believers to be influential in the world, but He wants Believers always to allow Jesus Christ to promote Himself through them (Galatians 2:20). Believers' obedience will cause them to find ultimate satisfaction in their labors, happiness in their lives, comfort while going through life's tribulations, and God's eternal rewards for obedient work well done.

God does not want Kroc's sometimes examples of performing callous, merciless, and heartless business practices in the Kingdom of God just to get financially successful in business. Matthew 6:24 says, "No man can serve two masters: for either he will hate the one and love the other; or else he will hold to the one and despise the other. Ye cannot serve God and mammon."

God is a rewarder of them that diligently seek Him (Hebrews 11:6). God rewards obedient Believers (and Believer Business ministers) with certain "crowns" in the life to come, including the "Crown of Life" (James 1:12), "Crown of Glory" (1 Peter 5:4), "Crown of Exultation" (2 Timothy 4:8), "Incorruptible Crown" (1 Corinthians 9:25), and "Crown of Rejoicing" (1 Thessalonians 2:19).

In Luke 22:28-30, Jesus spoke to His disciples and said, "Ye are they which have continued with Me in My temptations. (29) And I appoint unto you a kingdom, as my Father hath appointed unto me; (30) That ye may eat and drink at My table in My kingdom, and sit on thrones judging the twelve tribes of Israel."

JAMES AND JOHN'S UNRIGHTEOUS COMPETITIVENESS AS YOUNG APOSTLES

James and John, along with Peter and Andrew were businessmen, who owned their own fishing boats and had employees. These two brother businessmen came to Jesus, asking for a special position in His kingdom over and above what the other apostles were going to receive. This was sinful ambition and competitiveness.

Mark 10:35-44 says, "And James and John, the sons of Zebedee, come unto him, saying, 'Master, we would that thou shouldest do for us whatsoever we shall desire.' (36) And he said unto them, 'What would ye that I should do for you?' (37) They said unto him, 'Grant unto us that we may sit, one on thy right hand, and the other on thy left hand, in thy glory.' (38) But Jesus said unto them, 'Ye know not what ye ask: can ye drink of the cup that I drink of? and be baptized with the baptism that I am baptized with?' (39) And they said unto Him, 'We can.' And Jesus said unto them, 'Ye shall indeed drink of the cup that I drink of; and with the baptism that I am baptized withal shall ye be baptized: (40) But to sit on my right hand and on my left hand is not mine to give; but it shall be given to them for whom it is prepared.' (41) And when the ten heard it, they began to be much displeased with James and John. (42) But Jesus called them to Him, and saith unto them, 'Ye know that they which are accounted to rule over the Gentiles exercise lordship over them; and their great ones exercise authority upon them. (43) But so shall it not be among you: but whosoever will be great among you, shall be your minister: (44) And whosoever of you will be the chiefest, shall be servant of all.'"

In this passage of scripture, Jesus responds by requesting functioning apostles James and John to say what they want Him to do for them. Jesus already knew what they wanted to ask. In the same way God knows what we need or want before we make our requests known to Him. James 4:3 says, "Ye ask, and receive not, because ye ask amiss, that ye may consume it upon your lusts." God will not finance your lusts of the flesh, lust of the eyes, or pride of life. John was in his late teens and James was in his early twenties when they spoke this request to Jesus, so they were naturally immature because of inexperience. Immature Believer Business Employees sometimes ask for the wrong things that could stumble their spiritual growth and maturation or is not the path that the Godhead wants them to travel. Before the Godhead gives them more authority, He wants them to gain insight into their own immature questions and motives. Often, God invites them to speak out, so they can reveal to themselves their immaturity or their missing God's servanthood principles and God's perfect Will for them.

Names in the Bible have significance. Mark 3:16-17 says, "And Simon he surnamed Peter; (17) And James the son of Zebedee, and John the brother of James; and He surnamed them Boanerges, which is, the sons of thunder." Peter, James, and John were partners in their fishing business. Peter, James, and John saw Jesus' glory when Jesus invited the three of them to go with Him to the Mount of Transfiguration where the three saw Jesus' glory and saw God's eternal life (Matthew 17:1-9, Mark 9:2-8, and Luke 9:28-36). John later wrote in 1 John 1: 1-2, "That which was from the beginning, which we have heard, **which we have seen with our eyes**, which we have looked upon, and our hands have handled, of the **Word of Life**; (2) (For the **Life was manifested**, and **we have seen it**, and bear witness, and shew unto you that Eternal Life, which was with the Father, and was manifested unto us).

James and John asked Jesus to sit on His left hand and the other to sit on His right hand in His kingdom. James and John ignored what Jesus had just said that He, Jesus, had to suffer and/or die, and be resurrected. James and John apparently did not listen when Jesus said that all His functioning apostles will suffer and/or die and be with Him in heaven where He will be sitting on the throne at the right hand of His heavenly Father (Psalm 101:1; Acts 7:55-56; Hebrews 1:3; 12:2; 1 Peter 3:21). John was the only functioning male apostle who stood at the foot of the Cross watching Jesus die, so perhaps this is one of the reasons that John was the only functioning apostle who did not die a martyr's death as the other functioning apostles.

Before James and John's actions of requesting of Jesus that He grant them special honor, Jesus had just said in Mark 10:33-34, "Behold, we go up to Jerusalem; and the Son of Man shall be delivered unto the chief priests, and unto the scribes; and they shall condemn Him to death, and shall deliver Him to the Gentiles: (34) And they shall mock Him, and shall scourge Him, and shall spit upon Him, and shall kill Him: and the third day He shall rise again."

James and John did not comprehend Jesus' statement that His humanity nature must suffer and die prior to His resurrection, ascension, and exaltation to sit at the right hand of Father God. All that

James and John wanted to think about was Jesus' reign as the Messiah and being King over the whole earth and heaven, and then their own place in His kingdom. After His resurrection, Jesus did say in Matthew 28:18, "… All power is given unto me in heaven and in earth."

In addition to James and John's ambitious competitive desire for the best authoritative places in Jesus' kingdom, they represented personal ambition and unrighteous competitiveness at the exclusion of the other disciples. Ambition and unrighteous competitiveness belong together as being sinful, self-absorption, and self-exaltation. Once Jesus was arrested John and James were two of the first to flee, but John returned later out of *agape* love for Jesus and was the only functioning apostle who appeared at the foot of the Roman cross while Jesus was crucified and dying (John 19:25-27). Jesus had taken the opportunity to inform His disciples that they will suffer and die for Him before they will receive their rewards and honor. Jesus then takes the opportunity to teach all the young functioning apostles (save John) that they will go to heaven the same path as He; so, all the apostles suffered physical persecution and were martyrs, save John the Beloved (although suffered) who died of old age. Although His functioning apostles will experience bitter and harsh suffering, both inwardly and outwardly as part of their martyrdom, they will rule and reign with Christ throughout eternity.

Yet, Jesus' functioning apostles' suffering they were going to experience was not as extreme as the personal suffering that He was going to suffer. Jesus suffered cruel beatings and crucifixion although He never committed any sin and was not born with the sin principle inside Him, but took upon Himself the sins and punishment on behalf of sinners (2 Corinthians 5:21). Also, Jesus suffered by hanging on the Roman Cross, as He vicariously took on the curse of the Law to relieve Believers from the curse of the law (Galatians 3:13). It is one thing for someone to be punished when that someone had done some heinous crime deserving death, but for Jesus to be totally innocent of any sin or crime while experiencing His sinless body being beaten beyond measure and then crucified was a soulish suffering unlike any of His functioning apostles endured.

As for James and John's request, Jesus basically said that He is merely a Servant, and it is His Father who makes those decisions regarding a division of work and position in His Kingdom. God the Father gives a Believer as a child by adoption, his or her place and work assignments in the kingdom according to His wisdom and Will. God is still concerned about His Kingdom manifesting here on earth.

Acts 1:6-7 says, "When they (apostles) therefore were come together, they asked of Him, saying, Lord, wilt thou at this time restore again the kingdom to Israel? (7) And he said unto them, 'It is not for you to know the times or the seasons, which the Father hath put in His own power.'"

SERVANTHOOD IS THE GREATEST WORK BELIEVER BUSINESS MINISTERS CAN PERFORM AS THEY ARE LED BY THE HOLY SPIRIT

Jesus said in Matthew 23:1-11, "Then spake Jesus to the multitude, and to his disciples, (2) saying, 'The scribes and the Pharisees sit in Moses' seat: (3) All therefore whatsoever they bid you observe, that observe and do; but do not ye after their works: for they say, and do not. (4) For they bind heavy burdens and grievous to be borne, and lay them on men's shoulders; but they themselves will not move them with one of their fingers. (5) But all their works they do for to be seen of men: they make broad their phylacteries, and enlarge the borders of their garments, (6) And love the uppermost rooms at feasts, and the chief seats in the synagogues, (7) And greetings in the markets, and to be called of men, Rabbi, Rabbi. (8) But be not ye called Rabbi: for one is your Master, even Christ; and all ye are brethren. (9) And call no man your father upon the earth: for one is your Father, which is in heaven. (10) Neither be ye called masters: for one is your Master, even Christ. (11) But he that is greatest among you shall be your servant.'"

Jesus said in John 12:37, 42-43, which says, "But though He (our business Messiah) had done so many miracles before them, yet they believed not on Him. . . (42) Nevertheless among the chief rulers also many believed on Him; but because of the Pharisees they did not confess Him, lest they should be put out of the synagogue: (43) For they loved the praise of men more than the praise of God."

In John, chapter 13 Jesus ends His public ministry and decides to do a personal private ministry to His functioning apostles regarding the virtue of humility before the final hours remaining before His crucifixion. He gathered together these still young functioning apostles; all were younger than Him, and most in their twenties who would spread the gospel of the kingdom and gospel of repentance and remission of sins and disciple the new community of Believers that we now call the *Ekklesia* or church.

Humility and servanthood are the purpose that Jesus, as the Messiah, the only begotten Son of God, taught His functioning apostles by washing their feet as the kinesthetic example of how they are to be minister as humble servant *agapao* loving leaders of His *Ekklesia.* Jesus was about to suffer tremendous cruelty of beatings and then suffer crucifixion and death on the Roman cross, but Jesus used His precious remaining time before His suffering and death to train His functioning apostles through a kinesthetic example of humility to rid themselves of unrighteous competition as to who was going to be the greatest in His kingdom.

Washing another person's feet was very condescending in the Jewish culture at that time. Jesus even removed His outer garment and put a towel around Him, as if He was a slave. Jesus' Jewish functioning apostles were shocked to see what Jesus was doing, but they remained silent until Peter protested to Jesus in John 13:6-10. Peter succumbed to the kinesthetic training and conversed with the Lord in John 13:8-9, "Peter saith unto Him, 'Thou shalt never wash my feet.' Jesus answered him, 'If I wash thee not, thou hast no part with Me.' (9) Simon Peter saith unto Him, 'Lord, not my feet only, but also *my* hands and *my* head.'"

Jesus discusses the washing of feet of His functioning apostles as kinesthetic training of humility and servanthood in John 13:12-17, "So after He had washed their feet, and had taken His garments, and was set down again, He said unto them, 'Know ye what I have done to you? (13) Ye call Me Master and Lord: and ye say well; for so I am. (14) If I then, your Lord and Master, have washed your feet; ye also ought to wash one another's feet. (15) For I have given you an example, that ye should do as I have done to you. (16) Verily, verily, I say unto you, The servant is not greater than his lord; neither he that is sent greater than he that sent him. (17) If ye know these things, happy are ye if ye do them.'"

After Jesus explained His using kinesthetic training of humility and servanthood of His young functioning apostles, then Jesus sat down at the last supper table while Jesus was under stress that His crucifixion is within hours. He speaks to His functioning apostles at the last supper table sitting with Him, and He gave them the foundational commandment that His apostles must teach and train other Believers this act of humility and servanthood as they build the *Ekklesia.*

While at the last supper in John 13:34-35, Jesus reveals His new final New Commandment, "A new commandment I give unto you, 'That ye love one another; as I have loved you, that ye also love one another. (35) By this shall all men know that ye are My disciples, if ye have love one to another."

So, Jesus taught His chosen functioning apostles who would lead His *Ekklesia* to wash one another's feet—that is, to humble themselves and sacrificially serve others even in ways that most Believers might think are beneath them. Jesus' foot-washing humility and servanthood kinesthetic training has gone around the world, along with preaching the gospel of the kingdom and preaching repentance and remission of sins.

HUMILITY AND SUBMISSION PRECEDES PROMOTION, NOT COMPETITION AMONGST BELIEVERS

The fallen world's unrighteous competitiveness and the works of the flesh in commerce must be discontinued as soulish motivation, and the souls of Believer Business Owners and Believer Business Employees must be spiritually transformed into humility and servanthood, motivated by *agape* love.

The souls of Believer Business Owners and Believer Business Employees need submission to the Godhead's transformation of the soul unto spiritual humility and servanthood for maturation to curtail pridefulness, self-absorption, and self-promotion.

Likewise, seeking recognition in the warehouse or cathedral church pyramid structure has been in the traditional church since Constantine made Christianity a State religion which has caused divisions in the community of Believers. Church leadership elitism has no place in the true *Ekklesia* and the Body of Christ. Again, Mark 10:44 says, "And whosoever of you will be the chiefest, shall be servant of all."

What should be the motivation of every Believer Business minister of the Lord? Paul in Romans 12: 3 says, "For I say, through the grace given unto me, to every man that is among you, not to think of himself more highly than he ought to think; but to think soberly, according as God hath dealt to every man the measure of faith."

In the body of Christ all Believers must *agapao* love one another and be servants of other Believers in God's Kingdom. Since the Godhead lives in every Believer, then Believers must honor the Godhead that lives inside them, Who is there to transform the Believers' souls, to have intimate relationship, and to protect and guide them. All Vocations as kings, priests, lords, ambassadors, and soldiers are equal in stature. Also, there are no gifts superior to any of the other gifts. 1 Corinthians 12: 24-26 says, "For our comely parts have no need: but God hath tempered the Body (of Christ) together, having given more abundant honour to that part which lacked: (25) That there should be no schism in the Body (of Christ); but that the members (in the Body of Christ) should have the same care one for another. (26) And whether one member suffers, all the members suffer with it; or one member be honoured, all the members rejoice with it."

The Believer Business Owner must know the level of spiritual maturity of each Believer Business Employee by the aptness with which the business task assigned is accomplished, the humility of his or her soul, and whether he or she has moral ethics and likeminded and humble character of Christ.

Jesus said in Matthew 23:12, "And whosoever shall exalt himself shall be abased; and he that shall humble himself shall be exalted." Believer Business Owners and Believer Business Employees who are humble will not abuse others. They will work hard, learn how the work assigned shall be done, and do not seek his or her own self-aggrandizement; but will seek the betterment of the Believer

Business Owners, other Believer Business Employees, and the successfulness of the business. The humble Believer Business Employee should be looked upon as a candidate to be promoted to the position of a Believer Business Manager. Paul cautions against hasty promotion in 1 Timothy 5:22, "Lay hands suddenly on no man…."

SPEAK THE SAME THINGS IN ONE ACCORD WITH THE MIND OF CHRIST

1 Corinthians 1:10 says, "Now I beseech you, brethren, by the name of our Lord Jesus Christ, that ye all speak the same thing, and that there be no divisions among you; but that ye be perfectly joined together in the same mind and in the same judgment."

1 Corinthians 2:16 says, "For who hath known the mind of the Lord, that He may instruct him? But we have the mind of Christ." The mind is in the soul, and Jesus' humanity nature has a soul with a mind, emotions, heart, and will. Jesus' humanity nature mind is totally humble and submission to God the Father as He only said and did what Father God said and did (John 5:19 and John 12:49). Jesus humanity nature's mind is what we are to emulate with humility and servanthood. Again, Philippians 2:5-8 says, "**Let this mind be in you, which was also in Christ Jesus**: (6) Who, being in the form of God, thought it not robbery to be equal with God: (7**) But made Himself of no reputation, and took upon Him the form of a servant**, and was made in the likeness of men: (8) And being found in fashion as a man, He humbled Himself, and became **obedient unto death,** even the death of the cross."

Unlike Believer Business Owners and Believer Business Employees, Jesus' mind is resurrected and never had a sinful thought. Believers Business functioning ministers have received Christ's life as His resurrected humanity nature provided His seed for their born again spirits which are their new nature (2 Corinthians 5:17) as part of Jesus' Second Man (1 Corinthians 15:47). Since Christ Jesus' resurrected humanity nature is the *zoe* life of Believers' born again spirits, then Believers can invite their born again spirit in their soul to experience the mind of Christ. With the mind of their business Messiah, Savior, and Lord, then in Believer Business Owners' business dealings they are able now to receive the wisdom that was personified by Jesus Christ. 1 Corinthians 1:30 says, "But of Him are ye in Christ Jesus, who of God is made unto us wisdom, and righteousness, and sanctification, and redemption." To live with the mind of Christ, Believer Business Owners and Believer Business Employees must follow the admonition and instruction of Galatians 2:20, which says, "I am crucified with Christ: nevertheless I live; yet not I, but Christ liveth in me: and the life which I now live in the flesh I live by the faith of the Son of God, who loved me, and gave Himself for me."

Giving Jesus' functioning twelve apostles some grace because of their young ages when they were called when Jesus was only 30 years of age, and all the functioning apostles were younger than Peter. Jesus' oldest functioning apostle was Peter, who was married and probably was about 24 years old when Jesus called him to be a disciple and fisher of men. John the Beloved was the youngest and was just a teenager between 14 to 17. The rest of the functioning apostles had an age between John and Peter. The functioning apostles were arguing and competing because they were immature young men, not because they were overly sinful (except for Judas). They all were trying to make themselves important in the Kingdom of God that Jesus always preached was at hand (Matthew 4:17). Judas hanged himself through guilt as a young man because he committed treason against the King of kings, the business Messiah. What would have happened if Judas approached Jesus after His resurrection and asked for forgiveness? There is some evidence that Caiaphas sought Jesus' forgiveness after Jesus' resurrection, which was given. It was interesting that Caiaphas resigned as Head of the Sanhedrin shortly after Jesus' death, resurrection, and ascension.

Unfortunately, the self-centered ministry mentality organizes things, controls people, and sometimes builds something great to edify self. Ministers with these elitists and self-promotion personality traits start denominations, which creates a mixed seed, and spend millions on church buildings, and focuses merely on initial salvation to increase the membership but normally are not interested in activating the Believers for the work of the ministry as mandated in Ephesians 4:12-13.

In fact, this denomination ministry mentality is the old varnish which must be stripped off to bring forth the glorious *Ekklesia*, without spot, wrinkle, or blame, but is holy, *agapao* loving, and not competitive against others in the same *Ekklesia* (or business) (Ephesians 5:27; John 13:34-35). The Believer Business Owners must make it a strict rule for employees not to become a "business denomination" but remain always open and obedient, especially obedient to the leading of the Holy Spirit.

The phrase "old wineskins" is a metaphor from the Bible regarding the Pharisees, Sadducees, Herodians, who were joined together as members of the Sanhedrin. Today, there are religious denominations where the Holy Spirit is not invited to manifest in the congregations to follow rigid religious traditions. In the New King James, Matthew 9:17 says, "Nor do they put new wine into old wineskins, or else the wineskins break, the wine is spilled, and the wineskins are ruined. But they put new wine into new wineskins, and both are preserved."

When a denomination member seeks employment in the business, the Believer Business Owner must give instructions not to bring their denominational prejudices with him or her because the business is a foundational believing business, not majoring forcing other employees to accept their "elective" type beliefs. Yet, if a Believer practices Sabbath on Saturday, like the Seventh Day Adventist, then the Believer Business Owner must accommodate him or her as this is part of their foundational belief.

Psalms78:41 says, "Yea, they turned back and tempted God and limited the Holy One of Israel." The psalmist points out that Israel limited God by their lack of faith and thereby failed to receive God's promises and ultimate blessings because they rejected God and started worshipping false gods or idols. This was a violation of the First and Second Commandments of the Decalogue.

THE FALSE DICHOTOMY OF SECULAR VERSUS SACRED AGAINST BUSINESS LEADERS BEING MINISTERS

Ancient Greek philosophers, like Socrates, Plato, and Aristotle, valued intellectual pursuits of knowledge and virtue as the highest aims of human life. These Philosophers viewed business, manual labor, commerce, and political activities less valuable and even undesirable. These Philosophers in their writings revealed their prejudices. They believed that those involved in business were involved in "vulgar" pursuits because they were motivated by profit and self-interest rather than the higher pursuits of knowledge and virtue. This prejudice crept into the Christian church leadership and caused prejudice against seeing business as a work of ministry even to this day.

Thus, there is an unjustified historical prejudice in church leadership that sets a wall of separation of the secular business labor versus the sacred religious practices. This prejudice against business Believers is handed down throughout the church against the mandate of God. It is common for Believers to define life activities being divided between the sacred and the secular.

When Jesus was twelve years old, He said to His mother that He was about His Father's business (Luke 2:49). So, God is engaged in the business of saving unbelievers and transforming the souls of Believers here on earth. Jesus did not choose one of His functioning apostles who had studied for the priesthood or a religious position at that time, except for Paul later who first studied law and was a Pharisee. Jesus came as the Messiah after being trained as a Carpenter and Stonemason. Jesus chose fishermen and a tax collector as functioning apostles, as He wanted ministers who could be instructed with kinesthetic training.

Believers are taught by church leaders, impliedly or expressly, that owning or working in businesses, attending schools to learn business, (unless it is a Bible College), shopping, sharing a meal, raising children, traveling, and everything else Believers do, are only secular activities.

Likewise, Believers are taught by church leaders that activities are considered sacred when Believers are engaging in prayer, singing and worshipping God, performing as church musicians and worshippers, reading the Bible, witnessing, teaching at a church building, ministering as a Ephesians 4:11 functioning minister, working as a church secretary, training youth, and traveling as missionaries. Religious teachers promote that contemplating and worshiping God is sacred but training in government, businesses, professions, agriculture, plumbing, carpentry, electrical, computer programming, air conditioning, farming, animal husbandry, inventing new medical products, scientific research, reading, writing, and arithmetic in schools, and other disciplines are merely secular and not being about God the Father's business and entering into God's kingdom. Nothing could be farther from the truth.

God wanted the possession of the earth, world, and humans returned to Him, so He could give all authority in heaven and in earth to His only begotten Son and His Son's Bride as an inheritance. Jesus accomplished and fulfilled God's desire by dying on the Roman cross and defeating all the works of the devil (1 John 3:8). Since the Word became flesh (John 1:14), there is no distinction between secular and sacred. God does not make the distinction between secular versus sacred in His kingdom and in the *Ekklesia* because God's temple is in Believer Business functioning ministers who are working in business.

Wherever the Believer goes, God is with him or her. This means when the Believer Business Owners and Believer Business Employees come to the business venue to work, the sacred comes with them because he or she is bringing God's temple with them (2 Corinthians 6:16). Colossians 3:23-24 says, "And whatsoever ye do, do it heartily, as to the Lord, and not unto men; (24) Knowing that of the Lord ye shall receive the reward of the inheritance: for ye serve the Lord Christ."

This false dualism of secular versus sacred activities has relegated most Believers to think of their lives as being mostly secular since their sacred times are relegated to Sunday and one day in the evening during the weekdays. Instead of Believers' lives on earth as being a foretaste of the Kingdom of God "and have tasted the good word of God, and the powers of the world to come" that God has for us (Hebrew 6:5), life here on earth is seen as a mundane stop on the way to heaven. This false dualism of secular versus sacred outlook was foreign to Jesus and the early *Ekklesia*; and the teaching of false dualism by the historical non-Christian Greek culture has had an impact on the church leadership.

Also, this false dualism of secular versus sacred activity has caused elitism in the church, and this false dualism has made the laity think they are not sacred but are merely secular in life activities and are not qualified to be ministers, contrary to Ephesians 4:12. Jesus stated to the *Ekklesia* in Ephesus in Revelation 2:6, "But this thou hast, that thou hatest the deeds of the Nicolaitans, which I also hate." Nicolaitans (meaning hatred of the laity) were elitists who had disdain against the laity and did not want to activate the laity into the work of the ministry. Obviously, part of the reason for promulgating the false dualism of secular versus sacred is that the elites believed their ordination and personal spiritual calling qualifies them as "worthy" of receiving the tithes, offerings and all the accolades. Teachers teach and students pay tuition.

Jesus gave an example of the secular versus sacred of the wrongful spiritual elitism in the parable of the Pharisee and the repentant Publican. Luke 18:11-14, says, "The Pharisee stood and prayed thus with himself, 'God, I thank thee, that I am not as other men are, extortioners, unjust, adulterers, or even as this publican. (12) I fast twice in the week, I give tithes of all that I possess.' (13) And the publican, standing afar off, would not lift up so much as his eyes unto heaven, but smote upon his breast, saying, 'God be merciful to me a sinner.' (14) I tell you, this man went down to his house justified rather than the other: for every one that exalteth himself shall be abased; and he that humbleth himself shall be exalted."

Although Believer Business Owners and Believer Business Employees are ministers, local church and denomination leaders often suffer discrimination because of the false dualism of secular versus sacred activities. The reality is most all Believers who should be recognized as ministers are working in business and the marketplace and not in the warehouse church building. Ministry activity at the workplace or marketplace does not make it secular. God is omnipresent, and, again, the Godhead lives inside each Believer (2 Corinthians 6:16). God does not live in the warehouse church building, but in Believers' bodies.

Ephesians 4:12 states that all Believers are to be equipped or perfected for the work of the ministry. If Believers are engaged in business and commerce, and they are to be activated for the work of the ministry, then that daily work of activating them for the work of the ministry will be done best at the business workplace where incremental corrections, encouragement, and oversight by Believer Business Owners or Managers can speed up the work of the ministry at the workplace.

1 Peter 2:9 says that all Believers are part of a chosen generation, royal priesthood, holy nation, and peculiar people. Being kings and priests mean Believers working at business and in the marketplace have spiritual kingly and priestly authority there. Being priests of the order of Melchizedek, all Believers are activated to minister reconciliation of the unsaved to God the Father daily or as the opportunity rises (2 Corinthians 5:18-19).

This reconciliation with God ministry by Believer Business Owners and Believer Business Employees is done primarily at the business and the marketplace, not just in a church building. 1 Corinthians 12: 4-31 declares the diversity of spiritual gifts amongst all Believers, and the importance of each believer using their gifts for the common good. These gifts are practiced not just in a home fellowship but in business and the marketplace.

Believer Business Owners and Believer Business Employees are ministers working in commerce who God has appointed them in the ministry Vocations as kings, priests (Revelation 1:6), lords (1 Timothy 6:15), ambassadors (2 Corinthians 5:20), and soldiers (1 Timothy 2:3-4).

Therefore, why do some religious leaders and their denominational precepts foster this false dualism of activities as either secular or sacred?

THE DEVIL'S STRATEGY OF INFLUENCING THE STARTING OF ANOTHER DENOMINATION ALWAYS CAUSES DIVISION AND FUELS COMPETITION IN THE BODY OF CHRIST

Paul said in Philippians 2:2, "Fulfill ye my joy, that ye be likeminded, having the same love, being of one accord, of one mind." Similarly, Paul reiterated his concerns in 1 Corinthians 1:10, "Now I beseech you, brethren, by the name of our Lord Jesus Christ, that ye all speak the same thing, and that there be no divisions among you; but that ye be perfectly joined together in the same mind and in the same judgment."

Ephesians 4:14 says, "That we henceforth be no more children, tossed to and fro, and carried about with every wind of doctrine, by the sleight of men, and cunning craftiness, whereby they lie in wait to deceive." The devil will work overtime to keep Believer Business Owners away from an illumination and understanding of their Ephesians 4:7 grace given for the measure of their gift from Christ to try to deceive them that business must remain separate from ecclesiastical ministry.

We have a whole diverse *Ekklesia* where the Believers of Christ Jesus differ in their spiritual practices, and these denominational differences cause religious humanists to prefer denominational supportive scriptures as more important than others because they support their religious traditional practices. The problem is that religious traditional practices sow discord and competition amongst the Believers based upon the natural world's fallen ideas instead of God's Kingdom principles and moral virtues. This causes a response to defend their religious traditional practices, which often further causes an incendiary defense against rivals. Alienation and division occur, and they sometimes fall to the devices and strategies of the devil that weakens the Body of Christ through its divisions. Ministers that promote elitism based upon their spiritual doctrines, spiritual gifts, or spiritual practices should not be promoted in the Body of Christ.

One of the devil's strategies is to park Believer Business Owners in congregations where the pulpit belongs to a denomination onefold functioning priest, bishop, pastor, teacher, or reverend who ministers with a preset denominational doctrines, beliefs, or practices. This is not to disparage the solid doctrines of faith that are fundamental where the Believer Business Owners receive at least foundational teachings, which most all functioning priests, bishops, pastors, teachers, and reverends accept as truths.

However, often the onefold functioning priest, bishop, pastor, teacher, or reverend insists that his or her elective spiritual practices are foundational that will lead to soulish maturation. The Believer Business Owners are stuck in denominations that do not recognize them as ministers. The Believer Business Owners are not considered to be spiritual ministers because in the Greek businessmen and businesswomen were thought to be lower in stature than the philosophers, like Aristotle, Plato, and Socrates. Why? The reason why Greek Philosophers disdain businessmen and businesswomen was because they handled money transactions and sought after "filthy lucre."

Jesus, as the Messiah, was a businessman, working as a Carpenter and Stonemason, and He saw that doing business instruction by kinesthetic training met His functioning apostles' needs better than classroom lectures as previously discussed. The businesses and marketplaces are the Believer Business Owners' and Believer Business Employees' venue for ministry. The Holy Spirit wants to activate the Believer Business Owners as Ephesians 4:11 functioning ministers to train their Believer Business Employees with biblitarian principles of economics, ethical morality, servanthood, long run thinking, preaching the gospel of the kingdom and repentance and remission of sins, showing *agape* love, reading the Bible daily, and maturing through the daily incremental tasks during the eight to ten hours a day, five to six days week under the tutelage of spiritually mature Believer Business Owners.

Yet, the spiritual practices that are only unique to a particular denomination leadership causes division. Often, they rarely are not open to the movement of the Holy Spirit Who wants to do a new, fresh thing to bring revival. With these denominational distinguishments, they often cause them not to ascertain the movement of the Holy Spirit. Isaiah 43:19 says, "Behold, I (Holy Spirit) will do a new thing; now it shall spring forth; shall ye not know it? I will even make a way in the wilderness, and rivers in the desert."

On the other hand, some denomination priests, bishops, pastors, teachers, or reverends acknowledge Ephesians 4:11 functioning apostles and prophets are for today, but in practice they do not acknowledge that the functioning apostles and prophets are in their congregations or are functioning ministers in businesses or in the marketplaces. Traditionally, a few denomination church Leaders incorrectly believe that functioning apostles have more authority than functioning prophets because 1 Corinthians 12:28 says, "And God hath set some in the church, first apostles, secondarily prophets, thirdly teachers, after that miracles, then gifts of healings, helps, governments, diversities of tongues."

Yet, functioning apostles are first because their work in laying the foundation needs to be first. Functioning apostles are the steel rebar that must be properly placed before the liquid concrete is poured. The foundation is built first by laying down steel rebar in a tic-tac-toe formation, which is the functioning apostles' ministry; and then the liquid concrete is poured over the steel rebar, which is the functioning prophets' ministry. The functioning apostles' and functioning prophets' ministries are both needed to have a proper, solid spiritual foundation to correctly build the business. Thus, the functioning apostle's and functioning prophet's ministries are just a question of timing not stature of one over the other in the *Ekklesia*. This will be revealed most clearly in subsequent chapters.

At traditional ecclesiastical pulpits, visiting functioning ministers are allowed to come and preach because they are here today and gone tomorrow and are not competition against the local functioning priest, bishop, pastor, teacher, or reverend. Yet, the presence of functioning apostles and functioning prophets at the local church for the most part is not sought or practiced. Most functioning priests, bishops, pastors, teachers, or reverends believe and practice as a onefold evangelist, pastor, or teacher with the sole sovereign authority at the warehouse or cathedral lecture hall pyramid paradigm structure. What most functioning priests, bishops, pastors, teachers, or reverends do not recognize is that in their community of Believers there are anointed Believer Business Owners doing businesses as functioning apostles, prophets, evangelists, pastors, and teachers.

Believer Business Owners usually are not activated as ministers in the warehouse or cathedral lecture hall pyramid paradigm structure. Believer Business Owners almost never receive any invitation by the onefold evangelist, pastor, or teacher to preach the gospel of the Kingdom (Matthew 24:14) or repentance and remission of sins (Luke 24:47) or even teach the local *Ekklesia* congregation are supposed to be activated to do the work of the ministry. The local functioning priests, bishops, pastors, teachers, or reverends cut off spiritual potential competitors, who could be anyone who he or she suspects will become a better evangelist, pastor, or teacher than he or she is.

IT IS WRONG TO TRY TO INTELLECTUALIZE THE EXCLUSION OF FUNCTIONING APOSTLES AND PROPHETS

Scriptures allow differences of gifts, diversities of administrations, and varieties of operations by Believers (1 Corinthians 12:5-7), including the recognition of Believer Business Owners, Believer Business Employees, and each member of the whole Body of Christ as having spiritual Gifts and spiritual Vocations as previously discussed.

Denominational church Leaders can disagree on the non-essentials, but the basic foundational beliefs should be (and normally are) the same. The Body of Christ needs all members to have a full, functioning Body of Believers with differences of gifts, diversities of administrations, and varieties of operations of spiritual Gifts, but, again, with all Believers having the same Vocations. God's word teaches unity, not uniformity of the members of the Body of Christ. There is room for members who have different functions in the Body under the headship of Jesus Christ. There is no exclusive venue for the preaching of the gospel of the Kingdom and preaching of the gospel of repentance and remission of sins, so the place of leading someone to the Lord for salvation includes businesses and in the marketplaces. The Godhead is omnipresent, and He is in the marketplaces and businesses every day. The Godhead must wonder why Believers are not preaching the gospel of the Kingdom and not preaching repentance and remission of sins everywhere since the Godhead is everywhere.

No true scholar can conclude that functioning apostles and prophets are not for today, since "the gifts and the calling of God are irrevocable" (Romans 11:29). If God has purposely limited the *Ekklesia* here on earth by revoking the functioning ministries of the apostles and prophets, and especially those who exercise their gifts outside of the traditional church construct, why did God (as falsely taught) only revoke the functioning apostles and prophets but not the functioning evangelists, pastors, and teachers? Just because we have the canonized word does not mean we no longer need all Ephesian 4:11 functioning apostles, prophets, evangelists, pastors, and teachers. The problem is that reading the Bible, although good scholastically, is not kinesthetic hands on instruction and training that also is needed to activate Believers in their spiritual Vocations and spiritual Gifts.

Only by misreading scriptures with anemic interpretations do some denominational leaders conclude that spiritual gifts and functioning apostles and prophets are not for today. For example, they quote 1 Corinthians 13:8-10 which says in the New King James, "Love never fails. But whether there are prophecies, they will fail; whether there are tongues, they will cease; whether there is knowledge, it will vanish away. (9) For we know in part, and we prophesy in part. (10) But when that which is perfect has come, then that which is in part will be done away".

Paul surmises in 1 Corinthians 13:8-10 that prophecies, tongues, and inspired knowledge are gifts that are here to help our souls become spiritually transformed because our souls are in a state of spiritual imperfection, as we only know in part and only prophesy in part (verse 9). In other words, while our souls are undergoing transformation while alive, our souls are never absolutely righteous, holy, or perfect because our souls daily are influenced by the born again spirit (led by the Holy Spirit) and other times by the carnality of the flesh. Even after studying the scriptures, where there are many mysteries, Believers only know in part.

Paul said in 1 Corinthians 13:8, "Charity (*agape* love) never faileth: but whether there be prophecies, they shall fail; whether there be tongues, they shall cease; **whether there be knowledge, it shall vanish away**." These teachers who teach skip entirely the phrase in 1 Corinthians 13:8 of "**whether there be knowledge, it shall vanish away**" because these denominational teachers would lose their cleric jobs because they would not be allowed to teach anymore.

To teach that since the canonize word is here, there shall be no more inspired knowledge means that would put every functioning pastor and teacher out of a job. Thus, we need inspired knowledge still. Likewise, we still need inspired knowledge for soul maturation, so we need every one of the Ephesians 4:11 functioning ministers. In truth, the canonized word is great to bring the foundation truth in the *Ekllesia*, but there is so much more in the activating, spiritual word of God. For example, Hebrews 4:12 says, "For the word (*logos*) of God is quick, and powerful, and sharper than any twoedged sword, piercing even to the dividing asunder of soul and spirit, and of the joints and marrow, and is a discerner of the thoughts and intents of the heart."

Thus, 1 Corinthians 13:10 refers to the perfection of the *Ekklesia* as the Bride of Christ, not the canonize word. The Bride of Christ is what is being perfected as a glorious *Ekklesia* or Spouse of Christ, not having spot, or wrinkle, or any such thing; but that she should be holy and without blemish (Ephesians 5:27, Revelation 19:7-8).

Once the Lord returns, and Believers come with Him with a soul in a perfected state by the Godhead, there will be no need of gifts of tongues, prophecy, or inspired knowledge. In the perfected future life, with perfected holiness, righteousness, and wisdom, Believers will relate with God and the humanity nature of Christ in perfect communication, and with a knowledge that a capacity of glorified minds will allow. These are the two states of imperfection and eventual perfection that Paul describes.

Various spiritual gifts were particularly fitted for imperfect Believers in their souls making up of the *Ekklesia*. Yet, the knowledge and gifts cannot be compared to the supremacy of the Kingdom of God, *agape* love, mercy, repentance, forgiveness, grace, faith, wisdom, knowledge, and understanding that Believers are mandated to share with each other (Matthew 24:14; Matthew 13:34-35; Luke 24:47; Isaiah 33:6; Ephesians 3:10; James 3:17; Colossians 1:14; Hebrew 11:6; 2 John 1:3).

In the end when the Lord returns to earth with the New Jerusalem (Revelation chap. 21), and each Believer already has a perfect born again spirit that is righteous, holy, perfect, and sinless (Ephesians 4:24; Hebrews 12:23; 1 John 3:9), having a spiritually transformed soul (Romans 12:2), and then receives a resurrected body (1 Corinthians 15:23, 42-44).

At that time each Believer's *agape* love will be so pure that these other gifts in their imperfection will have less importance. It is anemic teaching that the "when the perfect has come" means the canonized word of God. This anemic teaching that functioning apostles and prophets, prophecies, tongues, and knowledge are no longer in operation since the canonized word do not stand up against other scriptures.

Why do religious denomination Leaders try to revoke the gifts of Ephesians 4:11functioning apostles and prophets by telling their congregations they are not for today? The effect is non-recognition and the robbing of the Body of Christ with those office engiftments, which lessens the activation of Believers for the work of the ministry.

Similarly, to allow religious tradition to silence Ephesians 4:11 Business ministers with a doctrinal position also robs Believers of the blessings of God, especially about the transfer of wealth generationally and providing a workplace where there is kinesthetically training of Believers in business ministry five to six days a week.

FAILURE TO ACCEPT THE EPHESIANS 4:11 MINISTRIES TODAY IS NOT DISCERNING THE ENTIRE BODY OF CHRIST

"Not discerning the Body of Christ" is one of the most serious problems in the *Ekklesia* today. The Believer Business Owner may not know what gifts a Believer Business Employee has. The Believer Business Owner may not know the strengths and weaknesses of each Believer Business Employee; but as the Believer Business Owner, you need to seek the discovery of their spiritual gifts. Therefore, the Believer Business Owner must know his or her Believer Business Employees and their families, along with knowing clients, customers, products, machines, and everything that is in the business.

Those denominations leaders espousing doctrinal religious traditions do not properly discern the Body of Christ if they do not recognize as part of the Body of Christ the functioning apostles and prophets are for today and especially do not discern that all the Ephesians 4:11 ministries can be operated outside of the *Ekklesia* warehouse lecture hall auditorium by starting a business and everywhere else in society.

Apostle Paul encourages every Believer to further admonish himself in 1 Corinthians 11:28, "But let a man examine himself (soul), and so let him eat of the bread and drink of the cup." How does a Believer do this spiritually. The Believer must examine his soul by comparing our darkness with the Lord Jesus Christ's lightness. Then we will discern the Lord's body. Believers are the light of this world (Matthew 5:14-16) because Jesus came as the Light of this world (John 8:12). He shared His light with His disciples. A Believer's examination of himself or herself is crucial before he or she takes part in communion. The reason is that a Believer sometimes hear, but he does not discern God's will and purpose.

Apostle Paul makes this point clear when teaching on having the right heart when taking of communion. 1 Corinthians 11:29-30 says, "For he who eats and drinks in an unworthy manner eats and drinks judgment to himself, not discerning the Lord's body. (30) For this reason, many are weak and sick among you, and many sleep."

If Christ Jesus through His divine nature, God the Word, is the one giving those engifted functioning ministries delineated in Ephesians 4:11 to the Body of Christ, then He also has the authority to determine their purpose and when they are no longer needed. If Jesus trained His disciples to minister in the businesses and marketplaces, and activated them to do so, where Peter walked down the public street and his shadow fell on people was honored by the Holy Spirit and caused the anointing to heal them (Acts 5:15). Then, the traditional church functioning priests, bishops, pastors, teachers, and reverends do not have the authority to cancel spiritual Vocations or spiritual Gifts mentioned in the Bible.

The Ephesians 4:11 ministers who function as apostles, prophets, evangelists, pastors, and teachers operating in business are needed to properly equip and mature the Body of Christ who consists of the Believer Business Owners and Believer Business Employees of the business and all those who encounter the business workers. When denominations deny the gifts of functioning apostles and prophets exist today, they lack discernment of the leadership that activates Believers in the work of ministry that edifies the Body of Christ (.Ephesians 4:12). With such denial, they cut off the financial blessings that Believer Business Owner functioning apostles, prophets, evangelists, pastors, and teachers operating in business and the marketplace that can bring an economic change in the culture to bless the Body of Christ and finance the mission of the Lord.

The lack of discernment by so many church functioning priests, bishops, pastors, teachers, and reverends in denominations that deny the entire Ephesians 4:11 leadership God wants in the workplace, businesses, and marketplace. Their denial causes strife, disunity, instability, lack of integrity, improperly joined together of Believers with the unsaved that lead to failure to equip the saints for the work of the ministry in business for the edification of the Body of Christ, which is the Father's business.

No wonder Believers in the Body of Christ are weak, sick, and dying before they fulfill the purpose God has called them because business activity is taught in the old church structure as not being the place where the Kingdom of God is and where the maturation of Believer Business ministers happens during the workweek. Denomination church functioning priests, bishops, pastors, teachers, and reverends must stop their anemic teaching that denies certain Ephesians 4:11 office ministries are functioning today. By denying these office ministries are functioning in business and marketplace is not being about Father God's business of maturing the Believer Business ministers for the work of the ministry.

Again, 1 Peter 2:9 says, "But ye (all Believers) are a chosen generation, a royal priesthood, a Holy Nation, a peculiar people; that ye should shew forth the praises of him who hath called you out of darkness into his marvelous light." This scripture speaks of ministry pluralistically as a "...chosen generation, a royal priesthood, a Holy Nation, and a peculiar people....." Each of these pluralistic participatory Vocations and designations in God's Kingdom include every Believer individually and all Believers pluralistically, not just a select group calling themselves priests, bishops, pastors, teachers, or reverends.

Believers are not going to be activated in their spiritual Vocations and spiritual Gifts while sitting in a pew or chair every Sunday in a warehouse lecture hall for forty years listening to sermons and teachings and paying tuition at every meeting to the religious leaders for those sermons and teachings. Is the primary purpose of these sermons and teachings only the transformation of the Believers' souls after initial salvation?

There is Vocational ministry work to be done by all Believers after initial salvation. Ephesians 2:10 says, "For we are His (God's) workmanship, created in Christ Jesus unto good works, which God hath before ordained that we should walk in them." The work of the Vocation ministries of God's Kingdom spiritual kings, priests, lords, ambassadors, and soldiers require every Believer to be activated and minister in their spiritual Vocations and with their spiritual Gifts. All Believers are mandated to take their spiritual Vocations and spiritual Gifts and minister with them locally, regionally, nationally, and internationally as Christ's witnesses (Acts 1:8) to make disciples of all nations, baptizing them in the name of the Father, Son (with His dual natures), and the Holy Spirit, teaching them all that Jesus commanded (Matthew 28:19-20).

God wants Believers to exercise their spiritual Vocations and spiritual Gifts to impact the unsaved people and the world system where Believer Business Owners and Believer Business Employees reside and work. Work is not a spectator's endeavor; that idea would be considered entertainment. In traditional church services today, the only Believers working are the praise and worship team performing on stage, children's ministry, secretarial workers, greeters, ushers, the preacher/teacher speaking the sermons, and sometimes prayer helpers who come up to assist after the altar call. This might be sufficient for initial salvation invitations, but not for activating Believers into their spiritual Vocations and spiritual Gifts. The venue that can do a better job is at the business office or work-place where Believer Business Employees work eight to ten hours a day, five to six days a week and are being paid to accept the kinesthetic training using biblical economics, being directed with a biblical moral compass, maintaining humility, focused on obedience to the Lord, following the leading of the Holy Spirit, exhibiting servanthood to clients, customers, and fellow workers, *agapao* loving people, and being activated into their spiritual Vocations and spiritual Gifts.

Under the current church lecture hall paradigm structure, it is not conducive to the equipping of Believes in their Vocations for the work of the ministry. Even if the old religious order at the warehouse lecture hall facility has a two-year Bible course for congregates to attend and study the precepts of the Bible and the denominational doctrines and traditions, there is little place at the old church paradigm where Believers can practice ministry with financial support after graduation? There is no room at the pyramid top of the old church structure he is attending. There is usually no money to pay him or her in the smaller church structures, where money is tight. This is why Jesus lived with His functioning apostles mostly 24 hours a day, 7 days a week, 3 ½ years before He was crucified and died on the Roman Cross, was resurrected, and finally was ascended to heaven to sit at the right hand of the Throne of God the Father.

God's only begotten Son, who was destined to be King over the entire spiritual and natural creative realities, said that His greatness was that He was the servant of all because He was laying down His humanity nature (*psuche*) life as a ransom to pay for the sins and iniquities of all those who believe and accept Him as Lord and Savior (Mark 10:45).

When leaders set up a pyramid type warehouse lecture hall onefold ministry structure, then this restricts the number of the ministry positions. In the old church structure of a local congregation there usually is only one priest, bishop, pastor, teacher, or reverend. Once the pyramid structure is set up, then the leader does not look for leaders but followers in the congregation of his or her ministry, which is not what Christ Jesus taught, as He kinesthetically trained the original twelve apostles and His disciples to take over the *Ekklesia* once Jesus ascended to heaven.

The Ephesians 4:11 functioning apostles, prophets, evangelists, pastors, and teachers, looking for followers to support him or her, abdicates his or her duty and God's commandment to focus his or her attention as stated in Ephesians 4:12-13, which is "… perfecting of the saints, for the work of the ministry, for the edifying of the Body of Christ (13) Till we ALL come in the unity of the faith, and of the knowledge of the Son of God, unto a perfect man (both men and women as ministers), unto the measure of the stature of the fulness of Christ (where Christ is living in and through them to minister to others -Galatians 2:20)."

THE LIFE OF BELIEVERS IN THE FIRST CENTURY *EKKLESIA*

In the early *Ekklesia*, the functioning apostles, prophets, evangelists, pastors, and teachers had a "V" shape home fellowship structure and meeting occasionally in the open forum at the Temple, where the Ephesian 4:11 ministers were the servants of all. The early *Ekklesia* increase daily, sometimes thousands at a time. Every Believer went out to preach the gospel of the Kingdom and preached repentance and remission of sins everywhere to everyone.

In the First Century *Ekklesia* there were Believer Business Employers as Ephesians 4:11 functioning ministers, and there were Believer Business Employees as ministers with the same work of the ministry mandate in Ephesians 4:12 as kings, priests (Revelation 1:6), lords (1 Timothy 6:15), ambassadors (2 Corinthians 5:20), and soldiers (2 Timothy 2:3-4).

In the First Century *Ekklesia*, Peter, Andrew, James, John, Thomas, and Nathanael were fishermen. Matthew had an accounting and tax collecting business. Paul worked with Priscilla and Aquila in their tent-making business. Dr. Luke was a medical doctor and traveled with Paul. Lydia was a businesswoman, whose business was making purple-dyed fabric for others to sew together to make clothing. In fact, Lydia was the first European that received the gospel of the Kingdom and the gospel of repentance and remission of sins. All these businessmen and businesswomen were ministers in the First Century *Ekklesia.*

Like the first century businessmen and businesswomen, the Lord, through the Holy Spirit, is again calling businessmen and businesswomen to become Believer Business Owners, bringing with them their skills, wisdom, knowledge, and understanding of business and marketplace interactions with people. These Believer Business Owners have been given the mandate scholastically to teach and kinesthetically to train and activate Believer Business Employees into ministry with their spiritual Gifts to do the work of ministry of their true Vocations as kings, priests, lords, ambassadors, and soldiers.

Also, the functioning apostle Paul never had one trained Pharisee ministering with him, even though he, himself, was trained as a Pharisee. This false dichotomy of secular versus the sacred has caused a prejudice in the church that Believer Business Owners and Believer Business Employees are strictly secular because they are engaged only in commerce with the goal of acquisition of money.

1 Peter 3:15 says, "But sanctify the Lord God in your (all Believers') hearts: and be ready always to give an answer to every man that asketh you a reason of the hope that is in you with meekness and fear." Every Believer is called to preach the gospel of the Kingdom (Matthew 24:14) and preach repentance and remission of sins (Luke 24:47). Every Believer is a Witness of the Lord (Acts 1:8). Colossians 4-5 says, "Walk in wisdom toward them that are without, redeeming the time. (5) Let your speech be always with grace, seasoned with salt, that ye may know how ye ought to answer every man."

Also, the first Century congregation after the Day of Pentecost normally met in homes of the Believers. While in the home fellowship meetings, the congregation ministered one to another, with each sharing their spiritual Vocations and spiritual Gifts, as servants helping others. Paul said in 1 Corinthians 12:28-29, "And God hath set some in the church, first apostles, secondarily prophets, thirdly teachers, after that miracles, then gifts of healings, helps, governments, diversities of tongues. (29) Are all apostle? are all prophets? are all teachers? are all workers of miracles?"

Ekklesia home fellowship meetings during Paul's time were in a "V" structure where everyone was a servant and was allowed to share their spiritual Gifts and spiritual Vocations for the edification of others, were allowed to speak, were allowed to read out loud the scriptures, not like today where Believers sit in pews, maybe participate in singing, but remaining quiet and perhaps taking notes of the sermon spoken by the priest, bishop, pastor, teacher, or reverend.

Paul said in 1 Corinthians 14:26-32,39 "How is it then, brethren? when ye come together, **every one of you hath a psalm, hath a doctrine, hath a tongue, hath a revelation, hath an interpretation. Let all things be done unto edifying**. (27) If any man speak in an unknown tongue, let it be by two, or at the most by three, and that by course; and let one interpret. (28) But if there be no interpreter, let him keep silence in the church; and let him speak to himself, and to God. (29) Let the prophets speak two or three, and let the other judge. (30) If anything be revealed to another that sitteth by, let the first hold his peace. (31) For ye may all prophesy one by one (in the meeting), that all may learn, and all may be comforted. (32) And the spirits of the prophets are subject to the prophets… (39) Wherefore, brethren, covet to prophesy, and forbid not to speak with tongues."

First Century fellowship was relational and daily, and this is why the Believer Business Owner and the Believer Business Employees today fulfill the mandate of making disciples and not just converts. They follow Jesus' pattern of discipleship kinesthetically training daily at the workplace eight to ten hours a day, five to six days a week. In the first Century *Ekklesia,* those Believers who were not employed during the day visited the temple but also had daily fellowship and meals from house to house as they engaged in close fellowship (*koinonia*).

Why was the First Century *Ekklesia* just after the Day of Pentecost so attractive to new Believers? Acts 2:42, 46-47 says, "And they (Believers)continued steadfastly in the apostles' doctrine and fellowship *(koinonia*), and in breaking of bread, and in prayers. . .(46) And they (Believers), continuing daily with one accord in the temple, and breaking bread from house to house, did eat their meat with gladness and singleness of heart, (47) Praising God, and having favour with all the people. **And the Lord added to the church (*Ekklesia*) daily such as should be saved."**

If the *Ekklesi*a leaders today will replace their traditions with intense fellowship with the goal of activating Believers into their spiritual Vocations and spiritual Gifts, then they will replicate the hearts that the first century Believers responding to Peter's sermon after the Holy Spirit came on Day of Pentecost. Then, again revival of the *Ekklesia* will come and multitudes will join daily. God will fill the home fellowships, fill the business fellowships, fill the school fellowships, fill the entire commerce with His presence. God's will is that Believers in the true *Ekklesia* express loving *koinonia* in the fellowship businesses while working in business, in the fellowship in homes when Believers are gathered after work, and in any activity where Believers are together in fellowship community.

In the First Century *Ekklesia*, Believer Business Owners and Believer Business Employees love the *koinonia* daily with other Believers, and this is what is available in the Believer Business ministers *koinonia* while they are about the Father's business at the workplace. Believer Business Employees will love coming to work because God's *agape* love, grace, mercy, righteousness, peace, joy and the triune nature of God the Father, God the Word, and God the Holy Spirit, Himself, is there. Matthew 18:20 says, "For where two or three are gathered together in My name, there am I in the midst of them."

The best place for activation of a Believer's spiritual Vocations and spiritual Gifts is at the businesses where the Believer Business Owners function as apostles, prophets, evangelists, pastors, or teachers during working hours of eight to ten hours a day, five to six days a week, that kinetically train and activate the Believer Business Employees in biblical economics, biblical moral ethics, servanthood in their spiritual Vocations while using their spiritual Gifts of God the Father (Romans 12:6-8), God the Word (Ephesians 4:11-13), and God the Holy Spirit (1 Corinthians 12:8-10). The Believer Business Owners through the daily incremental problem-solving and work assignments equip Believer Business Employees with biblical wisdom, knowledge, truth, understanding, strength, servanthood, *agape* love, and long run thinking practices that transform the souls of the Believer Business Employees to have the proclivity of having spiritual thoughts, spiritual feelings, spiritual beliefs and the heartfelt spiritual will to fulfill the vision of the Believer Business Owners that God gave them.

Paul instructed Timothy, "And the things that thou hast heard of me among many witnesses, the same commit thou to faithful men, who shall be able to teach others also" (2 Timothy 2:2).

In Ephesians 4:11 Jesus' divine nature, as God the Word, and Jesus' humanity nature as the only begotten Son of God, gave the offices of the functioning apostles, prophets, evangelists, pastors, and teachers; and the method that Jesus did with His apostles is the model for scholastic teaching and kinesthetically training the Ephesians 4:11 functioning ministers. Jesus is the Apostle of our profession (Hebrews 3:1), Prophet as Jesus' divine nature is God the living *Logo*s word (John 1:1; Mark 6:4; Hebrews 4:12), functioning *agape* loving Evangelist (Mark 1:14-15; Luke 10:2; John 4:35), the most caring Pastor/Shepherd (John 10:11; 1 Peter 5:4), and the most wise, knowledgeable, and understanding Teacher (John 1:38; 3:2).

Each Ephesians 4:11 Business minister brings that part of Christ's heart he or she is specially gifted and called to express into the task of equipping others with that part of Christ's anointing for the work of the business for the building up of the whole Body of Christ unto maturity and creating income streams and business opportunities for more of the Body of Christ to have the independence of being self-employed in business.

THE WORK ETHIC MANDATE IN THE BIBLE

Philippians 2:12-13 says, "Wherefore, my beloved, as ye have always obeyed, not as in my presence only, but now much more in my absence, work out your own salvation with fear and trembling. (13) For it is God which worketh in you both to will and to do of His good pleasure." Again, the Greek for work is *ergon,* which means, "toil". Toil means an effort or occupation by implication an act ,including a deed, doing, labor, or work at the workplace where God's business is conducted. The Greek word *ergon* is the same word as "work" in Ephesians 4:12.

The ongoing truth is that the Believer Business Owner's workplace is where the Believer Business Employees are paid to follow biblical principles of economics, hard work, moral ethics, and servanthood to fulfill God's purposes as our Business God and Jesus as our Business Savior. Through scholastic teaching and kinesthetic training repetition, Believer Business Employees are trained and discipled eight to ten hours a day for five to six days a week. The continuous repetition of incremental tasks with spiritual focus and spiritual inspiration, wisdom, knowledge, and understanding in the Believer Business Employees' souls unto spiritual transformation unto spiritual maturation.

Believer Business Owners need to encourage the Believer Business Employees that their scholastic teaching and kinesthetic training repetition eight to ten hours a day for five to six days a week is not just on Sunday mornings and one night a week at a warehouse or cathedral lecture hall pyramid church structure. Believer Business Employees need one on one and small groups of business ministry scholastic teaching of principles and hand-on kinesthetic training. Believer Business Owners and Believer Business Employees need to see their place of ministry as being outside of the four walls of the old church warehouse lecture hall building structure.

Believer Business Owners and Believer Business Employees need to have their souls put on Jesus Christ's humanity nature (Romans 13:14) and their souls put on their born again spirits, which is the New Man, as their covering of righteousness and holiness (Ephesian 4:24). Believer Business Owners and Believer Business Employees need to take the focus from warehouse or cathedral lecture hall pyramid paradigm structure sitting as spectators in pews or chairs as the only place of ministry, and instead focus on ministering in the businesses, marketplaces, home places, school places, government places, and every other place in the world.

All Believers are called to preach the gospel of the Kingdom, preach repentance and remission of sins, lay hands-on the sick to see them recover, teach God's wisdom for life instead of mere existence, pray for the needs of others, lead other Believers to seek first the Kingdom of God and His righteousness, and exercise strong belief and faith that all the things for which they are praying and seeking will be provided by our *agapao* loving, covenant-making and covenant-keeping God and Lord and Savior Jesus Christ.

Paul said in 1 Corinthians 8:6, "But to us there is but one God, the Father, of whom are all things, and we in Him; and one Lord Jesus Christ, by whom are all things, and we by Him." It would have been clearer if Paul had said, "But to us there is but one God, consisting of the Father, the word, and the Holy Spirit and the humanity nature of the Lord Jesus Christ."

Believers should be bringing already saved Believers to have community *koinōnia* with other Believers in home fellowships before they invite them to the warehouse or cathedral lecture hall pyramid paradigm structure, as the Believers will gravitate to the home fellowships where there is sincere *koinōnia.* Believers should lead their friends to the Lord in businesses, marketplaces, or other areas of our society where people gather during the workdays instead of only during the weekends; and then invite them into home fellowships a little at a time. First. invite the non-believer to your (as a Believer) home for lunch or dinner with both families attending, where the children can develop friends. Parents are protective, and they want their children to be safe but also saved. Children easily gravitate towards *koinōnia* as they are more trustworthy and make friends quickly. Then, invite them to a larger home fellowship where they can have *koinōnia* with other *agapao* loving Believers. This is how the first century church expanded so quickly. The gospel of Christ is relational, not just expounding and listening to sermons.

The first century Believers actions are stated in Acts 2:42, 46-47, "And they continued stedfastly in the apostles' doctrine and fellowship, and in breaking of bread, and in prayers… (46) And they, continuing daily with one accord in the temple, and breaking bread from house to house, did eat their meat with gladness and singleness of heart, (47) Praising God, and having favour with all the people. And the Lord added to the church (*ekklesia*) daily such as should be saved."

THE DEVIL'S REALM CAUSES COMPETITION, DIVISION, AND DISCORD

The devil causes divisions. Proverb 6:16-19 says, "These six things doth the LORD hate: yea, seven are an abomination unto him: (17) A proud look, a lying tongue, and hands that shed innocent blood, (18) An heart that deviseth wicked imaginations, feet that be swift in running to mischief, (19) A false witness that speaketh lies, and he **that soweth discord among brethren."**

Why did the devil move so purposefully to raise up divisions and denominations in the *Ekklesia* leadership and congregations? The reason is it causes competition and discord among the members of the *Ekklesia.* If there is competition and discord amongst different denominations, then that disunity causes less effectiveness in the war against the devil's realm of darkness. The devil wants to divide and conquer to weaken the prayer warriors. If the devil keeps different *Ekklesia* denomination leaders practicing elitism, isolationism, and arguing over pet religious practices, then the devil's work of competition, division, and discord intensifies by the *Ekklesia* itself. This is the devil's deception and strategy.

If Believer Business Owners and Believer Business Employees submit to being led by the Holy Spirit, who is omnipresent; then the Godhead will spiritually mature all business ministers at the workplace. God comes to the business by invitation. When the leaders in the old denomination church structure fail to recognize the maturity and calling of business ministers, then they are disobedient in not recognizing Believer Business Owners and Believer Business Employees as spiritual ministers in the Body of Christ.

There is a principle involved which Jesus taught in Matthew 12:25-26 and Luke 12:17-18, which was that **a** kingdom divided against itself cannot stand. Satan causes divisions. Competition causes division, and division is why the church members today are to a large degree not impacting the world. Believers come to the warehouse or cathedral lecture hall pyramid paradigm structure seeking *agapao* loving fellowship with other Believers, but they encounter strangers sitting in pews, not speaking with each other, and leaving immediately after the spiritual service has ended. Church is a spectator event, but it should be a ministry activating experience.

Most Believers are spectators in the *Ekklesia* because they are not activated for the work of the ministry under Ephesians 4:12. Also, most Believers are not taught the relevance of life benefits of reading and studying the Bible daily and memorizing scriptures, praying throughout the day, and as top priority daily seeking first the kingdom of God and His righteousness. As spectators they basically believe that those who study the Bible do so to speak to spectators in the warehouse or cathedral lecture hall pyramid paradigm structure on Sunday morning. These church leaders project the Bible verses that are relevant for the sermon being taught on the screen behind the functioning pastor or teacher, but there is very little, if any at all kinesthetic training of Believers for the work of the ministry. Most Believers think their leader minister would never ask them to teach or preach; so, what is the relevance of the rank and file studying the word of God or taking sermon notes? They may think, "Why should I have to share *agape* love with brothers and sisters in the Lord if I only meet them as strangers on Sunday morning or at a meeting on Wednesday evening sitting in chairs without any personal interaction with other Believers?"

ACTIVATING EVERY BELIEVER INTO MINISTRY, ESPECIALLY BELIEVER BUSINESS EMPLOYEES

What was Jesus' plan to use the work in ministry to bring Believers to the full measure of their engiftment with grace while they are working in a trade, product sales business, manufacturing industry, or service profession? There is no law of separation of God and business that forbids business personnel from collaborating with fellow Believer Business Owners and fellow Believer Business Employees at the workplace.

Each Believer is given a measure of grace according to the measure of the gift of Christ's divine nature, God the Word. These gifts can be operated anywhere and should be operated everywhere, including in businesses and the marketplace. The ministries of the functioning apostle, prophet, evangelist, pastor, and teacher are office ministry gifts, especially in business because the Godhead uses the solving of daily problems encountered in business to mature the saints as they see the spiritual lessons being applied in their daily interaction with Believers and non-believers. Thus, God teaches His children in business as Jesus was taught by His stepfather, Joseph, how to be a journeyman Carpenter and Stonemason. While Jesus walked on earth, Jesus used the same teaching skills to train His functioning apostles, prophets, evangelists, pastors, and teachers to be His witnesses throughout the known world.

Again, the foundation of this book is that the Believer Business Employer, who normally functions as an apostle, prophet, evangelist, pastor, or teacher (or a combination thereof) has the obligation to equip the Believer Business Employees for the work of the ministry as functioning kings, priests, lords, ambassadors, and soldiers to fight the good fight of faith while preaching God's gospel of the Kingdom and preaching the repentance and remission of sins, along with the goal of taking back possession of the earth, world, and humans for God the Father.

Every Believer is given a measure of faith to do ministry (Romans 12:3), and every Believer must build the faith received hearing the rhema word of God (Romans 10:17), maturing by studying the word of God (2 Timothy 3:16-17), and through kinesthetic training being activated to do the work of ministry (Ephesians 4:12), as spiritual kings, priests (Revelation 1:6), lords (1 Timothy 6:15), ambassadors (2 Corinthians 5:20), and soldiers (2 Timothy 2:3-4). Every Believer must be kinesthetically trained to hear the still small voice of God, Who speaks often when a particular scripture comes alive to deal with a particular difficulty in the Believer's life or from another Believer who is the gift of ministry is granted and directed.

Paul continues in Romans 12:6 and offers further instruction, "Having then gifts differing according to the grace that is given to us, whether prophecy, let us prophesy according to the proportion of faith." Thus, the gift has a portion of grace and a portion of faith bestowed by God for the Vocations as kings, priests, lords, ambassadors, and soldiers in business to operate his or her spiritual gifts.

In Ephesians 4:7-11, God reveals His plan in verse 7 to bring to every person grace for the measure of gift which he or she is called. Verse 8 starts out with "Therefore..." The word therefore means God essentially is saying, "Here's how I am going to bring you to a place where you recognize your grace for the measure of gift bestowed upon you by Jesus' divine nature, God the Word and Jesus' humanity nature as the only begotten resurrected and ascended Son of God and Sacrificial Lamb of God."

PURPOSE OF THE CHAPTERS THAT FOLLOW

In the chapters that follow, I will use the Ephesian 4:11 ministers as functioning apostles, prophets, evangelists, pastors, and teachers to motivate and reveal to you the fullness of your spiritual Vocation and spiritual Gifts through a measure of God's grace. The ministry of the Lord Jesus Christ through God the Word toward the Ephesians 4:11 foundation ministers of the functioning apostle and prophet (Ephesians 2:20) where Jesus is the Chief Corner Stone that the builders of the warehouse auditorium and Cathedral lecture hall paradigm structure have rejected historically by too many onefold traditional religious functioning priests, bishops, pastors, teachers, and reverends.

Regarding the activation of Believers to do the work of ministry at the workplace, God gives grace depending on the measure of the gift of Ephesians 4:11 Believer Business Owners for the purpose of equipping Believer Business Employees for the spiritual work of the ministry being conducted at the business. At the same time, the Believer Business Owner helps God transform the souls of the Believer Business Employees through daily repetitive kinesthetic training through work assignments using biblical principles of economics, moral integrity, servanthood, *agape* love, strong work ethic, and wisdom for the perfecting of the Believer Business Employees with their spiritual Vocations and assigned spiritual Gifts.

Believer Business Owners, who function as apostles, prophets, evangelists, pastors, or teachers are to use scholastic teaching and kinesthetic training for Believer Business Employees to be pure of heart, humble, and obedient to the instructions of the Believer Business Owners. Believer Business Employees will become witnesses of Christ that edifies others they encounter at the workplace. The Holy Spirit will encourage Believer Business Owners and Believer Business Employees to seek unity of the faith and vision of the business, with continuous increase in the knowledge of the Son of God, where souls are being spiritually perfected, unto the measure of the stature of the fullness of Christ in all working Believer Business Employees in the business.

The Believer Business Owners usually are Ephesians 4:11 functioning apostles, prophets, evangelists, pastors, and/or teachers, or a combination thereof. Thus, The Believer Business Owners' scholastic teaching and kinesthetic training process is for the spiritual maturation of the Believer Business Employees who see the business venue as the place of spiritual maturation and activation into the Lord's work of ministry.

Here is the primary principle for both Believer Business Owners and Believer Business Employees. Colossians 3:17 says, "And whatsoever ye do in word or deed, *do* all in the name of the Lord Jesus, giving thanks to God and the Father by Him."

CHAPTER SIX

THE COMMON FOCUS REQUIRED OF THE EPHESIANS 4:11 BELIEVER BUSINESS FUNCTIONING MINISTERS

GRACE, MEASURE, AND GIFT OF THE EPHESIANS 4:11 BELIEVER BUSINESS FUNCTIONING MINISTERS

This chapter primarily concentrates on what all the Ephesians 4:11 functioning apostles, prophets, evangelists, pastors, and teachers have in common as the focus of each of their functioning office ministries. Ephesians 4:7 says, "But to each one of us **grace** was given according to the **measure** of Christ's **gift.**" This preparatory foundational scripture is to elucidate the functions and primary mandate of the Ephesians 4:11 functioning ministries.

There are three defining words in Ephesians 4:7 that need commentary for further elucidation.

GRACE means God's divine attributes and unmerited favorable influence on a Believer. It particularly means God's divine indulgence to express His beauty, *agape* love, mercy, clemency, order, protection, favor, excellence, wisdom, knowledge, power, righteousness, holiness, and sanctification upon a Believer, usually to activate a particular gift or enablement of a gift bestowed upon the Believer. God's grace gives a minister's work beauty, honor, elegance, dignity, and crown jewels.

Grace is given as against the exercise of selfassertion and selfwill. Grace is the authority, power, and favor of God given to someone to complete the task or purpose God requested him or her to do. The grace given by God keeps spiritual matters flowing in a Godly manner. Grace carries with it the *exousia* authority, the *kratos* territorial assignment, and the *dunamis* power necessary to fulfill the functional work of the office ministry in the territory assigned especially to the Ephesians 4:11 minister and the activated ministry of every Believer. In the New King James, functioning apostle Paul declares in 1 Corinthians 15:910, "For I am the least of the apostles, who am not worthy to be called an apostle, because I persecuted the church of God. (10) But by the grace of God I am what I am, and His grace toward me was not in vain; but I labored more abundantly than they all, yet not I, but the grace of God *which was* with me." Thus, grace is the divine impartation of God's *agape* love, assignment, authority, power, and engiftment through His divine favor (or grace) bestowed upon the Ephesians 4:11 minister and all activated ministers called to accomplish God's purpose and will here on earth.

MEASURE refers to the dimension, quantity, or capacity as ascertained by comparison with a standard established by God. The measure of a Believer's spiritual Gift refers to the extent or degree, a fitting amount, and an action taken to an end. God's measure of a Believer's spiritual Gift means that God's poetic or artistic expression of the gift in and through a Believer is bestowed upon the Believer with God's order and purpose for its use. God's measure of a Believer's spiritual Gift is the degree of authority, power, anointing given by God to actuate the spiritual Gift. God's measure also means to mark off or apportion, usually with reference to a given unit of measurement. The spiritual Gift proves God has His mark on the chosen Believer. God's measure also means 1. A standard of comparison of the Believer's spiritual Gift with others having the same spiritual Gift: a. test, b. standard, c. mark, d. criterion, e. gauge, f. benchmark, g. touchstone, h. yardstick; 2. That which has a relative intensity or amount, as of a quality or attribute concerning the Godgiven spiritual Gift: a. degree, b. extent, c. proportion, d. magnitude; 3. That which is allotted in the dispensation by God of the spiritual Gift: a. part, b. lot, c. share, d. portion, e. allotment, f. allowance, g. allocation, h. ration, i. quota; 4. Measure also means the formal product of the function of an Executive, Legislative, or Judicial office or body in the operation of the duties of that office or body of the Believers involved. Thus, it refers to the anointed spiritual officegift function of establishing doctrines of the faith and handing them down to other Believers. It also means the adjudication over those doctrines of faith in disputes between Believers. Thus, each Ephesians 4:11 minister is to function in spiritual or legal measures while exercising his or her responsibilities in the authority of that office Gift. In this context, measure means law, b. act, c. legislation, d. statute, e. enactment; and 5. the regular recurrence of strong and weak elements, such as stressed and unstressed notes in music: a. rhythm, b. beat, c. meter, d. swing, e. cadence. It can mean that the spiritual Gift has with it the measures to be taken to maintain God's steps in fulfilling His purpose.

GIFT means not based upon work done or merit earned but bestowed upon a Believer by our benevolent God having a donative heart. Gift also means: 1. A God given spiritual capability: a. a new faculty, b. a new talent, c. a new aptitude, d. a new specific divine calling; 2. A thing, office, or power bestowed upon someone freely: In the context of Ephesians 4:11, it is the specific function and authority of the offices of the apostle, prophet, evangelist, pastor, or teacher; 3. Something bestowed upon or in another with a donative intent: a. contribution, b. charity, c. offering, d. donation, e. beneficence, or f. beneficiary of a trust.

THE PURPOSE OF EPHESIANS 4:7 BECOMING A SPIRITUAL REALITY

Again, Ephesians 4:7 says, "But unto every one of us is given grace according to the measure of the (spiritual) gift of Christ." Ephesians 4:11-16 reveals what happens when Ephesians 4:7 becomes a spiritual reality.

The preceding three verses before Ephesians 4:7 give an explanation of the purpose of Ephesians 4:7-16. Ephesians 4:4-6 says, "There is one Body, and one Spirit, even as ye are called in one hope of your calling; (5) One Lord, one faith, one baptism, (6) One God and Father of all, who is above all, and through all, and in you all."

God's purpose of Ephesians 4:11-16 is to activate Believers for the work of the ministry (Vocations), and through that work of ministry to mature Believers to become Christ like. Additionally, God's purpose is to have Believers stay on the narrow spiritual path to make every part of the Body of Christ spiritually functioning for the betterment of all Believers as they are transformed in holiness and righteousness as the mature Body of Christ and eventually the Bride of Christ.

The Ephesians 4:11 functioning ministers were established by Jesus' divine nature, God the Word, and Jesus' humanity nature, the only begotten Son of God, for the purpose of activating members in the Body of Christ with the given grace according to the measure of their spiritual Gifts of Christ. The Ephesians 4:11 functioning ministers will receive awareness of their spiritual calling. In that spiritual activation, the Ephesians 4:11 functioning ministers often will revealed the venue where the Believer will minister to fulfill God's purpose for which they were born.

The manifold grace of God will manifest as the Believer Business Owners teach scholastically and train kinesthetically the Believer Business Employees who gain incremental spiritual maturity by employing biblical economic principles, expressing *agape* love, maintaining biblical morality, developing heartfelt humility in serving others while faithfully working in business as a ministry to fulfill the needs of customers and clients. Through repetitive scholastic teaching and kinesthetic training daily, both the Believer Business Owners and Believer Business Employees experience *zoe* life abundantly in seeking first the biblical truth in God's Kingdom that manifests spiritual freedom and Christ's spiritual liberty with the manifold grace of God according to the measure of the spiritual Gifts ministered one to the other.

1 Peter 4:10 says, "As every man hath received the gift, even so minister the same one to another, as good stewards of the manifold grace of God."

There must be free flowing of engiftments in the Ephesians 4:11 functioning ministers by the grace given to them for the equipping of Believers for the edification of the Body of Christ. There are principles which bring the ministry activation by the functioning of the Ephesians 4:11 Business ministers that manifest while working daily in business at the workplace.

As pertains to Believer Business ministers, there must be trustworthiness in the relationship between the Ephesians 4:11 Believer Business Owners and the Believer Business Employees for continuous maturation of the souls of both the Believer Business Owners and Believer Business Employees. The task of Believer Business Owners as Ephesians 4:11 functioning ministers is effectively transforming the Believer Business Employees' souls through reading the Bible before work, praying, teaching biblical economics, elevating the activity of servanthood, demanding strict ethical morality, if possible sharing a percentage of profits with the employees as an incentive, clearly inculcating the foundational and directional plans of the business, the expectation of every Believer Business Employee to show *agape* love to others, with an expectation of excellence and continuous increase in talents and applied knowledge.

God's economic principles can be found in this author's book titled: How God Transfers Wealth to His Business Servant. Also, you can learn about the insidiousness of money where you can discern those people who have fractures in their personalities trying to mend with money in the author's book titled, The Personality Traits of Money.

This spiritual maturation at the workplace comes from a continuous spiritual fellowship with the Godhead and Jesus' humanity nature, along with spiritual fellowship with each Believer Business Owner and Believer Business Employee that works at the business, not just studying books.

A Believer is not activated into ministry just by graduating with a seminary degree, but rather being called, matured, and released through laying on of hands, and through further ongoing kinesthetic training by mature Ephesians 4:11 functioning ministers. The new minister must also have the impartation of the anointing for the activation of spiritual Vocations and spiritual Gifts and enter the process of his soul's spiritual transformation and maturation.

Timothy in the Bible is a good example. 1 Timothy 4:14 says, "Neglect not the gift that is in thee, which was given thee by prophecy, with the laying on of the hands of the presbytery." 2 Timothy 1:6 says, "Wherefore I put thee in remembrance that thou stir up the gift (Greek-*charisma*) of God, which is in thee by the putting on of my hands." These two scriptures show how the spiritual gift (*charisma*) of God was bestowed upon Timothy when Paul and the presbytery laid hands upon him. The laying on of hands is one of the six doctrines of the functioning apostles and is coming in agreement with the Holy Spirit to activate the Believer into ministry (Hebrew 6:1-2).

Some Ephesians 4:11 functioning ministers rely on their *charisma* and stop developing character through the spiritual transformation and maturation of their souls, which is the ridding the soul of the influence of the flesh. They can operate their *charisma* for a season, but eventually they will not be able to depend on their gifting and calling alone as their character flaws in their souls will become publicly known.

Romans 12:2 says, "And be not conformed to this world: but be ye transformed by the renewing of your mind, that ye may prove what is that good, and acceptable, and perfect, will of God." In 1 Timothy 4:12, Paul admonished Timothy, "Let no man despise thy youth; but be thou an example of the Believers, in word, in conversation, in charity, in spirit, in faith, in purity." Similarly, James counseled in James 1:2-4, "My brethren, count it all joy when ye fall into divers temptations; (3) Knowing this, that the trying of your faith worketh patience. (4) But let patience have her perfect work, that ye may be perfect and entire, wanting nothing."

Each Believer Business Owner and each Believer Business Employee must submit to spiritual transformation of their soul from carnality to spirituality through the loving discipline of God the Father (John 15:2), God the Word (Ephesians 5:26-27), and God the Holy Spirit (Romans 8:13). In submitting to this discipline, each Believer must develop his or her own humble relationship with Jesus' humanity nature and the Godhead. The goal of spiritual soulish transformation unto spiritual maturation is stated in Ephesians 4:13, which says, "Till we all come in the unity of the faith, and of the knowledge of the Son of God, unto a perfect man, unto the measure of the stature of the fulness of Christ." In Ephesians 4:13, the word "perfect" in the passage is the Greek *teleios* which means in Strongs G5046, "*complete* (in various applications of labor, growth, mental and moral character, etc.); neuter *completeness:* - of full age, man, perfect."

The Believer Business Servants must mature through transformation of their souls to match the spiritual perfection in their born again spirits. The Believer Business Servant's born again spirit is incorruptible (1 Peter 1:23), is perfect (Hebrews 12:23 - *teleios*), does not sin (1 John 3:9), is absolutely holy and righteous as the New Man (Ephesians 4:24), is joined with Christ as one spirit (1 Corinthians 6:17), because he is a new creature in Christ (2 Corinthians 5:17). The goal in soul maturation of each Believer servant of God in Ephesians 4:13 is the spiritual unity of the faith, and of the knowledge of the Son of God, unto a perfect man, unto the measure of the stature of the fullness of Christ.

This means the process of the Believer's mind, emotions, and heart emulating Jesus' humanity nature and emulating the Believer's born again spirit. As the soul matures to be more like Christ's humanity nature and the Believer's born again spirit, Jesus said in Matthew 18:19, "Again I say unto you, 'That if two of you shall agree on earth as touching anything that they shall ask, it shall be done for them of My Father which is in heaven.'" Besides agreement with a fellow Believer, this also means if your soul comes into agreement with your born again spirit, then whatever you ask of God, He will do it because it is in line with God's will.

This process of soul transformation unto maturation makes the Believer Business Owners and Believer Business Employees anointed, mature servants of the Lord Jesus Christ; and that is the reason that good character is more important than *charisma*. The Believer Business Servants must daily accept Galatians 2:20 as the submissiveness that is required for spiritual maturation, "I am crucified with Christ: nevertheless, I live; yet not I, but Christ liveth in me: and the life which I now live in the flesh I live by the faith of the Son of God, who loved me, and gave Himself for me."

Soul spiritual transformation unto spiritual maturity will take several years, and generally a lifetime. Each submitted, humble Believer continues to mature spiritually throughout his or her entire life. Each Believer also must continue in fellowship where the Lord's divine nature, God the Word, brings His presence in the gathering. There are different measures of spiritual Gifts, and there are different levels brought through humility as spiritual servants, as greater humility unto spiritual servanthood increases the stature of maturity of Believer Business functioning ministers here on earth.

The *Ekklesia* in business requires the functioning of the Ephesians 4:11 Believer Business Owner ministering incremental daily steps of maturation to the Believer Business Employees through spiritual scholastic teaching and hands on spiritual kinesthetic training eight to ten hours a day for five to six days a week, and the result will be that the *Ekklesia* in business is redefined to impact all of society, especially at the workplace and marketplace.

God has an order to bring forth the Ephesians 4:11 Believer Business Owners, and God has an order to equip His Believer Business Employees for the work of ministry for the edification of the Body of Christ while being about God the Father's business. God's plan is to expand and spiritually mature the *Ekklesia* by manifesting the full measure of Christ's grace gifts through His transformed and mature Believer Business Servants.

There is a diversity in the function of the Ephesians 4:11 Believer Business Owners, even though there is unity in all their joint goals of equipping and building up the total Body of Christ while they are working and earning needed finances through profits from the business. When a Believer comes to the workplace not only to earn money to pay living expenses but instead sees the business as his or her place of ministry, then he or she will be earning a living instead of just earning money for existence. There is a major difference in production when an employee works just to exist financially instead of working to experience *zoe* life at the workplace. Experiencing zoe life at the workplace is fulfilling a soulish desire to bring Christ's spiritual kingdom to earth for the betterment of mankind. Believer Business Servants must stop eating fruit from the Tree of the Knowledge of Good and Evil and choose to partake of the eternal spiritual fruit from the Tree of *zoe* Life.

Each of the Ephesians 4:11 Believer Business Owners work in equipping the Believer Business Employees for the work of the ministry to make Ephesians 4:7-13 a spiritual reality in their lives that affect the greater plurality of the Body of Christ, especially those who are called into business as their ministry.

Ezekiel 37:7-10 is a prophecy of the nation of Israel coming together, but it also can be seen as a prophecy of the Body of Christ by the anointing of the Holy Spirit that causes new *zoe* life, symbolizing the unification of Believers all fitting together as one Body of Christ. "So, I prophesied as I was commanded; and as I prophesied, there was a noise, and suddenly a rattling; and the bones came together, bone to bone. (8) Indeed, as I looked, the sinews and the flesh came upon them, and the skin covered them over; but *there was* no breath in them. (9) Also, He said to me, Prophesy to the breath, prophesy, son of man, and say to the breath, 'Thus says the Lord GOD: "Come from the four winds, O breath, and breathe on these slain, that they may live."'" (10) So I prophesied as He commanded me, and breath came into them, and they lived, and stood upon their feet, an exceedingly great army."

The regathering of Israel is a pattern of the reuniting of the various members of the Body of Christ, especially in the field of business for marketplace evangelism and transformation unto maturation of the souls of the Believer Business Servants because the work at the business is where the Lord's

Body of business Believers work eight to ten hours a day, five to six days a week. First, there is noise and activity. Then "bone to bone" members are joined together based on function, spiritual gifts, and grace given. Then the Holy Spirit becomes the breath of each Believer that exudes God's *zoe* life to everyone working in the business, along with the clients or customers that seek service or product being offered by God's Business Servants.

The measure of a Believer's spiritual Gift also is defined by the boundaries of ministry calling and the Ephesians 4:11 office authority granted by Jesus Christ humanity nature, in agreement with the entire Godhead. The measure of the Believer's gift is the magnitude of authority, and the gift is the function of the Ephesians 4:11 minister, along with the rulership assignment connected with it.

Every position of authority, whether the President of General Motors, the President of the United States, or the Governor of a State has a measure of authority that is inherent in the functional territorial authority based on the assignment given. For example, the Governor of the State of California has no territorial authority to exercise his or her official governmental functional executive authority and power concerning the governmental executive matters of the State of Arizona, although the Governor will be given great respect if he or she visits the Governor of Arizona. Likewise, the Governor has authority and power only when exercising the duties of his or her office, as opposed to the legislative or judicial branches of government. Thus, the Governor has no authority to decide a dispute between two litigants in a civil lawsuit, as a judge in the judicial branch of government has that authority. The authority granted Believer Business Owner ministers and Believer Business Employee ministers are assigned based upon the venue of the business. The functioning apostle, prophet, evangelist, pastor, and teacher can all exercise their spiritual Gifts in the business workplace in the venue assigned. The operational gifts of the Ephesian 4:11 ministers in business will have a dynamic effect in preaching the gospel of the Kingdom and preaching repentance and remission of sins in the workplace or marketplace in the assigned venue that is a given geographical territory, such as a city, county, state, country, or internationally.

Similarly, the measure of authority and power of the Ephesians 4:11 minister office depends on the territorial assignment and the specific ministry purpose of the office granted by God. For example, a General of the Army has a greater measure of authority because of his assignment and responsibility of that rank over a Captain in the same Army. Therefore, God appropriates authority and power based upon the office gift, responsibility, purpose, and the territorial assignment. God's grace will flow when the Believer is exercising his or her duties in the office engiftment and in the performance of the task assigned to him or her by God to fulfill God's purpose.

The General of the Army has little if any authority in the Navy. The Navy is run by Admirals, not Generals. Thus, the General of the Army has great authority in the Army, but no authority in the Navy, although the General of the Army would be respected by the Officers in the Navy when they come together. A functioning pastor gift is different than the functioning apostle, prophet, evangelist, or teacher, and a pastor gift of one congregation, and the Ephesians 4:11 functioning minister must submit to the local pastor's authority when visiting the local pastor's congregation. Again, the local functioning pastor must respect and recognize the anointing of the visiting Ephesians 4:11 functioning minister. However, since this territory visited is not the authoritative assignment of the visiting Ephesians 4:11 functioning minister, then to exercise the anointing and gift in the local congregation, the visiting Ephesians 4:11 functioning minister must seek permission and honor the Ephesians 4:11 functioning minister having authority over that territory. The territory jurisdiction is the Vocation as Lord, which references the area on earth that a Ephesians 4:11 functioning minister has been granted authority. This is why in law there are "landlords," and authority as a lord over a territory in ministry is a Vocation venue.

Chosen by Jesus' divine nature, God the Word and Jesus' humanity nature, as God's only begotten Son, the Believer Ephesians 4:11 functioning ministers must be satisfied with the **grace** flowing that determined the **measure** of the spiritual **Gift** bestowed. Paul discussed this point in 2 Corinthians 12:7-9, which says, "And lest I should be exalted above measure by the abundance of the revelations, a thorn in the flesh was given to me, a messenger of Satan to buffet me, lest I be exalted above measure. (8) Concerning this thing I pleaded with the Lord three times that it might depart from me. (9) And He said to me, 'My grace is sufficient for you, for My strength is made perfect in weakness.' Therefore, most gladly I will rather boast in my infirmities, that the power of Christ may rest upon me."

The functioning apostle Paul did not try to increase the measure of authority in his office gift. God's grace was sufficient for Paul, and God's grace is sufficient for every Believer if the Believer stays true to the Believer's calling, office gift, and specific portion of the world assignment as lord. Paul's specific assignment was primarily to the Gentile people living in nations outside Israel. If the Believer goes beyond the parameters and venue of his or her office, calling, and assignment, then the Believer will be attacked by the devil because the Believer trespassed someone else's world assignment. It is important for the Believer to stay in his or her spiritual office Gift, calling, and assignment to prosper being about the Father's business in that territory and assignment. If the Believer Business Servant stays in his or her assigned territory, God will give the Ephesians 4:11 Believer the grace to go through any trial or tribulation. Notwithstanding, if the world assignment is too large for one Ephesians 4:11 functioning minister, then God often sends a group of Ephesians 4:11 functioning ministers for that assignment for that given part the world that God wants to bring His Kingdom manifestation.

The obedient Believer Business Servant will prosper even when the economy is bad, as Isaac did because he stayed in the Promise Land during the famine and did not go to Egypt, which represents the world. In Genesis 26, God appeared to Isaac and instructed him not to go to Egypt, but instead to stay in the land that God gave him. Genesis 26:2-3 says "And the LORD appeared unto him (Isaac), and said, 'Go not down into Egypt; dwell in the land which I shall tell thee of: (3) Sojourn in this land, and I will be with thee, and will bless thee; for unto thee, and unto thy seed, I will give all these countries, and I will perform the oath which I sware unto Abraham thy father,'" Isaac obeyed and settled in Gerar, where he prospered greatly despite the famine and the hostility of the Philistines. Genesis 26:12-16 says "Then Isaac sowed in that land, and received in the same year an hundredfold: and the LORD blessed him. (13) And the man waxed great, and went forward, and grew until he became very great: (14) For he had possession of flocks, and possession of herds, and great store of servants: and the Philistines envied him. (15) For all the wells which his father's servants had digged in the days of Abraham his father, the Philistines had stopped them, and filled them with earth. (16) And Abimelech said unto Isaac, Go from us; for thou art much mightier than we."

If the Ephesians 4:11 functioning minister goes outside his or her office gift, calling, and assignment, the Ephesians 4:11 functioning minister could violate his or her spiritual office Gift. God expects the Ephesians 4:11 Believer to have integrity of the spiritual office Gift. The Believer is admonished to never go beyond the measure and assignment of his or her spiritual office Gift. Those who do usually will fall from grace.

The Ephesians 4:11 Believer Business Owners functioning apostles, along with the Believer Business Owners functioning prophets, must be about the Father's assignment of laying the foundation of Christ Jesus upon which to build His *Ekklesia* in the business (Luke 2:49; Ephesians 2:20). If they are faithful to this call, God will make sure that His grace is sufficient for them. What all the Ephesians 4:11 Believer Business Owners need is the grace that balances out the measure of the Gift that God bestowed upon him or her. God expects each Ephesians 4:11 Believer Business Owner to accomplish his or her assigned tasks in the territory that God assigned to him or her to minister and flourish there.

Christ was, within Himself, the Pattern for all that the Ephesians 4:11 Believer Business functioning ministers are to emulate. As the Business Messiah, while here on earth, Jesus fulfilled all the spiritual office Gifts of the apostle (Hebrews 3:1), prophet (John 1:1; Mark 6:4; Hebrews 4:12), evangelist (Mark 1:14-15; Luke 10:2; John 4:35), pastor/shepherd (John 10:11; 1 Peter 5:4), and teacher (John 1:38; 3:2).

Jesus often chose Ephesians 4:11 Believers who were in the marketplace and businesses to be His disciples and apostles, because to a degree they already had experience in dealing with people and knew how to take charge as leaders in the *Ekklesia* to lead other Believers. Believer Business Employers know how to assign work projects and how to choose the best Believer Business Employees to perform the business task to complete the assignment. The gospel flows through Believer Business Employers and Believer Business Employees in the government, schools, professions, businesses, and every place where people are drawn into relationships and business interactions. Jesus chose the Ephesian 4:11 functioning ministers having the experience in business because they already knew how to relate with the problems of people in the world that they already encountered in their daily workdays. As Believer Business Owners, Peter, Andrew, James, and John were fishermen who had employees, so they had authority experience. Likewise, the Centurion had experience with military authority and knew that Jesus, being a Jew, under the law, was forbidden to enter a Gentile home. The Centurion understood Jesus' authority from God because the Centurion was a man of authority over others and at the same time a man under authority to whom he was submitted. Jesus said He did not see such great faith in all of Israel (Matthew 8:5-13), and without Jesus touching the Centurion's servant, his servant immediately was healed.

Also, Peter's experience of authority over his employees in business inspired Peter to hear from God that Jesus' authority was from God as the Christ (Matthew 16:16-17). Thus, the Centurion and Peter recognized authority as connected with faith and revelation. In Acts chap. 10, the Holy Spirit gave Peter a vision of a sheet full of four-footed beasts of the earth, and wild beasts, and creeping things, and fowls of the air that were forbidden by the law to eat by the Jews, but the Holy Spirit told Peter three times to eat the unclean food. At first, Peter refused as the things in the sheet were forbidden by the law; so the Holy Spirit had to tell Peter three times to eat, knowing that Peter also denied Jesus three times by the time morning was about to come and the rooster crowed (Matthew 26:34; Luke 22:34; John 13:38).

Peter was stubborn and doubted the vision, so the Holy Spirit said in Acts 10:19-20, "While Peter thought on the vision, the Spirit said unto him, 'Behold, three men seek thee. (20) Arise therefore, and get thee down, and go with them, doubting nothing: for I have sent them.'" The unclean animals represented the Gentiles that Jews were forbidden under the law to enter into their homes as the Centurion acknowledged, but from that vision Peter heard and finally obeyed the Holy Spirit to accept the invitation and urging from the Gentile, Cornelius of the Italian Band. Peter led Cornelius' whole household to the Lord, and while Peter was speaking, the Holy Spirit fell upon them. Then, Cornelius' whole household started speaking in tongues. This was a definite sign to Peter that God wanted the Gentiles to become Believers, so Peter ordered that they be baptized. Peter was the first of Jesus' functioning apostles to lead Gentiles to the Lord, and Peter realized that Jesus and the entire Godhead wanted to fulfill the Abrahamic covenant that through Abraham's Seed all families and all nations on earth would receive the blessings of salvation and reconciliation back to God (Genesis 12:3, 22:18; Galatians 3:16).

THE BIBLITARIAN KINESTHETIC TRAINING SCHOOL OF BUSINESS IN MINISTRY

Jesus saw that Peter, Andrew, James, and John were not just fishermen, but He kinesthetically trained them to be "fishers of men" (Mark 1:17). The Ephesians 4:11 Believer Business Owners have business talents that will be enhanced by their functioning spiritual office Gifts and anointing. On the day of Pentecost, Peter stood up as a fisher of men, and through his functioning spiritual office Gift, 3,000 souls were saved that day. This was a great catch for this fisher of men.

Since God always anoints of the Holy Spirit and empowers Believers to accomplish His purposes here on earth for His Kingdom's sake, God calls and gives His special grace to engift His Ephesians 4:11 Believer Business Owners. Their assignment is to equip the Believer Business Employees in their spiritual Vocations and spiritual Gifts in ministry to edify Christ's body into the unity of faith and knowledge of the Son of God to fulfill His purpose in establishing His Kingdom and maturing the Body of Christ to the stature of the fullness of Christ (Ephesians 4:11-13).

Each Believer Business minister has been anointed with the Holy Spirit and with power. 2 Corinthians 1:21-22 says, "Now He who establishes us with you in Christ and has anointed us is God, (22) who also has sealed us and given us the earnest of the Spirit in our hearts."

God's restoration plan is to build a glorious *Ekklesia* without spot or wrinkle that she should be without blemish, blameless, and is holy at home with the family, at school with students, in the marketplace with customers, in business with Believer Business Owners and fellow Believer Business Employees, and every place to change people's lives in receiving initial salvation and then transforming and maturing their souls. God's gift to the *Ekklesia* of His Ephesians 4:11 Believer Business Owners as functioning ministers is an awesome responsibility to activate new Believer Business Employees to become soulishly transformed and mature Believer Business Managers who continue in scholastic teaching and kinesthetic training. Once Believer Business Managers have matured with God's Kingdom biblitarian principles and precepts, then a branch office or business can be established in other locations to continue being a scholastically teaching and kinesthetically training business ministry school where there is no tuition and where the students are paid to attend school. This new approach in business expansion could start a revival in every nation.

God's purpose is seen in Ephesians 3:9-11, "... to make all men see what is the fellowship of the mystery, which from the beginning of the world hath been hid in God, who created all things by Jesus Christ: (10) To the intent that now unto the principalities and powers in heavenly places might be known by the church the manifold wisdom of God, (11) According to the eternal purpose which he purposed in Christ Jesus our Lord."

EPHESIANS 4:11 FUNCTIONING BUSINESS MINISTERS ARE CALLED BY GOD THE WORD AND JESUS' HUMANITY NATURE, NOT BY A BELIEVER'S SELF APPOINTMENT

The Ephesians 4:11 Believer Business Owners functioning ministers are proclaimed and called into ministry by Jesus' divine nature God the Word and Jesus' humanity nature, as God's only begotten Son. The Ephesians 4:11 Believer Business Owners functioning ministers cannot be self-proclaimed by man's finite resolve. The Ephesians 4:11 Business ministers have a recognizable grace as a measure of the gift bestowed by Christ. This grace and measure of gift may be ascertained and confirmed by other Ephesians 4:11 Believer Business Owners functioning ministers. Paul said in Ephesians 3:7, "Whereof I was made a minister, according to the gift of the grace of God given unto me by the effectual working of His power." Ephesians 4:11 Believer Business Owners functioning ministers are spiritual office Gifts from Christ Jesus' divine nature and humanity nature, and these Ephesians 4:11 Believer Business Owners functioning ministers will be proven by the effectual working of the *dunimas* power, *exousia* authority, and the biblical illumination that is bestowed upon them. These Ephesians 4:11 Believer Business Owners functioning ministers have been given the awesome responsibility to activate the members of the Body of Christ.

The Ephesians 4:11 Believer Business Owner functioning minister is not earned but is a spiritual Gift from Jesus' divine nature, God the Word and Jesus' humanity nature as God's only begotten Son. One is not spiritually transformed and matured in business by God first and then as a reward is promoted to the spiritual office of an Ephesians 4:11 Believer Business Owner functioning minister. The office of an Ephesians 4:11 Believer Business Owner functioning minister is not an award or prize of great achievement. This would be selfish and an office acquisition through self-indulgence and self-promotion. One does not mature and be promoted to one or more of the spiritual offices of the Ephesians 4:11 ministries of the functioning apostle, prophet, evangelist, pastor, or teacher, as the minister was born with that functioning office gift (Galatians 1:15). Upon accepting God's appointment from eternity past, the Ephesians 4:11 Believer Business Owner functioning minister must submit to being transformed and matured incrementally and continuously. The Ephesians 4:11 Believer Business Owner functioning minister is not restricted exclusively to only one of the Ephesian 4:11 Believer Business Owners functioning minister. An Ephesians 4:11 Believer Business Owners functioning minister may be a Business functioning apostolic teacher, a Business functioning pastoral apostle, a Business functioning apostolic evangelist, Business functioning prophetic pastor, or any other combinations. Yet, the Ephesians 4:11 Believer Business Owner functioning minister is a spiritual office Gift from Jesus as God the Word and Jesus' humanity nature as God's only begotten Son and should be honored in that office gift because he or she received his or her authority from God and anointing from the Holy Spirit.

JESUS IS ALWAYS BELIEVERS' EXAMPLE TO FOLLOW REGARDING EVERYTHING THEIR SOULS THINK, EMOTE, BELIEVE, AND WILLFULLY DO IN BUSINESS

1 Peter 2:19-25 says, "For this is thankworthy, if a man for conscience toward God endure grief, suffering wrongfully. (20) For what glory is it, if, when ye be buffeted for your faults, ye shall take it patiently? But if, when ye do well, and suffer for it, ye take it patiently, this is acceptable with God. (21) **For even hereunto were ye called: because Christ also suffered for us, leaving us an example, that ye should follow His steps:** (22) Who did no sin, neither was guile found in His mouth: (23) Who, when He was reviled, reviled not again; when He suffered, He threatened not; but committed Himself to Him (Father God) that judgeth righteously: (24) **Who His own self bare our sins in His own body on the tree, that we, being dead to sins, should live unto righteousness: by whose stripes ye were healed.** (25) For ye were as sheep going astray; but are now returned unto the Shepherd and Bishop of your souls."

Jesus had to toil in business as a carpenter and stonemason because Adam was punished for his sin by having to work with the sweat of his brow. Genesis 3:19, God says to Adam, "In the sweat of thy face shalt thou eat bread, till thou return unto the ground; for out of it wast thou taken: for dust thou art, and unto dust shalt thou return." Although Jesus never sinned, Jesus suffered and took the heavy labor of our sins upon Himself; so, Believers could enter into the rest that Jesus provided. Jesus said in Matthew 11:28-30, "Come unto me, all ye that labour and are heavy laden, and I will give you rest. (29) Take My yoke upon you, and learn of Me; for I am meek and lowly in heart: and ye shall find rest unto your souls.(30) For My yoke is easy, and My burden is light."

John the Baptist baptized unto sin, but Jesus allowed Himself to be baptized even though He never sinned to fulfill the law. Jesus never sinned as the only begotten Son of God, but He had to learn obedience by the things that He suffered growing up as a child unto manhood. Hebrews 5:8-9 says, "Though he were a Son, yet learned He obedience by the things which He suffered; (9) And being made perfect (Greek *teleioō*, mature, accomplished, consummate in character), He became the Author of eternal salvation unto all them that obey Him."

Jesus never sinned, but Isaiah 53:5-6 prophesized, "But He was wounded for our transgressions; He was bruised for our iniquities: the chastisement of our peace was upon Him; and with His stripes we are healed. (6) All we like sheep have gone astray; we have turned everyone to his own way; and the LORD hath laid on Him the iniquity of us all."

When the prophet spoke, He spoke in the past tense, as if the Messiah had already suffered in the spiritual realm what He was going to experience in the natural realm. Revelation 13:8 says, "And all that dwell upon the earth shall worship him." 1 Peter 1:19-20 says, "But with the precious blood of Christ, as of a lamb without blemish and without spot: (20) Who verily was foreordained before the foundation of the world, but was manifest in these last times for you, whose names are not written in the book of life of the Lamb slain from the foundation of the world."

Jesus committed no sin, but He was crucified on the Roman Cross as an example for us to follow. Paul said in Galatians 2:20, "I am crucified with Christ: nevertheless I live; yet not I, but Christ liveth in me: and the life which I now live in the flesh I live by the faith of the Son of God, who loved me, and gave Himself for me."

Jesus was the Master, yet He washed His disciples' feet. Jesus said in John 13:12-15, "So after He had washed their feet, and had taken His garments, and was set down again, He said unto them, 'Know ye what I have done to you? (13) Ye call me Master and Lord: and ye say well; for so I am. (14) If I then, your Lord and Master, have washed your feet; ye also ought to wash one another's feet. (15) For I have given you an example, that ye should do as I have done to you."

Jesus never disobeyed the law, so He never was subject to the curse of the Law. Yet, for our sakes, Paul stated in Galatians 3:13-14, "Christ hath redeemed us from the curse of the law, being made a curse for us: for it is written, 'Cursed is every one that hangeth on a tree': (14) That the blessing of Abraham might come on the Gentiles through Jesus Christ; that we might receive the promise of the Spirit through faith."

Jesus never sinned, but for our salvation He took our sins and suffered the penalty of death; so, that we could receive the righteousness of God and be saved. 2 Corinthians 5:21 says, "For He hath made him to be sin for us, who knew no sin; that we might be made the righteousness of God in Him."

Jesus, the only begotten Son of God had the wealth of God the Father, but He suffered being poor here on earth to cancel the curse of poverty. So, Believers can become rich if they follow God's economic principles but without greed, avarice, or covetousness. Paul wrote in 2 Corinthians 8:9, "For ye know the grace of our Lord Jesus Christ, that, though He was rich, yet for your sakes He became poor, that ye through His poverty might be rich."

Jesus committed no sin, but He went to hell to free the Old Testament Faithfuls who looked forward for the coming of the Messiah. Jesus went to hell for Believers, so Believers did not have to go to hell. 1 Peter 3:17-21 says, "For it is better, if the will of God be so, that ye suffer for well doing, than for evil doing. (18) For Christ also hath once suffered for sins, the just for the unjust, that he might bring us to God, being put to death in the flesh, but quickened by the Spirit: (19) By which also he went and preached unto the spirits in prison; (20) Which sometime were disobedient, when once the longsuffering of God waited in the days of Noah, while the ark was a preparing, wherein few, that is, eight souls were saved by water. (21) The like figure whereunto even baptism doth also now save us (not the putting away of the filth of the flesh, but the answer of a good conscience toward God,) by the resurrection of Jesus Christ."

Ephesians 4:8-10 says, "Wherefore He saith, 'When He ascended up on high, He led captivity captive, and gave gifts unto men. (9) Now that He ascended, what is it but that He also descended first into the lower parts of the earth? (10) He that descended is the same also that ascended up far above all heavens, that He might fill all things."

John the Baptist declared in John 1:29, ". . .'Behold the Lamb of God, which taketh away the sin of the world.'" The sin of the world was the original sin of Adam and Eve by eating the forbidden fruit. Where did Jesus take the sin of the world? He took the sin of the world to hell and threw the sins of mankind into the bottomless pit in hell.

Jesus went to hell for Believers to overturn the law of sin and death. Jesus' descent first went into hell to carry away the sins of Believers, and went to hell to set free those who were in Abraham's Bosom. Jesus' descent into hell was a victory over sin and death. By entering the realm of the dead Jesus also confronted the ultimate consequence of sin, which is death itself. 1 John 3:8 says, ". . . the Son of God was manifested, that he might destroy the works of the devil." Jesus took away the keys of death and hell. Revelation 1:18 says, "I am He that liveth, and was dead; and, behold, I am alive for evermore, Amen; and I have the keys of hell and of death."

Jesus was sent to hell, and His subsequent resurrection broke the bonds of death. He paid the price for Believers' eternal life by His own precious blood (1 Peter 1:18-19), not just for himself but for all who believe in Him. His victory means that death is not the end for Believers but a passage of hope and of eternal life with God and Christ Jesus.

Jesus said in John 3:13, "And no man hath ascended up to heaven, but He that came down from heaven, *even* the Son of man which is in heaven." Before His death, His descent to hell, and His resurrection, the Gates of Heaven were closed to humanity due to the original sin of Adam and Eve by eating the forbidden fruit. Before Jesus Christ, the faithful children of Israel that believed in the Messiah, upon death, went to Abraham's Bosom. By Jesus defeating death by dying on the Roman Cross, His descending into hell, and His subsequent resurrection, Jesus made it possible for Believers to enter Heaven.

CHAPTER SEVEN

THE BELIEVER BUSINESS OWNER FUNCTIONING APOSTLE

THE BUSINESS FUNCTIONING APOSTLE IS GOD'S GIFT TO ACTIVATE BELIEVER BUSINESS EMPLOYEES AS THE WORKING ADMIRAL WHO LAYS THE FOUNDATION OF SEVERAL *EKKLESIA* BUSINESSES

Ephesians 4:11-16 is edited and provides relevance: "And He gave some as (Believer Business Owner functioning) apostles... (12) for the equipping (spiritual scholastic teaching and kinesthetic training) of the saints (Believers) for the work of ministry (spiritual Vocations and spiritual Gifts in business) for the edifying (help laying a foundation) of the Body of Christ (who are in business) (13) Till we all (Believers in business) come in the unity of the faith, and of the knowledge of the Son of God, unto a perfect (transformed and matured soul of a business) man (or woman), unto the measure of the stature of the fullness of Christ: (14) That we (Believer Business ministers) henceforth be no more children (immature Believers in business), tossed to and fro, and carried about with every wind of doctrine (fallen ideas in the world about business), by the sleight of men, and cunning craftiness, whereby they lie in wait to deceive; (15) but (Believer Business ministers) speaking the truth in love, may grow up (to become mature Believer Business ministers) in all things into Him who is the head even Christ (16) from whom the whole body, joined and knit together (in common purpose) by what every joint supplies (with their spiritual Vocations and spiritual Gifts), according to the effective working (in business) by which every part does its share (of the spiritual work in business), causes growth (spiritual maturation) of the body (of Christ working in business) for the edifying (help laying the foundation) of itself (in business) in (*agape*) love."

THE BELIEVER BUSINESS OWNER WHO FUNCTIONS AS AN APOSTLE IT IS LIKE THE ADMIRAL OF THE FLEET OF BUSINESS SHIPS, AND OFTEN WORKS WITH THE PASTORS OR TEACHERS OF BUSINESS WHO ARE THE CAPTAINS.

The Greek word ***apostolos*** came from the ancient Phoenician language and referred to the highest-ranking officer in the Phoenician Navy. The rank called ***apostolos*** was equivalent to our English word Admiral.

The Navy has many ships, and each ship has a Captain who has the primary authority over that ship. There are lots of ships in a fleet and lots of Captains. Yet, there is only one Admiral over the whole fleet of ships.

In the business of the Lord Jesus Christ and Father God, the Believer Business Owner functioning apostle is destined to be the working Admiral over several businesses. However, in the local business after the foundation has been laid by the Believer Business Owner functioning apostle, the Believer Business Owner functioning pastor or teacher is often the chief ranking officer who has the oversight in that local business. Yet, after the foundation has been laid, the Believer Business Owner functioning apostle can also function as any of the other Ephesians 4:11 functioning ministers. The Believer Business Owner functioning apostle, in furtherance of the maritime analogy, can also be the Captain of the local business; but the Believer Business Owner functioning pastor as the business administrator needs the ongoing authority and foundation overseer of the Believer Business Owner functioning apostle (Admiral). Sometimes, the Believer Business Owner functioning apostle can function as an apostolic prophet, apostolic evangelist, apostolic pastor, or apostolic teacher and will continue to operate and scholastically teach and kinesthetically train the Believer Business Employees.

The Believer Business Owner functioning apostle's real position of authority is to be the **chief among equals** in several businesses which also have Believer Business Owner functioning prophets, evangelists, pastors, teachers, that may perform duties as managers, or who may act as lower ranking officers below the Believer Business functioning apostle. The ranking Navy officers from Admiral top down are Captain, Commander, Lieutenant, Ensign, and Warrant.

Paul, as a Believer Business Tentmaker Owner functioning apostle, took those business skills, along with his scholastic instruction as a Pharisee and legal training "at the feet of Gamaliel" (Acts 22:3) and became the functioning apostle of various local *Ekklesia* where he laid the apostolic foundation. The Believer Business Owner functioning apostle should be identified with a local congregation outside the business, especially in a home gathering for continuous *agape* love, prayerful support, and spiritual *koinonia.* This can include a group of spiritual brothers and sisters who also are Believer Business Servants. This gives the Believer Business Owner functioning apostle, along with his or her family, a place to enjoy fellowship with other Believer Business ministers and to serve and operate in his or her Vocations and spiritual Gifts in a spiritual community setting.

For example, functioning as an apostle, Paul was part of the local *Ekklesia* at Antioch (Acts chapters 13-14), although he founded many congregations of which he functioned as the apostle overseer. Like a Believer Business Owner functioning as a prophet, the Believer Business Owner functioning as an apostle usually has an intimate relationship with leaders of several business *Ekklesia.*

A Believer Business Owner functioning apostle has the special assignment of maintaining and constantly encouraging the Believer Business Employees to work promoting the established spiritual foundation and purpose of the business (1 Corinthians 12:26-29). The Believer Business Owner functioning apostle uses scholastic teaching and kinesthetic training the Believer Business Employees being led by the Holy Spirit and inculcating in the business what the Believer Business Owner functioning apostle hears from God regarding biblical economics, morality, strong work ethic, servanthood, grace, mercy, *agape* love, long run thinking, capturing a market share, and deciding what local charities to donate money, and is motivated to work wholeheartedly and competently as unto the Lord (Colossians 3:17, 23). Using biblical economic laws, economic truths, and biblical clarity as the foundation of the business, customer referrals will be more frequent, which leads to evangelism by preaching at the workplace the gospel of the Kingdom (Matthew 24:14) and by preaching repentance and remission of sins (Luke 24:47). As heartfelt biblical beliefs are expressed by the Believer Business Owner functioning apostle lays the foundation of biblical principles, ongoing soulish transformation, servanthood, humility, morals, truths, obedience, grace, mercy, and *agape* love into the souls of Believer Business Employees, the spreading of God's biblitarian principles, motives, salvation, and actions, then God's Kingdom government will come and God's Will here on earth will be done as it is in heaven (Matthew 6:10).

Customers, clients, and purveyors coming to the business will experience the foundation of righteousness, peace, and joy in the Holy Spirit being exhibited by all the Believer Business ministers in the business, and they will find themselves engaged in the goodness of God by the business entire personnel doing their work with righteousness, peace, and joy. Normally, the visitor to the business will be inspired to partake of the pleasure of God's goodness, seeing the work of faith with God's power being accomplished by the Believer Business ministers (2 Thessalonians 1:11). At the least these customers, clients, and purveyors of the business will become curious because they experience the goodness of God with the testimonies and behaviors of the Believer Business Owner and Believer Business Employees and will come to repentance. This is true business ministry witnessing.

The Believer Business Owner functioning apostle, like an Admiral will set sail of God's business ministry group of business ships of which he or she oversees in divine order and protects all the Believer Business Officers and Sailor Employees, so they will not be in business ships tossed to and fro and carried about with every wind of doctrine in the sea of humanistic dangerous waters of the fallen world oceans (1 Corinthians 11:34; 7:17; 16:12; Ephesians 4:14; 2 Thessalonians 3:14; Colossians 2:5).

Galatians 1:1 says, "Paul, an apostle, (not of men, neither by man, but by Jesus Christ, and God the Father, who raised Him from the dead)." Paul was chosen as a Believer Business Owner and functioned as an apostle while he was yet in his mother's womb. Galatians 1:15, "But when it pleased God, who separated me from my mother's womb, and called me by His grace." In fact, a Believer Business Ephesians 4:11 gift calling is purposed by God before time began, just like God called him or her to be in Christ before the foundation of the world (Ephesians 1:4-5). 2 Timothy 1:9 says, "Who hath saved us, and called us with a holy calling, not according to our works, but according to His own purpose and grace, which was given us in Christ Jesus **before the world began**."

Colossians 1:1 says, "Paul, an apostle of Jesus Christ by the will of God, and Timotheus our brother." 1 Timothy 1:1 says, "Paul, an apostle of Jesus Christ by the commandment of God our Savior, and Lord Jesus Christ, which is our hope." 2 Timothy 1:1 says, "Paul, an apostle of Jesus Christ by the will of God, according to the promise of life which is in Christ Jesus."

Although Paul was primarily a functioning apostle, Paul and Barnabus were functioning in the offices of either an apostolic prophet or apostolic teacher when the Holy Spirit at Antioch set them apart to function in the office as functioning apostles and apostolic teachers and sent them forth to preach and teach the Gospel of the Kingdom and repentance and remission of sins to the Gentiles (Acts 13:13). In Acts 19: 9-10 Paul exercised his gift as an Ephesians 4:11 apostolic teacher and taught daily in the university school of one Tyrannus.

To be clear, Paul was from the beginning called by God and the Lord Jesus Christ to be primarily a Believer Business Owner functioning apostle. Again, a functioning apostle can fulfill any of the other Ephesian 4:11 ministries. Romans 1:1 says, "Paul, a bondservant of Jesus Christ, called to be an apostle, separated to the gospel of God." Likewise, 1 Corinthians 1:1 says, "Paul, called to be an apostle of Jesus Christ through the will of God. . . ."

The Ephesians 4:11 minister functioning as an apostle can fill any of the other functioning minister positions as a prophet, an evangelist, a pastor or a teacher because he or she, along with the minister functioning as a prophet, lays the foundation for the other Ephesians 4:11 ministries (Ephesians 2:20).

The fivefold Ephesians 4:11 functioning ministers are like the fingers on your hand. The **thumb** on the hand is like the **apostle** and is the only digit that can touch all the other fingers. The **forefinger** is like the **prophet** that points the way and is the oracle of God but never contradicts the written scriptures. The **longest finger** is like the **evangelist** that reaches out in the world that preaches the gospel of the kingdom and repentance and remission of sins to draw sinners to God's and Christ for salvation. The **ring finger** is like the **shepherd/pastor** that loves the sheep and leads them to green pastors and still waters. The ring finger is where the wedding ring is worn and is symbolic of one engaged as the Bride of Christ. (Note: There is an ancient belief that a vein, known as the *vena amoris*, meaning vein of love, ran from the ring finger directly to the heart is a myth. While the tradition of wearing an engagement ring or wedding ring on the ring finger persists, the myth is rooted in cultural and symbolic beliefs rather than physical fact.) The **small finger** is like the **teacher** that brings balance, as the teacher illuminates the light, truth, and divine covenant and authority of the Godhead and the Lord Jesus Christ's humanity nature, who are the primary focus and personalities in the Bible. The small finger is like the person drinking a cup of coffee or tea, allowing the small finger to not be in the handle but sticks out to balance the cup.

Saul discarded his Hebrew name and started using his Roman name of Paul because Paul received his call to be an apostle of Jesus Christ directly from Jesus' divine nature God the Word and Jesus' humanity nature as God's only begotten Son when he encountered Him face to face on the road to Damascus. Acts 26:15-17 says, "And I (Paul) said, 'Who art thou, Lord?' And He said, 'I am Jesus whom thou persecutest. (16) But rise, and stand upon thy feet: for I have appeared unto thee for this purpose, to make thee a minister and a witness both of these things which thou hast seen, and of those things in the which I will appear unto thee; (17) Delivering thee from the people, and from the Gentiles, unto whom now I send thee."

A Believer Business Owner functioning apostle is one who is sent by God to a specific place and to specific Believer Business Employees, whom the Believer Business Owner functioning apostle is charged to train through the daily work assignments through scholastic study and kinesthetic training of biblical principles of economics, development of moral character, exhibiting grace, learning truths, being submissive, becoming spiritually mature, and having a heartfelt will for servanthood. Paul was called primarily to function as a Believer Business Owner functioning apostle while he worked as a tent maker and when and where working in his tent making business also shared the gospel of the Kingdom and the repentance and remission of sins. Paul did not distinguish the sacred from the secular, and he did not discard his spiritual calling while he was doing the tent-making business.

Paul reaffirms that he was called and given the revelation as a Believer Business Owner functioning apostle in business as a ministry directly from Christ Jesus' divine nature and humanity nature. Again, Galatians 1:12, 15-17 says, "For I neither received it of man, neither was I taught it, but by the revelation of Jesus Christ.. … (15) But when it pleased God, who separated me from my mother's womb, and called me by His grace, (16) To reveal His Son in me, that I might preach Him among the heathen; immediately I conferred not with flesh and blood: (17) Neither went I up to Jerusalem to them which were apostles before me; but I went into Arabia, and returned again unto Damascus."

Ephesian 4:11 Believer Business Owner functioning apostles must scholastically teach and kinesthetically train Believer Business Employees under God's direction to instill in them biblical words of wisdom, knowledge, and understanding (1 Timothy 2:7; 2 Timothy 1:11). Ephesian 4:11 Business Owner functioning apostles inculcate Godly economic principles, strong work ethic, humility, servanthood, strong ethical morals, daily studying of the Bible, daily praying without ceasing, seeking first the kingdom of God and His righteousness (Matthew 6:33), while always expressing *agape* love as revealed and commanded by God and the Lord Jesus Christ while operating the business and making Jesus Christ's disciples of Believer Business Employees (Matthew 13:34-35; 28:19; Hebrews 6:12).

Believer Business Owner functioning apostles are often called to ordain ministering Believer Business managers or overseers in business. Paul and Barnabas ordained elders in every *Ekklesia* they founded, being obedient to the Holy Spirit (Acts 14:23). For example, Paul took time off from his tentmaking business to be a member of the presbytery that participated with others in the impartation of spiritual gifts at Timothy's ordination (1 Timothy 1:18; 4:14; 5:22; 2 Timothy 1:6; 4:6; Romans 1:11).

In the business venue, the Believer Business Owner functioning apostle should be involved in leading the unsaved to the Lord and leading Believer Business Employees into the baptism of the Holy Spirit; so, they know how their spiritual Vocations and spiritual Gifts function in the Body of Christ (Acts 8:14-17). 1 Corinthians 12: 4-7 says "Now there are diversities of gifts, but the same Spirit. (5) And there are differences of administrations, but the same Lord. (6) And there are diversities of operations, but it is the same God which worketh all in all. (7) But the manifestation of the Spirit is given to every man to profit withal."

The blessing of business profit is not just money in God's Kingdom. A Believer Business Owner functioning apostle, along with the other Ephesians 4:1 Believer Business Owner ministers, have to consider what God determines as profit. There are great spiritual profits in God's Kingdom as His blessings from heaven (Matthew 6:19-21). Ephesians 1:3 says, "Blessed be the God and Father of our Lord Jesus Christ, Who hath blessed us with all spiritual blessings in heavenly places in Christ." God's spiritual blessings are eternal; whereas, the natural blessings of money, assets, and stature received here on earth are indeed to be enjoyed during Believers' lifetimes. Yet, the Believers should always seek the greater rewards and crowns given to faithful servants of the Godhead and the humanity nature of the Lord Jesus Christ for submitting and following the will of God and the Lord Jesus Christ.

Similarly, Isaiah 48:17 says, "Thus saith the LORD, thy Redeemer, the Holy One of Israel; I am the LORD thy God which teacheth thee to profit which leadeth thee by the way that thou shouldest go." Jesus said in Mark 8:36, "For what shall it profit a man, if he shall gain the whole world, and lose his own soul?"

Believer Business Owner functioning apostles should be involved in the scholastic teaching and kinesthetic training of other business ministers the spiritual foundation of how to be entrepreneurs that take the steps to form new businesses or purchase existing businesses and transform them into God's Kingdom businesses. Paul raised up ministers and ordained them to teach faithful men who would also teach other faithful men (2 Timothy 2:2). Paul ordained Dr. Luke, a medical doctor, and Priscilla and Aquilla, who were tent makers to work in the apostolic and teaching ministries. Also, Paul met Lydia, a business woman who made purple dye fabric to sell that fabric to customers, and he led her to the Lord. We all in the Western World owe a lot to Lydia because while Lydia continued in business, she started the first home fellowship *Ekklesia* community in Western Europe.

THE KINGDOM SPECIFIC ASSIGNMENTS AND AUTHORITIES OF THE BELIEVER BUSINESS OWNER FUNCTIONING APOSTLE.

The Believer Business Owner functioning apostle must know the area of his or her assignment.

Some Believer Business Owner functioning apostles are called in business to sell consumer products. Other Believer Business Owner functioning apostles are called into business in the construction industry. A few Believer Business Owner functioning apostles are called as professionals in medicine, dentistry, law, education, or other areas of higher learning.

Romans 11:13 says, "For I speak to you Gentiles, inasmuch as I am the apostle of the Gentiles, I magnify mine office." Paul was specifically called, was given the assignment, and was told by God and the Lord Jesus Christ to preach the gospel of God's Kingdom and repentance and remission of sins to the Gentiles, set in order various engiftments and ministries, and to ordain other *Ekklesia* ministers amongst the Gentile nations, without degradation of the Jewish nation. Paul was a Roman citizen (Acts 22:28) and a Jewish Pharisee (Philippians 3:5-6) before his conversion to Christianity. Paul remained a spiritual apostle while working in his tentmaking business.

Paul declared himself to be a preacher, apostle, and teacher to the Gentiles in 1 Timothy 2:7, which says, "Whereunto I am ordained a preacher, and an apostle, (I speak the truth in Christ, and lie not), a teacher of the Gentiles in faith and verity." (Verity is the unwavering truth of scriptures.) Paul felt it was important to reconfirm his calling to Timothy in 2 Timothy 1:11, which says, "Whereunto I am appointed a preacher, and an apostle, and a teacher of the Gentiles."

Since the Believer Business Owner functioning apostle is the true entrepreneur, who, along with the Believer Business Owner functioning prophet who has the vision, can lay the foundational purpose of the business and determine what steps to activate the Believer Business Employee for God's Kingdom purpose to be fulfilled.

The tentmaking Paul, functioning as a business apostle, like an Admiral of different local congregations where other ministers are functioning as evangelists, pastors, and/or teachers are gathered with the other Believers to express God's Kingdom government, repentance and remission of sins, and the ongoing spiritual transformation of their souls after initial salvation. Ephesians 1:1 says, "Paul, an apostle of Jesus Christ by the will of God, to the saints which are at Ephesus, and to the faithful in Christ Jesus."

Likewise, Scripture shows that the fisherman Peter that was functioning as a business apostle, like an Admiral, also had a specific assignment and sphere of influence over a particular people in various Gentile nations. 1 Peter 1:1-2 says, "Peter, an apostle of Jesus Christ, to the strangers (Greek- *parepidēmos* resident aliens in foreign nations) scattered throughout (Greek- *diaspora*) Pontus, Galatia, Cappadocia, Asia, and Bithynia. (2) Elect according to the foreknowledge of God the Father, through sanctification of the Spirit, unto obedience and sprinkling of the blood of Jesus Christ: Grace unto you, and peace, be multiplied." The word rendered by "strangers" means Jewish Christians who are resident for a time among Gentiles in other nations. In 1 Peter 1:1, Peter, as a fisherman Owner functioning apostle, was a Jewish Christian writing to Jewish Christians in Pontus, Galtian, Cappadocia, Asia, and Bithynia. In 1 Peter 1:2, Peter's addition of the words "sprinkling of the blood of Jesus Christ" show that the recipients of Peter's letter were Christian Jews.

Similarly, James 1:1 says, "James, a servant of God and of the Lord Jesus Christ, to the twelve tribes (Jewish Christians) which are scattered abroad (Greek- *diaspora*), greeting." The same Greek word in 1 Peter 1:1 is used, and, in fact, it seems to have been the same description for all Jewish Christians who did not live in Palestine. 1 Peter 2:11-12 says, "Dearly beloved, I beseech you as strangers (Greek- *paroikos* Jewish Christians resident aliens in a foreign nation) and pilgrims, (Greek- *parepidēmos* Jewish Christians resident aliens in a foreign nation) abstain from fleshly lusts, which war against the soul; (12) Having your conversation honest among the Gentiles: that, whereas they speak against you as evildoers, they may by your good works, which they shall behold, glorify God in the day of visitation."

In each of these scriptures Peter and James contrasted the Jewish Christians in Palestine as the homebase tacitly contrasted with Pontus and those scattered abroad in Gentile nations as the place where the Jewish Christians sojourned.

What is happening in these scriptures is that Peter and James were not recognizing yet that the "Promise Land" was not the strip of land that is called Judah at that time or Israel today, but the true Promise Land where Believers would live that Jesus Christ died for on the Roman Cross was the whole earth. Jesus made that clear in Acts 1:8, where He commanded, "But ye shall receive power, after that the Holy Spirit is come upon you: and ye shall be witnesses unto Me both in Jerusalem, and in all Judaea, and in Samaria, and unto the uttermost part of the earth."

Thus, the venue for ministry of the Believer Business Owners of Ephesians 4:11 functioning apostles, prophets, evangelists, pastors, and teachers scholastically teaching and kinesthetically training of Believer Business Employees is throughout the whole earth.

THE BUSINESS OWNERS FUNCTIONING AS APOSTLES ARE GIVEN DIRECT COMMANDS AND DECREES FROM CHRIST'S DIVINE NATURE THROUGH THE HOLY SPIRIT WHAT TO TEACH AND TRAIN THE BUSINESS EMPLOYEES IN THE BUSINESS.

Acts 1:2 says, "Until the day in which he was taken up, after that He through the Holy Spirit had given commandments unto the apostles whom He had chosen."

Acts 16:4 says, "And as they went through the cities, they delivered them the decrees for to keep, that were ordained of the apostles and Elders which were at Jerusalem."

God sends to His Believer Business Employees special instructions through His foundational ministries of the Believer Business Owner functioning apostles and functioning prophets.

Tentmaking Paul writes in Ephesians 3:4-7, "Whereby, when ye read, ye may understand my knowledge in the mystery of Christ, (5) Which in other ages was not made known unto the sons of men, as it is now revealed unto His holy apostles and prophets by the Spirit; (6) That the Gentiles should be fellow heirs, and of the same body, and partakers of His promise in Christ by the gospel: (7) Whereof I was made a minister, according to the gift of the grace of God given unto me by the effectual working of His power."

The words of the Believer Business Owner functioning apostle have special governmental authority. 2 Peter 3:2 says, "That ye may be mindful of the words which were spoken before by the holy prophets, and of the commandment of us the apostles of the Lord and Saviour." Similarly, Jude 1:17-18 says, "But, beloved, remember ye the words which were spoken before of the apostles of our Lord Jesus Christ; (18) How that they told you there should be mockers in the last time, who should walk after their own ungodly lusts."

The decrees, foundational scholastic teachings, kinesthetic training, along with apostolic doctrines of the New Testament *Ekklesia* were established by God and the Lord Jesus Christ and then were delivered through the functioning apostles, prophets, evangelists, pastors, and teachers, but especially the functioning apostles. Acts 2:42 says, "And they continued steadfastly in the apostles' doctrine and fellowship, and in breaking of bread, and in prayers." Hebrew 6:1-2 says, "Therefore leaving the principles of the doctrine of Christ, let us go on unto perfection; not laying again the foundation of repentance from dead works, and of faith toward God, (2) of the doctrine of baptisms, and of laying on of hands, and of resurrection of the dead, and of eternal judgment." Thus, the spiritual governmental decrees and doctrines of the *Ekklesia* were established by Believer Business Owner functioning apostles of our business Messiah and Savior, Jesus Christ, whose humanity nature worked in business as a carpenter and stonemason, whose humanity nature submits to His business Father God. Jesus was anointed and empowered by the Holy Spirit, Who went around doing good and healing all those oppressed by the devil (Acts 10:38).

The Believer Business Owner functioning apostles sat as those who judged spiritual governmental matters. Acts 15:2-6 says, "When therefore Paul and Barnabas had no small dissension and disputation with them, they determined that Paul and Barnabas, and certain other of them, should go up to Jerusalem unto the apostles and elders about this question. (3) And being brought on their way by the church (*Ekklesia*), they passed through Phenice and Samaria, declaring the conversion of the Gentiles: and they caused great joy unto all the brethren. (4) And when they were come to Jerusalem, they were received of the church (*Ekklesia*), and of the apostles and elders, and they declared all things that God had done with them. (5) But there rose up certain of the sect of the (Christian) Pharisees which believed, saying, 'That it was needful to circumcise them, and to command them to keep the law of Moses.' (6) And the apostles and elders came together for to consider of this matter."

For example, the council of functioning apostles and elders sent a letter signed by James to Paul and the leaders. Acts 15:19-21 states, "Wherefore my sentence is, that we trouble not them, which from among the Gentiles are turned to God: (20) But that we write unto them, that they abstain from pollutions of idols, and from fornication, and from things strangled, and from blood. (21) For Moses of old time hath in every city them that preach him, being read in the synagogues every sabbath day." While the scriptures do not explicitly mention circumcision, the council's decision was that Gentiles did not need to be circumcised and did not need to adhere to most of the Law of Moses. This decision was communicated to the Gentile Believers in Antioch, Syria, and Cilicia through the same letter.

The Believer Business Owner functioning apostles have the authority, grace, and anointing of the Holy Spirit to send, receive, confirm, and ordain other ministers and to lead in laying the foundation of a new work of the Lord. For example, Jesus' Believer Business Owner functioning apostles installed the first deacons of the New Testament *Ekklesia* in Acts 6:56, which says, "And the saying pleased the whole multitude: and they chose Stephen, a man full of faith and of the Holy Ghost, and Philip, and Prochorus, and Nicanor, and Timon, and Parmenas, and Nicolas a proselyte of Antioch: (6) Whom they set before the apostles: and when they had prayed, they laid their hands on them."

Apostles were given the authority to send ministers to put things in order. Acts 8:14 says, "Now when the apostles which were at Jerusalem heard that Samaria had received the word of God, they sent unto them (Business Owner fishermen and apostles) Peter and John." Acts 9:27 says, "But Barnabas took him (Business Owner tentmaker and apostle Paul), and brought him to the apostles, and declared unto them how he had seen the Lord in the way, and that He had spoken to him, and how he had preached boldly at Damascus in the name of Jesus."

POWERFUL SIGNS AND WONDERS FOLLOW THE APOSTOLIC MINISTRIES.

Acts 2:43 says, “And (reverent) fear came upon every soul: and many wonders and signs were done by the (functioning) apostles.”

Acts 4:33 says, “And with great power gave the apostles witness of the resurrection of the Lord Jesus: and **great grace was upon them all**.”

Acts 5:12, 15-16 says, “And by the hands of the apostles were many signs and wonders wrought among the people; and they were all with one accord in Solomon's porch . . . (15) Insomuch that they brought forth the sick into the streets, and laid them on beds and couches, that at the least the shadow of Peter passing by might overshadow some of them. (16) There came also a multitude out of the cities round about unto Jerusalem, bringing sick folks, and them which were vexed with unclean spirits: **and they were healed everyone**.”

2 Corinthians 12:12 says, "Truly the signs of an apostle were wrought among you in all patience, in signs and wonders, and mighty deeds.”

THE ORDER OR RANK OF BELIEVER BUSINESS OWNER FUNCTIONING APOSTLES.

There are 81 references in the Bible to the functioning apostles, with 79 of the references in the New Testament. Although the Old Testament doesn't have direct references to apostles as there is as the New Testament specifically states, it does contain examples of two individuals who performed leadership roles that are theoretically and practically correlated to the work of the functioning apostles in the New Testament.

The business shepherd Moses was a leader and lawgiver, and Moses was sent by God to deliver and lead the Israelites out of Egypt; and he communicated God's Commandments and laws to the Israelites. Also, Moses was led by God to ordain the Levite and Aaron priesthood and followed the instructions of God to establish the Tabernacle in the wilderness and the offerings and much more. Moses was used to lay the foundation of the Israelite religious practices.

While the Bible does not unequivocally state that Joshua had military experience by being in the Egyptian army, it is implied that he would have been involved in some form of military activity during the Israelites' time in Egypt. Joshua immediately became the leader of the Israelite army under Moses, and he led the Israelite army in many battles. Joshua knew how to take orders from Moses and knew how to form an army, establish a battle plan, and knew how to choose leaders in the army, and how to give orders. So, Joshua’s kinesthetic training had to have been from military service as he was accepted as the leader by the Israelite citizens as the Commander in Chief as they headed toward and when they arrived in the Promise Land. Joshua succeeded Moses and led the Israelites across the Jordan River into God’s Promised Land; and obeying God’s command, Joshua declared war and conquered the giants and fought the heathens living in the land. Finally, Joshua divided up the Promise Land amongst the Israelite tribes. These were apostolic foundational functions.

Again, the Greek word *apostolos* is interpreted in English as apostle.

Christ, a journeyman carpenter and stonemason, and His humanity nature as the only begotten Son of God with His divine nature, God the Word, and His humanity is "The apostle and high priest of our confession" (Hebrews 3:1).

God sent Jesus to the earth, to bring the Kingdom of God to earth, to die for sinful mankind, to defeat all the works of the devil, and to bring salvation to all those who accept Jesus Christ as Lord and Savior. God was the One sending Christ Jesus to earth (Galatians 4:4), but then Christ Jesus was the One sending His apostles throughout the whole earth (Acts 1:8). Jesus chose several businessmen to be His apostles, so they could be about His Father's business and could preach the gospel of the kingdom and repentance and remission of sins with signs following (Mark 16:2) . Jesus' miracle signs caused Jewish people to believe that He was sent by God. Matthew 10:40 says, "He that receiveth you receiveth Me, and he that receiveth Me receiveth Him that sent Me." John 3:2 says, "The same (Nicodemus) came to Jesus by night, and said unto Him, 'Rabbi, we know that thou art a teacher come from God: for no man can do these miracles that thou doest, except God be with Him.'"

THE TWELVE APOSTLES OF THE LAMB OF GOD.

The number 12 is the number of governments, especially the government established by the apostolic foundational ministers.

The 12 sons of Jacob were the Foundation Sons of Old Testament Israel (Genesis Chaps. 4849).

The 12 wells of water dug by Abraham symbolized the 12 tribes of Israel and the 12 functioning apostles to come (Exodus 15:27).

The 12 pillars at Mt. Sinai symbolized the 12 tribes of Israel and the 12 functioning apostles to come (Exodus 24).

The 12 princes and their offerings for the dedication of the brazen altar also symbolized the 12 tribes of Israel and the 12 functioning apostles to come (Numbers 7).

The 12 stones with the 12 names of the 12 tribes in the breastplate of the High Priest pointed to the 12 functioning apostles of the Lamb.

The 12 loaves of showbread on the table pointed to the 12 tribes of Israel and the 12 functioning apostles to come (Exodus 25:23-30).

The 12 lions on Solomon's throne (1 Kings 10:20), and the 12 oxen upholding the molten sea in the temple courts pointed to the 12 tribes of Israel and the 12 functioning apostles to come (1 Kings 7:25, 44), and the 12 porters at the gates of Jerusalem, likewise (1 Chronicles 26:13-19).

The City of God, the New Jerusalem, has 12 gates, 12 foundations, 12 names, 12 manners of fruits, 12 gates of pearls, etc. All point to the foundational apostolic governmental ministries.

Jesus said that the authority of the 12 functioning apostles of the Lamb is to sit on 12 thrones in the regeneration and rule over the 12 Tribes of Israel (Matthew 19:28).

POST ASCENSION FUNCTIONING APOSTLES WERE MANY,
WITH VARIOUS MEASURES OF THE GRACE OF APOSTLESHIP.

Matthias (Acts 1:26). Matthias was chosen to fill the position of Judas. Matthias had been with Jesus from the beginning of His ministry and was a witness to His resurrection. The event of filling Judas' position was important because it focused the necessity to maintain the foundation of the 12 apostles of the early church, which symbolized the 12 tribes of Israel and the number of governments.

James, the Lord's brother, who, like Jesus, worked in the family business as a carpenter and stonemason (Acts 1:14; 1 Corinthians 15:7; Galatians 1:19; 2:9) was an apostle, but not one of the twelve apostles.

Paul, a tent maker (Acts 14:14; 22:21), and he also studied law at the feet of Gamaliel (Acts 22:3). From Paul's writings, one can surmise that he had a very educated and complex understanding of the law, especially the law of Moses. Paul affirmed the law's value and holiness (Romans 3:31; 7:12,), while at other times Paul argued for the law's limitations or even the law's end in Christ (Galatians 3:19-26, Romans 10:4). Paul argued that the purpose of the law given to Israel was to reveal sin and the need for a Savior, which is Jesus Christ (Galatians 3:19-26). Finally, Paul also underscored that salvation comes not from following the law, but through faith in Christ (Galatians 2:16).

Barnabas, a landowner, (Acts 4:36-37; 11:22-30; 14:1, 4; 1 Corinthians 9:6). Barnabas was called an apostle in Acts 14:14, and the first century Ekklesia recognized him as an apostle. The book of Acts chronicles Barnabas's significant role in mentoring the functioning apostle Paul. Although Barnabas was not a businessman, his sale of land to support the new Ekklesia demonstrated his financial activity and pure heart to contribute to the needed finances for the birth of the Ekklesia post Jesus' ascension.

Apollos (1 Corinthians 4:69). His work was apostolic. Apollos is described as "an eloquent man, and mighty in the scriptures" (Acts 18:24), so, it is reasonable to believe he was a Jewish Christian. However, he started as a follower of John the Baptist, but Priscilla and Aquilla sat him down and taught him all about Jesus and the gospel of the kingdom and the repentance and remission of sins as the two messages that Jesus commanded to be preached. He worked full time in ministry, going on many missionary trips. He traveled to Ephesus and Corinth, preaching and teaching about Jesus.

Andronicus (Romans 16:7). Andronicus was an apostle, and the Bible describes him in his relationship with Paul, describing Andronicus as being a relative of Paul and an apostle imprisoned with Paul.

Junia was a woman functioning apostle (Romans 16:7). Junia was also a relative of Paul and was in prison at times for the sake of faith. Roman inscriptions from the first century confirm that Junia was a common female name. There's no evidence of a masculine form, "Junias," being used for men in that era. The early church, including Greek and Latin fathers, consistently viewed Junia as a woman. Many early church fathers, including Origen, John Chrysostom, and others, identified Junia as a woman. Remember, the 12 apostles of Jesus were all young men. Apparently, Junia was an older woman and many thought of her as the "mother of the apostles." Because of the prejudice toward women, Mary Magdalene's writings were not canonized. Also, in the 13th century interpreting Junia as a male functioning apostle was likely influenced by patriarchal biases toward women as leaders and limiting their roles in the Catholic Church. The Protestant Reformation started on October 31, 1517, when Martin Luther nailed his 95 Theses challenging the Catholic Church's practices regarding indulgences, was posted on the door of the Castle Church in Wittenberg, Germany. Yet, Martin Luther made changes including cancellation of celibacy of priests, and allowing marriage, but he was prejudice against women having a governing voice in the church. Yet, the consensus among biblical scholars and early church leaders overwhelmingly supported Junia as a mature female apostle.

Epaphroditus (Philippians 2:25 – "messenger" or functioning apostle).

Titus (2 Corinthians 8:23 – "messenger" or functioning apostle delegate).

Two unnamed functioning apostles (2 Corinthians 8:23).

Timothy (Acts 9:22; 1 Thessalonians 1:1; 2:6). Timothy is referred to as an apostle in the sense of being sent with authority from Paul to establish churches, like how Paul was sent by Christ. Timothy was with Paul as stated in 1 Thessalonians 1:1, and Paul stated that those with him were apostles at the same meeting in 1 Thessalonians 2:6.

Judas Barsabbas (Acts 15:23). Acts 15:23 speaks of Judas Barsabbas, who was a leader among the early Christians in Jerusalem. He was sent with Silas (Silvanus) to Antioch. It is believed that along with others he was an apostle that Paul mentioned in 1 Thessalonians 2:6.

Silvanus (Acts 15:23; 1 Thessalonians 1:1, 2:6). Silvanus (also called Silas) who was a leader among the early Christians in Jerusalem. Also, Silvanus was with Paul as stated in 1 Thessalonians 1:1, and Paul stated that those with him were apostles at the same meeting in 1 Thessalonians 2:6.

Erastus (Acts 19:22). In Romans 16:23 Erastus is mentioned as the city treasurer of Corinth and thus was a businessman. Erastus was an apostle delegate who was sent by Paul in the missionary field. Erastus is mentioned alongside Paul in Acts 19:22 and 2 Timothy 4:20. Erastus' role as city treasurer demonstrates the integration of faith and public service within the early Christian community. Since functioning apostles are considered as those who are sent, Acts 19:22 says, "So he (Paul) sent into Macedonia two of them that ministered unto him, Timotheus and Erastus; but he himself stayed in Asia for a season."

Tychicus (2 Timothy 4:12; Titus 3:12). Tychicus as an apostle delegate served the first century Christian *Ekklesia* and was sent by Paul as a messenger, carrying letters and news from Paul to various churches, including those in Colossae and Ephesus. He also was sent to Ephesus to relieve Timothy. Paul sent and described Tychicus in Ephesians 6:21, "But that ye also may know my affairs, and how I do, Tychicus, a beloved brother and faithful minister in the Lord, shall make known to you all things."

In totality, there are 28 functioning apostles mentioned in the New Testament, and several of them were Believer Business Owner functioning apostles while many others were apostle delegates that were sent to do apostolic work.

Ekklesia history, up to the present day, reveals men and women too numerous to name who were or are functioning apostles. Thus, Believer Business Owner functioning apostles are both men and women. Male or female preference has nothing to do with the office of the Believer Business Owner functioning apostle or any of the other Ephesians 4:11 functioning ministers (Galatians 3:28). To exclude women as Ephesians 4:11 functioning ministers is trying to build the Lord Ekklesia on the works of the flesh, not the spirit.

Christ gave the gift of the Believer Business Owner functioning apostle, like the Believer Business Owner functioning prophet, evangelist, pastor, and teacher, according to God's grace and the measure of the gift that He desires to manifest through a particular Believer Business Owner functioning minister (Romans 12:16; Ephesians 4:7).

The businesses and marketplaces will need tens of thousands of Believer Business Owner functioning apostles and/or other Ephesians 4:11 functioning ministers to complete the perfection of the *Ekklesia* in the businesses and the equipping of the Believers for the work of the ministry in their Vocations of kings, priests, lords, ambassadors, and soldiers of the Believer Business Employees to build Christ's glorious *Ekklesia* in business to serve customers and clients in marketplace and lead them to the Lord and serve them with their spiritual gifts.

Paul typifies the last days Believer Business Owner functioning apostles, and Paul stated in 1 Corinthians 15:8, "And last of all He was seen of me also, as of one born out of due time." There is a teaching by some scholars that 12 major functioning apostles like Paul will be born and will lead the *Ekklesia* in the last days to usher in the Lord's return to earth to set up His everlasting Kingdom where He will rule and reign as King with His Spouse and Bride, which is the multi-member Believers (Revelation 5:10). This teaching is a common theme particularly with those that teach on eschatology and the Second Coming of Christ. This teaching of the coming of 12 major functioning apostles like Paul in the end times draws parallels to the 12 functioning apostles chosen by Jesus in the New Testament, who were seen as the foundation of the early *Ekklesia*.

Believer Business Owner functioning apostles today are men and women who are humbled because they know they are unworthy to be Believer Business Owner functioning apostles in the natural, who are like undeveloped, almost aborted fetuses incapable of sustaining any spiritual life by themselves, but through the intervention, anointing, and empowerment of the Holy Spirit (2 Corinthians 1:21; 1 John 2: 18, 20, 27) have been chosen as Believer Business Owner functioning apostles, often sent to deliver God's people out of the evil and corrupt society where they live. These Believer Business Owner functioning apostles will be used to lay the foundation where Believers will be led by the Holy Spirit to end the *Ekklesia* Age and begin the dynamic Kingdom Age (Revelation 21:1-3), which is the business of Father God in fulfilling His desire to take back possession of the earth.

FUNCTIONING APOSTOLIC TEAMS WERE SENT OUT TO LAY THE FOUNDATION OF THE *EKKLESIA*.

At the time of Jesus and after the Feast of Pentecost, there were functioning apostolic teams who went with other Ephesians 4:11 functioning ministers, some of which were businessmen and businesswomen. Luke was a professional Medical Doctor who was a Believer Business Owner functioning apostle. Priscilla and Aquilla were tent maker owners with Paul. Lydia was a purple dye fabric manufacturer.

Our Messiah, Lord, and Savior, Jesus Christ, as the greatest Business Owner functioning Apostle of our confession and high Priest (Hebrews 3:1-2), worked as a carpenter and stonemason which He taught through kinesthetic training of His step brothers to become journeymen carpenters and stonemason, Who then using the same methods kinesthetically trained the 70 disciples two by two as ministers (Luke 10:120).

The Believer Business Owner functioning apostles, as Peter and John, were fishermen by trade, and were sent to Samaria to help Philip, the functioning evangelist, to bring the presence of the Holy Spirit (Acts 8:14) and to rebuke Simon, the magician.

Barnabas, (a landowner functioning apostle), Paul, (a tentmaker Business Owner functioning apostle), and Mark, (nephew of Barnabas, a functioning deacon and evangelist) ministered together (Acts, chapters 13-15).

Paul, (a tentmaker Business Owner functioning apostle) and Silas, (a prophetic apostle), were partners in ministry (Acts 15: 35, 40).

Paul, (a tentmaker Business Owner functioning apostle), Silas (functioning prophetic apostle), Timothy (functioning evangelistic apostle), Luke (a medical doctor functioning apostle delegate), Erastus (city treasurer of Corinth and business functioning apostle delegate) Gaius (baptized by Paul in Corinth and acting as Paul's host who had financial means), Aristarchus (a close companion of Paul, was imprisoned with Paul, traveled with Paul as a functioning apostle delegate through Greece and Asia, and traveled with Paul on his trip to Rome) (Acts 16:1, 18:24, 19:21-41; 20:4; 27:2; Romans 16:23; 1 Corinthians 1:14; 2 Timothy 4:11; 1 Thessalonians 1:1, 6).

Paul (functioning apostle), Silas (functioning prophetic apostle), Timothy (functioning evangelistic apostle), Luke (physician functioning apostle delegate), Aquilla and Priscilla (business functioning apostolic teachers), and Apollos (functioning teacher) (Acts 18:2-24; 2 Timothy 4:11; 1 Thessalonians 1:1, 1:6).

There are many more examples in the Book of Acts, representing team ministries with the Believer Business Owner functioning apostles.

There are functioning apostles by rank, maturity, and calling, and some of them were referred to as the "chiefest apostles." Apostle Paul said in 2 Corinthians 11:5 that, "For I suppose I was not a whit behind the very chiefest apostles." Again, the functioning apostle Paul said in 2 Corinthians 12:11 that, "I am become a fool in glorying; ye have compelled me: for I ought to have been commended of you: for in nothing am I behind the very chiefest apostles, though I be nothing."

THE PURPOSE OF THE MINISTRY OF A BELIEVER BUSINESS OWNER FUNCTIONING APOSTLE.

The Believer Business Owner functioning apostle is given by Christ Jesus to the body of Believers Business Employees in the business and marketplace who has the responsibility to do the following:

First, the Believer Business Owner functioning apostle is to bring foundational order in using scholastic teaching and kinesthetic training to activate, transform, and mature the souls of Believer Business Employees in their Vocations as Kings, Priests, Lords, Ambassadors, and Soldiers for the work of business along with their spiritual Gifts at the workplace. Receiving on the job training by kinesthetic methods, Believer Business Employees will acquire the wisdom, knowledge, and understanding of biblical economic principles, while being directed by a moral compass, a heart for servanthood, a quest to seek first the kingdom of God and His righteousness, having a strong work ethic, motivated by *agape* love, operate with anointing, are not haughty, are not self-centered or vainglory, are not motivated by greed, avarice, or covetousness, are submissive and humble, are not intemperate, extend mercy, are kind, and are generous in sharing the fruit of the spirit.

Second, the Believer Business Owner functioning apostle is to use scholastic teaching and kinesthetic training of Believer Business Employees in applying the principles of the Bible and with humility receive the anointing and power of the Holy Spirit in the workplace unto the Lord, and in furtherance of God the Father's business and the Lord Jesus Christ's business here on earth.

Third, the Believer Business Owner functioning apostle's duties include the ensuring that the business work by the Believer Business Employees are edifying the Body of Christ, advancing the kingdom of God, and building the Father's business and the Lord Jesus Christ's business in the marketplace, recognizing that God is omnipresent and is concerned about the livelihood and wellbeing of His adopted children (Matthew 6:33; Romans 8:15, 28; Ephesians 1:3; Philippians 4:19).

Fourth, the Believer Business Owner functioning apostle is to unify Believers Business Employees in the business with the mandate of Ephesians 4:2-6, that says, "with all lowliness and meekness, with longsuffering, forbearing one another in love; (3) Endeavoring to keep the unity of the Spirit in the bond of peace; (4) There is one body, and one Spirit, even as ye are called in one hope of your calling; (5) One Lord, one faith, one baptism, (6) One God and Father of all, who is above all, and through all, and in you all."

Fifth, the Believer Business Owner functioning apostle is to bring Believer Business Employees to the knowledge of how the Son of God through the Holy Spirit works perfectly the business mandated by Father God to bring the Believer Business Employee into continuous spiritual soulish transformation leading to spiritual soulish maturation unto a perfect man to the stature of the fullness of Christ (Luke 2:49, Ephesians 4:13).

Sixth, the Believer Business Owner functioning apostle should do spiritual counseling with the Believer Business Employees about the foundation of their beliefs in their hearts. Most Believer Business Employees have fractures in their souls, which need to be mended. Yet, the Believer Business Owner functioning apostle cannot spend everyday counseling with each Employee, but the Believer Business Owner functioning apostle should teach each employee the truth that the Godhead lives inside of them as they, individually and collectively, are the temple of God (2 Corinthians 6:16; 1 Corinthians 3:17; Ephesians 2:21). The Believer Business Owner functioning apostle must remind the Believer Business Employees that they have a responsible purpose to submit to Godhead's transformation of their souls because they must mature spiritually with good people skills and business acumen to become Managers in the current business or another business to be started by the Believer Business Owner functioning apostle as an entrepreneur.

In support of these apostolic duties, also read again Ephesians 4:11-16; Colossians 1:25-29, and Hebrews 6:12.

For example, Paul said in Colossians 1:25-29, "Whereof I am made a minister, according to the dispensation of God which is given to me for you, to fulfill the word of God; (26) even the mystery which hath been hid from ages and from generations, but now is made manifest to His saints: (27) to whom God would make known what is the riches of the glory of this mystery among the Gentiles; which is Christ in you, the hope of glory: (28) Whom we preach, warning every (business) man (and woman), and teaching every (business) man (and woman) in all wisdom; that we may present every (business) man (and woman) perfect (spiritually transformed and matured in their souls) in Christ Jesus: (29) whereunto I also labour, striving according to His working, which worketh in me mightily."

The purpose of the Believer Business Owner functioning apostle in laying a foundation in business is to bring forth the Body of Christ as Believer Business Employees in their fullest splendor with manifold Vocations and Giftings in the business and spreading to the marketplace to be used to establish God's Kingdom in business and commerce here on earth.

Functioning apostle Paul proclaims that God is One and there is the humanity nature of the Lord Jesus Christ. Paul stated in 1 Corinthians 8:6, "But to us there is but one God, the Father, of whom are all things, and we in Him; and one Lord Jesus Christ, by whom are all things, and we by Him." Galatians 1:3 says, "Grace be to you and peace from God the Father, and from our Lord Jesus Christ." Colossians 1:3 says, "We give thanks to God and the Father of our Lord Jesus Christ, praying always for you." 1 Thessalonians 3:13 says, "To the end He may stablish your hearts unblameable in holiness before God, even our Father, at the coming of our Lord Jesus Christ with all His saints."

The submission is a private matter between the Believer Business Employee and the Godhead and the Lord Jesus Christ. The entire Godhead is involved in the transformation of the Believer Business Owner and the Believer Business Employees' souls. God the Father prunes away the flesh's influence out of the Believer Business Employees' souls to bear more spiritual fruit (John 15:2). God the Word uses the *rhema* word of God to cleanse the dirty carnal flesh out of the Believer Business Employees' souls and sanctify the soul with the goal of not having spot, or wrinkle, or any such thing but is spiritually holy and without blemish of carnality (Ephesians 5:26-27). God the Holy Spirit mortifies (kills or starves) the deeds of the flesh that are in the Believer Business Employees' souls to bring greater *zoe* life (Romans 8:13).

When the local *Ekklesia* fellowship has many Believer Business Owners and Believer Business Employees, then the foundation of the Lord's *Ekklesia* and the fruit of the Holy Spirit and His anointing and power are present, it will turn the City, County, State, Country, and the whole world right side up because God's authoritative Kingdom is present and God's Holy Nation is manifesting in glorious revival with God's substituted *zoe* life. The Believer Business Owner functioning apostle will always be involved to some degree in the Christian community at large. The Believer Business Owner functioning apostle has the anointing of God's foundation of morality and biblitarian economic principles to understand how the secular government politicians and bureaucrats in the society should administrate under the leadership of the Holy Spirit and the children of God seeking and promoting God's righteous kingdom here on earth.

The holy and righteous Believer Business Owner functioning apostle bringing his or her knowledge, wisdom, and understanding, along with his or her strong anointing in the community, then the Believer Business Owner functioning apostle becomes a vital part of the plan of secular government because the Believer Business Owner functioning apostle plants the requirement to obey the Godly secular government's business laws that are in line with God's absolute holy and righteous laws. Yet, the Believer Business Owner functioning apostle also has the knowledge, wisdom, understanding, and fortitude to disobey when the secular business regulations are immoral against the foundational absolute laws of God. For example, the Believer Business Owner functioning apostle will try to work around the laws to get the job of building the business accomplished before he or she is advising the Believer Business Employees and Associates to protest and disobey the immoral laws or regulations.

BELIEVER BUSINESS OWNER FUNCTIONING APOSTLES IN MANIFESTING EPHESIANS 4:7-16 SPIRITUAL GOALS

A foundational relevant question is: "What is the God-given primary tasks of the Believer Business Owner functioning apostle as his or her gift relates to the goal of bringing Ephesians 4:7-16 into reality through scholastic teaching and kinesthetic training for the purpose of activating each Believer Business Employee for their work of ministry?"

The Believer Business Owner functioning apostle may be led by the Holy Spirit to use the profits from his or her business to establish homes for unwed mothers with the goal of stopping abortion on demand. The Believer Business Owner functioning apostle may be led by the Holy Spirit to provide foundational finances to build homes that will right other wrongs in the culture. The Believer Business Owner functioning apostle may be led by the Holy Spirit to do godly purposes for the use of business profits in line with God's word. In other words, building homes for the poor is good, but building homes to stop abortions would be better in this time of history because it would be stopping mothers from killing their babies, which is a violation of God's laws of killing the innocent.

The common tasks of all the Ephesians 4:11 Believer business owner functioning ministers is to pray for God's grace needed for the measure of the gift of the Believer business owner functioning ministers in the marketplace as stated in Ephesians 4:7 to edify, activate, and mature the Believer Business Employees into their spiritual Vocations and spiritual Gifts. Every Believer is a functioning minister having a ministry call and a place to exercise the grace given according to the measure of the gift bestowed by God. Many Believers will find their ministry call is in business, whether as Owners or Employees.

The chief purpose of the Believer Business Owner functioning apostle (and the other Ephesians 4:11 functioning ministers) is not to build businesses for just profit. The Believer Business Owner functioning apostle is to lay the foundation to activate business functioning ministers in the workplace, and this primary purpose is the same with the other Ephesians 4:11 functioning ministers as they work with their specific gifts. With God's mandate to seek first the Kingdom of God and His righteousness (Matthew 6:33), it is important to follow God's purpose, grace, and calling and not just launch a good business idea that is profit motivated.

Since most people in Western World society come to businesses as customers to purchase products or as clients to retain services, this influx of potential unbelievers is greater than trying to convince these same unbelievers in society to come to a church building on Sunday morning to go forward in a church meeting to confess their sins and vocalize the sinner's prayer in front of hundreds of people. Thus, the Lord wants Believer Business Owners and Believer Business Employees to take advantage of this phenomenal influx to reach unbelievers in the business to preach the gospel of the Kingdom of God and preach repentance and remission of sins. These unbelievers may not go to a church building, but they will go to a business building that has products and services they want and has mature Believer Business Owners and mature Believer Business Employees that have been spiritually friendly.

Thus, the foundation of the business must be very inviting with friendliness to the public along with selling excellent products and services. The best plan to attract unbeliever clients and customers is to find out what these customers and clients want and provide the best for them, and then start conversations about how good God is and if they have a relationship with Jesus Christ? The goodness of God leads an unbeliever unto repentance (Romans 2:4). Romans 2:4 suggests that witnessing God's kindness and grace, rather than His judgment, can awaken a sense of remorse, guilt, and finally repentance to a change of heart of the unbeliever customer or client, causing them to turn away from sin and toward God by believing that Christ Jesus rose from the dead and confessing Him as Lord (Romans 10:9). Accepting Jesus Christ as Lord is much more submissive than Him as Savior. Accepting Jesus Christ's lordship over the Believer's life is submitting to having his or her soul being spiritually transformed by being scholastically taught and kinesthetically trained in the foundational principles of the Bible and in the spiritual activation for the work of ministry as vocational Kings, Priests, Lords, Ambassadors, and Soldiers, along with spiritual Gifts.

The Believer Business Owner functioning apostles (along with the functioning prophets) will do the first acts of laying down the foundation of the business. The Holy Spirit can then start a spiritual revival in the business where God's holy Kingdom Nation (1 Peter 2:9) also is manifested in the country to reach the unsaved people in the fallen world. The spiritual revival and presence of the Holy Spirit will cause repentance, salvation, becoming born again, and then start the process of spiritually renovating the Believer Business Employee's soul in the ways of the Kingdom for the goal of his or her soul's spiritual cleansing, transformation, maturation, and submission for the purpose of activation in the work of ministry spiritual Vocations and spiritual Gifts (Ephesians 4:12-13; Revelation 1:6; 1 Timothy 5:16; 2 Corinthians 5:20; 2 Timothy 2:3-4; Romans 12:2, 6-8; Ephesians 4:11; 1 Corinthians 12:8-10).

The ultimate maturation of the soul is found in the Believer Business Owner functioning apostle Paul's personal maturation in Galatians 2:20, "I am crucified with Christ: nevertheless I live; yet not I, but Christ liveth in me: and the life which I now live in the flesh I live by the faith of the Son of God, who loved me, and gave Himself for me." Similarly, the Believer Business Owner functioning apostle Paul said in Philippians 3:7-11, "But what things were gain to me, those I counted loss for Christ. (8) Yea doubtless, and I count all things but loss for the excellency of the knowledge of Christ Jesus my Lord: for whom I have suffered the loss of all things, and do count them but dung, that I may win Christ, (9) And be found in him, not having mine own righteousness, which is of the law, but that which is through the faith of Christ, the righteousness which is of God by faith: (10) That I may know him, and the power of his resurrection, and the fellowship of his sufferings, being made conformable unto his death; (11) If by any means I might attain unto the resurrection of the dead."

At the business venue, the Believer Business Owner functioning apostle may be led by the Holy Spirit to work signs and wonders at the business venue. Certain signs, such as physical and soulish healings, prophetic words, words of knowledge, words of wisdom, demonic deliverances, and miracles of finance as the Holy Spirit leads, evidenced of God's presence while doing business (Acts 4:23, 5:12; 2 Corinthians 10:18, 12:12; 1 Corinthians 4:19-20; Romans 11:13, 15:18-19; Acts 3:18, 9:36-43; 16:18).

THE FUNCTIONING APOSTLES ARE EMPOWERED TO ORDAIN MINISTERS IN THE *EKKLESIA*

The Believer Business Owner functioning apostle Paul said in 1 Corinthians 7:17, "But as God hath **distributed to every man**, as the Lord **hath called every one**, so let him walk. And so ordain (Greek- *diatasso*) I in all churches (*Ekklesias*)." The Greek word *Ekklesia* means government assembly or military assembly, depending on the context. The word "churches," anemically translated from the Greek *Ekklesia,* did not and does not mean where church buildings are located. Paul indicates that ordination "in all the *Ekklesias*" is confirming on Believers in that local fellowship that grace and forgiveness are given by God the Father, God the Word, and God the Holy Spirit through the sacrificial work of the Lord Jesus Christ to each Believer, and the Godhead will dispense the measure of grace for each Believer's spiritual Gift to start working in his or her spiritual Vocations as a spiritual king, priest, lord, ambassador, and soldier while seeking first the Kingdom of God and His righteousness and while submitting to the leading of the Holy Spirit.

What Paul confirms is that "God hath distributed to every man" because the Lord has "called every one" as ministers. Christianity is not a spectator business. In God's businesses every worker must work, every worker is gifted, and every worker is blessed of the Lord for their service. 2 Thessalonians 3:10-11 says, "For even when we were with you, this we commanded you, that if any would not work, neither should he eat. (11) For we hear that there are some which walk among you disorderly, working not at all, but are busybodies." The passage encourages a strong work ethic and discouraging being a burden on the local community's resources.

The activation into ministry of 1 Corinthians 7:17 above is close to the activation into ministry of every Believer in Ephesians 4:7, which says, "But unto **every one of** us is given grace according to the measure of the gift of Christ." Again, the Greek word for "ordain" in 1 Corinthians 7:17 is *diatasso,* which means in Strongs G1299, "to arrange thoroughly, i.e., institute, prescribe, appoint, command, give, set in order, ordain." 1 Corinthians 7:17 speaks about activating the **spiritual Vocations**. On the other hand, Ephesians 4:7 speaks about activation of **spiritual Gifts**, especially the functioning gifts as apostles, prophets, evangelists, pastors and teachers. Then using the Ephesians 4:11 engiftments, in Ephesians 4:12 all Believers are to be activated with their spiritual Vocations and spiritual Gifts.

Dia The channel of an act.

Tasso A primary verb which means to arrange in an orderly manner, i.e., assign or dispose to a certain position, to appoint, decide, ordain, or set in order.

The Believer Business Owner functioning apostle confirms by illumination from scriptures and leading of the Holy Spirit that all Believers Business Employees have the same spiritual Vocations but have diversified spiritual Gifts. The Believer Business Owner functioning apostle also may reach out to other Believer Business Owners to disciple them in the ways of Kingdom business principles and how to spiritually scholastically teach and spiritually kinesthetically train their Believer Business Employees. Then, the Believer Business Owner functioning apostle puts the business in order by assigning each Believer Business Employee their work duties where using their spiritual Vocations, using their spiritual Gifts, following God's spiritual principles of economics, seeking first the Kingdom of God and His righteousness, while being guided by moral ethics, servanthood, strong work ethic, repentance, humility, forgiveness, grace, mercy, and *agape* love.

It bears repeating over and over again that all Believer Business Employees must receive on the job biblical scholastic teaching and kinesthetic spiritual training to work with sincerity displaying the fruit of the Spirit. Paul enumerated the fruit of the Spirit in Galatians 5:22-23, which says, "But the fruit of the Spirit is love, joy, peace, longsuffering, gentleness, goodness, faith, (23) Meekness, temperance: against such there is no law."

Paul also admonished Believers in Galatians 5:16-17, "This I say then, 'Walk in the Spirit, and ye shall not fulfil the lust of the flesh. (17) For the flesh lusteth against the Spirit, and the Spirit against the flesh: and these are contrary the one to the other: so that ye cannot do the things that ye would.'"

Paul further reproved in 1 Corinthians 11:31-34, "For if we would judge ourselves, we should not be judged. (32) But when we are judged, we are chastened of the Lord, that we should not be condemned with the world. (33) Wherefore, my brethren, when ye come together to eat, tarry one for another. (34) And if any man hunger, let him eat at home; that ye come not together unto condemnation. And the rest will I set in order when I come."

In the last sentence, "And the rest I will set in order when I come" has the same Greek word. Again, the English word, "order" in the Greek is *diatasso.*

Therefore, Believer Business Owner functioning apostles set things in order or *diatasso* particularly in business foundation matters and procedures.

The Believer Business Owner functioning apostles, who are true to their calling, often proclaim how another Believer Business Owner, who is in fellowship, in a loving way, has a business that is out of order and is in need of change to be in order. Then, those in the business may request a Believer Business Owner from another business to come and set things in order.

Titus 1:5 says, "For this reason I left you in Crete, that you should set in order (*diatasso*) the things that are lacking and appoint elders in every city as I commanded you."

Again, the important Greek word in this verse for "order" is *diatasso.* Therefore, the ministry of the Believer Business Owner functioning apostle toward Believer Business ministers is to "...set in order the things that are lacking and appoint elders (managers in business)…." The elders are the Business Managers, who have come of age or spiritual maturity to help run the Believer Business Owner functioning apostle's business; so, the Believer Business Owner functioning apostle has time to set up other businesses or do other spiritual work for the Lord, as traveling to another country on a missionary trip.

Whenever the Believer Business Owner that requests counseling is not moving in his or her Giftings and Vocations in his or her business, the spiritually mature Believer Business Owner functioning apostle will come and set in order the things that are lacking. The purpose of God is for the Believer Business Owner functioning apostle is to keep the ongoing continuous kinesthetic training of Believer Business Employees, especially those being kinesthetically trained to be Believer Business Managers in the business. Thus, the Believer Business Owner functioning apostle is kinesthetically trained in business and, if invited, can come to help the pastor or teacher in the *Ekklesia* to put things in order. The Believer Business Owner functioning apostle, if invited, can activate other Believer Business Owners or Managers in the *Ekklesia* congregation's business members that will cause growth in spiritual maturity, which will attract other Believer Business Owners to come to this *Ekklesia* congregation. Finally, the Believer Business Owner functioning apostle will raise the awareness of the ministry available in business and the marketplace which can increase the tithes and offering for the local *Ekklesia.* Instead of seeking only the money earned by Believer Business Owners, priests, bishops, pastors, teachers, and reverends should utilize these foundational spiritual gifts of the Believer Business Owner functioning apostles for the betterment of all in the local fellowship *Ekklesia* community.

1 Corinthians 16:1 says, "Now concerning the collection for the saints, as I have given order to the churches (*Ekklesia*) of Galatia, even so do ye." When a collection is taken, this is where the prosperous Believer Business ministers can exercise their gift of donation without covetous or greed, but with simplicity and purity of heart (Romans 12:8). Again, the Greek word for "order" is *diatasso.*

Here, as a Believer Business Owner functioning apostle Paul declares what is the proper order (*diatasso*) for taking the collection; and he exhorts the Business ministers to be cheerful givers.

1 Corinthians 14:40 says, "Let all things be done decently and in order." Again, the Believer Business Owner functioning apostle Paul declares that all things are to be done decently and in order (***diatasso***). Paul never taught that spiritual gifts were not to be expressed; he merely set forth in 1 Corinthians chap. 14 how to set in order the use of those spiritual Gifts. In fact, Paul encourages all the spiritual Gifts. Paul said 1 Corinthians 14:18, 40 "I thank my God, I speak with tongues more than ye all.... (40) **Let all things be done** decently and in order." Some pastors and teachers read 1 Corinthians chap. 14 calling public display of spiritual Gifts "out of order." Yet, Paul makes it clear by saying "let all things be done...." Paul wanted all spiritual gifts to be operative and manifested in the meetings, but he wanted to put things in order. Life from the River of Life in Revelation 22:1 flows from the Throne of God, the seat of authority. Understanding submission to authority shows you have great faith like the Centurion. God wants the Ekklesia members to exercise spiritual Gifts orderly; otherwise, it may look and sound like it is not from a very ordered God. Yet, order does not mean to stop the spiritual spontaneity of the Holy Spirit.

Matthew 10:5 says, "These twelve Jesus sent out and **commanded** them, saying: 'Do not go into the way of the Gentiles, and do not enter a city of the Samaritans.'" Here the word **"commanded"** is the Greek word *diatasso.* This is an example of Jesus acting as the Chief Business Functioning Apostle, Who was about His Father's business of apportioning and giving orders to His disciples. Here, Jesus brought His disciples into a greater measure of their gifting and calling by putting things in order (*diatasso)*.

This is the pattern. Jesus could have said something like, "You are functioning apostles. I am sending you out, so you can talk about My Father's and My spiritual business. Go and pray for the sick, deliver the demon possessed, preach the gospel of the Kingdom of God, preach repentance of sins; teach Believer Business Owners to establish their businesses on Biblical principles. Kinesthetically train the Believer Business Owners as functioning ministers to mature their Believer Business Employees in the ways of Godhead and all that I have commanded. You functioning apostles take with you and share the vision for God's Kingdom government here on earth as it is in heaven. The words that I have spoken to you are spirit and life. So, put things in order. Instruct Believer Business Owners to kinesthetically train their Believer Business Employees the word of God, which will cause the word of God to flow with decency and order throughout your business, the marketplace, and society as all believers are the real *Ekklesia* and receive grace in a measure according to their spiritual Gifts and activate them in their spiritual Vocations."

Jesus discipled His functioning apostles and other disciples to start and doing ministry work in building His *Ekklesia.* After His ascension, He sent the Helper, the Holy Spirit, who came on the day of Pentecost and spiritually baptized everyone in the Upper Room with spirit and with power to do signs and wonders. As the Business Messiah and Savior Who was about God the Father's business, Jesus released His disciples into a greater measure of their spiritual gifts and callings than they had ever walked because He scholastically taught and kinesthetically trained them how to put spiritual matters in order (*diatasso*).

Since the disciples did not earn the grace that brought this new measure of gifts, power, and anointing of the Holy Spirit, there is a stewardship responsibility of someone else's grace as a requirement attached to every minister's gift, anointing, and calling. The grace gifts given mean your time as a Believer Business Owner or Believer Business Employees, whether man or woman, is not going to be just to make a profit and lots of money. The Believer Business Owner and Believer Business Employees are *doulos,* bond servants of Jesus Christ, seeking first the Kingdom of God and His righteousness.

Revelation 22:1 says, "And he shewed me a pure river of water of life, clear as crystal, proceeding out of the throne of God and of the Lamb." What is taught in this verse is that life flows from God's seat of authority. God never creates chaos; God always creates by putting what is created first, then second, then third, then fourth, then fifth, and then sixth, and so on in that order. Then on the seventh day, God rested after He worked, not before He worked. Genesis 2:2 says, "And on the seventh day God ended His work which He had made; and He rested on the seventh day from all His work which He had made."

Luke 12:48 says, "But he that knew not, and did commit things worthy of stripes, shall be beaten with few stripes. For unto whomsoever much is given, of him shall be much required: and to whom men have committed much, of him they will ask the more."

As did the disciples in Matthew 10 and Acts 2:42-47, the local Believer Business Owner functioning apostles will be coming into a greater measure of their gifts and calling. They will be establishing at the business venue a Christ-centered business, applying biblical economic principles, moral ethics, *agape* love, servanthood, *dunamis* power, and fruit of the Spirit by Believer Business Employees, which will cause a business atmosphere that is attractive to customers and clients.

This spiritual business atmosphere will cause referrals, which will increase the cash flow and the profit in the business. The Believer Business Owner functioning apostle will not promote the "New World Order" of the humanists. Rather, the Believer Business Owner functioning apostle will lay the foundation to build the business with God's order of the Bible. The Believer Business Owner functioning apostle will institute the leading of unbelievers to receive initial salvation by sharing the gospel of God's kingdom, along with repentance and remission of sins, which will be enhanced by daily prayer and studying God's word by the Believer Business Owner functioning apostle leading the Believer Business Employees. Additionally, the Believer Business Owner functioning apostles will use biblical wisdom and knowledge with those seeking counseling, will show heartfelt *agape* love, granting grace, operating spiritual gifts, practicing spiritual *koinonia,* throughout the day of praising God for His blessings, maintaining favor with all the employees in the business, and dedicating himself or herself as the spiritual leader in business and eventually the local community outside the business.

What is it going to take to bring the Believer Business Employees to the full measure of their spiritual Gifts and spiritual Vocations? It will be the continuous, consistent, spiritual walk with faith, humility, and maturity that the functioning apostle Paul reached, which he said in Galatians 2:19-20, "For I through the law am dead to the law, that I might live unto God. (20) I am crucified with Christ: nevertheless I live; yet not I, but Christ liveth in me: and the life which I now live in the flesh I live by the faith of the Son of God, Who loved me, and gave Himself for me."

Of all verses, Galatians 2:19-20 are my most favorite verses which I often teach when I minister the word of God. After initial salvation, if you practice these two scriptures, your life experience will soar in Christ Jesus by fellowship with the Holy Spirit and other born again Believers.

God's purpose is to bring those lost in all places in the marketplace venue to Jesus where there is the greater gracing of the whole Body of Christ, as Jesus said in Matthew 11:28-30, "Come unto me, all ye that labour and are heavy laden, and I will give you rest. (29) Take My yoke upon you, and learn of Me; for I am meek and lowly in heart: and ye shall find rest unto your souls. (30) For My yoke is easy, and My burden is light."

Christ's Body membership will be moving under the grace, anointing, and power of the Holy Spirit. God wants the *Ekklesia* to stop gathering to enjoy entertainment and start working with their God-ordained Vocations for God the Father, Christ Jesus, and their Kingdom as you are led by the Holy Spirit. The triune nature of the Godhead wants each Believer to close their toy box and open their tool box and start preaching, building, and expanding God's Kingdom in everyplace here on earth, especially in the businesses, schools, professions, media, and families.

In The Passion Translation (2017), Proverbs 24:3, 5 says, "Wise People are Builders – They build families, businesses, communities. And through intelligence and insight their enterprises are established and endure. . . (5) Wisdom can make anyone into a mighty warrior and revelation-knowledge increases strength."

The Holy Spirit's spiritual revival in the U.S., or any other country, will not be done solely by the pulpit ministries, but spiritual revival will come *en mass* by the activated and equipped whole Body of Christ working in businesses through the foundation laid by the Believer Business Owner functioning apostle and prophet and their Believer Business Employees. The Holy Spirit is moving and calling forth Believer Business Owner functioning apostle and prophet owners to go into Ekklesia worship and teaching centers, marketplaces, business offices, hospital facilities, court houses, school campuses, entertainment centers, government buildings, military bases, and home places to lay the foundation for God's kingdom government in every place. This includes local, regional, and federal areas in every country in the world. The Holy Spirit is calling Believers to minister and to seek first the Kingdom of God and His righteousness, in their places of employment owned by Believer Business Owners in addition to attending a local community *Ekklesia* fellowship. Conversely, God calls Believer Business Owners and Believer Business Employees to give God and Jesus Christ their best during the business hours to focus to be about God the Father's business (Luke 2:49). God wants His business ministry done every day, during the working hours, and where people in the world come to find their needs met, especially during the workweek.

If parents believe that it is important to send their children to Schools where there are Christian teachers that not only teach the basic fundamentals of reading, writing, arithmetic, and science, but also teach the biblical economic principles, servanthood, *agape* love, moral ethics, avoiding temptations of the world, and the attacks of Satan's evil realm, then they should do homeschooling or attend a Christian school and encourage their children to seek employment with a Believer Business Owner. Why stop your children's kinesthetic biblical training after graduating from High School or College? Every good Christian parent wants their children to marry a Christian spouse and raise children as Christians. Parents should discourage their adult children from seeking non-believer business jobs where they will be taught alternative humanistic and secular ways of conducting business to make a living. Parents should teach their children as adults not to bring any humanistic or secular ideas home to feed the minds of their Christian children. The New International version of 1 Corinthians 15:33 says, "Do not be misled: Bad company corrupts good character."

The *Ekklesia* needs spiritually mature Believers to become prayer warriors against the forces of darkness in every local, regional, and federal areas in every country where Believers live. God is bringing forth a Body of Believers in the businesses and marketplaces that are anointed spiritual soldiers of God's Kingdom because He wants His *Ekklesia* to go into the enemy's territory.

There has been over one hundred thousand of youth dying each year in the United States because they had illegally ingested fentanyl that was smuggled in by Mexico and Venezuela drug cartels. The global fentanyl supply chain overwhelmingly starts with chemical companies based in China that is shipped to Mexico, Venezuela, and other countries who put the fentanyl in pills that are then smuggled across the U.S. southern border and by small boats sneaking into places along shoreline on the Pacific Ocean and the shoreline on the Gulf of America. To break this critical link in the fentanyl supply chain, God wants Believer Prayer Warriors spiritually confronting the evil spirits behind these drug cartels. These drug cartels should be specifically targeted and are arrested, prosecuted, and imprisoned. Why is the Chinese Government not stopping companies in its country from manufacturing and delivering fentanyl to kill the youth of the United States? Could it be for the purpose of killing off potential soldiers in the U.S. of military age to lessen our military personnel and military strength?

Matthew 11:1 says, "And it came to pass, when Jesus had made an end of commanding His twelve disciples, He departed thence to teach and to preach in their cities." Again, the word, "commanding" is the Greek word, ***diatasso.***

In Matthew 10:5-42, Jesus, as the Chief functioning Apostle of our confession, Jesus told His disciples where to go and where not to go, what to preach and what not to say, what to do and what not to do, and what were the principles that would govern the disciples' ministries. He told them about the rewards for obedience by the people who receive the Gospel of the Kingdom and repentance and remission of sins; and Jesus trained His disciples through kinesthetic training. Jesus taught them the goals of being about God the Father's business.

Matthew 10:5-42 is the example of the apostolic anointing flowing in the marketplaces to activate and send forth business disciples of Jesus moving with the Holy Spirit's anointing they never had before.

As a Believer in business, Matthew 10:5-42 apostolic activating principles will be continuously repeated in your life before your time is over here on earth if you make the decision to become a Believer Business Owner Ephesians 4:11 functioning minister or a Believer Business Employee working in that business. God has business plans, as He wants to bring His business in the workplace of His Kingdom. God's Kingdom economy will be based not only upon buying and selling but also on giving and receiving. Proverbs 19:21 says, "There are many devices in a man's heart; nevertheless, the counsel of the LORD, that shall stand."

However, instead of just Jesus' 12 functioning apostles, with some being businessmen, God will release millions of Believer Business Owners as functioning apostles (or one of the other Ephesian 4:11 functioning ministers) with a grace that increases the measure of their gifting and calling in business.

FIRST THE BELIEVER BUSINESS OWNER FUNCTIONING APOSTLES, SECOND THE BELIEVER BUSINESS FUNCTIONING PROPHETS

1 Corinthians 12:28 says, "And God has appointed these in the church (*Ekklesia* in business): first (business functioning) apostles, second (business functioning) prophets, third (business functioning) teachers, after that miracles, then gifts of healings, helps, administrations, varieties of tongues." I am emphasizing Believer Business Owner functioning apostles because this is the topic of this chap-

ter. I do so because most Believer Business Owner functioning apostles are outside of the *Ekklesia* warehouse lecture hall structure paradigm where the majority of Believers are not being activated as ministers or Leaders but are seen as rank and file followers, who are blessed by the functioning pastor's teachings, but are seen as financially supporting followers of that ministry that help pay the expenses of the building and the small percentage of those working in church leadership under a single priest, bishop, pastor, teacher, or reverend.

The obedient Believer Business Owner functioning apostles are the ones who release the Believers of God out of the bondage of religious tradition into a grace with a greater measure of their gifts and activation in their Vocations as spiritual kings, priests, lords, ambassadors, and soldiers of God.

God's favor cannot start until Believer Business Employees are released into the grace God wants to give them, so they are activated as mandated in Ephesians 4:12 "work of ministry" with the measure of the gift bestowed by God the Word, as Jesus' divine nature and God's only begotten Son, Jesus' humanity nature. This releasing and activating are the first steps that needs to be done, which is primarily the ministry of the Believer Business Owner functioning apostles and Believer Business Owner functioning prophets, who lay the foundation of the ministry in business. Notwithstanding, all the Ephesians 4:11 Believer Business Owner functioning ministers have a responsibility in their area of their calling to bring God's grace and measure of gift as stated in Ephesians 4:7 to scholastically teach and kinesthetically train their Believer Business Employees in their Vocations as mature kings, priests, lords, ambassadors, and soldiers in God's Kingdom, along with helping them operate in their spiritual Gifts.

Believer Business Owner functioning apostles are not superior to the other Ephesians 4:11 Believer Business Owner functioning ministers. The Believer Business Owner functioning apostles are merely "first" in function, not stature, because they put down the iron rods as the first work in laying the foundation of the kingdom business. God is no respecter of Believers (Acts 10:34) but does bestow His anointing, authority, and power based upon His Sovereign Will. In Truth, Believer Business Owner functioning apostles' work is the first in function in establishing the foundation of the business in the task of equipping the Believer Business Employees for the work of the ministry at the workplace.

The Believer Business Owner functioning apostle says to the Believer Business Employees, "The Lord through me wants to lay the foundation of this business. The principles that you Believer Business Employees will follow and promote are all have a biblically-based origin. I expect all of you Believer Business Employees to daily pray for each employee, for me, and for the success of this business. We will have prayer time before the workday begins every day. We then will read one chapter of Proverbs and five chapters of Psalms before the workday every day for the next two years. This is a time I encourage you to dedicate yourself to the Lord while working in this business. I will scholastically teach you God's Kingdom government while you work here, and you will be kinesthetically trained in biblical economic principles, morality, grace, mercy, *agape* love, work ethic, humility, and servanthood. The attendance in the morning prayer time and reading the Bible is not compulsory, but it will cause much faster spiritual maturity if you do."

"Notwithstanding, you also will have to learn through scholastic self-study God's biblical economic principles, morality, grace, mercy, *agape* love, work ethic, humility, and servanthood as foundational beliefs and work standards in this business. You will not be paid to come here and pray and read your Bible together with me or a supervisor and with other employees, as this is your personal spiritual growth which is of higher value than money. As we grow in numbers, and you mature spiritually, you may be selected to lead the group. If you attend these Bible study and prayer time, it will be your testimony that you see God as your source, and you are here to dedicate the day and your labor unto Him. If and when we open a branch business, we will select one or more of you who have become Managers because you have been scholastically taught and kinesthetically trained to use the biblical economic principles, morality, grace, mercy, *agape* love, work ethic, humility, and servanthood to other Believer Business Employees and customers. Your spiritual maturation in this business also will be continuous spiritual scholastic teaching and kinesthetic training, and being a Manager will include your level of spiritual maturity. This activating and releasing you in your spiritual Vocations and spiritual Gifts through daily incremental business work is to populate the world with God's Kingdom kings, priests, lords, ambassadors, and soldiers. You will be praying to bind the army of Satan's evil realm and releasing God's Kingdom government, Kingdom military to do His Will that He wants done here on earth as it is in heaven."

GOD'S BELIEVER BUSINESS OWNER FUNCTIONING APOSTLES LAY THE FOUNDATION "SO NOTHING BE LOST"

John 6:5-13 says, "When Jesus then lifted up His eyes, and saw a great company come unto Him, He saith unto Philip, 'Whence shall we buy bread, that these may eat? (6) And this He said to prove Him: for He Himself knew what He would do. (7) Philip answered Him, 'Two hundred pennyworth of bread is not sufficient for them, that every one of them may take a little.' (8) One of his disciples, Andrew, Simon Peter's brother, saith unto Him, (9) 'There is a lad here, which hath five barley loaves, and two small fishes: but what are they among so many?' (10) And Jesus said, 'Make the men sit down.' Now there was much grass in the place. So the men sat down, in number about five thousand. (11) And Jesus took the loaves; and when He had given thanks, He distributed to the disciples, and the disciples to them that were set down; and likewise of the fishes as much as they would. (12) When they were filled, He said unto His disciples, **'Gather up the fragments that remain, that nothing be lost.'** (13) Therefore they gathered *them* together, and filled twelve baskets with the fragments of the five barley loaves, which remained over and above unto them that had eaten."

God sends Believer Business Owner functioning apostles (and Believer Business Owner functioning prophets) to ensure that a proper foundation is laid "so nothing be lost." The kinesthetic training of the Believers Business Employees by the Believer Business Owner functioning apostle who works, so nothing is lost which is built. This is the fruit of true functioning apostolic and functioning prophetic business ministries. Because the Godhead is God of Abraham, Isaac, and Jacob, God's business plans are designed, if followed, to last for at least three generations.

Proper foundational preparation, function, and order in the business must be paramount and have priority. Without a solid foundation, everyone in business suffers loss. Psalms 11:3 says, "If the foundations be destroyed, what can the righteous do." If Jesus did not set the people down in ranks in hundreds and in fifties before He started multiplying the fish and the loaves of bread, there would have been a stampede while trying to grab the food.

BELIEVER BUSINESS OWNER FUNCTIONING APOSTLES BRING DIVINE ORDER OR ORDINATION.

The Business Owner functioning apostle releases his or her Believer Business Employees into their business grace, measure of gift, and spiritual Vocations and spiritual Gifts under the anointing of the Holy Spirit. The Believer Business Owner functioning prophet says, "Here is the divine vision and purpose, so find your place in the vision and revelation as God uses you to fulfill it." The Believer may ask, "How do I fit in?" The Believer Business Owner functioning apostle says, "This is how you fit in by accepting the vision and purpose that God has given us, and how to request the Holy Spirit's anointing and power to be about the Father's business through the incremental daily steps in furtherance of God's vision and purpose. Eventually, Believer Business Employees' habits and actions will cause them to see how God's vision and purpose is being accomplished, and how they have accomplish an important part of that vision and purpose, with accountability; so, nothing is lost. Business Believer Employees must stay humble, obedient, and then they will be promoted. As Business Believer Employees mature in working in fulfilling God's vision and purpose, they will be assigned as a Manager functioning as teachers of new employees that need to learn to flow and do their parts to also fulfill God's vision and purpose." The Believer Business Employees' requirement to study scripture is stated in 2 Timothy 2:15, which says, "Study to shew thyself approved unto God, a workman that needeth not to be ashamed, rightly dividing the word of truth."

Luke 11:43-44, 47-50 says, "Woe unto you, Pharisees! For ye love the uppermost seats in the synagogues, and greetings in the markets. (44) Woe unto you, scribes and Pharisees, hypocrites! for ye are as graves which appear not, and the men that walk over them are not aware of them.... (47) Woe unto you! for ye build the sepulchers of the prophets, and your fathers killed them. (48) Truly ye bear witness that ye allow the deeds of your fathers: for they indeed killed them, and ye build their sepulchers. (49) Therefore also said the wisdom of God, I will send them prophets and apostles, and *some* of them they shall slay and persecute: (50) That the blood of all the prophets, which was shed from the foundation of the world, may be required of this generation."

God sends the Believer Business Owner functioning apostles and Believer Business Owner functioning prophets to reveal what is in the hearts of the leaders in business. They come with the message from the Lord, and God will honor their submission and office ministry. God will bring foundational order in the *Ekklesia* to His business purpose through His Believer Business Owner functioning apostles and Believer Business owner functioning prophets.

The Book of Acts concerns the works of the Lord's functioning apostles, prophets, evangelists, pastors, and teachers, but especially the apostles. Believer Business Owner functioning apostles are action-minded and release people in God's grace in the measure of their spiritual Gift. Believer Business Owner functioning apostles' primary goal is activating all Believers for the work of the ministry (Vocations as kings, priests, lords, ambassadors, and soldiers) in laying the foundation of the Father's business. The Believer Business Owner functioning apostles must be about the Father's business of edifying or building the Believer Business Owner's business on the solid foundation of the Lord Jesus Christ (1 Corinthians 3:11).

The work of the Believer Business Owner functioning apostles coming into their businesses in the end times shall be greater than the Believer Business Owner functioning apostles which have gone before because the spiritual battles need greater wisdom from above. The end time businesses run by anointed men and women Believer Business Owner functioning apostles will be more glorious, as they will be an integral part of God's plan to wrap up the *Ekklesia* Age and pour out His Spirit on all flesh. The Believer Business Owner functioning apostles will play a significant role in laying the foundation of the final move of the Holy Spirit to have a glorious *Ekklesia* in business that will help transform the souls of Believer Business Employees as God's business ministers that are without spot or wrinkle, that will be holy.

THE FURTHER WORK OF MINISTRY OF BUSINESS FUNCTIONING APOSTLES

The Believer Business Owner functioning apostle is given by Christ Jesus to selected Believer Business Employees who are functioning ministers or in the marketplace and have the responsibility:

For the perfecting and maturity of Believers as employees or those in business through stewardship business scholastic teaching and kinesthetic training.

For bringing Believers working in business to the place where the business activity becomes a ministry.

For edifying the selected Believer Business Employees who are functioning ministers, who have found their place of ministry in the business, workplace, and marketplace.

For unifying Believer Business Owners and Believer Business Employees under one faith, one body, one Spirit, one Lord, and one God.

For bringing Believer Business Owners and Believer Business Employees to the knowledge of how the Son of God while doing the incremental labor in Father God's business.

(See Luke 2:49; Ephesians 4:11-16; Colossians 1:25-29; 3:23; Hebrews 6:1-2)

AGAIN, THE APOSTLES (AND PROPHETS) LAY THE BUSINESS FOUNDATION.

Even though the foundation functioning ministry belongs to both the functioning apostles and functioning prophets with Christ Jesus as the Chief Cornerstone (Ephesians 2:20), this chapter shines light on the Believer Business Owner functioning apostles. Much of what will be said also applies to the Believer Business Owner functioning prophets.

The Believer Business Owner functioning apostle must activate each Believer Business Employee in their spiritual Vocations and spiritual Gifts as Christ did with His disciples to build His *Ekklesia.*

Therefore, all Believer Business functioning ministers must study scriptures regarding the apostles and prophets, and both the Believer Business Owner and Believer Business Employees can then focus their activities first in laying the foundation in establishing the business as the venue for their ministry.

Again, the Business Believer Owner functioning apostle, is one who is sent to lay the foundation of the business. As the Business Believer Owner functions as an apostle, he or she puts things in order, as he or she is normally the entrepreneur that does everything that opens the business and establishes it as a Christ-centered business. The Business Believer Owner functioning as an apostle or prophet is to work together in laying the foundation of the business. The Believer Business Owner functioning prophet is the one who has a vision and purpose for the business or sees the condition of the business already operating and that changes are needed. The Believer Business Owner functioning apostle knows how to flow in the prophetic vision and conform the actions and plans in conformance to the vision, or that facilitates changes in the business. The Believer Business Employees can be scholastically taught and kinesthetically trained to work with the anointing and power of the Holy Spirit to fulfill the vision and purpose of the business by taking steps in making needed changes in line with the business vision and purpose. The Believer Business Owner functioning apostle and Believer Business Owner functioning prophet can pray and hear from God His plan that conforms with His teleology. God's teleology is achieving His ultimate multigeneration purpose rather than immediate causes. Essentially, it's looking at the "why" the business by focusing on the "end result," with the Greek roots of the word meaning "purpose" (telos) and "study of" (-logy).

The Believer Business Owner functioning apostle is an envoy, who especially works as a king, priest, lord, ambassador, and soldier in God's Kingdom who is about the Father's business in laying the foundation of God's grace and gifting (Ephesians 4:7). The Believer Business Owner functioning apostle's faith that was bestowed upon him or her by God the Word for the establishment of God's Kingdom here on earth as it is in heaven (Matthew 6:10).

The Believer Business Owner functioning apostle's engiftment is more than as a business servant initially establishing a business in a particular location to manifest God's Kingdom government in the marketplace. The Believer Business Owner functioning apostle's engiftment is given for the primary purpose of perfecting of Believer Business Employees for the work of the ministry through spiritual Vocations and spiritual Gifts, for the edifying of the body of Christ that is working in businesses and taking back possession to God of the earth, the *cosmos*, and the people that reside in the culture where the Believer Business Owner functioning apostle resides and has influence.

There is a pattern to duplicate and follow in the Bible regarding the Ephesians 4:11 engiftment of the foundational ministries of the Believer Business Owner functioning apostles and functioning prophets and applying them to the business, workplace, and marketplace. The pattern in the Bible for the Believer Business Owner functioning apostle is Christ Jesus' own profession and work experience as a carpenter and stonemason as thoroughly discussed in previous chapters.

As a carpenter and stonemason in business, Jesus exemplified all the Ephesian 4:11 office functioning ministries in business and in the marketplace. Hebrews 3:1 says, "Wherefore, holy brethren, partakers of the heavenly calling, consider the Apostle and High Priest of our profession, Christ Jesus." As with all the office gift ministries, Jesus is the pattern.

The Believer Business Owner functioning apostle must ordain leaders in business and help recognize each Believer's grace engiftment and business calling because Christ Jesus gave Believer Business Owner functioning apostles to contribute to the foundation in building His *Ekklesia* in business that is serving others in the marketplace and bringing to the forefront in conversation the gospel of the kingdom of God, repentance and remission of sins, and from God's point of few to bring possession of the earth, world, and people back to God through the original under ruler, submitted authority granted to mankind (Genesis 1:26-28).

The Lord Jesus Christ, with His dual natures, uses Believer Business Owner functioning apostles and Believer Business Owner functioning prophets literally to build the foundation of the *Ekklesia* being servants to fellow employees and customers in business and in the marketplace, which is built on Christ Jesus, the Chief Corner Stone. The Believer Business Owner functioning apostle can lay no other foundation in business than that of Christ Jesus (1 Corinthians 3:11).

Therefore, daily scripture scholastic study regarding the Believer Business Owner functioning apostles and Believer Business Owner functioning prophets is all important. Scriptures relate them to their activities in laying the foundation in establishing the businesses with the purpose of manifesting God's Kingdom government here on earth in commerce to impact the world with God's kingdom principles, wisdom, knowledge, ways, purpose, and anointing. Scripture scholastic studying daily matures Believer Business Owners and Believer Business Employees along with the daily handling of business problems by using biblical principles, wisdom from above, moral ethics, servanthood, grace, faith, mercy, and *agape* love. Believer Business Owner functioning apostles must submit to being led by the Holy Spirit Who anoints and empowers them to manifest the Kingdom of God and to diminish the presence and power of Satan's evil realm in the area where the business is being conducted and has influence.

Bodies of each Believer Business Owner and bodies of each Believer Business Employee are the Temple of God where God resides (2 Corinthians 6:16). God in His temple likes to exhibit holiness, righteousness, peace, joy, grace, *agape* love, wisdom, truth; so, *zoe* life in the Holy Spirit as the manifestation of His Kingdom permeates the souls of the Believer Business Owners and Believer Business Employees, along with the very environment of the business premises.

In considering the laying of the foundation in business, what are the ingredients? Most foundations of any building are formed with wrought iron rods and concrete. The Believer Business Owner functioning apostles are the wrought iron rods, and the Believer Business Owner functioning prophets are the liquid concrete. The wrought iron rods are made from iron ore placed in the fiery furnace and remolded into the likeness needed for the building the foundation. This is the life of a Believer Business Owner functioning apostle. The Believer Business Owner functioning apostle is hard as nails in their faithful resolve to submit to entering the crucifixion of Christ and allowing Christ to live His life in them (Galatians 2:20). The Believer Business Owner functioning apostle has been humbled through the test of fiery circumstances encountered in life. In fact, fire is the main ingredient that causes the iron to be in the shape it is in. Exposure to fire becomes the purifying agent for metal. The metal comes from the results of God's holy fire. The wrought iron rods are placed in perfect order like a tic tac toe to distribute their strength throughout the foundation base.

The entire Godhead inhabits Business Believers at the workplace, and the Holy Spirit will manifest in a business setting and environment when the ministry opportunity for salvation of someone or the healing of someone who is being oppressed by Satan's evil realm (Acts 10:38). Ephesians 2:19-22 says, "Now therefore ye are no more strangers and foreigners, but fellow citizens with the saints, of the household of God; (20) And are built upon the foundation of the apostles and prophets, Jesus Christ Himself being the chief corner stone; (21) In whom all the building fitly framed together groweth unto an holy temple in the Lord: (22) In whom ye also are builded together for an habitation of God through the Spirit."

Hebrew 12:29 says, "For our God is a consuming fire." Believer Business Owner functioning apostles are prepared for the task of submitting to God's consuming fire for purification prior to allowing them bringing any soulish fractures that will hurt God's Believer Business Employees. God starts building the foundation of His business by exposing the character flaws in business Believers' lives through His exposing, purifying fire of circumstances. As the heat of God's fiery circumstances is turned up, there is first a melting of the hard elements in Believer Business' functioning ministers' souls. Flaws in the foundation of a Believer Business Owner functioning apostle's soul might be a formless void, a hurt during childhood, a season of negative growth, causing an inner spiritual circumspection, or a need to forgive. It is not always that the fire in one's life is ignited by the devil, but sometimes fire is ignited by Jesus' divine nature, God the Word and Jesus' humanity nature to prepare the minister to become loving and helpful, not resentful or hurtful toward Believer Business Employees.

John the Baptist said in Matthew 3:11, "I indeed baptize you with water unto repentance: but He that cometh after me is mightier than I, whose shoes I am not worthy to bear: He shall baptize you with the Holy Ghost, and with fire." There is a baptism of fire that seems to burn up the briers and brambles in Believers' souls that are ignited to test the works being done by the Believer. 1 Corinthians 3:13, 15 says, "Every man's work shall be made manifest: for the day shall declare it, because it shall be revealed by fire; and the fire shall try every man's work of what sort it is. . . (15) If any man's work shall be burned, he shall suffer loss: but he himself shall be saved; yet so as by fire. " Sometimes, the Godhead removes a sinful partner or a sinful employee to protect others in the business and to protect God's venue where Believer Business Employees are spiritually transformed and matured in their souls. The fire seems to purify the iron and brings forth pure steel, usable by God in His Body of Believers being expressed and working in the business. Believer Business Owner functioning apostles and Believer Business Employees are being purified with fire because they will be ministering representatives of God and His Kingdom in the business and marketplace. When God moves with a new movement of the Holy Spirit, He is much stricter with His ministers in the venue where the Holy Spirit is moving.

God demands that Believer Business Owner functioning apostles build the business on God's absolute and eternal foundational principles and not finite natural world's ideas. This necessary season of negative growth is best described as a Gideon's Revival. It seems the business gets smaller but has Believer Business Employees that are more spiritual experience with developed natural talents that qualify them in the industry or profession that the business is engaged. The business runs efficiently, and profits are greater with a smaller, but wholly trained, hardworking, and loyal Believer Business Employees. Not every Believer Business Employee can stand the heat of God's refiner's fire. Some Believer Business Owners and Believer Business Employees will resist God and are not willing to pay the price of the fire burning away their pride, sin, and self-centeredness out of their souls. The Believer Business Owners' souls constantly are being transformed, purified, made righteous, peaceful, and holy after initial salvation. God will bring mature Believers into business relationships that will love them while challenging the darkness in their lives. All Believer Business Owner functioning apostles, along with their Believer Business Employee managers are called from the outset to go through the refiner's fire for purification. Malachi 3:2 says, "But who may abide the day of his coming? And who shall stand when He appeareth? For He is like a refiner's fire, and like fullers' soap." God wants righteousness and holiness inside the souls of Believer Business Owners and Believer Business Employees, so they will not be tempted by the money being made or tempted to do things as short cuts to obtain money that involve risks of loss. Also, God wants His Believer Business servants to be representative as Vocational kings, priests, lords, ambassadors, and soldiers in His Kingdom as they go out and represent His Kingdom in the business and marketplace venues.

Many Believers in the business community have been so thrilled over the baptism of the Holy Spirit and spiritual gifts that they forgot there was also a baptism of fire involved in laying the foundation in the business, including bringing the living words of scriptures, promoting the goodness of God, *agpapao* loving people, and allowing wisdom and knowledge by the stability of your times and the strength of your salvation. In these end times, we are seeing God's holy fire being poured out as a cleansing fire on God's Believers Business Owners and Believer Business Employees. The Lord's holy baptism of fire is not sent to kill, steal, or destroy Believers. It is sent to purify Believers' souls and make them vessels of honor who are doing God's business here on earth! Functioning apostles are office gifts from Jesus' divine nature, God the Word, and Jesus' humanity nature as the only begotten Son of God, and functioning apostles submitted souls are being purified with fire to produce the wrought iron rods for the foundation in building of the Body of Christ. Additionally, God the Father's discipline is to make purified, humble, and submitted hearts of Believer Business Owners as functioning apostles build the foundation upon which God can build His *Ekklesia* working and ministering in the business and marketplace.

On the other hand, the Believer Business Owner functioning prophets contribute liquid concrete to the foundation of the *Ekklesia* in the business. Concrete is a mixture of rocks, sand, cement, and water, which hardens into solid rock. It is the ***petros*** Believers who have the ***petra*** of the divine revelation of Christ upon which the *Ekklesia* doing God's business is built. The rocks, cement, sand, and water are all part of the revelation word of God applied to specific Believer's circumstances of self-centered lives to be transformed by the renewing of souls (Romans 12:2). However, it is not until the active ingredient of water is applied do the elements of rock, sand, and cement mixed and over time becomes the solid foundation material of Christ's revelatory redemptive gospel message. Ephesians 5:26-27 says, "That he might sanctify and cleanse it with the washing of water by the word. (27) That he might present it to Himself a glorious church, not having spot, or wrinkle, or any such thing; but that it should be holy and without blemish." The liquid concrete is then poured over the strategically arranged wrought iron rods, and when the liquid concrete hardens, it becomes a very solid foundation. Thus, the Believer Business Owner functioning prophet is used with the Believer Business Owner functioning apostle to lay the foundation of the ministry in business and how to then build upon that foundation God's Kingdom of righteousness, peace, and joy in the Holy Spirit.

Neither the wrought iron rods nor the liquid solidified concrete by themselves alone can be the foundation to manifest the *Ekklesia's* expression of God's Kingdom in the business. Yet, when the concrete of the functioning prophet is poured over the crisscrossed wrought iron rods of the functioning apostle, the foundation hardens with great strength to support skyscrapers of any business as ministry. 1 Corinthians 12:28 says, "And God has appointed these in the church (*Ekklesia*): first (functioning) apostle, second (functioning) prophets. . . ."

Psalm 127:1 says, "Except the LORD build the house, they labour in vain that build it:..." No local *Ekklesia* expressed in the business can be built upon the proper spiritual foundation unless they have the foundational business ministry gift influence and anointing of the Holy Spirit upon the Believer Business Owner functioning apostle and the Believer Business Owner functioning prophet. There are so many businesses that lack the proper spiritual foundation and are void of the expedition of signs and wonders of the foundational ministries or are not following the biblical principles of truths (Mark 16:15-17, 20).

Many businesses are built on the sinking sand of social agendas and popular messages which allows the lust of the flesh, lust of the eyes, and the pride of life. Also, if the purpose of the business is focused only on working to make money instead of intimately-involved in the maturing of the Believer Business Employees in business in their spiritual Vocations and spiritual Gifts, then God will not bless the Believers business endeavor. Yet, there are many Believer Business Employees searching for the pure heart of the foundational revelations of the Believer Business Owner functioning apostle or functioning prophet who has gone into the business, commerce, and marketplace to establish the *Ekklesia* of the Lord and God's kingdom there.

In Acts, the functioning apostles and functioning disciples were generally sent out two by two to do ministry. Often, a Believer functioning apostle and Believer functioning prophet were sent out together to lay the foundation of the early *Ekklesia.* If it was needed when Jesus walked here on earth to lay the foundation ministries of the Believer Business Owner functioning apostle and Believer Business Owner functioning prophet of every new business and every older business that have fallen away from being biblitarians.

The New King James version in Matthew 28:19 Jesus said to His Believer functioning apostles, many of whom were trained in business and or handling their family estate, "Go therefore and make disciples of all nations. . . ." Jesus commanded in Mark 16:15, "… Go ye into all the world and preach the gospel (gospel of the Kingdom and gospel of repentance and remission of sins) to every creature." Jesus' chosen Believer Business functioning apostles were not part of the religious hierarchy but worked in their businesses at times; and they carried the gospel of the Kingdom back to the unsaved working in their businesses and marketplaces. Jesus and His chosen Believer 12 apostles learned to be about God the Father's business. They preached the gospel of the Kingdom and the God and the gospel of repentance and remission of sins, healed the sick, cast out demons, and learned how to minister by Jesus' scholastic teaching and kinesthetic training.

THE *EKKLESIA* IN BUSINESS MUST BE BUILT UPON THE SOLID FOUNDATION LAID BY BELIEVER BUSINESS OWNER FUNCTIONING APOSTLES AND FUNCTIONING PROPHETS

The definition of a **business foundation**: "To lay something down upon which you can build." The proper business foundation is the indispensable prerequisite. The business foundation will be either the solid rock which is Christ Jesus or the shifting sand which is the fallen world's humanistic philosophies.

Every Believer Business Owner functioning apostle must lay the foundation of his or her business on the solid rock, Christ Jesus. 1 Corinthians 3:10-11 says, "According to the grace of God which is given unto me, as a wise master builder, I have laid the foundation, and another buildeth thereon. But let every man (or woman) take heed how he (or she) buildeth thereupon. (11) For other foundation can no man lay than that is laid, which is Jesus Christ."

Ephesians 2:16, 19-22 says, "And that he might reconcile both unto God in one body by the cross, having slain the enmity thereby: . . . (19) Now therefore ye are no more strangers and foreigners, but fellow citizens with the saints, and of the household of God; (20) And are built upon the foundation of the apostles and prophets , Jesus Christ himself being the chief corner stone; (21) In whom all the building fitly framed together groweth unto an holy temple in the Lord: (22) In whom ye also are builded together for an habitation of God through the Spirit. "

The Believer Business Owner functioning apostle and Believer Business Owner functioning prophet know and accept the foundation of his or her business is Christ Jesus and Him crucified, resurrected, ascended on high, and is the Believer Business Employees acceptance of Jesus Christ as Savior and Lord. As Savior, Jesus mandates making converts; but as Lord, Jesus mandates making disciples (Matthew 28:19, Romans 10:9, 13). Conversion is the starting point. The biblical concept of conversion involves receiving a perfect, sinless, holy, righteous born again spirit as a new creature in Christ (2 Corinthians 5:17; 1 Peter 1:23; Hebrews 12:23; 1 John 3:9; Ephesians 4:24). On the other hand, Galatians 2:20 refers to being a disciple who submits to being "crucified with Christ" and allowing Christ's life to be the disciple's life. A disciple is one who lives out his spiritual life by submitting to God's transforming work of pruning (John 15:2), cleansing, sanctifying (Ephesians 5:26), and mortifying the deeds of the flesh (Romans 8:13) to rid the carnality in the disciple's soul. The purpose is to make the disciple an obedient and mature servant of Christ who is motivated by Christ's love in all that he does (Colossians 3:17) as an adopted child of God (Romans 8:15) and who will make other disciples as Christ's faithful functioning minister.

Both the Believer Business Owner and Believer Business Employees are to emulate Christ Jesus as the aspiration. Believer Business Owner functioning apostles and Believer Business Owner functioning prophets must work with living stones that are Believer Business Employees, and all are to lay the foundation of Christ Jesus in the business. Believer Business Servants in the marketplace can enter the crucifixion of Christ and submit to allowing Christ to live His life in them and through them to lead others to repent and receive remission of sins (Luke 24:47). Then, Christ can live in and through His *Ekklesia,* which are both the Believer Business Owners and Believer Business Employees in the business and marketplace. Five of the ten Virgins waiting for the coming of the Bridegroom bought their oil for their lamps from the businesses in the marketplace (Matthew 25:9).

Again, Ephesians 4:7 says, "But unto every one of us is given grace according to the measure of the gift of Christ." What do Believer Business Owner functioning apostles do to bring the grace according to the measure of the gift to activate the Believer Business Employees to do the work of the ministry through their spiritual Vocations and spiritual Gifts? The Ephesians 4:12 work of ministry of the Believer Business Ministry is the Vocations as kings, priests, lords, ambassadors, and soldiers is in the business and marketplace and especially working in the Believer Business Owner functioning apostle's business. Believer Business Owner functioning apostles bring a solid foundation order to every employee working in the business.

Romans 16:20 says, "And the God of peace shall bruise Satan under your feet shortly. The grace of our Lord Jesus Christ be with you." The apostle Paul proclaimed the grace of the Lord Jesus Christ be with the Roman Believers. Grace is the donative intent of God Who measures the size and nature of the Ephesians 4:11 spiritual office gift of God.

As a sheepherder, Moses was a man in business of his father-in-law, Jethro, but he was God's Believer Business functioning apostle and Business Believer functioning prophet of the Old Testament who after leading the children of Israel out of Egypt (meaning world system) went to Mount Sinai, spent time with God, brought down the Ten Commandments and laws, established the anointed Levitical and Aaron priesthood because of the children of Israel's rebellion, received the pattern for building the Tabernacle and the things inside, and received the wisdom how to govern God's *Ekklesia* in the wilderness. However, Moses committed the sin of vainglory by saying "we" instead of the Lord alone and striking the rock twice to bring forth water instead of speaking to the rock as the Lord commanded. With all that Moses did during his life, he was not permitted to enter the Promised Land (Exodus chapters 2031; Numbers 20:10-11; Deuteronomy 3:25-28). After Moses death, his spirit/soul was allowed to appear with Elijah along with Christ Jesus on the Mount of Transfiguration (Matthew 17:1–8, Mark 9:2–8, and Luke 9:28–36). Thus, Moses finally made it into the Promise Land.

When Moses met the Lord at the burning bush in Exodus 4:1-3, it says, "And Moses answered and said, 'But, behold, they (Israelites) will not believe me, nor hearken unto my voice: for they will say, "The LORD hath not appeared unto thee." (2) And the LORD said unto him, 'What is that in thine hand?' And he (Moses) said, 'A (business) rod.' (3) And He (the LORD) said, 'Cast it on the ground.' And he (Moses) cast it on the ground, and it became a serpent; and Moses fled from before it." Moses' sign that proved he was the LORD's anointed servant is what the LORD did to his simple sheepherder business rod. The rod that Moses had in his hand that God used to do a spiritual work. What thing do you have in your hand in business? God can have you use that thing as a sign of your spiritual anointing and as the LORD's servant?

Exodus 4:2-3 provides a valuable lesson for business by highlighting the importance of using and investing in the resources you already have, no matter how insignificant they may seem. The passage teaches that what you possess is enough for God to create something extraordinary, a principle that can be applied to innovation and resourcefulness in business.

The rod Moses had in his hand he had been using for 40 years in his father-in-law's business. Moses' rod was a common, everyday tool of a shepherd. The Believer Business Owner functioning apostle may not see the potential of a most basic, and even undervalued, common asset. A seemingly insignificant tool or product, a specific skill set within the team, or a simple business process could be the key to unlocking major growth.

For example, in 1968, Spencer Silver, a scientist at 3M, was attempting to create a super-strong glue for use in aircraft construction. Mistakenly, he developed a low-tack, reusable, but pressure-sensitive adhesive that would not work in aircraft construction. However, it did stick to surfaces without bonding permanently and could be removed without leaving residue. For years, Silver pitched this mistake to try to find a usefulness as a product to be sold by 3M but the company rejected his ideas. However, in 1974, a fellow colleague that also worked at 3M, named Art Fry, attended one of Silver's seminars at 3M. Fry was a Believer who sung in the choir with his church congregation and always was frustrated that the paper bookmarks he used kept sliding down the page of his hymnal book which made it too long to find the song next to be sung. Then, God put in Fry's mind the presentation at Silver's seminar about his repositionable adhesive paper made by mistake. Fry knew that using the repositionable adhesive paper would stick on the pages of his hymnal without damaging the pages. He thought that this also could be used in white collar businesses, schools, and everywhere.

Fry contacted his 3M colleague, Silver, and they together co-invented the Post-it Note for 3M. Fry developed the product's practical application. Fry and Silver worked together at 3M to develop the "post-it," which was eventually test-marketed in 1977 and launched nationally in 1980 by 3M. 3M secured both utility patents (for the process and materials) and trademarks (for the brand name "Post-it"); and 3M successfully secured its product from competitors through lawsuits. "Post-it" was one of the greatest profitable successes for 3M, but the idea started as a mistake, which God used another Believer Business Employee, Fry, at 3M that Silver, the 3M scientist did not see. God help create a repositionable adhesive paper to help the choir turn to the assign hymns in the hymnal books, so God used a Believer Businessman to help the church choir, and 3M profited millions of dollars in the secular world. God can use mistakes in business as a new product.

Likewise, what is significant was that Moses worked for forty years in his father-in-law's business of herding sheep and selling the wool and meat from the sheep, but he never realized that the very rod with which he guided the sheep would be anointed by God as an instrument to help bring forth the ten plagues of Egypt and to stretch forth over the Red Sea to depart the water so the children of Israel to cross over, and then for hitting the rock to bring forth water out in the desert. Those whom God calls He clothes with humility because those who are the most fit for God's service are the most humble servants. Moses' job was as a sheepherder, which was the lowliest work at that time; and Moses merely had a Shepherd's rod he used in Jethro's business for 40 years. Moses did not own the business; he was an employee of Jethro. When Moses questioned his ability to be the LORD's minister, the LORD simply asked what was the business instrument that Moses had in his hand? Moses responded by showing the LORD that he held a simple, everyday Shepherd's rod that he used for forty years shepherding another man's sheep.

God will cause Believer Business Owner functioning apostles and Believer Business Owner functioning prophets, along with the Ephesians 4:11 functioning ministers to work in business for many years to show them that their own business is their ministry. Your business profession can be as a medical doctor, dentist, lawyer, teacher, flower shop owner, mechanic shop owner, a small grocery store owner, or a funeral parlor owner. Then God can anoint your hands, feet, eyes, ears, mouth, and soul to become a leader perfected through scholastic teaching and kinesthetic training to fulfill the purpose of God. When people in the marketplace come to you for service or a product, then the Lord wants you to use what you have been using in business for years and preach the gospel of the Kingdom and the gospel of repentance and remission of sins, heal the sick, help the needy, give wisdom from above to solve a problem, and always be ready to pray for and with people. What Believer Business Owners and Believer Business Employees have in their hands and souls attract "sheep," and they will listen to them as spiritual leaders that know the narrow path that seeks first the Kingdom of God and His righteousness and the goodness of God that leads to repentance.

All foundational illuminations by Believer Business Owners functioning apostles and Believer Business Owners functioning prophets, and all acts done by them in laying the foundation of a business must be in the fulfillment of the Godly purpose of the Godhead, along with Jesus' humanity nature, and not from self-aggrandizement. For example, like Peter, Martha also declared the foundational revelation that Jesus was the Christ in John 11:27, which says, "She saith unto Him, 'Yea, Lord: I believe that Thou art the Christ, the Son of God, which should come into the world.'"

If the Believer Business Owner functioning apostle has relationships with other local Believer Business Owners, he or she may pass corrections in a loving manner about the activities in another local Believer Business Owner, if the other Believer Business Owner invites and submits to his or her wisdom, knowledge, and anointing.

Believer Business Owner functioning apostles are given binding and loosening ministries (Matthew 16:16-19; 18:15-20; 1 Peter 4:7).

Sapphira and Ananias were judged by the Lord through the Believer Business Owner functioning apostle Peter, a fisherman by trade, for their lying to the Holy Spirit (Acts 5:1-11).

Elymas, the Jewish sorcerer and false prophet was blinded by the Lord through the Believer Business Owner functioning apostle Paul, a tent maker, for resisting the Gospel (Acts 13:11).

The Corinthian fornicator was disciplined under apostolic instruction by the Believer Business Owner functioning apostle Paul (1 Corinthians 4:21; 5:1-13; 2 Corinthians 2:6-11; 13:2, 10).

The arrogance of Diotrephes was dealt with by the Believer Business Owner functioning apostle John, a fisherman by trade (2 John 9, 10).

Again, the Believer Business Owner functioning apostle Paul, a tent maker, dealt with those who were espousing false doctrines (1 Timothy 1:20).

Believer Business Owner functioning apostle Paul, a tent maker, disciplined those who caused divisions and offenses through carnal manipulation and works for their own gain (Romans 16:17-18).

The Believer Business Owner functioning apostle judges who are the false Believer Business Owner functioning apostles! The Believer Business Owner functioning apostle Paul set forth the teaching as to who were false functioning apostles. 2 Corinthians 11:13 says, "For such are false apostles, deceitful workers, transforming themselves into the apostles of Christ."

The Believer Business Owner functioning apostle may have to discipline another Believer Business Owner functioning apostle. Paul brought discipline against the Believer Business Owner functioning apostle, Peter. Galatians 2:11-13 says, "But when Peter was come to Antioch, I withstood him to the face, because he was to be blamed. (12) For before that certain came from James, he did eat with the Gentiles: but when they were come, he withdrew and separated himself, fearing them which were of the circumcision. (13) And the other Jews dissembled likewise with him; insomuch that Barnabas also was carried away with their dissimulation."

The Believer Business Owner functioning apostle must have a vision that will look out for and better the lives of all the Believer Business Employees and customers in the business with whom he or she comes in contact (Ephesians 3:19; 4:16).

The Believer Business Owner functioning apostle will care for the business for which the Cross of Jesus Christ is laid as the foundation (2 Corinthians 11:28).

The Believer Business Owner functioning apostle will be gifted with God's knowledge and wisdom concerning business decisions, investments, staying out of debt, knowing the times and seasons, and how to prosper during famines (2 Peter 3:15, 16; 1 Corinthians Chapters 1, 2 and 3). In Genesis 26:12-13, Isaac planted crops during a famine which yielded a hundredfold under challenging circumstances because the Lord blessed him. Isaac continued to follow the Lord's counsel in business and accumulated great wealth and gave birth to Jacob, who later was named Israel, and was the father of the twelve tribes of Israel and the great, great, great, etc of King David, and through the Virgin Mary, the Messiah, Christ Jesus.

The Believer Business Owner functioning apostle is noted for his or her "words of wisdom" (1 Corinthians 12:8). Likewise, Believer Business Owner functioning apostles need to have divine inspiration of the seasons and times regarding the things that prosper and the things that do not prosper. 1 Chronicles 12:32 says that Sons of Issachar became a great counsel for the head of government, King David, because they knew, understood, and had wisdom about the seasons and times for the nation.

The Believer Business Owner functioning apostle may minister in any of the other functioning gifts of the Ephesians 4:11 ministries, although he or she usually minors in one of the other Ephesians 4:11 office gifts in addition to being a Believer Business Owner functioning apostle.

Paul was a business functioning teacher/apostle (2 Timothy 1:11).

Paul and Barnabas together were functioning teachers/prophets but then were sent out as functioning apostles at the Antioch *Ekklesia* (Acts chap. 13).

Peter functioned as a pastor/apostle (John 21:15-17).

Timothy was a functioning evangelist/apostle (2 Timothy 4:5).

LIFE OF THE FUNCTIONING APOSTLE IN BUSINESS USUALLY HAS AN INORDINATE AMOUNT OF SUFFERING AND PERSECUTION

The Believer Business Owner functioning apostle will be a suffering servant for the business (Acts

5:18-40; Acts chapter 7; Colossians 1:23-29; 1 Corinthians 4; 2 Corinthians 6:3-10; 2 Corinthians, chapters 11 and 12).

The Believer Business Owner functioning apostle will be known for his or her humility. 1 Corinthians 15:9 says, "For I am the least of the apostles, that am not meet to be called an (functioning) apostle, because I persecuted the church (*Ekklesia*) of God." 1 Corinthians 4:9 says, "For I think that God hath set forth us the apostle last, as it were appointed to death: for we are made a spectacle unto the world, and to angels, and to men."

In Matthew 20:16 Jesus said, "So the last will be first and the first last." 1 Corinthians 12: 28 says in relevant part that "And God hath set some in the church (*Ekklesia*), first apostle, secondarily prophets, thirdly teachers, after that miracle, then gifts of healings, helps, governments, diversities of tongues." Since Believer Business Owner functioning apostles are first, they are destined to be last.

The foundation is that part of the house upon which people walk. The foundation is where the dirt is kicked off people's feet. The Believer Business Owner functioning apostles and functioning prophets that lay the foundation of the business have dirt thrown at them with gossip and false accusations. The most important part of a house is the foundation. It must be the sturdiest, the most solid, the most hardened, and needs the most preparation time to build; because when earthquakes or storms come, it is the solidity of the foundation that will make the house fall or stand.

Jesus spoke the beatitude about the necessity of building on a solid foundation in Matthew 7:24-27, which says, "Therefore whosoever heareth these sayings of Mine, and doeth them, I will liken him unto a wise man, which built his house upon a rock: (25) And the rain descended, and the floods came, and the winds blew, and beat upon that house; and it fell not: for it was founded upon a rock. (26) And every one that heareth these sayings of mine, and doeth them not, shall be likened unto a foolish man, which built his house upon the sand: (27) And the rain descended, and the floods came, and the winds blew, and beat upon that house; and it fell: and great was the fall of it."

The point made by Jesus was that the rains, floods, and strong winds will come in business; so the Believer Business Owner functioning apostles and Believer Business Owner functioning prophets have to build the business on the solid foundation of Christ Jesus.

I had a client that was very wise in business, even as a young man. For example, he would not employ another employee until he had one year's salary for the employee in a savings account. His rent of his business was hard negotiated and had the lowest rent in a newly built strip mall as the first tenant, and he negotiated hard to keep the rent increases low. After a few years, the strip mall was sold, and the new owners tried to renegotiate his ten year lease with renewal options; but with my legal help, they failed in trying to force him to sign a new lease. His employees were very high tech educated, but were Believers who prayed together each morning before work. He made a handsome profit, but he shared this profit with his employees each year during the Christmas season. Yet, his functioning pastor of a local church where he attended would not recognize his spiritual maturity in using financial biblical principles in operating his business that led to much profit. He came to me, and I prayed and ordained him as a Believer Business Owner functioning apostle of his business, as he really had sound and spiritual foundational business skills, more than anyone else that I knew. I came to his business often and started teaching his employees the Bible, giving them Scriptures to study, having each of them read out loud to the group the Scriptures being studied that day. I laid hands on each of his employees and prayed for wisdom, knowledge, understanding, and witty inventions. Eventually this Believer Business Owner functioning apostle opened up his home for fellowship. He kinesthetically trained his employees to operate in their spiritual Vocations and to be led for truth revelation by the Holy Spirit of their spiritual Gifts. Most of his employees became spiritual leaders in opening their homes for fellowship with their families, friends, and neighbors. He eventually paid off his home and sent his children to Christian School. Although I moved out of the area, every once in a while over the years, I called him to fellowship over lunch. He is now a wealthy Believer Business Owner functioning apostle who has retired from his business. He showed everyone that his business was his place of ministry. With my encouragement, he enjoys meeting other Believer Business Owners, and he teaches my lessons that business is a ministry and the owners are Ephesians 4:11 functioning ministers.

The Believer Business Owner functioning apostle will be **tested by the word of God** as to whether his or her work has become a true business ministry and whether it will pass through the fire (1 Corinthians 3:12-15). He or she always must be ready to perform servanthood to others in the business and in the marketplace, ready to bring God's principles and word to every business transaction (Revelation 2:2; Galatians 2:11-13; Acts 17:10-12). After eight years, I left my partnership law firm, and I became a sole practitioner lawyer, which I still am today in my late seventies. When I had employees, I would be the first person at the law office if I did not have a court appearance. My practice was to set up a coffee thermos with cups for my employees, where we sat to read five books of Psalms and one book of Proverbs before the phones started ringing and the employees started performing their assigned tasks.

GOD'S GREAT MYSTERY IS REVEALED TO THE FUNCTIONING APOSTLES AND PROPHETS

God promotes and commands unity. In Psalms 133:1 David proclaims, "Behold, how good and how pleasant it is for brethren to dwell together in unity!" Paul writes in Ephesians 4:3,13, "Endeavouring to keep the unity of the Spirit in the bond of peace. . . (13) Till we all come in the unity of the faith, and of the knowledge of the Son of God, unto a perfect man, unto the measure of the stature of the fulness of Christ."

Paul reveals unity of Jews and Gentiles in Ephesians 2:11-22, "Wherefore remember, that ye being in time past Gentiles in the flesh, who are called Uncircumcision by that which is called the Circumcision in the flesh made by hands; (12) That at that time ye were without Christ, being aliens from the commonwealth of Israel, and strangers from the covenants of promise, having no hope, and without God in the world: (13) **But now in Christ Jesus ye who sometimes were far off are made nigh by the blood of Christ.** (14) **For He is our peace, who hath made both one, and hath broken down the middle wall of partition between us**; (15) Having abolished in His flesh the enmity, even the law of commandments contained in ordinances; for to **make in Himself of twain one New Man**, so making peace; (16) And that He might reconcile both unto God **in one body by the cross**, having slain the enmity thereby: (17) And came and preached peace to you which were afar off, and to them that were nigh. (18) **For through Him we both have access by one Spirit unto the Father.** (19) **Now therefore ye are no more strangers and foreigners, but fellow citizens with the saints, and of the household of God**; (20) **And are built upon the foundation of the apostles and prophets, Jesus Christ himself being the chief corner stone**; (21) In whom all the building fitly framed together groweth unto an holy temple in the Lord: (22) In whom ye also are builded together for an habitation of God through the Spirit."

Again, the greatest mystery of Jesus Christ for Believers that was revealed to Paul was the unity as fellow heirs of both the Jews and the Gentiles with Christ Jesus. Paul said in Ephesians 3:1-11, "For this cause I Paul, the prisoner of Jesus Christ for you Gentiles, (2) If ye have heard of the dispensation of the grace of God which is given me to you-ward: (3) **How that by revelation He made known unto me the mystery**; (as I wrote afore in few words, (4) Whereby, when ye read, ye may understand my knowledge in the mystery of Christ) (5) Which in other ages was not made known unto the sons of men, as it is now **revealed unto His holy** (functioning) **apostles and** (functioning) **prophets by the Spirit**; (6) **That the Gentiles should be fellow heirs, and of the same body, and partakers of His promise in Christ by the gospel**. (7) Whereof I was made a minister, according to the gift of the grace of God given unto me by the effectual working of His power. (8) Unto me, who am less than the least of all saints, is this grace given, that I should preach among the Gentiles the unsearchable riches of Christ; (9) **And to make all men see what is the fellowship of the mystery, which from the beginning of the world hath been hid in God, who created all things by Jesus Christ:** (10) **To the intent that now unto the principalities and powers in heavenly places might be known by the church (Ekklesia-government assembly and military assembly) the manifold wisdom of God**, (11) **According to the eternal purpose which he purposed in Christ Jesus our Lord**."

Likewise, Paul declared in Galatians 3:28-29, "There is neither Jew nor Greek, there is neither bond nor free, there is neither male nor female: for ye are all one in Christ Jesus. (29) And if ye be Christ's, then are ye Abraham's seed, and heirs according to the promise."

Romans 10:12 says, "For there is no difference between the Jew and the Greek: for the same Lord over all is rich unto all that call upon him."

Acts 10:34-35 says, "Then Peter opened his mouth, and said, 'Of a truth I perceive that God is no respecter of persons: (35) But in every nation he that feareth Him, and worketh righteousness, is accepted with Him.'"

The foundational belief of Christ Jesus that must be expounded by the Believer Business Owner functioning apostles and Believer Business Owner functioning prophets is that Jesus broke down the barrier between Jews and Gentiles to create a new unified Body of Believers of all races in the world.

In America, there is a reaction to Palestinian people dying because of the Israel and Hamas war. Yet, instead of blaming the terrorist Hamas, these anti-semites put all of the blame on Israel instead of Hamas. Hamas started the war by attacking Israel on October 7, 2023, launching missiles and coordinated armed incursions on Israel from the Gaza Strip. Approximately 1,200 Israeli civilians and soldiers were killed in the Hamas-led attack, while around 250 Israelis were kidnapped on that horrific day. Hamas rejected several cease fire and peace propositions but finally accepted a cease fire and peace. Yet, the Palestinian people were victims of the war. Even after the latest cease fire and peace agreement, Hamas started assassinating Palestinians who they believed were sympathizers with Israel. President Trump has negotiated the rebuilding of the Palestinians territory, and President Trump has other Arab nations paying most of the cost for the rebuilding.

Christ Jesus' mother was a Jew, so Jesus was Jew, even though He was the only begotten Son of God. When He walked here on earth, He came to bring the Abrahamic blessing of reconciliation with God to all mankind as one people with Christ Jesus who together are the Temple of God here on earth (2 Corinthians 6:16; 1 Corinthians 3:17; Ephesians 2:21).

God's covenant was with Abraham to be a blessing to all nations (Genesis 18:18) and all families

(Genesis 12:3) on the earth. This promise of blessing is through Abraham's descendant, Christ Jesus (Galatians 3:16), spiritual unity of all people is the great mystery that is implied in the gospel of the Kingdom (Matthew 24:14) and repentance and remission of sins (Luke 24:47). The Jews and Gentiles can and must come together as all people who are descendants of Adam and Eve as the *Ekklesia* under the headship of Jesus Christ (Ephesians 1:22-23; 5:23; Colossians 1:18). Following the example of Gentiles and Israelites becoming as one Kingdom nation of God under Christ Jesus, even the Democrats and Republicans in the U.S., and the political parties in every nation, can be joint citizens of the Kingdom of God. All true Believers are to enter the kingdom of God as one worldwide holy nation (1 Peter 2:9).

The Believer Business Owners and Believer Business Employees must be supportive of all people, and especially must be supportive of the Jews as this race of people are the source of our Messiah and Savior.

Paul wrote in his letter to Ephesus in Ephesians 4:1-6, "I therefore, the prisoner of the Lord, beseech you that ye walk worthy of the Vocation (kings, priests, lords, ambassadors, and soldiers) wherewith ye are called, (2) With all lowliness and meekness, with longsuffering, forbearing one another in love; (3) **endeavoring to keep the unity of the Spirit in the bond of peace**. (4) There is one body, and one Spirit, even as ye are called in one hope of your calling; (5) One Lord, one faith, one baptism, (6) One God and Father of all, who is above all, and through all, and in you all."

CHAPTER EIGHT

THE BELIEVER BUSINESS OWNER FUNCTIONING PROPHET

BUSINESS FUNCTIONING PROPHETS ARE GOD'S GIFT TO ACTIVATE BELIEVER BUSINESS EMPLOYEES WITH GOD'S PROPHETIC WORDS TO EDIFY, EXHORT, COMFORT, AND MATURE THEM INTO THEIR SPIRITUAL VOCATIONS AND SPIRITUAL GIFTS

Ephesians 4:11-16 provides in relevant part, "And He gave … some as (Believer Business Owner functioning) prophets... (12) for the equipping (spiritual scholastic teaching and kinesthetic training) of the saints for the work of ministry (in business) for the edifying (help laying a foundation) of the Body of Christ (who are in business) (13) Till we all (saints in business) come in the unity of the faith, and of the knowledge of the Son of God, unto a perfect (business) man (or woman), unto the measure of the stature of the fullness of Christ: (14) That we henceforth be no more children (immature saints in business), tossed to and fro, and carried about with every wind of doctrine, by the sleight of men, and cunning craftiness, whereby they lie in wait to deceive; (15) but speaking the (prophetic) truth in love, may grow up (become mature Business ministers) in all things into Him who is the head even Christ (16) from whom the whole body, joined and knit together (common purpose) by what every joint supplies (with their talents), according to the effective working (in business) by which every part does its share (of the spiritual work in business), causes growth of the body for the edifying (help laying the foundation) of itself (business) in love."

Although much about the Believer Business Owner functioning prophets were discussed about prophets in the previous chapter regarding Believer Business Owner functioning apostles, it was because they share the same obligation of laying the foundation of the business with Jesus Christ as the Chief Corner Stone (Ephesians 2:20). So, I need to emphasize this foundation building mandate of the prophet but from a slightly different perspective that you will find edifying and revealing.

1 Corinthians 12:28 says, "And God has appointed these in the church (*Ekklesia* in business): first (business functioning) apostles, second (business functioning) prophets, third (business functioning) teachers, after that miracles, then gifts of healings, helps, administrations, varieties of tongues."

The Believer Business Owner functioning prophets' duty is to equip the Believer Business Employees for the work of ministry (of spiritual Vocations with spiritual Gifts) for the edification of the body of Christ.

Again, Vocations that all Believers are called as the work of ministry (Ephesians 4:12) is the labor as kings, priests (Revelation 1:6), lords (1 Timothy 6:15), ambassadors (2 Corinthians 5:20), and soldiers (2 Timothy 2:3-4). All Believers have the same Vocations, but they have different spiritual Gifts to be used in the furtherance of the work of their ministries.

1 Corinthians 12:5-7 says, "And there are **differences of administrations**, but the same (Jesus as) Lord (Ephesians 4:11). (6) And there are **diversities of operations**, but it is the same (Father) God which worketh all in all (Romans 8:6). (7) But the **manifestation of the (Holy) Spirit** is given to

every man to profit withal. (1 Corinthians 12:10)."

The Bible says that the ministry of the functioning prophet and prophecy is in the spiritual Gifts of God the Father (Romans 12:6), spiritual Gifts of God the Word and the Lord Jesus Christ's humanity nature (Ephesians 4:11), and spiritual Gifts of God the Holy Spirit (1 Corinthians 12:10). Unlike the functioning prophet and prophetic gifts, neither the functioning apostles, functioning evangelists, functioning pastors, nor functioning teachers are mentioned in all three ministry spiritual Gifts of the Godhead.

God is no respecter of Believers, and speaking of the functioning apostle as first is merely for the timing of the functioning apostles and functioning prophets' performing their duties in laying the foundation for the business. The truth is that 1 Corinthians 12:28 does not place upon the Believer Business Owner functioning apostle a higher stature than the Believer Business Owner functioning prophet, or any other Ephesians 4:11 functioning minister. 1 Corinthians 12:28 just means that the functioning apostle ministry is first in time and order for proper laying of the business foundation and then followed by the Believer Business Owner functioning prophet in completing the step of laying the business foundation, which has been previously discussed.

THE HEBREW WORDS FOR PROPHECY OR PROPHESY IN THE OLD TESTAMENT

The Hebrew word *chazah* means to gaze and to see as a Seer in the ecstatic state, and this Hebrew word was translated as:

BEHOLD-- Job 23:9, Psalm 17:2; 27:4.

LOOK-- Isaiah 33:20; Micah 4:11

PROPHESY-- Isaiah 30:10

PROVIDE-- Exodus 18:2

SEE-- Isaiah 1:1; 13:1; Ezekiel 13:6-8

The Hebrew word *masa* means a burden, a tribute, figuratively an utterance, chiefly a doom, especially singing, mental desire, and translated as:

BURDEN-- Isaiah 13:1; 15:1; 17:1; 19:1; Jeremiah 23:33,34,36; Habakkuk 1:1.

CARRY AWAY-- 2 Chronicles 20:25

PROPHECY-- Proverbs 30:1; 31:1

SONG--1 Chronicles 15:22,27

TRIBUTE-- 2 Chronicles 17:11

The Hebrew word *naba* means to prophesy, speak or sing by inspiration under divine spiritual anointing and translated as:

PROPHESY-- 1 Samuel 10:11; Jeremiah 2:8; 26:11; Ezekiel 37:7; Joel 2:28; Amos 3:8.

BUILD ONE-SELF UP AS A FUNCTIONING PROPHET-- Jeremiah 29:26,27

The Hebrew word *nebuwah* means a verbal or written prediction translated as:

PROPHESY-- 2 Chronicles 9:29; 15:8; Nehemiah 6:12

The Hebrew word *nataph* means to ooze, distill gradually, to fall in drops, to speak by inspiration, prophesy, discourse, a dropping down of inspired speech translated as:

DROP-- Judges 5:4; Ezekiel 21:2; Amos 7:16

PROPHESY-- Micah 2:6, 11

THE NATURE OF PROPHECY

FORTH-TELLING is a form of prophetic preaching, communicating the thoughts of God for the present movement of the Holy Spirit. Often, the past will be used to state the present. This includes prophecy which exhorts, reproves, warns, edifies, and comforts.

FORE-TELLING is a form of prophetic prediction of future events. The past and present are often used to explain the future events to come.

The purpose of prophetic prediction is to produce present godliness, faith, calmness, and hope for the future because God exercises His sovereign Will, teleology, authority, power, and God's *agape* love as Creator and covenant making and covenant keeping God to maintain is plan for mankind.

Believers' assurance is stated in John 3:16, and in particular 1 John 4:16-18, which says, "And we have known and believed the (*agape*) love that God hath to us. God is (*agape*) love; and He that dwelleth in (*agape*) love dwelleth in God, and God (dwelleth) in him. (17) Herein is our (*agape*) love made perfect, that we may have boldness in the day of judgment: because as He is, so are we in this world. (18) There is no fear in (*agape*) love; but perfect love casteth out fear: because fear hath torment. He that feareth is not made perfect in love."

VARIOUS TYPES OF PROPHETIC FUNCTIONS

THE SPIRIT OF PROPHECY -- Revelation 19:10 says "The testimony of Jesus is the Spirit of Prophecy."

The Spirit of Prophecy is seen when the Holy Spirit comes upon men and women and causes them to speak divinely inspired utterances.

Adam prophesied concerning His wife and the marriage estate (Genesis 2:20-25). Then in Genesis 3:20 Adam prophesied the hope of the future because God spoke about the coming Redeemer in Genesis 3:15 by naming his spouse, "Eve" because she was going to be the mother of all living.

Enoch prophesied of the Second Coming of Christ (Jude 14-15)

Abraham was called a prophet (Genesis 20:7)

Isaac and Jacob exercised the Spirit of prophecy during their paternal blessings upon their sons (Genesis chaps. 27,48, & 49; Hebrews 11:20-21)

Joseph prophesied of the exodus from Egypt (Genesis 50:24; Hebrews 11:22)

The Spirit of prophecy came upon the 70 Elders appointed by Moses (Numbers 11:24-30)

The Spirit of prophecy was on Saul who was not a prophet (1 Samuel 19:20-24; 10:10)

THE GIFT OF PROPHECY --This gift of prophecy is mentioned in 1 Corinthians 12:10; Romans 12:6; Acts 2:18

THE OFFICE OF THE PROPHET--Hosea 12:10 and Hebrews 1:1 says that God speaks to His people by way of the prophets. The prophet wears a prophetic mantle. In Numbers 11:29 Moses said, "Would God all His people were prophets." The Office Gift of the functioning prophet is mentioned in Ephesians 4:11.

THE PROPHECY OF SCRIPTURE --2 Peter 1:19-21 has the expression "prophecy of the scripture" which refers to the prophetical books of the Old Testament. All spoken prophetic utterances must conform to the written word of God. 2 Peter 1:19-21 says, "We have also a more sure word of prophecy; whereunto ye do well that ye take heed, as unto a light that shineth in a dark place, until the day dawn, and the day star arise in your hearts: (20) Knowing this first, that no prophecy of the scripture is of any private interpretation. (21) For the prophecy came not in old time by the will of man: but holy men of God spake *as they were* moved by the Holy Ghost.

THE WORD OF GOD THROUGH PROPHECY

The *rhema* of the Lord is indued with spirit and *zoe* life. John 6:63 says, "It is the spirit (*pneuma*) who gives life (*zoe*); the flesh (*sarx*) profits nothing. The words (*rhema*) that I speak to you are spirit (*pneuma*), and they are life (*zoe)*."

Some would ponder the thought that nothing can be added to the written word that we call the Bible, so functioning prophets or prophetic gifts were terminated in the Catholic Church after the canonized New Testament Scriptures. They would rationalize that verbal prophecy is not allowed today as it would add to or subtract from the words of prophecy in the Bible and thus violate the admonition. Yet, this interpretation is misleading at best and false at worst.

These proponents that prophecy is not needed or authorized today often quote improperly Revelation 22:18-19, which says, "For I testify to everyone who hears the words of the prophecy of this book; if anyone adds to these things, God will add to him the plagues that are written in this book; and if anyone takes away from the words of the book of this prophecy, God shall take away his part from the Book of Life, from the holy city, and from the things which are written in this book."

The correct interpretation of the admonition of Revelation 22:18-19 is that it applies in context to only the book of Revelation, not the entire New Testament. Revelation 22:18-19 warned that one was not to prophesy to change scripture in the book of Revelation but must accept what is revealed in this endtime prophetic written word of eschatology. I agree that one is not supposed to come up with a new Book of the Bible, as it has now been canonized in its final form. Yet, true prophecy may not add to or subtract from scripture, but illuminates, enlarges, and enhances the scriptures to bring greater understanding. If Believers just spue denomination doctrine that are not following truth of scriptures and have the audacity to think they have "The Truth" of interpretation of scriptures, then they are elitists and closed minded.

I know that those who honor God's written word do so mostly with a pure heart, but they still may be anemic in their thinking. I also honor God's word because Hebrews 4:12 says, "For the (*logos*) word of God *is* quick, and powerful, and sharper than any two-edged sword, piercing even to the dividing asunder of soul and spirit, and of the joints and marrow, and is a discerner of the thoughts and intents of the heart."

God is alive, and God still speaks today through His prophets, and no religious tradition can mussel God's thoughts, emotions, and foundational design, purpose, plan, and Will. He wants His adopted spiritual children to preach, teach, and prophesy to a lost and decadent world, and especially to an overly religious church. Those who teach that functioning prophets are not for today are like deists who believe that God is far away in heaven and allows mankind to rule over the society and people on earth without His twenty four-seven life-sustaining, life producing presence. Yet, the Bible says that obedient Believers are theists because they accept the truth that God is with us. Matthew 1:23 says, "Behold, a virgin shall be with child, and shall bring forth a Son, and they shall call his name Emmanuel, which being interpreted is, God with us." God lives inside each Believer as God's Temple. 2 Corinthians 6:16 says, "And what agreement hath the temple of God with idols? For ye are the temple of the living God; as God hath said, 'I will dwell in them, and walk in them; and I will be their God, and they shall be My people.'" Therefore, trying to mussel functioning prophets of God as not a legitimate ministry for today means these religious denominationalists try to mussel God from speaking through His holy functioning prophets (Amos 3:7). May it never be.

We need to hear from God today for the world under humanism is in a real mess, where murder of human beings is fostered and seen as good by deranged killers to promote humanistic philosophies.

RADICAL POLITICAL LEFT WING KILLINGS

Charlie Kirk's Assassination in 2025: Charlie Kirk of Turning Point USA was assassinated on September 10, 2025, because he spoke the Lord's truths in both the Old Testament and New Testament. Authorities say alleged shooter Tyler Robinson, age 21 was in a "romantic relationship" with his roommate, a "biological male… undergoing a gender transition."

Annunciation Catholic School in Minneapolis: On August 27, 2025, Robin Westman, a 23-year-old, gender transition from suburban Minneapolis, shooting through stain glass windows, was obsessed with killing children. The attack during the school's first Mass of the year left two children, aged 8 and 10, dead and 17 others injured. Westman, a former student, fired 116 rifle rounds through stained-glass windows. Police uncovered chilling writings, videos, and a manifesto revealing violent fantasies, regret over gender transition, and plans to target kids. Westman's mother worked at the Annunciation Catholic School until she left in 2021. Robert (changed to Robin after transgender surgery) Westman had previously attended the school. Westman was a man who became a transgender woman, blamed his/her mother for the mass shooting of the Christian kids, writing to her he stated, "Your words, mother, made me stay in my discomfort unable to ask for help to avoid admitting defeat. You were right mama, but the way you handled it led me to wanting to kill so so many people," Gender and weed f_ _ _ _ _ up my head," he claimed.

A Mormon Ward in Grand Blanc Township, Michigan: On September 28, 2025, in Grand Blanc Township, Michigan. Thomas Jacob Sanford, a 40-year-old Marine veteran from Burton, Michigan, did a mass shooting, who was killed by police at the scene. Sanford rammed his pickup truck into the front doors of the church, opened fire on the congregation with an assault rifle, and set the building on fire. The attack killed four churchgoers and injured eight other churchgoers. According to officials, Sanford harbored a deep hatred for the Mormon faith. He was killed by police in a shootout in the church parking lot. According to friends, his animosity reportedly stemmed from a failed relationship with a Mormon woman several years earlier.

These assassinations and killings are by no means all of that has and will be happening in the U.S. and other parts of the world.

FAR LEFT DEMOCRAT SOCIALIST THINK THEIR CONSTITUENTS ARE STUPID

The Democrat party in America is trying to stop the Judea-Christian foundation of the United States. People from other countries have come to America for 250 years because the U.S. society historically was basically founded on the principles and precepts of the Old Testament and New Testament, as we are basically a Judeo-Christian culture where there are rights and freedoms guaranteed under our U.S. Constitution. Yet, the church is anemic in the U.S. and are silent as the Lutheran Church was silent during the Nazi reign in Germany.

Although we have had decades of decline of Christian biblical truths that were enshrined in our Declaration of Independence, U.S. Constitution, and moral ideas, there is a spiritual revival that has begun by hundreds of thousands of GenZ young people who were influenced by Charlie Kirk and young men by people like Jordan Peterson.

There is a problem when people have become the silent majority regarding their Christian beliefs because the church leaders have dumb down the congregation. When you go to college you have to study hard because you want your education to be a good prerequisite to obtaining employment with a business owner. When you go to church listing to sermons for 20 to 30 years, you are not told the purpose for being taught the Bible is for you to learn scriptures because your spiritual profession is as a minister, and you are mandated in Ephesians 4:12 to do the work of the ministry. Yet, you are treated as a spectator when you arrive at the warehouse or cathedral lecture hall auditorium structure, and most Believers just get their spiritual shot every Saturday or Sunday, but the scriptures are not applied to the spectators' lives. The church leaders do not tell the congregation members they are all functioning ministers, and they never hear quoted Colossians 3:17, which says, "And whatsoever ye do in word or deed (personally, in family, in business, or in employment), do all in the name of the Lord Jesus, giving thanks to God and the Father by Him."

In his 1943 after ten years in prison, Dietrich Bonhoeffer wrote an essay titled "Theory of Stupidity," which argues that stupidity is a moral failing, not an intellectual one, and is in some ways more dangerous than evil. He observed that highly intelligent people can be stupid, while intellectually dull individuals might be wise, moral, and kind. Bonhoeffer says stupidity appears when people voluntarily surrender their critical thinking, inner independence, and sense of responsibility to the overwhelming force of rising power or group thinking. Bonhoeffer offered that a stupid person is a "mindless tool," and is a mere puppet in the hands of malicious forces. Stupid people can be guided and manipulated to do evil things without being able to recognize that their actions are evil.

Bonhoeffer said that reasons and facts "fall on deaf ears" of stupid people. If facts contradict stupid people's pre-judgments, they simply don't believe them, or they push them aside as inconsequential. Attempts to convince stupid people through debate are futile. An evil person who knows what he does is evil may have a sense of unease, but the stupid person is utterly self-satisfied in his beliefs. When challenged for their facts are totally wrong, they become easily irritated and dangerous, lashing out or going on the attack, even sometimes physical attacks.

The Christian Germans in the Lutheran church and other Christian denominations as Bonhoeffer's audience that he was addressing as being silent and stupid, he saw that stupidity was a social phenomenon in Germany. He believed that mass stupidity is a form of mass delusion that spreads especially when there is an "overwhelming impact of rising power" which is the takeover of the Democrat Party by a radical far left of Socialists.

For example, let's look at Zohran Mamdani.

Zohran Mamdani: Primarily **y**oung people came out in groves on November 4, 2025, voted to elect a self-proclaimed Democrat Socialist, Zohran Mamdani as the mayor of New York City. Mamdani refers to himself as a Democratic Socialist, but his positions come out of the Communist ideas of Karl Marx. **First,** Mamdani promises to **r**aise the corporate tax rate and taxes on the wealthy. When asked if billionaires have a right to exist, Mamdani replied, "I don't think that we should have billionaires because, frankly, it is so much money in a moment of such inequality." **Second,** Mamdani proposed starting a pilot program for one city-run grocery store in each borough, with the stated goal of seeing if removing the profit motive makes groceries cheaper. **Third,** He proposed subsidizing New York City buses to make them free to riders which may become filled by the homeless during the winters, so regular people would rarely be able to use the buses. **Fourth**, Mamdani**'s** platform included making childcare free for all New Yorkers, but government paid childcare has always been unaffordable. **Fifth**, Mamdani advocated for freezing rents for many tenants in rent-controlled apartments. **Sixth**, Mamdani in 2020 was a fierce critic of the NYPD and called for it to be defunded, although during his campaign he said he no longer holds that policy. **Seventh**, he is a vocal advocate for Palestinian rights and a strong critic of the Israeli government's actions. **Eighth**, Mamdani said he would have the Prime Minister of Israel, Benjamin Netanyahu arrested if he ever comes to New York City. **Ninth**, Mamdani said in a 2021 video of a Q&A session at a "Young Democratic Socialists of America" (YDSA) conference, that he identified with "seizing the means of production" as an "end goal" of the socialist movement, which is a core tenet of Marxist communism, as articulated by Karl Marx. **Tenth**, in a 2020 social media post on X (formerly Twitter), Mamdani used a version of "Each according to their need, each according to their ability". This statement is a famous line from Karl Marx's *Critique of the Gotha Program* and is widely associated with communist ideology. **Eleventh**, in 2020, Mamdani wrote a post on X suggesting that New York City's next mayor should be like "Comrade Arya Rajedran," a communist mayor in India. **Twelfth**, Mamdani made statements in the past on abolishing private property, which seems to be "fundamentally anti-American" and a threat to a cornerstone constitutional principle of freedom from government intrusion of private lives and *laisa fair* economy. Some legal immigrants from former Soviet Union bloc countries and other communist regimes found Mamdani's comment are communists and anti-American, arguing that such policies lead to a loss of personal freedom, single-party authoritarian rule, and human suffering.

If this is a trend for the Democrat far left, and it becomes popular, this is not a policy of affordability but for Socialism which throughout the world has been horrible for the country and its residents because it violates all principles in the Bible, especially in the parables of the minas (Luke 19:11-27) and the parable of the talents (Matthew 25:14-30). Socialism does not care what the U.S. Constitution says.

This is a time we really need God's functioning prophets who have a special ear for hearing God's voice about the future.

Those of us who lived during the Cold War with the Soviet Union, and Red China are very concerned of voters electing a far left Socialist or Communist.

Between the mid-1930s and 1938, Stalin orchestrated the Great Purge (also known as the "Great Terror") with the intent to eliminate perceived enemies within the Communist Party, military, and general populace. Hundreds of thousands of Soviet Union citizens were accused of political crimes and summarily tried in mock trials and immediately executed by shooting. The estimated death toll from the Great Purge is between 700,000 to 1.2 million. Additionally, millions of Soviet Union people were sent to the Gulag, which was a vast network of forced labor camps across the Soviet Union, often in remote regions such as Siberia. Also, Stalin's policy of forced Collectivization of Agriculture aimed to consolidate private farms into state-controlled collective units took away the incentives of hard work that farming owners did not mind doing since they would receive a profit. On the hand, Collectivization of Agriculture was a disaster, as the government took away free enterprise. Wealthier peasants, known as "kulaks," were seen as a threat to the Communist Government and were dispossessed, murdered, or exiled to labor camps and "special settlements." This effectively wiped out an entire upper social class in the Soviet Union. The Communist policies led to widespread famine in the early 1930s, especially in Ukraine, which is known as the Holodomor (meaning "death by hunger"). Stalin sealed Ukraine's borders to keep people from fleeing in search of food and imposed harsh grain requisitions and blacklisting measures. Millions of people perished from starvation and related diseases. There was no freedom of religions, freedom of speech, or freedom of redress of grievances.

In Communist China, after WWII and the defeat of Japan, the Chinese Civil War resumed between the Nationalist and Communist parties. This conflict resulted in millions more deaths and immense suffering before the Communists won and established the People's Republic of China in 1949. Mao Zedong's plan to rapidly industrialize China backfired spectacularly. It disrupted agriculture, caused a collapse in food production, and led to catastrophic famine, with estimates of deaths ranging from 15 to 55 million people. A political and ideological campaign launched by Mao Zedong to focused on purging capitalist and traditional elements from Chinese society. Millions of Chinese were persecuted, tortured, and killed by Red Guards, often their fellow students or colleagues. An estimated 1 to 2 million people died. Again, typically, there was no freedom of religions, freedom of speech, or freedom of redress grievances.

Persecution, loss of freedoms, and starvation, and excuses by government politicians follow wherever country has Socialism or Communism as their government.

Socialism generally fails financially due to issues with incentives, the absence of a market-based price system, or better known as the free enterprise system with less government intrusion and regulation. There also are the resulting problems with resource allocation, crime, chaos, and all resulting in an economic calculation problem. Finally, the Socialist always have an enemy's list who they can blame the enemy for the social distress and economic problems, not blame the fundamentals of Socialism or Communism. Socialism is a bad idea, and Communism is even worse, as the government controls the means of production, and thinks the government can provide cradle to grave, womb to tomb government economic welfare, which always increases government debt and regulates businesses out of existence.

Karl Marx, an Atheist coined the phrase "religion is the opiate of the masses," which he meant that religion provides a form of psychological relief to the mass of people experiencing hardship, similar to how opium can dull physical pain. It suggests that religion gives people illusory happiness and the strength to endure oppressive conditions, economic hardships, distracting them from their real-world problems and preventing them from seeking fundamental changes to throw Socialist politicians out of government.

While as Mayor of New York, I suggest that Mamdani will weekly attack Republicans, has Trump derangement syndrome, will be formulating lies to broadcast, will not swear allegiance to the U.S. Constitution, will not honor Veterans, as he believes the U.S. is an oppressive military government toward the Islamic religion, comes from a rich family, wants power, is a hypocrite, and is anti-American. He is an antisemite. He might eventually outlaw Christmas Trees and Nativity scenes in New York City.

The devil attacks unsaved people with ideas that sound as if they are egalitarian and that promote liberty, which often means promoting sin, and the ideas sound like liberty when they actually cause bondage. These ideas sound like they are non-discriminatory. If the ideas of the devil are acceptable to fallen mankind, then the devil goes home and rests because humans are doing his bidding.

For example, such as the devil came up with the idea of abortion on demand, the women of a whole generation got like-minded justices on the U.S. Supreme Court that held that abortion on demand is the sole right of the mother, not the father of the unborn. It is impossible to know the exact number of abortions worldwide since 1973 due to variations in record-keeping but estimates suggest that around 1.5 billion abortions have occurred globally. In the U.S. the number of abortions since 1973 is approximately 65 million abortions, which is the biggest holocaust against children in history.

PROPHECY IS ENCOURAGED AS A SPIRITUAL GIFT IN THE NEW TESTAMENT

Again, prophecy is encouraged in the New Testament in the spiritual gifts of Romans 12:6-8, 1 Corinthians 12: 8-10, and Ephesians 4:11. Revelation 19:10 says in relevant part that: "...For the testimony of Jesus is the spirit of prophecy." Similarly, 1 Corinthians 14:39 says, "Wherefore, brethren, covet to prophesy, and forbid not to speak with tongues." Even more compelling is 1 Thessalonians 5:19-21, which says, "Quench not the Spirit. (20) Despise not prophesyings. (21) Prove all things; hold fast that which is good." Yet, all prophecy must conform to Scripture and cannot be explained by its own meaning. It must be conformed to the *logos.* 2 Peter 1:19-21 says, "We have also a more sure word of prophecy; whereunto ye do well that ye take heed, as unto a light that shineth in a dark place, until the day dawn, and the day star arise in your hearts: (20) Knowing this first, that no prophecy of the scripture is of any private interpretation. (21) For the prophecy came not in old time by the will of man: but holy men of God spake as they were moved by the Holy Ghost."

A Believer Business Owner functioning prophet gives new light through direct application of Scripture to Believer Business Employees and other people concerning edification, exhortation, and comfort (1 Corinthians 14:3). The Believer Business Owner functioning prophet will confirm not only Scripture but also what God is already telling him or her. The Believer Business Owner functioning prophet can help Believer Business Employees see their ministry gift upon maturity and as their destiny. Psalm 119:130 says, "The unfolding of Thy words gives light; it gives understanding to the simple."

Believer Business Owner functioning prophets will use God's written word in the Old and New Testaments to support their prophetic words and cause an increase in illumination, so that the word of God can be put to living use in the lives of Believers, especially Believer Business Owners and Believer Business Employees. No one Believer throughout the history of the church has seen all the light in God's word. God's word is living and powerful (Hebrews 4:12) and constantly is giving off its light to enhance the lives of Believers in each generation.

Illumination of and from God's word is birthed out of previous insights. The Holy Spirit illuminates His revelation in the words already prophesied or already revealed and written down, then the Holy Spirit enlightens that word and amplifies and illuminates understanding of the revelation through His still small voice and signs.

In the Protestant Bible, it contains thirtynine books in the Old Testament and twentyseven books in the New testament, all written by approximately forty Believers, inspired by the Godhead. Each writer has his own personality, style, focus, peculiarities, and phraseologies. Although the Book of Job may have been the first book written, the first five books written by Moses stand at the beginning of a continuous line of God inspired thought that is totally dependent on what was previously written. Joshua wrote his book on the foundation laid by the Torah or Pentateuch. Joshua ministered based upon what he knew from the Pentateuch, not independent knowledge outside the Torah or Pentateuch. The same was true of all the other Books. There is not one contradiction in all the Bible in God's perspective, but the illumination of one writer may have a different facet of the same diamond that sends out a different color of light. There were many writers, but they all wrote on the foundation of the previous writings and what they heard and vision they received from God.

The writers in the New Testament merely enlarged, illuminated, enlightened, and enhanced the previous revelations, illuminations, and mysteries of truth revealed in the Old Testament. There are more than a thousand five hundred direct quotations of Old Testament Scriptures in the New Testament. Thus, even the New Testament is not independent, nor can it stand alone apart from the Old Testament. God is the same yesterday, today and forever; so, His word yesterday is the same for today and it will be the same in the future.

Prophecy must be spoken by voice or vision by God the Father, first, then transmitted to God the Word, then conveyed to God the Holy Spirit, then spoken to a functioning prophet's born again spirit, afterwards to the soul of the functioning prophet by the Holy Spirit's still small voice or by vision, and finally to the receiver of the prophetic word that the Holy Spirit instructed to direct the prophecy. This is God's redemptive word of communication, and it is spoken at the speed of thought. Words of knowledge, words of wisdom, tongues, and interpretation of tongues happen the same way (1 Corinthians 12:8-10). Thus God's prophecy is full of spirit and *zoe* life. As God the Word, Jesus' divine nature instructed Jesus to say in John 6:63, "It is the spirit that quickeneth; the flesh profiteth nothing: the words that I speak unto you, they are spirit, and they are life."

God partnerships with His chosen prophets to minister His prophetic word and *rhema* from the written word. There is not only God's written word but also the ministering of God's *rhema* word or prophetic word by the functioning prophet. Although occasionally God would use an angel to deliver His prophetic word to man, He normally used functioning prophets, especially in the Old Testament. God also uses functioning teachers that are revealed a *rhema* word from God's *logos* word. Since God's word is generally ministered by mankind, the functioning minister of the word, whether the functioning apostle, functioning prophet, functioning evangelist, functioning pastor, or the functioning teacher, becomes a strict oversight for God.

In the Old Testament God use functioning prophets to spread and taught His word. In the New Testament, the prophetic word is first spread by Jesus, Who is in a class all by Himself. Then God in the New Testament would use His functioning apostles, prophets, evangelists, pastors, and teachers. God will use His Believer Business Owner functioning prophets today, especially as the Holy Spirit is moving the *Ekklesia* to manifest His Ephesians 4:11 functioning apostles, prophets, evangelists, pastors, and teachers in businesses for the equipping and activating the Believer Business Employees for the work of their spiritual Vocations and spiritual Gifts.

2 Chronicles 20:20 says, "Believe in the Lord your God, and you shall be established; believe His (functioning) prophets, and you shall prosper."

ALL PROPHECY IS CONDITIONED UPON THE BELIEVER'S OBEDIENCE AND FAITH

Since the Godhead is resident in all business Believers (2 Corinthians 6:16), a Believer Business Owner functioning prophet and Believer Business Employees may prophesy under the prophetic anointing of the Holy Spirit, although not all are prophets. If the Holy Spirit can speak through an Old Testament donkey (Numbers 22:21-39), who was not an Ephesians 4:11 prophet, nor was human who had the gift of prophecy, He is well able to speak through any Believer Business owner or Believer Business Employee.

2 Peter 1:19-21 says, "We have also a more sure word of prophecy; whereunto ye do well that ye take heed, as unto a light that shineth in a dark place, until the day dawn, and the day star arise in your hearts: (20) Knowing this first, that no prophecy of the scripture is of any private interpretation. (21) For the prophecy came not in old time by the will of man: but holy men of God spake as they were moved by the Holy Ghost."

The Holy Spirit will not trespass a Believer's will to make a personal prophecy come to past. Thus, all personal prophecies are conditional! Assume that a Believer Business Owner receives a genuine prophecy that he is going to be wealthy. Even though this prophecy was spoken by a tested and mature Believer functioning prophet, the Believer Business Owner ripped off several investors by a concocted financial scam and goes to prison for 12 years does not make the functioning prophet a false prophet.

The personal prophecy speaks of God's best for a Believer, or what God's will is, or what God would like to have happen in the Believer's life; but the Believer can nullify the prophecy through his own sin or reject the prophetic word by the exercise of his will in his heart.

The Believer Business Owner functioning prophet speaks a prophetic word that reveals God's will for a better tomorrow in a Believer Business Employee's life to edify, comfort, and exhort him or her. Yet, it is God's desire for the Believer, not necessarily what is going to happen to the Believer Business Employee, especially if the Believer Business Employee becomes a reprobate and go into sinful rebellion. Also, there may be human or demonic intervention that interferes with and cuts off the perfect will of God.

A Believer Business Employee can commit himself or herself to different courses of action than

God's Will, and those courses of action are subject to the law of sowing and reaping (Galatians 6:7-8), which may cause a different harvest or effect than prophesied. Also, the devil can send his demons to come in and steal the word planted as they become the "fouls of the air" (Matthew 13:4, 19; Luke 8:5, 12). God does not coerce people to fulfill His prophetic personal words, just as he did not coerce Adam and Eve to "not eat the fruit from the Tree of the Knowledge of Good and Evil." Eating the forbidden fruit was the exercise of their "sovereign wills." God will not violate His moral attributes of respecting free moral agents just to fulfill a personal prophecy.

When a Believer Business Owner or Believer Business Employee receives a personal prophecy, he or she should write it down, pray over the prophetic word, check the prophetic word whether against or in favor of the written word of God, and meditate on the prophetic word from the prophet. These steps should be taken just like we daily must meditate on the written word of God.

Additionally, God's spiritual blessings in the Bible are written in conditional form. "If my people, who are called by my name will humble themselves. . . then I will hear from heaven and will forgive their sin and heal their land" (2 chronicles 7:14). "But you shall meditate in it day and night. . . then you will make your way prosperous, and then you will have success" (Joshua 1:8). "Beloved above all else I wish you would prosper and be in health even as your soul prospers" (3 john 2). Most all spiritual blessings are conditional, even salvation, because you must confess Jesus Christ as Lord and believe in your heart that God has raised Christ Jesus from the dead for Believers to be saved (Romans 10:9-10). By the same standard personal prophecies are conditioned upon other principles not being violated. If a prophecy does not come to pass, then perhaps other dependent conditions were not met. Perhaps the Believer receiving the prophecy was not obedient to the word of God. Additionally, the prophecy may be connected to a season which has not yet arrived. A prophecy also might be connected to a level of maturity that the Believer has yet not obtained in the Believer's soul.

Leaders who say that the New Testament prophets are to be stoned, as they were in the Old Testament, if their prophecies do not come true, are just ignorant. These religious leaders have a predisposition to believe that God exercises His sovereign will in a dictatorial way and treats human beings as robots, which is false. God does not force His word or will on anyone. God created mankind as free moral agents, with the cognitive ability to exercise volition. God is not capricious.

All prophecy should illuminate God's written word through a specific application to a particular Believer, season, event, or place. Therefore, a true Believer Business Owner functioning prophet continuously studies God's word in both the Old and New Testaments. All words from God are progressive and are not in opposition to the word already written or spoken. Prophecy will only illuminate, enlarge, or enhance that which is already written, but will not add to, subtract from, or contradict that which is written in scripture.

Some Believers improperly prophesy strictly out of the beliefs or thoughts from their souls without first hearing and receiving the redemptive flow of God's word. Although this is immaturity for a New Testament Believer to prophesy out of his soul, a word that is only a soulish prophecy is irresponsible and can be hurtful to the recipient if followed. Although being stoned by falsely prophesying were the reference to the rules of the Old Testament prophecies, Jeremiah 23:16 shows how God is upset with even New Testament Believers that use soulish prophecies for self-exaltation or self-promotion. "Thus, saith the LORD of hosts, 'Hearken not unto the words of the (false or immature) prophets that prophesy unto you: they make you vain: they speak a vision of their own heart (soul), and not out of the mouth of the LORD.'"

There were exceptions in the Old Testament when a true prophecy did not come true, even though when it was given, it came through God's redemptive communication to the prophet. Elisha's final prophecy was not entirely fulfilled, as it was modified and unfulfilled because of an attitude of Joash, king of Israel. Elisha was the prophet with the double anointing, with twice as many miracles as Elijah, but still part of his final prophecy did not come to past completely. God's perfect will was not done following a legitimate prophetic word. In 2 Kings 13:14-25 the first part of Elisha's prophecy to Joash, the king of Israel was to take a bow and shoot the arrow through the east window, which the king obeyed. Functioning prophet Elisha then said in 2 Kings 13:18-19, "… Take the arrows. And he (King Joash) took them. And he said unto the king of Israel, 'Smite upon the ground.' And he smote thrice and stayed. (19) And the man of God was wroth with him, and said, 'Thou shouldest have smitten five or six times; then hadst thou smitten Syria till thou hadst consumed it: whereas now thou shalt smite Syria but thrice.'" The king did not do the act constituting God's will as pronounced by God's prophet, Elisha. Because of King Joash's lack of enthusiastic commitment to the prophetic word, King Joash did not totally win the war against Syria but just had three smaller victories in battle where he recaptured and regained lost territory that had been taken during his father's reign (see 2 Kings 13: 22-25).

Thus, even in the Old Testament, when the Believer receiving a personal prophecy had to be obedient to the prophetic word for it to be fulfilled. Therefore, prophecy fulfillment is conditional, but this fact does not diminish the accuracy of the prophet nor the anointing on his or her life, nor on the perfect will of God.

The final prophecy of Elisha to King Joash was followed by Elishs's death where a dead man was buried in the tomb of Elisha. When the dead man was put down on the bones of Elisha, he was raised from the dead. The double anointing was even in Elisha's bones (2 Kings 13:21). Therefore, the Old Testament prophet Elisha was subject to both the will of God and the will of man. Likewise, the New Testament prophet would certainly be subject to the same principle, except the New Testament prophet can allow his or her personality in giving a particular prophecy as the word became flesh or personality (John 1:14).

PROPHETS OF THE OLD TESTAMENT

The first man called a Believer Business Owner functioning prophet was Abraham, and his ministry office was verified by a heathen king named Abimelech. Genesis 20:7 says, "Now therefore, restore the man's wife; for he is a (functioning) prophet, and he will pray for you, and you shall live. But if you do not restore her, know that you shall surely die, you and all who are yours."

Abraham walked, lived, and ministered as a functioning prophet of God, becoming an excellent example of God's grace extended to an individual when the Lord decides the individual is going to be God's Business functioning minister. Although Abraham did not walk in perfect obedience in his early life, he did have a heart to obey God, and the Lord worked with him until he grew to maturity.

Abraham was a true Believer Business Owner functioning prophet. Abraham was a very successful Believer Business Owner functioning prophet who had large herds of animals, many servants, and much wealth which he handed down to his child of promise, Isaac.

1 Kings 17:1 shows Elijah in scripture, without reference to his training or preparation in a violent confrontation. "As the Lord God of Israel lives, before whom I stand, there shall not be dew nor

rain these years, except at my word."

God alone can make an individual stand before Him, receiving what needs to be said and delivering it with a boldness and anointing necessary to bring forth repentance and direction!

The Old Testament functioning prophets were known under the following designations:

THE MAN OF GOD –(1 Samuel 9:6; 1 Kings 12:22).

THE SEERS –(1 Samuel 9:9; 2 Chronicles 33:18; 35:18; 2 Samuel 24:11; Amos 7:12; Isaiah 29:10)

THE INTERPRETERS – (Isaiah 43:27). The prophets were the interpreters of the Law and the history of the Nation.

THE MESSENGERS OF THE LORD TO THE NATION – (Isaiah 43:19; Malachi 3:1)

THE SERVANTS OF THE LORD – (Haggai 2:3)

THE FUNCTIONING PROPHETS – (Hosea 12:10). They were public expounders and preachers of the word of the Lord. "Holy men of God spoke as they were moved of the Holy Spirit" (2 Peter 1:21).

THE FUNCTIONING PROPHET MOSES--THE LETTER OF THE LAW – Moses was the prophet who received the Law of God on Mt. Sinai. This was a true example of a foundation ministry, and all succeeding functioning prophets were tested by the law given to Moses by the LORD. The LORD communicated with Moses face to face, and he became a type of Messiah who would be "like unto Him" (Acts 3:22-33).

THE FUNCTIONING PROPHETS FROM SAMUEL TO MALACHI – THE SPIRIT OF THE LAW – It was under Samuel there was a distinct development of the prophetic office. The Scriptures clearly mark Moses and Samuel as being key men in the prophetic ministry of the Old Testament.

"For Moses truly said..." (Acts 13:22). "Yea, and all the prophets from Samuel and that follow after..." (Acts 3:24). "And after that He gave them judges about the space of 450 years, until Samuel the (functioning) prophet..." (Acts 13:20; Hebrews 11:32). Samuel was the last of the Judges and first of the line of functioning prophets. In the school of the functioning prophets was where young men were trained and instructed out of the Law of Moses and were taught how to respond to the Spirit of the Lord in worship and prophecy (1 Samuel 9:20).

There were training centers where the sons of the functioning prophets gathered for the preparation of the ministry gift. Ramah – 1 Samuel 19:18-24. Bethel--2 Kings 2:3. Jericho--2 Kings 2:5,7,15 and Gilgal – 2 Kings 4:38; 2:1.

Since Israel was set up as a theocracy, the functioning prophets often spoke prophetically to the Kings. Saul and David had the functioning prophet Samuel (1 Samuel 9, 10, 16). David also had the functioning prophets Nathan and Gad (2 Samuel 12; 24:11). Solomon had the functioning prophet Nathan (1 Kings 1:38). Rehoboam had the functioning prophet Sheminial (1 Kings 12:21,22). Ahab had the functioning prophets Elijah and Elisha (1 Kings 17:1; 19:16).

There were functioning prophets who wrote Historical Books, prophets who wrote Poetical Books, and prophets who wrote prophetical Books.

There were local functioning prophets who spoke to their own present generation.

There were national functioning prophets who wrote about the future destiny of Israel as a nation and the destiny of the Gentile nations as well.

There were Messianic functioning prophets who spoke concerning the Jewish Messiah and the *Ekklesia*, from His first coming to His second coming. The Messianic prophecies deal with the first coming of Christ, the *Ekklesia* of Jesus Christ, and the second coming of Christ.

The functioning prophet of the Old Testament was one who spoke for God as His mouthpiece where God used the functioning prophet merely as a tape recorded. The functioning prophet was to boil forth prophetic words as a hot spring or fountain.

The functioning prophet under the Old Testament law was not living in the dispensation of grace brought by Jesus' crucifixion and resurrection. The Old Testament functioning prophet was most strictly judged by the law as whether the prophecy was true. Normally, if a prophecy did not come true, the functioning prophet was stoned to death. Yet, some prophecies were so futuristic that the truth or falsehood of the prophecy could not be ascertained. This can be seen in Moses' prophecy of a futuristic functioning prophet (Jesus Christ) in Deuteronomy 18:15, which says, "The LORD thy God will raise up unto thee a functioning Prophet (Jesus Christ) from the midst of thee, of thy brethren, like unto me; unto Him (Jesus Christ) ye shall hearken."

On the other hand, in the New Testament, the functioning prophet can be chastised by the Godhead but not stoned to death because the word became personality and dwelt among us (John 1:14).

THE MINISTRY OF GOD'S WORD BY THE OLD TESTAMENT FUNCTIONING PROPHETS

The many functioning prophets of God in the Old Testament spoke by the visions which they had received. The word had to come to them from God under the anointing the prophets had from His Spirit.

In the Old Testament God set aside the functioning prophet's emotions and thoughts and illuminated him by vision. The functioning prophet was like a tape recorder and just played the tape recording of what God revealed to him. In other words, God merely employed the Believer's mouth to speak His word.

Under this method, the Holy Spirit so controlled the functioning prophet that there could be no error in God's word as revealed by Him. There was little if any beliefs, emotions, or thoughts of the Believer involved.

For example, Numbers 22:9 says, "Then God came to Balaam and said, 'Who are these men with you?'" After Balaam answered Him, Numbers 22:12-13 says, "And God said to Balaam, 'You shall not go with them; you shall not curse the people, for they are blessed.' So, Balaam rose in the morning and said to the princes of Balak. 'Go back to your land, for the Lord has refused to give me permission to go with you.'" After the princes of Balak took Balaam′s refusal to Balak, he sent others to entreat Balaam with offers of riches to prophesy and curse the Jews. Number 22:20 says, "And God came to Balaam at night and said to him, If the men come to call you, rise and go with them; but only the word which I speak to you that shall you do.'"

Balaam saddled his donkey and did as the Lord commanded him. On the way, an Angel of the Lord stood in the narrow path, blocking their way. Numbers 22: 27-31 says, "And when the donkey saw the Angel of the Lord, she lay down under Balaam; so, Balaam′s anger was aroused, and he struck the donkey with his staff. Then the Lord opened the mouth of the donkey, and she said to Balaam, 'What have I done to you, that you have struck me these three times?' And Balaam said to the donkey, 'Because you have abused me. I wish there were a sword in my hand, for now I would kill you!' So, the donkey said to Balaam, 'Am I not your donkey on which you have ridden, ever since I became yours, to this day? Was I ever disposed to do this to you?' And he said, 'No.' Then the Lord opened Balaam's eyes, and he saw the Angel of the Lord standing in the way with His drawn sword in His hand; and he bowed his head and fell flat on his face."

In the Old Testament God would employ even a donkey's tongue to speak His will. The Scriptures show that when Balaam came to prophesy, his personal feelings toward the children of Israel were wrong, yet he prophesized the word of God as commanded. Nevertheless, as soon as Balaam spoke outside of the revelation of God, he manifested sin, error, and darkness.

Since God did not want any human mind, emotions, or heart of the soul involved, then He used the tongue of the human functioning prophet or donkey to sound forth His prophetic words like He would use a tape recorder. Numbers 11:25 says, "Then the Lord came down in the cloud, and spoke to him and took of the Spirit that was upon him and placed the same upon the seventy elders; and it happened, when the Spirit rested upon them, that they prophesied, although they never did so again." This was the operation of the Spirit of Prophecy as they were not God's chosen prophets.

However, there were exceptions with functioning prophets Moses, David, Isaiah, and Jeremiah. With these functioning prophets, God allowed the men to interject their own thoughts, feelings, and will in the delivery of His word. During three occasions Moses spoke to God as he felt, and Moses' word changed God′s mind. Thus, Moses' word became God's word or decision. The same is true with Isaiah. Similarly, David and Jeremiah expressed their own feelings and ideas before God. The New Testament Believer Business Owner functioning prophets must have an intimate relationship with the Holy Spirit, so the Believer Business Owner functioning prophet knows the voice of the Holy Spirit.

In the Old Testament the penalty for a functioning prophet if the prophecy that did not come true was stoning unto death. Deuteronomy 13:10, "And you shall stone him with stones until he dies, because he sought to entice you away from the Lord your God, who brought you out of the land of Egypt, from the house of bondage."

Are we now under the Law? Are the functioning prophets of the New Testament *Ekklesia* to be stoned if their prophetic words do not come to pass? Also, Deuteronomy 13:10 has a purpose of stoning and that was, "....because he (prophet) sought to entice you away from the Lord your God...." What God wanted was no false prophets enticing Believers away from Him, as this was what Lucifer, Satan, and the devil did in using the serpent (or dragon) to entice Eve to eat the forbidden fruit (Genesis 3:1-6).

THE MINISTRY OF GOD'S WORD IN THE GOSPELS BY CHRIST JESUS

Only one Greek word was used to encompass all of prophecy in the New Testament. The Greek word, *Euo* means to foretell events, divine speech, speak under divine inspiration, to proclaim a divine revelation, to prophesy, to foretell and forth-tell of the future, and *Euo* is translated in English as prophesy (Matthew 15:7; Luke 1:67; 22:64; John 11:51; Acts 2:17-18; 21:9; 1 Corinthians 14:1,3-5; 1 Peter 1:10; Revelation 1:3).

Again, Jesus' divine nature is God the Word, and this is why Hebrew 4:12 says, "For the (*logos*) word of God is quick, and powerful, and sharper than any two-edged sword, piercing even to the dividing asunder of soul and spirit, and of the joints and marrow, and is a discerner of the thoughts and intents of the heart."

Repeating, John 1:14 says, "And the Word (*logos*) was made flesh, and dwelt among us, (and we beheld His glory, the glory as of the only begotten of the Father,) full of grace and truth."

In the Old Testament God merely engaged the functioning prophets' tongues to propagate His word. Even John the Baptist was only "The voice of one crying in the wilderness" (John 123). God simply used John's voice when he ascertained that the word had become flesh by the appearance of Jesus. Later, Jesus was crucified and was resurrected from the dead. After Jesus' ascension, and the Day of Pentecost, the Holy Spirit poured out and empowered the Believers to be Jesus' witnesses throughout the world (Acts 1:8). John the Baptist operated as an Old Testament prophet and Jesus declared that he was the greatest functioning prophet of the Old Testament. Yet, Jesus said in Matthew 11:11 says, "Verily I say unto you, 'Among them that are born of women there hath not risen a greater than John the Baptist: notwithstanding he that is least in the kingdom of heaven is greater than he."

However, Jesus' humanity nature was the *logos* word made flesh. Jesus' divine nature, as God the Word is living and sharper of any two-edged sword. God did not have to send His word to Jesus as He had done to the Old Testament prophets, even John the Baptist. The living God the *Logos* was already the distinguishable part of Jesus as one of His dual natures, and this living *Logos* became flesh and dwelt amongst us here about 2,000 years ago.

Jesus' divine nature, God the *Logos* took on His humanity nature personality with His thoughts, emotions, and will of a Sinless Man, the Last Adam and Second Man (1 Corinthians 15:45,47), the only begotten Son of God and the chosen Lamb of God, that took away the sins for those who become His Believers. Jesus' divine nature, God the *Logos* had unhindered use of Jesus' sinless Humanity Nature and fulfilled the purpose of God to partnership with Man regarding His word. Even though God the *Logos* was embodied in Jesus' humanity nature, God the *Logos* did not lose any of its purity because Jesus' divine nature was distinguished from His humanity nature. Therefore, when Jesus took on sins of mankind, God the *Logos* was not damaged nor tarnished.

God did not intend that God the *Logos* remain merely in the spiritual realm but intended that God the *Logos* become incarnate separately attached but distinguishable to Jesus' humanity nature and thereby took on human personality living in a mortal body. God delighted in God the *Logos* becoming flesh with His Only Begotten Son. God wanted His word to carry human feelings, thoughts, and beliefs, which were totally submitted to Him.

Jesus' divine nature, God the *Logos* was not touched by the sin (2 Corinthians 5:21) or the curse of the Law (Galatians 3:13) placed upon Jesus' humanity nature when He was crucified, as His divine nature was totally separate but distinguishable from His humanity nature. This fact about Jesus explains the great mystery and principle of how an imperfect Believer can have the abiding word of God and have the holy and righteous born again spirit within him or her and yet still be immature and involved in sin in the soul. Jesus paved the way for the *rhema* word of God to remain pure even while being filtered through man's immature or sinful thoughts, feelings, and heart where his or her will manifested.

Jesus said in Matthew 5:17 to "Think not that I am come to destroy the law, or the prophets: I am not come to destroy, but to fulfil." The fulfillment of the Law and the Old Testament prophetic insights through the prophets were by the *Logos* becoming personified in Christ Jesus.

Again, Christ Jesus' humanity nature worked as a carpenter and stonemason, lived with His divine nature, God the *Logos*; and God the *Logos* was fully expressed through His mindful thoughts, emotional feelings, and heartful beliefs of His humanity nature without the hindrance of sin. Thus, the word of God was advanced from mere revelation to taking on the humanity of an individual personality. Jesus' sinless humanity nature did not have to wait on the word of God coming to Him from heaven outside of His humanity nature, as God the *Logos* was Jesus' divine nature; and Jesus' sinless human spirit, soul, and body was joined to His divine nature, although separate, not commingled together, distinguishable, and inseverable. In Jesus, God's word was unaffected and unrestricted like it is in a sinful man's soul being transformed but chosen as a functioning prophet. Thus, every Believer who has the gift of prophecy, merely prophesies in part. 1 Corinthians 13:9 says, "For we (Believers) know in part, and we prophesy in part." Jesus' humanity nature took on the sin of fallen humanity, while Jesus' divine nature, God the *Logos,* acted as the High Priest that offered Jesus' humanity nature as the Sacrificial Lamb of God. Thus, Jesus laid down His own humanity life to pay the price for the sins of fallen humanity who believe in Him (John 15:13; Romans 5:8; Ephesians 5:2; Titus 2:14; 2 Corinthians 5:21).

The Old Testament functioning prophets did not have the indwelling Godhead because Jesus had not as yet been sent to earth according to Galatians 4:4. However, the New Testament functioning prophets have the entire Godhead residing in them. Unlike Jesus, New Testament functioning prophets do not have transform souls, so they have some sins in their souls. In Christ Jesus' humanity nature, there was no sin as He was perfectly holy and righteous. Like Jesus, God the *Logos*, along with God the Father and God the Holy Spirit, indwells each Believer, including New Testament functioning prophets, but they only prophesy in part because of their imperfect souls.

THE SIGNIFICANCE OF THE NEW TESTAMENT PROPHETIC WORD MADE FLESH OR PERSONALITY

Acts 3:22 says, "For Moses truly said unto the fathers, 'A prophet shall the Lord your God raise up unto you of your brethren, like unto me; Him shall ye hear in all things whatsoever He shall say unto you.'"

One of the major purposes of the functioning prophets is to stand in the gap when God reveals pending judgment, so a prophet is an intercessor for the Body of Christ that brings repentance for the judgment to be averted. After repentance salvation and deliverance will come.

Functioning prophets also produce in people an understanding of how God operates as well as putting in Believers a heart-felt desire to go into the inner chamber with God to intercede and stand in the gap for revival.

For example, Abraham was so successful in his intercession that the Angel of the Lord literally led Lot and his family out of Sodom outside the city before the impending destruction (Genesis 19:15-17). .

Believer Business Owner functioning prophets also are called to be confronters and stand up and say things that are true, even as against religious traditions. This is one of the functioning prophets' primary assignments which is to instill and equip the New Testament Believers for the work of Vocations. The functioning prophets must re-instill the commitment to speak God's truth what they hear from the Holy Spirit and do not be afraid of being attacked by the religious leaders. Only when all Believers start speaking the truth to those in the world and the Body of Christ and its leaders, can those Believers truly be used by God as a prophet in its major measure of grace.

Prophets of the New Testament by the power of the Holy Spirit also see and expose wrong motivation. In the application of the topic of this book, Believer Business Owner functioning prophets operate strongly in the gift of discernment which they must express in the End-time *Ekklesia.* This is especially true since the major sign of the end time is deception.

Believer Business Employees must be activated by the prophetic gift to discern both good and evil in business. This spiritual discernment will also be instilled in the *Ekklesia* to discern the motivation of the heart of people. There are people that have obsessive and compulsive behaviors with money, where they seek money to feel safe, to have control, to establish freedom, to be romantic, to be attractive, or other maladies that lead to avarice, greed, or covetousness.

Again, I suggest you purchase my book at Amazon, titled The Personality Traits of Money for one of the most comprehensive studies from a Christian point of view regarding the good attachment of money as opposed to the evil use of money to enhance a person's personality maladies.

Believer Business Owner functioning prophets are also called to reproduce in the Believer Business Employees a heart which hates impurity, selfishness, manipulation, greed, covetousness, or avarice. There is a divine integrity in business which must come upon the Believer Business Owners and Believer Business Employees in the last days. The very heart of God for holiness is one shown by the true prophets of God, and the pure prophet's heart is a pattern for all Believers' hearts in the Body of Christ that must be transformed unto righteousness and holiness. It is when the Body of Christ has been activated to show God the Father's heart to the unsaved, that we will see the kind of fruit God wants to have remain.

1 Corinthians 13:2 says, "And though I have the gift of prophecy, and understand all mysteries and all knowledge, ...but have not love, I am nothing." In fact, all spiritual gifts must be exercised with *agape* love and faith.

Paul said in 1 Corinthians 14:3, "But he who prophesies speaks edification (to build up) and exhortation (to stir up encouragement) and comfort (to bind up) to men." Further, Paul said in 1 Corinthians 14:24-25 says, "But if all prophesy, and there come in one that believeth not, or one unlearned, he is convinced of all, he is judged of all: (25) And thus are the secrets of his heart made manifest; and so falling down on his face he will worship God, and report that God is in you of a truth." Thus, the functioning prophets were to bring secrets of his heart made manifest (to open up) and so falling down on his face (to change heart).

The Believer Business Owner functioning prophet when in charge of a business by himself or herself, often brings forth both positives and negatives according to what he or she sees and hears from God. A Believer Business Owner functioning prophet can build up the positive and brutally tear down the negatives in business that do not correspond to the vision. Truth is of paramount concern with the Believer Business Owner functioning prophets, which is contained in the vision given by God for the business.

Believer Business Owner functioning prophets do not tolerate deviation from the vision of the business. The prophetic vision is foundational. If a Believer Business Owner functioning prophet catches a Believer Business Employee doing something wrong that is harmful to the business, the Believer Business Owner functioning prophet is normally not gentle in correction or confrontation, as truth is more important than feelings of the Believer Business Employees or Believer Business Owners.

Believer Business Owner functioning pastors are much more understanding and seem to work hard to bring change through conciliation instead of confrontation. It is not that the Believer Business Owner functioning prophet lacks love; it is that he or she loves truth over any failings, excuses, or falsehoods. All actions must conform to the prophetic vision, and the prophetic word. Loyalty to the vision or prophetic is of paramount concern for the supervisors and leaders of the business, so the business is headed in the right direction, and the anointing is not lost.

Believer Business Owner functioning prophets hate cover-ups or excuses. Believer Business Owner functioning prophets must bring all problems out in the open and examine the problems as to whether actions taken to solve the problem further the vision and purpose of the business.

The Believer Business Owner functioning prophet forbids Believer Business Employees from having contact with customers outside the business hours to talk about other business or for personal intimate contact is strictly forbidden, the violation of which results in immediate dismissal from employment. Things are usually black and white with the Believer Business Owner functioning prophet, as there are rarely any gray areas. The Believer Business Owner functioning prophet often goes through many Believer Business Employees until they find someone with a similar dedication to the vision and truth of what the business is called to accomplish.

1 Corinthians 14:1,3 says, "Follow after charity (*agape* love), and desire spiritual gifts, but rather that ye may prophesy… (3) But he that prophesieth speaketh unto men to edification, and exhortation, and comfort."

The advantages of Believer Business functioning prophet leadership are clarity of vision, love for truth, activating Believer Business Employees at the business venue, with the purpose that all Believers connected with the business to fulfill God's purpose of manifesting God's Kingdom, and that all Believers are prepared to face the future. Also, with the prophetic anointing, the Believer Business Owner functioning prophet can release the spirit of prophecy where employees can hear clearly from God and be able to come up with God's creative ideas in furtherance of God's teleology.

On the other hand, some of the disadvantages of Believer Business Owner functioning prophet leadership when trying to run a business is the tendency to reproduce a degree of coldness and hardness about following procedures, and roughness in communication because truth is paramount over Believer Business Employee's immature and wrongful thoughts, unstable feelings, and unbiblical beliefs. This is especially true in modern day tendency of even young Believers being self-absorbed, working to satisfy emotions, and disregarding biblitarian truths. This can cause immature Believer Business Employees to figure a problem out themselves instead of trying to get a consensus of ideas for fear of ridicule. Unfortunately, living in a fallen world society has both godly good and anti-biblical bad ideas and mores. Likewise, other Believer Business Employees may emulate the Believer Business Owner functioning prophet's harshness and coldness toward fellow employees and customers because biblical truth is paramount, which will be counterproductive of God's Kingdom principles of economics. Galatians 5:6 states "… faith which worketh by (*agape*) love." *Agape* love for others is a commandment of the Lord (John 13:34-35).

Believer Business Owner functioning prophets are almost at times the opposite of the people-pleasing Believer Business Owner functioning pastors in business whom the Believer Business Employees tend to love and go to for help because the Believer Business Owner functioning pastors encourage loving relationships, thoughtfulness, gentleness, and helpfulness as servants toward each other.

Yet, discipline, which is discipleship training that is the responsibility of all the Believer Business Owner Ephesians 4:11 functioning ministers. It is be better if the Ephesians 4:11 minister as a Believer Business Owner is a functioning prophetic pastor, where he or she demands truth and loyalty to the business vision, but is kinder, empathetic, and shows *agape* love. With a Believer Business Owner functioning prophetic pastor, Believer Business Employees are not afraid to admit they are ignorant on what to do.

On the other hand, the Believer Business functioning prophet will think that the Believer Business Employee lacking knowledge means the Believer Business Employee is undisciplined and unwilling to be discipled. The Believer Business Employee may be terminated. The Believer Business Employee is harshly informed that he or she must acquire the knowledge and training needed or he or she will be replaced. God's discipline is sound and teaches the Believer Business Employee that discipleship is a tough life, but he or she will mature quickly, will discard fallen world false principles of economics, and will be promoted with higher responsibilities. Thus, discipline unto maturity enhances the spiritual fruit of *agape* love.

Believer Business Owner functioning prophets usually produce employees who begin to hear the words of the Holy Spirit and will recognize the words of the Holy Spirit from the Believer Business Owner functioning prophet. The problem is the employees and people in business can be too dependent on the Believer Business Owner functioning prophet for guidance, rather than developing an on-going relationship with the Godhead and the Lord Jesus Christ's humanity nature, submitting to God's leadership, and establishing a firm foundation of their principles and beliefs from the written word of God as they are led by the Holy Spirit.

The Believer Business Owner functioning prophets are required to have the Godly character qualities of moral business leaders if they are to be all that God would have them to be in the business and marketplace. They must not be greedy, covetous, or avarice but must be funnels of God's outpouring to those in need of wealth and prosperity in business.

Believer Business Owner functioning prophets can bring the spirit of prophecy with them for others to partake, and they carry with them the gift of prophecy. They will have a word from God for Believer Business Employees with expected futuristic trends, how to start working to provide what customers want, which will prosper the business and how God's economic principles when applied will prosper everyone in the business.

As with the other Ephesians 4:11 functioning ministers, the Believer Business Owner functioning prophet is to operate with signs and wonders to prove the word has become flesh or personality, and that the Kingdom of God is now manifesting within Believers. God will use the Believer Business Owner functioning prophets to speak His vision, wisdom, and truth to those working in the business as they encounter the marketplace.

The Believer Business Owner functioning prophets are the planners, the visionaries, the seers, the inventors, the imaginators, and have the divine word from God. Believer Business Owner functioning prophets are revolutionary and are usually the first to see the changes needed and how the Kingdom principles of economics are to be applied in the marketplace that will bring more customers. On the other hand, the Believer Business Owner functioning apostles are the ones that bring these needed changes and these new ideas into the marketplace and the steps to be taken to achieve that purpose and vision revealed by the Believer Business prophet. This is how the Believer Business Owner functioning apostles and functioning prophets lay the foundation of the business together.

The Believer Business functioning prophet may have visions, dreams, words of wisdom, words of knowledge, miracles, healings, the gift of faith, discerning of spirits, along with gift of prophecy which edifies, exhorts, comforts, and convicts other people in business. The ministry in business of the Believer Business functioning prophet is a great gift for any business, as he or she is not afraid of new ideas and is usually on the cutting edge of any industry.

FURTHER TRUTHS OF GOD'S PROPHETIC WORD BY THE NEW TESTAMENT BELIEVERS

The ministry of God′s prophetic word in the Old Testament was strictly objective. The ministry of God′s prophetic word through Christ Jesus′ sinless humanity nature in the New Testament was/is purely subjective.

The ministry of God's prophetic word by New Testament functioning prophets is both objective and subjective. Again, unlike Jesus, New Testament functioning prophets' thoughts, emotions, and beliefs in their souls are not sinless. Therefore, Believer Business Owners functioning prophets' minds, emotions, and hearts in their souls need transformation to become incrementally purer vessels of God's word for the purpose of more accuracy in speaking words of prophecy.

Since Christ Jesus′ incarnation, crucifixion, resurrection, and ascension, God decided to intertwine human personality with His word. God the Word desires His *Ekklesia* to submit their minds, emotions, and hearts to Him for sanctification. Ephesians 5:26-27 says, "That He might sanctify and cleanse it with the washing of water by the (*rhema*) word, (27) That He might present it to Himself a glorious church (*Ekklesia*), not having spot, or wrinkle, or any such thing; but that it should be holy and without blemish." The reason is that God wants His children to be vessels of purity to minister His prophetic word and minister God's truths from scripture to others.

Although God has decided to allow His word to filter through Believer Business ministers' untransformed souls. Nevertheless, to protect and foster the purity, holiness, and truth of His word, God must deal with Believer Business ministers' carnal soulish disobedience, pride, sin, unbelief, doubt, fears, stubbornness, and emotional problems in the Believer Business ministers' fractured personalities. These carnal maladies interfere with Believer Business ministers' expressing God's word and fruit of the Spirit with purity at the workplace while doing business.

God directs His Believer Business Owners and Believer Business managers to scholastically teach and kinesthetically train the Believer Business Employees through the daily incremental problem solving while using biblical principles and insisting on servanthood with the goal of transforming, maturing, and purifying all Believer Business minsters' souls through God's spiritual transformation, righteousness, holiness, and purification. God wants to use Believers' soulish thoughts, feelings, and beliefs in ministry, but He will put Believers' souls in the washing machine and take Believers to the beauty parlor. The Lord not only wants His prophetic words spoken but also exhibited through Believers' real life testimony of Believers' personal relationship with Him. Similarly, God wants His word to have the diverse flavors of Believer human personalities. Since prophetic words are sent into and through the Believers' soul, while the soul is being washed and sanctified (Ephesians 5:26), this is why Believers only prophesy in part. The more spiritually mature the soul of the functioning prophet, the more accurate the prophecy is spoken.

Again, Paul said in 1 Corinthians 13: 9, "For we know in part, and we prophesy in part." Why would Paul say that it was okay to prophesy in part since the prophets of the Old Testament had to prophesy accurately in full, not part, or suffer being stoned to death.

For examples, Peter's and John's scriptures show they used words differently than in Paul's scriptures. Luke's gospel and the book of Acts used words like a medical doctor and often uses medical words to explain his revelations. For example, Luke wrote in Acts 2:2, "And suddenly there came a sound from heaven as of a rushing mighty wind, and it filled all the house where they were sitting." The Greek used by Luke for the word "wind" was *pnoe*, which is the first inhaling of air of a newborn baby. Luke meant that the inhaling of the *pnoe* was the birth of Jesus' New Testament *Ekklesia.*

Each New Testament author used his own special phraseology and words. For example, Mark used "immediately" or "straightway" often in his gospel. Mark's words emphasized that Jesus' words were repeated from God the Father, and Jesus' actions were swift and decisive in obedience to God the Father. The immediate responses by Jesus' to God's words and immediate actions duplicating the actions of God, along with operating with the Holy Spirit's anointing and power doing the work of the ministry. Matthew used the phrase a "kingdom of heaven" but Luke used the phrase "kingdom of God." Matthew wrote primarily to the Believer Jews, while Luke wrote to both Believer Jews and Believer Gentiles. Irrespective of the individual personality and focus of the author, each Book is the inspired word of God.

The reason why God allows individual styles to be used in expressing His word is because God loves diversity, and He loves watching as His children do their best to quote what God is saying. This does not mean He wants error, but He is patient with His functioning prophets and the prophetic word because souls are being transformed that takes a lifetime for maturation, as the souls are not perfected when the Believer is born again with a new spirit. Every Ephesians 4:11 become mature over the years, as their souls spiritually mature.

Here is another illustration. Let's suppose that three musicians came in during a special worship service at the church, with the first playing the piano, the second playing the saxophone, and the third playing the trumpet. Each is given the song "Amazing Grace" to play. As each Believer with his or her own instruments would play the same notes, a different sound would fill the room. Yet, the audience would understand the song being played but would have a diversity in the sound. Each musician is disciplined on his or her own instrument to play the music correctly with proper beat and pitch but with a different sound. This is like the Bible written by different authors, especially the New Testament. This is the word rendered through different personalities. It remains the pure word of God unhindered, but their personalities make the word come alive.

Therefore, Jesus' crucifixion, death, resurrection, ascension, glorification, and now intercession provided and now allows the word of God to be intertwined with the imperfect personalities of Believers. The prophetic expression is as different as the personalities that speak God′s prophetic words. Some New Testament functioning prophets have unique accents, and a few functioning prophets use poor grammar while others sing the prophetic word. Some New Testament functioning prophets give a Scripture as the prophetic word. A good number of New Testament functioning prophets are loud when they speak, while other New Testament functioning prophets are softly spoken. Yet, this is the prophetic word that has become flesh within Jesus′ body or mixed with personalities that are unique with a particular New Testament functioning prophet.

Since God's word is to be filtered through man′s soul, then God wants to clean up the soul, mature the soul, deliver the soul, and make the soul pure in handling the prophetic word of God. To the extent that "self" in the soul gets in the way, the Believer is that much ineffective in ministering the word of God. God deals with His ministers as a Father would a son or daughter. As the best Father, God is very strict to cause the sanctification of the souls of His adopted children. Until the Believer is up to God′s standard, he or she will be limited in being used by God. This is why Believer Business Owner should not allow Believer Business Employees, who are young converts to minister the prophetic word of God. Immature, untransformed souls do not know how to impart spirit and *zoe* life to others because of the fractures, sin, and immaturity in their own personalities.

A Believer must submit in allowing the process of crucifixion to take place in one's soul where the Believer no longer lives for himself but desires to allow Christ to live in the Believer and through the Believer to impart spirit and *zoe* life to others (Galatians 2:20). God the Father takes the Believer through a pruning away the flesh in the soul process, often by the harsh circumstances of life to bear more spiritual fruit (John 15:2). God the Word washes and sanctifies the Believer's soul after initial salvation, so that He might present it to Himself a glorious *Ekklesia*, not having spot, or wrinkle, or any such thing; but that it should be holy and without blemish (Ephesians 5:25-27). God the Holy Spirit mortifies the deeds of the flesh in the soul, so the Believer can experience more *zoe* life (Romans 8:13).

Once Believer Business Employees have been broken in their souls and are opened to receive spiritual truth and a willingness to submit to God, then God can pour His spirit and life in their souls. By submission to God, Believer Business Employees become obedient servants; and they can receive and accept prophetic words because they have an ear to hear. Believer Business Employees become submitted, humbled, and useable. Without this process of soul spiritual transformation unto spiritual maturation being done, the Believer Business Employees' souls would remain closed to receive God's prophetic word blocked inside soul without release to a chosen recipient. They would be ineffective. Thus, in the New Testament, God deals with cleaning up Believer Business Employees' souls through the transformation process by the Believer Business Employees to actively submit to allowing the Godhead to make their souls righteous and holy. Ephesians 4:24 says, "And that ye put on the new man (born again spirit), which after God is created in righteousness and true holiness." Thus, the Godhead will do a transformation of Believer Business Employees' souls before He does work through the Believer Business Employees as ministers to touch the lives of others.

Paul said in 2 Corinthians 2:4 that: "For out of much affliction and anguish of heart I wrote unto you with many tears; not that ye should be grieved, but that ye might know the love which I have more abundantly unto you." What Paul wrote was the word of God, but the word written was also full of his many feelings and personal thoughts. The word of God inside him caused him to be remolded into the image of Christ. Paul wrote through his suffering and tears that transformed his soul and personal experience in his teaching and preaching without damaging the word of God.

God's word is not just a bunch of commandments, not just delineated doctrines or principles to live by, but is full of vibrant personality and testimony of personal experience under the headship of Christ and leadership of the Holy Spirit. God's word is fulfilled when it has the sanctified human flavor enlarging its relevancy to everyday life. This is the word of God becoming human personality in this four-dimensional world.

The word of God becoming flesh does not mean that somehow it is now lowered to become man's soulish immaturities and frailties. It means that the word of God has now the savor of distinct humanity without sacrificing any of the word's purity. This is Christ with His Divine Nature and Humanity Nature being expressed through mankind.

God's word is magnified and becomes relevant through the human experience, but the human element does not change the absolute truth or impartation of the Lord's spirit and life.

Therefore, it is an awesome responsibility to handle and minister God's prophetic word. When a minister preaches under the anointing with accuracy of the meaning of scripture, the *rhema* word preached is not only bringing spirit and life to the hearers but also is transforming the preacher to further refine and mature his soul.

Often, a word that God gives me to preach convicts me first before anyone ever hears it. I personally find myself in tears late at night caused by the further working of the *rhema* word of God in me.

Ministering God's word by any of the Ephesians 4:11 Business functioning ministers is not just an objective teaching but must be subjectively pronounced by the illumination of God's word through the Believer Business Owner's or Believer Business Employees' own enlightenment, personal relationship with God, and personal experience. The word of God is first deposited in the Believer's heart in the soul for transformation and then is released through his or her soul and body to others to bring spirit and life. Any defect in the minister's personality or soul will be wrought upon by God, as the defect will hinder the releasing of the intended spirit and life inherent in God's word to others.

Therefore, as a Believer Business Owner or Believer Business Employee, if you are going to preach the word of God, please understand that you will be dealt with severely by a loving and disciplining Father God who wants you to handle His word with the Holy Spirit's anointing, spirituality, and *zoe* life. The biggest burden Believer Business Owner or Believer Business Employees must face in preaching the word is not whether research or study is proper but whether the delivery of the prophetic word speaks forth eternal spirit and life. God is more concerned whether the Believer Business Owner functioning prophet word is personally right before the Lord than whether He has delivered a perfect prophecy. If the Believer Business Owner functioning prophet has hidden sin that has not been dealt with, has bitterness, suffers from victimization, or other defects, the prophetic word does not have the effect on the Believers listening as it should. When a mature Believer Business Owner functioning prophet of God's word is teaching or preaching the gospel of the kingdom or repentance and remission of sins, God is even more glorified as the minister's personal life has been become righteous and holy. Also, his spiritual life is magnified by the lifegiving truth transforming his or her soul and enhancing his relationship with the Godhead, family, and those Believer

Business Employees and ministers at work.

Because the word is mingled with personality, and because Believers have imperfect minds, emotions, and hearts, unlike Jesus, Believers can only know and prophesy in part. 1 Corinthians 13:9-10 says, (9) "For we know in part, and we prophesy in part. (10) But when that which is perfect has come, then that which is in part will be done away." As stated in the Introduction, some theologians have used these verses to try to prove that prophecy is no longer needed for today. They argue that the reference to when the "perfect has come" means when the Canonized word came. Yet, the true meaning in line with other Scriptures is when a whole new world comes which is a reference to the coming of another creative event of Believers when the Lord returns to a new heaven and a new earth (Revelation 21:1). The reference is to the coming of the perfection of His Bride in all Her radiant adornment. To this end, the last clause in verse 8 says "whether there is knowledge, it will vanish away." Obviously, knowledge has not vanished since the coming of the Canonized word. Therefore, why would prophecy vanish away with the coming of the Canonized word? Those theologians interpreting this Scripture as a reference to the coming of the Canonized word instead of the perfected soul and the resurrected body of the Bride have a prejudice against prophecy and the speaking in tongues. In any event, the ministry of the word of God, whether a word of knowledge, a word of wisdom, or a word of prophecy, is perhaps the most important function of every born again Believer.

Paul reminds Believers that all gifts must be expressed with order. Paul says in 1 Corinthians 14:22-25, "Therefore tongues are for a sign, not to those who believe but to unsaveds; but prophesying is not for unsaveds but for those who believe. (23) Therefore, if the whole church (*Ekklesia*) comes together in one place, and all speak with tongues, and there come in those who are uninformed or unsaveds, will they not say that you are out of your mind? (24) But if all prophesy, and an unsaved or an uninformed Believer comes in, he is convinced by all, he is convicted by all. (25) And thus the secrets of his heart are revealed; and so, falling down on his face, he will worship God and report that God is truly among you."

HOW THE FUNCTIONS OF THE APOSTLE AND PROPHET DIFFER

Along with the Believer Business Owner functioning apostles and the Believer Business Owner functioning prophet's efforts work together to build the proper foundation in the business, but the construction and future repair or change of the direction of the business is needed as well. Believer Business Employees just cannot work on a slab of concrete that is the foundation of the business. Believer Business Employees want more in their life with the Lord and each other. Believer Business Employees want fellowship with Believer Business Owners and fellowship with other Believer Business Employees and want teaching from the Bible and hands on business kinesthetic training. Believer Business Employees want to excel in their employment, want promotions, want positive reinforcement and affirmation, want prayer when they have a need, want shepherding by leading them instead of mere negative discipline. Believer Business Employees want to minister to fellow employees and customers with their spiritual Vocations and spiritual Gifts. Believer Business Employees want to learn through kinesthetic hands on training how to contact and participate in leading the unsaved unto salvation by accepting Jesus as Lord and Savior; they want to be shown by kinesthetic training how to bring healing virtue to restore the sick with good health. They want to be activated with their spiritual Vocations and spiritual Gifts. They want a kinesthetic training school, not just a classroom lecture.

The Believer Business Owner functioning prophet sees a little of your tomorrow and brings it into your today. The vision of the Lord will stabilize you as a Believer Business minister who waits on the Lord for the business vision to manifest. Proverbs 29:18 says, "Where there is no revelation (prophetic vision), the people cast off restraint." The Believer Business Owner functioning prophet speaks what God tells him or her to speak, and it could be a new illumination from scripture, an answer to a serious question, an area of a need to change in the Believer Business Owner's soul, a change in a Believer Business Employee's life, when to change a product, or take a new direction and plan for the business.

If the Believer Business Owner and Believer Business Employees stay close to the Holy Spirit, He will reveal and how to flow in His perfect will for the Believer Business Owner's trade or profession. The Holy Spirit can lead customers to a Believer Business minister because he or she may have a need for prayer but also will purchase the business products, and the customer or client will spread a good recommendation to others that Christians are working in the business.

The Believer Business Owner functioning prophet causes you to look in the prophetic mirror, so you can see the image of your maturity or immaturity as a Business minister. The Believer Business Owner functioning prophet says you can have what you can see in image form when you ask God for provision to fulfill God's purpose. 2 Corinthians 3:18 says, "But we all, with unveiled faces, beholding as in a mirror the glory of the Lord, are being transformed into the same image from glory to glory, just as by the Spirit of the Lord."

The Believer Business Owner functioning prophet gives you the revelation; whereas the Believer Business Owner functioning apostle makes the plans and handles the revival that flows from the manifested prophetic vision concerning the business. Again, the Believer Business Owner functioning prophet is not that concerned with *when* the vision or prophetic word will manifest because it is the word of God which is true and will not fail, so long as the Believer Business Owner does nothing that negates the prophecy. On the other hand, the Believer Business Owner functioning apostle declares *when* the prophetic word concerning your business ministry has been manifested and how you and your Believer Business Employees are to enter the flow of that prophetic word to fulfill God's purpose for the business and each Believer Business Owners and Believer Business Employees' lives.

When Mary was pregnant with Jesus, and she went to visit her cousin, Elizabeth, who was pregnant with John the Baptist, the prophet of God leaped in his mother's womb when the Lord, even before He was formed, came into the prophet's presence. In Luke 1:44-45 Elizabeth said, "For, lo, as soon as the voice of thy salutation sounded in mine ears, the babe leaped in my womb for joy. (45) And blessed is she that believed: for there shall be a performance of those things which were told her from the Lord." Jesus was not even formed completely in His mother's womb; yet, while in his mother's womb, John the Baptist, as the functioning prophet of God received the divine vision and revelation that he was in the presence of the Messiah, the Christ.

Starting with John 1:29, Jesus was coming to the Jordan River to be baptized by John the Baptist. "The next day John seeth Jesus coming unto him, and saith, 'Behold the Lamb of God, which taketh away the sin of the world.'" Later, in John 1:33 John the Baptist goes on to say, "And I knew Him not: but He that sent me to baptize with water, the same said unto me, 'Upon Whom thou shalt see the Spirit descending, and remaining on Him, the same is He which baptizeth with the Holy Ghost.'" This Scripture started being fulfilled in John 20:21-22, which says, "Then said Jesus to them again, Peace be unto you: as my Father hath sent me, even so send I you. (22) And when He had said this, He breathed on them, and saith unto them, 'Receive ye the Holy Spirit.'" The allusion is obvious in these verses to Genesis 2:7 where God "breathed" life into Adam.

The old creation started with a breath of God, and through the great business functioning Apostle, Lord Jesus Christ, the new creation started with the breath of Jesus' divine nature, God the Word. In this meeting the disciples went through what Paul later writes about in Romans 10:9. This was the first time these functioning apostles truly confessed Jesus as resurrected Lord and could then believe in their hearts that God raised Jesus from the dead. The functioning apostles who were trained to be about God the Father's business now entered into salvation and received their born again spirits. The regeneration experience of 2 Corinthians 5:17 suddenly became reality and the functioning apostles were cleansed of all unrighteousness and ready to do the Father's business. On the Day of Pentecost, those in the Upper Room received the Baptism of the Holy Spirit in full measure.

Before Jesus was tempted in the wilderness; before Jesus attended the wedding feast and changed water into wine; before Jesus casted out one demon; before Jesus healed one sick Believer, John the Baptist, the functioning prophet saw that Jesus was the Messiah. John the Baptist saw in a vision as a functioning prophet who the Messiah would be, and he did not have to see any other evidence of Jesus' anointing and office. After the manifestation and fulfilment of the vision, John the Baptist declared his business assignment in the Kingdom of God was over here on earth. Once the word or vision of God which was given by God to the functioning prophet had manifested and was fulfilled, the functioning prophet's authority and assignment over that word or vision was over. John the Baptist later said, "He must increase, but I must decrease" (John 3:30). Why? Because a mature Ephesians 4:11 minister does not go beyond his or her assignment, authority, venue, and anointing; for to do so would encroach on someone else's assignment, authority, venue, and anointing.

On the other hand, the Believer Business Owner functioning apostle is the one who declares that the word of God, the prophetic vision or revelation from God, is now manifesting in the Believer Business ministers' presence. The Believer Business Owner functioning apostle declares, "The prophetic word or *rhema* Scripture has manifested and has been fulfilled in your presence." After the Holy Spirit came into the Upper Room like a mighty wind, and people started speaking in tongues and there appeared on those in the Upper Room divided tongues as of fire, the Believer Business Owner functioning apostle Peter stood up on that day of Pentecost and declared that the signs that had just manifested were merely the commencement of the fulfilment of what the functioning prophet Joel said in Joel 2:28-32 concerning the visitation of the Holy Spirit. Peter further said that Jesus Christ is the "Lord" referred to in the prophetic Scripture by the prophet David, who said in Psalm 110:1, "The LORD said to my Lord, 'Sit at My right hand, till I make Your enemies Your footstool.'" Peter declared that the manifestation of the prophetic Scriptures had just occurred in the presence of the people. When people see that prophetic words have manifested and have been fulfilled, then the faith of the unsaved people rise to acceptance of Jesus as their Lord and Savior. Believer Business Owners and Believer Business Employees must wait on the Holy Spirit to declare "the time for My visitation is now!" Romans 10:17 says, "So then faith cometh by hearing, and hearing by the (*rhema*) word of God." Jesus said in Matthew 4:4 says, "... It is written, Man shall not live by bread alone, but by every (*rhema*) word that proceedeth out of the mouth of God."

As the great Business functioning Apostle, Jesus, stood up in a synagogue in Luke 4:18-19 where He read the prophetic scripture found in Isaiah 49:8-9. Then in Luke 4:21, Jesus said, "Today this Scripture is fulfilled in your hearing." As the great Business functioning Apostle, Jesus declared when His Father's business would start to fulfill all prophetic words of the Old Testament prophets. Jesus taught His functioning apostles, who would conduct His Father's business, how to flow into God's timing of the release of that prophetic word in its fullness. The Believer Business Owner functioning apostle not only declares when the Spirit of God is moving; but he or she activates leaders into that divine move.

As has been said, the early New Testament functioning apostles had the perseverance to endure great hardships. They knew they were a sacrifice for the cause of laying the foundation of Christ. All the original functioning apostles, save John, were executed, crucified, beheaded, boiled in oil, or skinned alive. Through all the persecutions, the functioning apostles laid the foundation of the Father's business here on earth based upon Biblical principles to be applied in God's Kingdom government.

Those who learn to be the survivors of the affliction qualify to be revivers. The revival to come will be those who are referred to in Hebrews 12:3, which says, "For consider Him who endured such hostility from sinners against Himself, lest you become weary and discouraged in your souls."

With every new level of God's spiritual revelation and illumination from God's word, there comes a new level of confrontation by the world and Satan's evil realm. This is why learning to do spiritual warfare is a strategic mandate. With every new level, there is a new devil. The Believer Business Owner functioning prophet shows you who you are going to be from God's point of view. The Believer Business Owner functioning prophet is not concerned about your current business circumstances or your past business failures. To the Believer Business functioning prophet, timing is not important.

When the Believer Business functioning prophet informs the Believer Business Employees that the business where they work is a ministry and not just for making profit, the Believer Business Employees receive a new paradigm of understanding how Believer Business Employees will receive spiritual activation when they most likely would never be activated attending warehouse or cathedral lecture hall pyramid paradigm structure.

When new Believer Business Employees are first hired, they generally have very little experience in being a minister themselves because their *Ekklesia* experience was just as a spectator at the warehouse or cathedral lecture hall pyramid paradigm structure where they sat in a chair or pew sometimes for years. The new Believer Business Employees will most likely expect to be just spectators watching the Believer Business Owner functioning prophet ministering while they watch. No, Believer Business Employees will learn that all aspects in the daily incremental work at the business will be both a scholastic teaching and kinesthetic training center where they are required to have a much stronger work ethic, much stronger faith, and much stronger daily concentration in using their spiritual Vocations and spiritual Gifts and fine tuning them during interaction with other people. Believer Business Employees will learn to submit to the Godhead's work in the transformation of their souls by accepting that the other Believer Business Employees also are going through the same process of spiritual maturation.

Simply, the workers building a house can explain the work of each of the Ephesian 4:11 functioning ministers. Believer Business Employees need spiritual doors to open and walk in and out of the business will allow them to enter a new venue of ministry they had never experienced which are Believer Business Owners as functioning evangelists. Believer Business Employees need illumination from the windows in the business, which are Believer Business Owner functioning teachers. Believer Business Employees need a roof over their heads for protection from the prince of the power of the air and the storms from the world, which are Believer Business Owner functioning pastors. Yet, more than anything else, Believer Business Employees need a solid business foundation that are laid by Believer Business Owner functioning apostles and functioning prophets, which is built upon the solid foundation of Christ Jesus (1 Corinthians 3:11).

As a reminder, 1 Corinthians 12:29 says, "Are all (business functioning) apostles? are all (business functioning) prophets? are all (business functioning) teachers? are all (business functioning) workers of miracles? "

Jesus came in part as a prophetic fulfillment of God's covenant with King David, as Acts 13:23 says, "Of this man's (David's) seed hath God according to His promise raised unto Israel a Saviour, Jesus." As God's only begotten Son, Jesus spent approximately twenty years as a business carpenter and stonemason, and He demonstrated every ministry office of all the Ephesians 4:11 functioning ministers. Jesus was, and is, our foundational functioning Apostle (Hebrews 3:1). Jesus was specially sent by the Father, Himself, and is, the supreme functioning Prophet to fulfill prophecy to build the foundation of the *Ekklesia* that is the redeemed Second Man who is reconciled to God (Acts 3:22; 1 Corinthians 15:47; 2 Corinthians 5:17-19).

Jesus also moved and spoke with authority as the foundation ministry of the supreme functioning Prophet where God the *Logos* Word, Jesus' divine nature, became manifested and fully attached but not commingled with His humanity nature with a mortal body that died for Believers on a Roman Cross but was resurrected on the third day. Jesus' witness was, and is, also the open door functioning evangelist who preached the gospel of the Kingdom and repentance and remission of sins. Jesus was, and is, additionally, the covering Good Shepherd or functioning Pastor. Jesus was the consummate functioning Teacher who was, and is, the Light of the world and the Truth personified.

Each of the Ephesians 4:11 Business functioning ministers must reproduce that part of the expression of Jesus' heart toward His *Ekklesia* for the maturing of Believers to reflect the character and nature of Christ Jesus.

The goal of each Ephesians 4:11 Business functioning minister is to reproduce Jesus' heart in the business to activate every Believer Business Employee in their spiritual Vocations and spiritual Gifts unto maturity and accomplishing God's assignments, missions, engiftments, and business purpose. Every Believer Business minister is called to spiritually impact others as they touch the world in the marketplace who want to engage in commerce.

CHAPTER NINE

THE BELIEVER BUSINESS OWNER FUNCTIONING EVANGELIST

BUSINESS FUNCTIONING EVANGELISTS ARE GOD'S GIFTS TO ACTIVATE BELIEVER BUSINESS EMPLOYEES TO EXTEND GOD'S GRACE AND SALVATION TO THE WORLD.

Ephesians 4:11, 12 & 16 says in relevant part, "And He gave some as (Believer Business Owner functioning) evangelists...(12) for the equipping (spiritual scholastic teaching and kinesthetic training) of the saints for the work of ministry (in business) for the edifying (building up by increasing) the Body of Christ (who are in business) (16) from whom the whole body, joined (evangelists equip others to recruit) and knit together (common purpose) by what every joint supplies (with their talents and gifts), according to the effective working (in business) by which every part does its share causes growth (expansion through evangelism) of the body for the edifying (building through evangelism) of itself in (*agape*) love."

The Believer Business Owner functioning evangelists emphasize obtaining more sales, so their proclivity is to direct their Ephesians 4:11 functioning ministry in the sales department. The Believer Business Owner functioning evangelists use primarily kinesthetic training of the Believer Business Employees how to sell the company's products or services. They often will train the Believer Business Employees in the importance of telling the public the excellent attributes of the products or services.

Yet, the spiritually mature Believer Business Owner functioning evangelists create a Christ-centered company looking for opportunities to offer the gift of eternal life by sharing the gospel of the Kingdom and repentance and remission of sins to employees, customers, and clients. Believer Business Owner functioning evangelists establish standards of integrity by guaranteeing their products being sold to consumers will perform as represented, so the products and services match the representations of the Believer Business Employee salespersons. Also, the Believer Business Owner functioning evangelist will always say with sincerity, "For any reason that you do not like our products and want to return them, we have a money back guarantee for 90 days." In other words, the Believer Business evangelists reach out to the public with utmost integrity, so customers will return and purchase more products. Believer Business Owner functioning evangelists want the reputation as the honest and friendly Christian owned company for certain products or services in that community.

I have several Believer Business functioning evangelists who I challenged to come out of the closet and let their businesses be a ministry. I have activated many Believer Business Owner evangelists since I came back to the Lord in 1978, which was three years after I became an Attorney. For example, I had a salesman functioning evangelist who took my challenge. He had contracted with several office supplies companies as a wholesaler buyer, where he was able to obtain office supplies at wholesale cost, usually at a 35% discount, and he passed on a 10% discount off the retail price at stores to his customers, collecting the sales tax, and his profit was about 15%. It was great business for him while it was a good deal for us customers as my office staff would call him for the supplies needed, and he would deliver the office supplies to my office within days. This was before Amazon, and no one was delivering products to a customer's office in those days at a discount price. So, he targeted Attorney Offices, which my office was one. When he came to my office, I enjoyed his stories of evangelizing and spreading the gospel, so I cherished his fellowship. He would relay his testimony to me of how he led a secretary to the Lord at one office, or how he prayed for someone who was sick because the owner said she was a Believer and gave him permission.

I taught him and activated him into his work of ministry in his spiritual Vocations and spiritual Gifts (as mentioned throughout this book), and afterwards he would say a quick prayer for success of the customers before he left their office he said. I gave him referrals of other attorneys, tax preparers, and other Believer Business Owners to contact. He broadened his customer base into other professions. Within one year, by becoming a Believer Business Owner functioning evangelist, he nearly doubled his business. Then I taught him how I trained my Believer Business Employees through scholastic teaching and kinesthetic training, as he was so busy he needed help. He hired a couple of men to become Believer Business Employees of his business, who came to his home each morning early where he had a list of customers that day to deliver the office supplies, to pick up products, along with the names, addresses, and the persons to contact at every customer business, and provided to them an invoice to obtain a check from each customer.

The Believer Business Owner functioning evangelist's Believer Business Employees delivered the products, brought back a check the next morning, and continued the cycle. He would fellowship with his employees, pray with them for travel safety, invite them to his home fellowship at his house once a week, and taught them the importance of integrity and biblical principles of servanthood. Never once did he ever have a theft by his Believer Business Employees of the check picked up from a customer. Since he was dealing with white collar businessmen and businesswomen, most of whom were Believer Business Owners, he was prosperous.

Yet there was one customer that he personally would deliver the office supplies, which was me. It was because he wanted to spend time with me in fellowship. I would continue to give him biblical principles and truths to take back to his Believer Business Employees to share with them, and he would give me the testimony of himself and his employees. Over the years, his business grew and grew, and he had to lease a warehouse, and hire additional Believer Business Employees, establish routes for each. They all would meet at the warehouse, get their orders, customer information, and then he and his employees would read out loud five books of Psalms and one book of Proverbs every morning. Then all the Believer Business Employees knew the names of customers, would always pray for the customers and their businesses, and then go to the next customer.

Eventually, this Believer Business Owner functioning evangelist, and his wife, became my legal clients, and I prepared their estate planning documents for them, transferring their home into their revocable trust. Of course, I charged him a very substantial wholesale discount price. He eventually sold his business to the senior Believer Business Manager on a long-term contract where he and his wife received regular monthly payments. His Believer Business Manager learned through kinesthetic training and studying biblical economic principles, which he continued to use in the business. My friend and client would occasionally attend his old Believer Business manager's morning meetings of prayer and studying the Bible before his employees were sent out for deliveries. His Believer Business Owner prior manager just duplicated what my friend and client did, who duplicated what I did with my Believer Business Employees each morning. My Believer Business friend eventually passed, and at the memorial his wife told me that I had made her husband a business functioning evangelist, and that he would tell her what he learned from me at our fellowship meetings over the word of God in my law office. She said that her husband became a wonderful loving husband because I helped him become a mature businessman of God. In his business, as a Believer Business Owner functioning evangelist, he led hundreds of men and women to the Lord while he was doing business.

The Believer Business Owner functioning evangelist must be ready to preach the gospel of the Kingdom (Matthew 24:14), preach repentance and remission of sins (Luke 24:47), and must be able to impart and use biblical economics, share God's *agape* love, lead people to initial salvation, and live as a servant of others. Servanthood, honesty, biblical principles, *agape* love, humility, submission, faith, and fruit of the Spirit expressed to others are the most important character traits of the mature Believer Business Owner and mature Believer Business Employee. These mature spiritual character traits were purposefully repeated and discussed multiplied times in every chapter of this book because spiritual kinesthetic repetition transforms the soul.

Thus, preaching the gospel of the Kingdom in the workplace blesses both God and the Believers, as the Kingdom manifested here on earth brings back possession of the earth to God. On the other hand, preaching solely repentance and remission of sins, which is good, but it primarily benefits the new Believer with eternal life, telling the Believer to look to a futuristic blessing of going to heaven. Each of these gospel messages are equally important for the Believer Business Owner and Believer Business Employees to present to customers, clients, and fellow workers in business.

Again, the purpose of the Believer Business Owner functioning evangelist, as are the other Ephesians 4:11 functioning ministers, is to grant grace given by the measure of the gift by Christ Jesus' divine nature and humanity nature to each Believer Business Owner and Believer Business Employee to spread the gospel messages to the other Believer Business Owners, customers, clients, and the Believer Business Employees. This is such a good spiritual habit where both Believer Business Owner functioning evangelists and the Believer Business Employees will be led by the Holy Spirit to spread the good news in every restaurant or coffee shop, every fuel station, every store cashier, and every fellow shopper doing business commerce in the marketplace. This is lifestyle evangelism doing God's business in the workplace, marketplace, and commerce area. At least 75%, or more, of the people attending most warehouse or cathedral auditorium lecture hall building pyramid paradigm structure already have initial salvation. So, that is the least place Believer Business Owner functioning evangelists and Believer Business Employees should be looking for unbelievers needing initial salvation. Leading unbelievers to the Lord.

THE MINISTRY OF THE FUNCTIONING EVANGELIST DEFINED.

Euaggelizo is a Greek word which means to announce good news or glad tidings. Jesus was an Announcer of good tidings (Matthew 11:5; Luke 1:19; 2:10; 8:1; 16:16; Acts 8:4, 12, 25, 35; 13:32; Ephesians 2:17). This Greek word is used 45 times in the whole New Testament.

Euaggelion is a Greek word which means the gospel or the good news message. It generally is used to pertain to the message that in the business the Believer Business Owner functioning evangelist trains Believer Business Employees to share the gospel of the kingdom and repentance and remission of sins with others. Functioning evangelists often preach or teach the death, burial, resurrection, ascension, intercession, and return of Christ Jesus. (Mark 1:1; Matthew 24:14; Acts 15:7; 20:24; 16:25; Galatians 2:2-7; Revelations 14:6; Ephesians 2:17) Yet, functioning evangelists will address the idea that the future is uncertain, so today is the day of salvation (2 Corinthians 6:2). Yesterday is gone, your tomorrow may not come, so today is your day for salvation and eternal life. The functioning evangelists might ask, "Will you with a heartfelt sincerity right now repent of all your sins?" After that, then the functioning evangelist may then ask them to repeat, "I believe that Jesus Christ died on a Roman Cross and rose from the dead. I confess Jesus as my Lord and Savior." If this was a heartfelt confession, then the unbeliever will be saved, born again, and receive eternal life. If the unbeliever hesitates, then the functioning evangelist may say, "When will be the next time that you will have someone personally sharing one on one the gospel of the kingdom and the gospel of repentance and remission of sins for your eternal salvation? What if this day, or next week, is the last day of your life?" I have never had one unbeliever that decided not to participate with me to receive forgiveness of sins and receive eternal life.

The best one on one witnessing unto salvation is done by my long time dear friend, Dr. Bill Henderson, who is like a brother to me. He will not leave a restaurant without inquiring if the waiter or waitress is saved. If he or she is not, he has a whole plethora of statements that makes him or her want to be led to repent of their sins, believe that Jesus rose from the dead, and confess Jesus is Lord. If the waiter or waitress says that they don't have enough time, then Dr. Bill will say to him or her, "Then just call on the name of the Lord Jesus Christ as your Lord and Savior?" Probably, 99% will follow his lead. (Again, I never saw one unbeliever say "no") Dr. Bill has a very pure heart for the lost, and he lives to lead people to the Lord for initial salvation. However, when he teaches Believers in congregations, he focuses on the Believers' transformation and maturation of their souls and activating them to lead the unsaved to the Lord. Those of you who know Dr. Bill will agree with me that this assessment of him is true. One of Dr. Bill's favorite scriptures is 2 Timothy 4:5, where Paul tells Timothy, "But watch thou in all things, endure afflictions, do the work of an (functioning) evangelist, make full proof of thy ministry."

Euanggelistes is a Greek word which means a preacher or messenger of good news. The word is from *Eu,* meaning "well" and *angelos*, meaning "a messenger." This word *Euanggelistes* speaks of the man or woman, who is the Believer who is a functioning evangelist. In the business world, the functioning evangelists would be both the Believer Business Owner and the kinesthetic trained Believer Business Employees. This Greek word *Euanggelistes* is used only three times in the New Testament. It is the ministry work of Philip who was the functioning evangelist in Acts 21:8, of the functioning evangelists listed in Ephesians 4:11, and of Paul when he exhorted Timothy to do the work of a functioning evangelist in 2 Timothy 4:5.

In the Old Testament, there was a Hebrew word which was *basar*, which was a similar word to the Greek root words for evangelism.

The Hebrew word *basar* is translated "messenger" in 1 Samuel 14:17, "preach" in Psalms 40:9 and Isaiah 61:1, "publish" in 1 Samuel 31:9, "shew forth" (bear, carry, bring, preach, good, tell good) in 1 Chronicles 16:23 and Isaiah 60:6, "tidings" in Isaiah 61:11, Jeremiah 20:15, Psalm 68:11 and several other passages of scripture in the Old Testament.

However, the word *basar* in the Old Testament is mainly used to refer to the first coming of the Messiah and of those who bring good tidings, as in Isaiah 40:9; 41:27; 52:7; 61:1; Psalms 68:11 and Proverbs 25:25. In truth, it refers to Christ Jesus, the Messiah, and the Great Evangel!

CHRIST JESUS WAS AND IS THE GREAT BUSINESS OWNER FUNCTIONING EVANGELIST

Christ Jesus was the greatest business functioning Evangelist while He worked as a carpenter and stonemason. He was the Messenger of God, the One Who brought, preached, and published the good tidings. Jesus learned through being a business carpenter and stonemason how to know people and how to speak with them. Jesus always followed what God the Father said and what God the Father did through kinesthetic training by God the Father of Jesus, and Jesus as His only begotten Son.

Yet, it was not easy for Jesus' humanity nature, who had to grow up as a baby. Hebrews 5:8 says, "Though He were (God's only begotten) Son, yet learned He obedience by the things which He suffered."

Jesus experienced suffering while working in His family business as a carpenter and stonemason. Jesus was a business owner with Joseph and his laboring brothers growing up. Jesus' four brothers were James, Joses (or Joseph), Judas (or Jude), and Simon. Mark 6:3 says, "Is not this the Carpenter, the son of Mary, the brother of James, and Joses, and of Juda, and Simon? and are not his sisters here with us? And they were offended at Him." So, this scriptures mentions four brothers and at least two sisters. Although the names of Jesus' half-sisters are not specified in the gospels, but later tradition suggested their names were Mary and Salome. The Catholic leadership believes as doctrine that these listed children were either children of Joseph's prior marriage, or they were cousins in order for them to maintain the Catholic church doctrine that Mary maintained her virginity and did not have sex with Joseph. Exodus 12:10 says that a husband shall not withhold conjugal rights of a wife, so she can have children, and the Rabbinic teachings have said the wife shall not withhold conjugal rights of a husband. Thus, I do not know any Protestants historically that believe that Mary never had conjugal relationships with her husband. It makes no sense because God merely wanted a virgin woman to plant the holy seed for His only begotten Son would have a body.

A baby girl and baby boy from a man under the lineage of Adam and Eve has 46 chromosomes in 23 pairs, which a baby receives 23 chromosome pairs from each parent. The first 22 pairs are the same in both males and females, while the 23rd pair are sex chromosomes, which determine the baby's sex. The genetic material is passed from a sperm cell (23 chromosomes) and an egg cell (23 chromosomes) to form a zygote with a full set of 46 chromosomes. The first 22 pairs are called autosomes and are identical in males and females. The remaining 23rd single pair determine the sex of the baby, whether boy or girl. Mothers always have two X chromosomes while fathers have X and Y chromosomes.

However, Jesus was different. As the female child lineage from Adam and Eve, Mary provided 23 chromosomes in her egg cell (one X sex chromosome and 22 autosomes). The remaining 23 chromosomes, including the essential one Y sex chromosome that was necessary to make Jesus a male baby were miraculously implanted in Mary's womb by the Holy Spirit to make Jesus phenotypically male and not female. This immaculate conception bypassed the need for a human father of the lineage of Adam and Eve to provide a sperm (seed) to make Jesus a male baby. This divine intervention meant Jesus did not inherit the "original sin" or "sinful nature" as the sin was passed down through the Adamic (male) lineage. Because Jesus' mother, Mary, was from the lineage of Adam and Eve, then Jesus' humanity nature through Mary was genetically related to Abraham and David. With Jesus, the precise biological mechanism and birth is considered a divine mystery and a miracle that surpasses human understanding.

However, as a young boy being taught by His step-father, Joseph, did Jesus ever hit is thumb with a hammer trying to drive a nail? Did Jesus ever cut Himself while working? Did Jesus ever have sore back muscles after carrying stone to set in place? Did Jesus ever fall when he was very little, hurt Himself, and came crying to His mother who had to bandage the womb and perhaps kiss the bandage to make the pain go away? In business, did Jesus have customers that did not pay on time, but

He had to deal with them lovingly? In business, did Jesus have to redo a door or a window that did not fit? Of course He did. Did Jesus grumble when He had to redo the carpentry work? He learned spiritual lessons of forgiveness of debt, spiritual forgiveness of those who trespassed against Him, and spiritual lessons of love and kindness. Jeus was disciplined by Father God as He matured into manhood. Thus, Jesus, from His own experience learned to do what Father God did, and He learned to say what Father God said through kinesthetic training by Father God. Jesus taught His business disciples and all His disciples the same way that Father God taught Him.

Did Jesus continue to speak to people with phenomenal spiritual knowledge and wisdom as He did at age 12? Luke 2:46-49, 52 says, "And it came to pass, that after three days they found him in the temple, sitting in the midst of the doctors, both hearing them, and asking them questions. (47) And all that heard him were astonished at his understanding and answers. (48) And when they saw Him, they were amazed: and His mother said unto Him, 'Son, why hast Thou thus dealt with us? behold, thy father and I have sought thee sorrowing. (49) And He said unto them, 'How is it that ye sought Me? wist ye not that I must be about My Father's business?'... (52) And Jesus increased in wisdom and stature, and in favour with God and man."

Jesus, Himself, was and is the Good News personified that must be preached, as He is the King of the kingdom here on earth; and He is the Savior who brought forgiveness of sins by taking on the sins on behalf of unsaved people (2 Corinthians 5:21) and taking away the curse of the law by hanging on the Roman Cross (Galatians 3:13).

In the Old Testament, the functioning evangelistic prophet, Isaiah, prophesied the coming Messiah as the One Who brings good tidings (Isaiah 41:27; 52:7; 40:9).

Christ Jesus, as the Great Business Functioning Evangelist, quotes Isaiah 61:1-2 in Luke 4:18, "The Spirit of the Lord is upon Me, because He has anointed Me to preach the Gospel (of the Kingdom and repentance and remission of sins) to the poor...."

Jesus primarily preached the Gospel and glad tidings of the Kingdom of God in His ministry (Luke 4:43; 7:22; 8:1; 16:16; 20:1; Matthew 10:35, 36), but He also preached repentance for forgiveness and remission of sins (Matthew 4:17; Luke 5:32; 13:5; 24:47).

AS THE GREAT BUSINESS FUNCTIONING EVANGELIST BEING ABOUT HIS FATHER'S BUSINESS, CHRIST JESUS PREACHED A PLURALISTIC AND AN INDIVIDUALISTIC GOSPEL

Jesus kinesthetically trained His young Believer Business Owner functioning evangelistic apostles the art of evangelism. He told Peter, Andrew, James and John, "Come and I will make you fishers of men" (Matthew 4:19).

The gospel of the kingdom and gospel of repentance and remission of sins are a pluralistic and individualistic message, not one or the other. The gospel of the kingdom and gospel of repentance and remission of sins cover all aspects of life. Both messages must be preached in the businesses, marketplaces, schools, governments, news reporting, all professions, and the arts, and not just in a warehouse or cathedral lecture hall pyramid paradigm structure. The newly evangelized Believer must come into the Kingdom and be workers in the Kingdom after initial salvation with those understandings.

Jesus said in Matthew 28:19, "Go therefore and make disciples of all the nations (Greek- *ethnos*)..." "Nations" denote a discipleship of pluralism of all races. What God wants to have manifested on earth are Believers who are a chosen generation, a royal priesthood, a holy nation, and a peculiar people (1 Peter 2:9).

The Gospel of the kingdom and gospel of repentance and remission of sins are not self-actualizing, self-centered, bless me messages. The Gospel of the kingdom and gospel of repentance and remission of sins are the initial rebirth into God's Kingdom where there are new creatures in Christ Jesus' humanity nature as Believers living in community with God's *agape* love, *zoe* life, grace, and mercy. All new Believers then are supposed to be activated for the work of the ministry as spiritual kings, priests (Revelation 1:6), lords (1 Timothy 6:15), ambassadors (2 Corinthians 5:20), and soldiers (2 Timothy 2:3-4). Yet, this is best done with Believer Business Owner Ephesians 4:11 functioning ministers where the Believer Business Employees work eight to ten hours a day, five to six days a week under godly supervisors who use scholastic teaching but more importantly kinesthetic hand-on practical training in how to be ministers of Christ Jesus.

God is all good that is defined by God, and it is the "goodness of the Lord that leads you to repentance" (Romans 2:4). This "goodness" means Believers are invited to join the household and family of God as adopted children (Romans 8:15; Ephesians 2:19-20).

All Believer Business Employees while working must accept that they are being about God the Father's business of adding new Believers as citizens of God's Kingdom, household, family, and temple. Ephesians 2:19-22 says, "Now therefore ye are no more strangers and foreigners, but fellow citizens with the saints, and of the household of God; (20) And are built upon the foundation of the apostles and prophets, Jesus Christ Himself being the chief corner stone; (21) In whom all the building fitly framed together groweth unto an holy temple in the Lord: (22) In whom ye also are builded together for an habitation of God through the Spirit."

So, every Believer Business Owner and Believer Business Employee must dedicate themselves as being employed by the one Godhead, consisting of God the Father, God the Word, God the Holy Spirit, along with the Lord Jesus Christ's humanity nature, the only begotten Son of God. Again, Colossians 3:23-24 says, "And whatsoever ye do, do it heartily, as to the Lord, and not unto men; (24) Knowing that of the Lord ye shall receive the reward of the inheritance: for ye serve the Lord Christ." Colossians 3:23-24 encourages Believer Business Employees to work with all their heart and beliefs in the heart and will in the soul because they are working in establishing God's Kingdom here on earth as the primary mandate of the Lord Jesus Christ as the Great Evangelist in preaching the gospel of the Kingdom and gospel of repentance and remission of sins.

The Believer Business Owner functioning evangelist must scholastically teach and kinesthetically train the Believer Business Employees that they are not just working for a human boss, but for the Lord Jesus Christ and the Godhead. It is evident in Colossians 3:23-24 that Believer Business Employees are not getting just a paycheck for their work, but they are promised an eternal inheritance as a reward for their faithful work of ministry and seeing and honoring the business as their place for activation into ministry and soulish spiritual transformation and spiritual maturation.

Romans 8:17 says each Believer Business Employee working in the business is a joint heir of the Lord Jesus Christ, and each Believer Business Employee will be together with Christ in heaven for a season and back here in a new heaven and new earth (Revelation 21:1) and will rule and reign with Christ over the entire earth for all eternity (Revelation 5:10). To this end, Believer Business Owners and Believer Business Employees should be steadfast in their resolve not to create any schisms, abusive competition, unnecessary arguing, and behind the scenes backbiting. These negatives divisive activities have to be strictly forbidden, as all Believers are receiving God's blessings as joint heirs with the Lord Jesus Christ (Romans 8:17).

As each individual Believer Business Employee reaches the full measure of his and her Gifting, Vocation, and Calling together, then they become the fullness of Christ (Ephesians 4:13) for the edifying or building up of the Body of Christ for the work of the ministry (Ephesians 4:12), not just the individual alone. However, each Believer Business Employee individually must be equipped with the fullness of their grace according to the measure of Christ's gift (Ephesians 4:7) to edify or build up the whole Body of Christ, especially with the fellow workers in the business.

Therefore, preaching by some of the traditional American individualistic self-fulfillment religious gospel is only half the message, at best, because the functioning pastors or functioning teachers normally do not preach the gospel of the kingdom that Jesus mandated to be preached along with repentance and remission of sins. Consequently, the gospel of the individual salvation, although true and paramount, that is being presently preached as the sole message without the gospel of the Kingdom results bringing new born again Believers with birth defects in their souls, even though their born again spirits are new creatures in Christ, are perfect, do not sin, and are holy and righteousness (2 Corinthians 5:17; Hebrews 12:23; 1 John 3:9; Ephesians 4:24). God just does not want His unsaved people to become saved and join His family as His children and joint heirs with Christ Jesus, but He also wants through His adopted children, being led by the Holy Spirit, to manifest His spiritual Kingdom here on earth as a Holy Nation within the secular country where the residents are God's chosen generation, royal priesthood, and peculiar citizens.

In truth, the immature and anemic souls of Believer Business Employees are carnal and not spiritual, so they often do not exercise their wills in their hearts in their souls to seek first the Kingdom of God and His righteousness. Believer Business Employees that become spiritually mature relate in their souls with each other for the purpose of edifying and building up each other as the pluralistic Body of Christ. This attitude is to quelch carnal competition in the business. Believer Business Employees that become spiritually mature can spiritually join and knit together in unity of the spirit, supplying to other Believers with that which Christ has engifted and graced each Believer.

The message to the Believer Business Owner functioning evangelists and Believer Business Employees by Paul in 1 Corinthians 12:7 is "But the manifestation of the Spirit is given to every man to profit with all." The purpose of leading someone to the Lord and maturing the new Believer Business Employee, or perhaps a customer brought to a home fellowship, is "to profit with all" as opposed to profit of the individual alone.

Both Believer Business Owners as functioning evangelists and Believer Business Employees must represent an underlying *agape* love for each other and *agape* love toward customers and clients doing business with them and carrying God's goodness that leads unbelievers to God through Christ Jesus. *Agape* love must be the foundational motivation for leading an unbeliever to the Lord. Galatians 5:6 says, "... faith which worketh by (*agape*) love."

Agape love is a major underlying message of Paul in 1 Corinthians 13:4-8 that the engiftments given were nothing unless the Believer has *apape* love for the unsaved, along with *agape* love for the brothers and sisters in the kingdom and living in God's holy nation. Paul said in 1 Corinthians 13:4-8 that "Charity (*agape* love) suffereth long, and is kind; charity (*agape* love) envieth not; charity (*agape* love) vaunteth not itself, is not puffed up, (5) Doth not behave itself unseemly, seeketh not her own, is not easily provoked, thinketh no evil; (6) Rejoiceth not in iniquity, but rejoiceth in the truth; (7) Beareth all things, believeth all things, hopeth all things, endureth all things. Charity (*agape* love) never faileth…."

Similarly, 1 Corinthians 13:3 says, "And though I bestow all my goods to feed the poor, and though I give my body to be burned, and have not charity (*agape* love), it profiteth me nothing." The economy in God's Kingdom is giving and receiving, so *agape* love is the means of exchange, not money.

Since the Believer Owners functioning evangelist will start or rededicate the business as a focal point of ministry unto the Lord Jesus Christ, then the Believer Business Owner who is a functioning evangelist and Believer Business Employees must learn truths from the Bible and through kinesthetic training how to individually and jointly with other Believer Business Employees as a business group to establish a business ministry venue to reach the unsaved in society.

In a similar message, Paul spoke of the Body of Believers in 1 Corinthians 14:12, which says, "Even so you, since you are zealous for spiritual gifts, let it be for the edification (building up) of the church (*Ekklesia* defined as either a government assembly or military assembly) that you seek to excel."

The Believer Business functioning evangelists at the workplace speaking to unbelievers should stand ready to preach repentance and remission of sins but especially preach the benefits of the Kingdom of God and the Kingdom's attributes in their daily living. Romans 14:17 says, "For the Kingdom of God is not eating and drinking, but righteousness and peace and joy in the Holy Spirit." Thus, the Believer Business Owner and the Believer Business Employees are mandated to inform unbelievers they can seek and find righteousness, peace, and joy in the Holy Spirit when they accept Jesus as Lord and Savior.

Are Believers to have peace with the fallen world and with Satan or his realm? No! Is there righteousness in the fallen world and in Satan realm? No! The righteousness, peace, and joy are only in the Holy Spirit, under His authority, under His anointing, under His leading, under His kinesthetic training, and under His comforting *agape* love that manifests the kingdom of God. In whom does the Holy Spirit dwell? The Holy Spirit indwells in the Body of Christ corporately and individually (2 Corinthians 6:16; 1 Corinthians 3:17; Ephesians 2;21). Every Believer Business Owner and Believer Business Employee, as members of the Body of Christ are to seek daily God's Kingdom and His righteousness (Matthew 6:33), which is righteousness, peace, and joy in the Holy Spirit (Romans 14:17). Every Believer Business Owner and Believer Business Employee are mandated to share these blessings of the kingdom to other members of the Body of Christ. The Kingdom of God's attributes manifest best while in fellowship with other Believers.

In conducting business, **"righteousness"** means doing what is right and just, being honest, fair, and treating others with *agape* love, kindness, and respect, while having a good relationship with God, other Believers, and that part of the creation which God gives you to care for, which also means living justly, honestly, and faithfully as a biblitarian, along with living a life of integrity, holiness, and virtue. In conducting business, **"Peace"** means not as the world thinks of peace (John 16:33). Jesus' peace means a spiritual restored relationship with God, free from sin, guilt, and condemnation. Jesus' peace means a spiritual good relationship with other Believers and means a state of living where Believer servants in business show *agape* love and support to other's well-being as opposed to conflict. Jesus' peace means a state where differences are celebrated as rights for the good of all Believers, so, peace means seeking reconciliation with fellow Believer Business Employees and all Believers. In conducting business, **"Joy"** means a settled emotional tranquility that comes from intimacy with the Godhead and the Lord Jesus Christ's humanity nature. The Holy Spirit's joy means a fruit of the Holy Spirit that grows from seed form into a fruit producing fruit tree in your soul for others to partake. A fruit tree does not eat its own fruit, but inside the fruit is a seed, when planted, breaks open, and dies and starts the beginning of an orchard of fruit trees. An orchard of fruit trees is a specific-cultivated area where fruit trees are planted, most often for commercial purposes. The Holy Spirit's joy means a choice to trust that God is a covenant making and covenant keeping personal Sovereign Creator and the Holy Spirit is the joyful Comforter.

Therefore, when Believer Business Owners and Believer Business Employees are saved out of Satan's evil realm and transferred into the Kingdom of the Son of God's love (Colossians 1:13), then the gospel of salvation has been preached to include becoming a new family member by adoption into the Household of God. As a member of the family of God, Believers have family responsibilities of loyalty, love, and work. The family of God includes God the Father, God the Word, God the Holy Spirit, Jesus' humanity nature, and all Believers as a pluralistic Body of Christ. The family of God is not the experience that is defined as a self-centered spiritual relationship between the Believer and God. Being the gospel of the Kingdom should be presented as a message of pluralistic relationships and responsibilities to unify or care for other Believers, who are brothers and sisters in the Lord.

It is the pluralistic *agape* loving, righteous, and holy Body of Christ which Jesus will return to receive as His Bride, not a group of individual immature Believers living as if they do not know or care for each other. Thus, Jesus wants a loving, holy Bride and does not want a Bride that is full of selfishness and animus toward others.

God has called Believers Business Owner functioning evangelists in Christ Jesus to be the chosen of God, and salvation is an emphasis on both the individual salvation and pluralistic salvation whom as a "people who have obtained God's mercy." Believer Business ministers are royal priests individually but expressed corporately as a royal priesthood. Believers belong individually to a pluralistic holy nation. Again, the emphasis is upon a pluralistic Body of Christ who becomes matured as Christ's multi-peopled Bride.

The dual message of the gospel of the kingdom, coupled with the gospel of repentance and remission of sins, is what is the correct message to preach in evangelism.

God is calling forth Believer Business Owner functioning evangelists who will extend God's *agape* love, grace, mercy, and salvation to Believer Business Employees, sharing the gospel of the Kingdom and gospel of repentance and remission of sins to customers and every one that comes to the business. Every Believer Business functioning minister must present an invitation to others to be reconciled with God individually and to be joined to the Body of Christ pluralistically as members of this new spiritual family with God the Father by way of adoption (Romans 8:15). This is the business of God the Father. Good loving fathers seek and care for their children. Jesus' humanity nature, as our business Messiah, is the "everlasting Father" of our born again spirits (Isaiah 9:6; 1 Peter 1:23). Malachi 4: 5-6 says, "Behold, I will send you (the spirit of) Elijah the prophet (John the Baptist) before the coming of the great and dreadful day of the LORD: (6) And he shall turn the heart of the fathers to the children, and the heart of the children to their fathers, lest I come and smite the earth with a curse." The family that has many absentee fathers causes a big problem in society. The true Gospel of the Kingdom and repentance and remission of sins will reconcile each man or woman back to Father God and His Kingdom. God's holy nation within every country is where Father God manifests His fatherly love, discipline, and provision.

In the world where the family unit has been disintegrated, the Gospel of the Kingdom and the gospel of repentance and remission of sins bring healing because Jesus is the everlasting Father of Believers' born again spirits (Isaiah 9:6, 1 Peter 1:23) and are children of God the Father by adoption (Romans 8:15). Healing is a call to all fathers unto reconciliation who take on the characters of fatherhood as the loving, covenant-making and covenant-keeping Godhead and the Lord Jesus Christ's humanity nature.

PHILIP WAS AN EXAMPLE OF A NEW TESTAMENT FUNCTIONING EVANGELIST.

Philip was the first one chosen of the seven deacons in the local *Ekklesia* at Jerusalem (Acts 6:1-6) before he became a functioning evangelist (Ephesians 54:11). Philip was approved in his ministry first as a deacon in the local *Ekklesia* before he was sent out as a functioning evangelist.

Philip as a functioning evangelist was sent out to preach the good news of Christ as the gospel of the Kingdom and the gospel of repentance and remission of sins to the Gentiles in Samaria (Acts 8:4-5).

Acts 8:7, 12 says, "For unclean spirits, crying with loud voice, came out of many that were possessed with them: and many taken with palsies, and that were lame, were healed. . . But when they believed Philip preaching the things concerning the kingdom of God, and the name of Jesus Christ, they were baptized, both men and women."

Philip brought great joy to the city of Samaria (Acts 8:4). Although Philip's ministry included evangelism with a pluralistic goal of saving the whole city of Samaria, he was sensitive to the Lord concerning individual salvation.

Philip, as a functioning evangelist was led by the Holy Spirit and was sensitive to the voice of the Lord through His divine nature, God the Word (Acts 8:26). Philip had no fear when called of God to minister salvation to the eunuch who was a man of authority for a wealthy man or a royal family (Acts 8:27, 29).

Philip had spent much time learning the scriptures and was able to preach the Gospel of the Kingdom and repentance and remission of sins. Philip preached Christ from a passage of the Old Testament looking ahead to Christ's sacrificial death. (Acts 8:30-34).

Philip, as a functioning evangelist preached Christ Jesus to the eunuch, not some religious doctrine (Acts 8:37). Philip took the time to make sure the eunuch, as a new Believer was baptized in water (Acts 8:38-39).

Philip led the sorcerer, Simon, to the Lord and probably had baptized him in water. However, Philip did not discern the heart of Simon the Sorcerer. Neither did Philip lead the new Believers of Samaria into the baptism of the Holy Spirit.

THE WORK OF THE EVANGELISTS WITH OTHER FIVE-FOLD MINISTERS.

After Philip left Samaria, Peter and John, who were functioning apostles, came and led the Samarian new Believers into the baptism of the Holy Spirit. Afterwards, Peter and John allowed Simon the

Sorcerer to expose his covetous heart under the right circumstances (Acts 8:13-14).

Obviously, Simon's quick repentance from trying to buy the spiritual gifts and anointing was probably because of the stature of Peter. Simon may have heard what happened in Acts 5 to Ananias and Sapphira by the Holy Spirit through Peter.

Philip recognized the foundational ministry of the functioning apostles and did not try to teach the apostolic doctrines, nor try to organize and put in order a Samaritan congregation. Philip did not try to be the servant Shepherd to God's Believers in Samaria.

TYPES OF EVANGELISM AND PEOPLE IN THE MARKETPLACE.

In business, evangelism is similar to promoting the positive attributes of a product or service to a wide audience to increase a company's customer base. Evangelistic business marketing relies on recommendations from scientists, specialists, or well-known individuals.

In Romans 16, Paul mentioned ten women who were fellow-workers, helpers, or co-laborers in ministry, and some of these women were wealthy and gave into his ministry. Also, most scholars agree that the Bible identifies Junia as a woman functioning apostle. Priscilla and Acquilla were Believers who worked with Paul as tent makers and helped in ministry as functioning evangelists. Also, Paul mentioned women functioning evangelists such as Eudodias and Syntyche, who "labored with him in the Gospel" (Philippians 4:2, 3). Throughout history, both men and women were and are functioning evangelists. Therefore, what is said in the Bible concerns both Believer Business Owners men and women functioning evangelists.

The Gospel of the Kingdom and repentance and remission of sins are to be preached to every person in every place of society. This includes in the garden and parks evangelism (John 3:1-5); child evangelism (Matthew 19:14); rest home evangelism (Psalm 71:9).; hospital evangelism (Matthew 25:36, 43); prison evangelism (Matthew 25:36, 43); home fellowship evangelism (Acts 20:18-21); workplace evangelism (1 Peter 3:15; Colossians 4:6); one on one personal evangelism (Acts 8:27-40); small and large crowds evangelism (Acts 8:1-26).

The Believer Business Owner functioning evangelist is not just someone who wears white shoes, brightly-colored jackets and ties, who plays a guitar, who is an Internet personality, or who blitz the media or rent large civic auditoriums for crusades. The Believer Business Owner functioning evangelist can often have lifetime effectiveness in leading the unsaved to the Lord for initial salvation.

The message of the gospel is delivered in different ways and in different places as the opportunity arises, which calls for "life-style evangelism" as the most important method of evangelism.

Some will come to Christ Jesus in search of a philosophy of truth (John 18:38). Others will respond to the "goodness of the Lord" (Romans 2:4). A few will be won through curiosity of the supernatural (John 4:29, 30). Yet many poor people will receive salvation by a response to a functioning minister's acts of charity and *agape* love (Acts 10:19-48).

The key then to being a successful Believer Business Owner functioning evangelist is following the leading and direction of the Holy Spirit. It is the Holy Spirit that ultimately draws a Believer to repentance and confession by faith in Christ Jesus for salvation.

The Holy Spirit reveals to the mature Believer Business Owner functioning evangelists the condition of the person with the unsaved heart as the goodness of God the Father draws them nearby.

John 16:8, 13 says, "And when He has come, He will convict the world of sin, and of righteousness, and of judgment. (13) However, when He, the Spirit of truth, has come, He will guide you into all truth; for He will not speak on His own authority, but whatever He hears He will speak; and He will tell you things to come."

John 6:44 says, "No one can come to Me unless the Father who sent Me draws him; and I will raise him up at the last day."

Therefore, Believer Business evangelism is a cooperative effort with the Holy Spirit. The Holy Spirit knows the unsaved person, his needs, past childhood, his sinful habits, and the demonic spirits that bind him.

Most importantly, the Holy Spirit has the power to translate the unsaved from Satan's evil realm into God's Kingdom where Christ Jesus has been elevated as King of kings and Lord of lords (Colossians 1:13; 1 Timothy 6:15).

Since Matthew 28:19 commands Believers to make disciples of all nations, it is obvious the work of the Believer Business Owner functioning evangelists is only the initial step. The entire Ephesians 4:11 functioning ministers are needed to equip and bring the unsaved from initial salvation with a born again spirit to having a spiritually transformed and mature soul as a disciple of Christ to perform their Vocations and Gifts.

The Lord said that the gospel of the Kingdom shall be preached in all the world and then the end will come (Matthew 24:14). Jesus never talked about evangelizing the lost with the gospel of heaven, the gospel of eternal life, the gospel of Christ, or the gospel of salvation, even though these blessings are part of the gospel of the Kingdom and other functioning apostles mentioned some of these names, but they all are part of the gospel of the Kingdom and gospel of repentance and remission of sins. Jesus did not say to seek first eternal life and God's righteousness, and all these things will be added to you. Jesus said in Matthew 6:33 says, "But seek ye first the kingdom of God, and his righteousness; and all these things shall be added unto you."

Matthew 4:23 says, "And Jesus went about all of Galilee, teaching in their synagogues, and preaching the gospel of the kingdom, and healing all manner of sickness and all manner of disease among the people." Similarly, Matthew 9:35 says, "And Jesus went about all the cities and villages, teaching in their synagogues, and preaching the gospel of the kingdom, and healing every sickness and every disease among the people."

Finally, Mark 1:14 says, "Now after that John was put in prison, Jesus came into Galilee, preaching the gospel of the kingdom of God, And saying, 'The time is fulfilled, and the kingdom of God is at hand: repent ye, and believe the gospel.'"

THE EVANGELIST'S VENUE FOR PREACHING THE GOSPEL OF THE KINGDOM AND REPENTANCE AND REMISSION OF SINS

Jesus pronounced the Great Commission for everyone in Mark 16:15, "...Go ye into all the world, and preach the gospel [of the Kingdom (Matthew 24:14) and repentance and remission of sins (Luke

24:47)] to every creature." The Greek for the word "world" in this scripture is *kosmos,* which means according to Strongs G2889, "… by implication the *world* (in a wide or narrow sense, including its inhabitants, literally or figuratively [morally]): - adorning, world."

In the New King James Version, Jesus said in Matthew 28:19, "Go therefore and make disciples of all the nations (ethnic groups)…." Jesus said to all Believers to "go into all the world" (Mark 16:15) not park yourself in your favorite seat in a warehouse or cathedral lecture hall pyramid paradigm structure for thirty years. Jesus mandates all Believers to go to the lost because they will rarely come to you. The *kosmos* is every part of the world where Believers are mandated to go, not just in other countries, but in your town, your city, your county, your state, where your federal legislatures are and preach the gospel of the Kingdom and repentance and remission of sins to every unbeliever, and after initial salvation train them to be disciples of Christ. Preach to unbelievers concerning Christ Jesus, the history of His life, death, resurrection, ascension to heaven while alive, and our eternal hope of His return back here in a new heaven and a new earth. Share Believers' eternal hope of ruling and reigning with Christ Jesus here in the new heaven and a new earth throughout eternity as kings and priests (Revelation 5:10).

Matthew 24:14 says, "And this gospel of the kingdom shall be preached in all the world for a witness unto all nations; and then shall the end come." The Greek for the word "world" in this scripture is *oikoumenē,* which means according to Strongs G3624, "…*land*, that is, the (terrene part of the) *globe*; specifically, the Roman *empire:* - earth, world."

Matthew 28:20 says, "Teaching them to observe all things whatsoever I have commanded you: and, lo, I am with you always, even unto the end of the world." The Greek for the word "world" in this scripture is *aion,* which means according to Strongs G165, "…an *age*; by extension *perpetuity* (also past); by implication the *world*; specifically (Jewish) a Messianic period (present or future): - age, course, eternal, (for) ever (-more), [n-]ever, (beginning of the, while the) world (began, without end).

The importance of showing these various Greek words for the English word "world" or "earth" as places to preach the gospel of the kingdom of God and repentance and remission of sins. The scriptures never mandated that the teaching and preaching had to be done exclusively in selected buildings like the Jewish Synagogues, the Temple, or today exclusively and jurisdictionally in the Christian warehouse or cathedral auditorium lecture hall pyramid paradigm structure. The gospel of the Kingdom and repentance and remission of sins are to be preached in every place in the society and culture in every city, county, state, and country, and in every part of the culture, including businesses. This witnessing and leading people to the Lord includes every Believer, including Believer Business Owners and Believer Business Employees as they engage other employees, customers, clients, or purveyors that visit the workplace.

The mandate by Jesus in Matthew 28:19 in making disciples of all ethnic groups is different than making mere converts. Making disciples is a daily process of God the Father's pruning to bear more spiritual fruit (John 15:2); God the Word's cleansing and sanctifying by the water of the *rhema* word to have an *Ekklesia* without spot, wrinkle, blemish and that she is holy (Ephesians 5:26-27), and God the Holy Spirit mortifying the deeds of the flesh, so the soul has more *zoe* life (Romans 8:13). This soul transforming work by the Godhead is after initial salvation.

As functioning evangelists, along with the other Ephesians 4:11 functioning ministers, Believer Business Owners can make disciples of their Believer Business Employees by using both scholastic teaching from the word of God and by hands on kinesthetic training with repetitive demonstrations. Kinesthetic training is by far what is missing by the leaders in the warehouse or cathedral lecture hall pyramid paradigm structure. Kinesthetic training is activating disciples in the work of the ministry by showing them how to lead unbelievers to the Lord for initial salvation and by guiding and watching the young Believer Business Employees leading someone to the Lord. Kinesthetic training means helping the young Believer Business Employee prepare and then watch the young Believer Business Employee leading a Bible study in the morning before work begins, or at a home fellowship meeting and having an invitation for newcomers to accept Jesus Christ as Lord and Savior. It also means the Believer Business Owner (or spiritually mature manager) watching a young Believer Business Employee leading a customer or another employee to the Lord for their initial salvation.

Both men and women were called as witnesses to preach the gospel of the Kingdom (Matthew 24:14) and the repentance and remission of sins (Luke 24:47) to the unsaved people in all the *kosmos* in society. Thus, these two messages of the gospel shall be preached to the whole world in every place to every ethnic group, in businesses, in marketplaces, in highways and byways, in restaurants, in schools, and every place where fallen mankind congregate together.

CHAPTER TEN

THE BELIEVER BUSINESS OWNER FUNCTIONING PASTORS

THE BUSINESS FUNCTIONING PASTOR IS GOD'S GIFT TO THE BODY TO TEND AND FEED THE FLOCK OF GOD IN THE MARKETPLACE.

Ephesians 4:11, 12 & 16 says, "And He gave some as (Believer Business Owner functioning) pastors...(12) for the equipping (spiritual scholastic teaching and kinesthetic training) of the saints (employees) for the work of ministry (using spiritual gifts, power, knowledge, and fruit in business) for the edifying (building up by leading to green pastures and still waters) the Body of Christ (who are doing business in the marketplace) . . .(16) from whom the whole body (the employer and employees engaging other Believers in the marketplace), joined (as one flock of God) and knit together (being about the Father's business) by what every joint supplies (with their talents), according to the effective working (in doing the Father's will in the marketplace and in business) by which every part does its share causes growth (in talents, servanthood, stewardship, and profit through the leading of the business shepherd) of the body for the edifying (building the business according to Biblical principles as the flock of the Lord) of itself in love (*agape* as the primary motive of all business actions).

Again, the purpose of the Believer Business Owner functioning pastor is to build up and activate Believer Business Employees, partners, and those other purveyors, customers, and clients with whom the Believer Business Owner functioning pastor meets and extends to them that measure of grace given by Christ Jesus as the Believer Business Owner functioning pastor engages in business in the marketplace.

The Believer Business Owner functioning pastor has the spiritual responsibility to intimately become involved in the lives of the Believer Business Employees and lead them to green pastures and beside still waters. This functioning ministry shepherds Believer Business Employees, so they can reach their own God-ordained purposes as good stewards and servants who are joined together being about the Father's business of maturing His children by enhancing skills, and instilling wisdom, knowledge, understanding, and servanthood. In other words, the Believer Business Owner functioning pastor has the duty to impart God's wisdom, knowledge, principled with grace and agape love to make each Believer Business Employee an activated leader in God's kingdom. In doing this, the focus and shepherding is designed to impart the measure of grace each Believer Business Employee is given according to Ephesians 4:7 becomes a reality. Thus, the Believer Business Owner functioning pastor goal is to transform the soul of each Believer Business Employee to be mature functioning ministers themselves. This is God's mandate for the Believer Business Owner functioning pastor to establish and activate scholastically teaching and kinesthetically training for activating business ministers.

Similarly, this is God's mandate for all the Ephesians 4:11 functioning ministers, with differences depending on the functioning office gift of each Believer Business Owners.

THE HISTORICAL AND CULTURAL USAGE OF THE WORD "SHEPHERD" OR "SHEPHERDING" AS USED IN THE AGRARIAN SOCIETY WHEN THE SCRIPTURES WERE WRITTEN, THAT DEFINES THE FUNCTIONING PASTOR AS A SHEPHERD.

The Hebrew word in the Old Testament for shepherd is *raah*, which means in Strongs H7462, "to *tend* a flock, that is, *pasture* it; intransitively to *graze* (literally or figuratively); generally to *rule*; by extension to *associate* with (as a friend): - X break, companion, keep company with, devour, eat up, evil entreat, feed, use as a friend, make friendship with, herdman, keep [sheep] (-er), pastor, + shearing house, shepherd, wander, waste."

Herding sheep, goats, cattle, and camels, but mostly sheep and goats, was a wealthy business that multiplies by doubling in size as ewe sheep and nanny goats give birth at least once a year. Who has a business that multiplies at least one fold (100%) each year? Cattle, sheep, and goats are a wealth asset that multiplies.

In the Old Testament Abraham, Isaac, Jacob, Moses, and David all worked their businesses as herdsmen of sheep and goats. God compares the pastoring of people like the shepherding of sheep. **Psalm 78:52** says God led the Israelites "like a flock;" **Jeremiah 50:6** calls them "lost sheep," and **Psalm 95:7** refers to them as "the sheep of His pasture" and "the sheep of His hand." Likewise, Ezekiel 34:23 says, "I will set up one shepherd over them, and he shall feed them, even my servant David; he shall feed them, and he shall be their shepherd." The famous verse in Psalms 23:1 says, "The Lord is my Shepherd; I shall not want." Finally, in the Messianic prophecy, Isaiah 53:6 says, "All we like sheep have gone astray."

In the New Testament, the word "pastor" as a person is only in one scripture, which is in Ephesians 4:11, and the Greek word for the functioning pastor is *poimēn,* but this Greek word is generally translated as shepherd. Believers also are compared to sheep in need of a good functioning shepherd. John 10:1-16 is where Jesus calls Himself the "good Shepherd" Who lays down His life for the sheep, and John 10:27 is where Jesus says, "My sheep listen to My voice; I know them, and they follow Me." In Matthew 10:16 Jesus sends His twelve functioning apostles and instructs them that they are "... as sheep in the midst of wolves: be ye therefore wise as serpents, and harmless as doves." In Matthew 25:32-34 is where God separates "the sheep from the goats."

The Hebrew word *raah* in the Old Testament is translated in the King James into English as:

Pastor or priest in Jeremiah 2:8; 3:15; 10:21; 12:10; 17:16; 22:22; 23:1, 2.

Shepherd in Genesis 46:32, 34; 47:3; Exodus 2:17, 19; 1 Kings 22:17; Psalms 23:1; 80:1; Isaiah 44:28; Jeremiah 6:3; Ezekiel 34:2-23.

Herdsman in Genesis 13:7,8; 26:20; 1 Samuel 21:7; as "Keeper" in Genesis 4:2; Exodus 3:1; and

Feed in 1 Samuel 17:15; 1 Chronicles 17:6; Psalm 68:71; Ezekiel 34:10; Zechariah 11:4, 7; Isaiah 40:11.

The Greek words in the New Testament for functioning pastor, shepherd, flock, or fold or the verb shepherd, are:

Poimen is translated shepherd 17 times, and functioning pastor only once. Matthew 9:36; 25:32; Mark 6:34; Luke 2:8; 1 Peter 2:25; Hebrews 13:20; and John 10:2 translated the word as shepherd, and Ephesians 4:11 as functioning pastor.

Poimaino is a verb meaning to tend as a shepherd. It means to feed or rule. Matthew 2:6; Luke 17:7; John 21:16; Acts 20:28; 1 Corinthians 9:7; 1 Peter 5:2; Jude 12; Revelations 2:27.

Poimne is translated flock, fold. Matthew 26:31; Luke 2:8; John 10:16; 1 Corinthians 9:7.

Poimnion is translated as flock or a group of Believers. Luke 12:32; Acts 20:28; 1 Peter 5:2, 3.

Basko is a verb which means to feed, pasture, to fodder, to graze, to feed, to keep. Luke 15:15; Matthew 8:30, 33; John 21:15-17.

Therefore, a Believer Business Owner functioning pastor is one who tends, herds, feeds, guides, and superintends the flock who are Believer Business Employees and/or customers of the business in ministry.

The shepherding husbandman was despised by the Egyptians (Genesis 46:34). Egypt is a word that stands for the world system, so the world system hates the mentors or Believer Business Owner functioning pastors that shepherd Believer Business Employees to obtain biblical wisdom, knowledge, and understanding and are trained in servanthood and expressing faith, hope, and the greatest is *agape* love (1 Corinthians 13:13). In the world, to give someone your wisdom, knowledge, and understanding is to make them a potential competitor, and if they are a thief they can steal your customers or clients. This is why every Believer Business Employee should sign an "At Will" employment agreement with a strong non-competition paragraph and a prohibition from soliciting other Believer Business Employees into the new business of the departed employee.

The Kingdom of God is based upon respect, honor, loyalty, integrity, grace, faith, hope, and *agape* love in dealing with other people in business. It is a different system than that of the world, so Believer Business Employees must be trained to be sharp as the serpents in the world to avoid the snakes, foxes, and wolves in sheep clothing, but be gentle as doves and not hurt anyone. Furthermore, the pastoral functioning ministry will be despised by a fallen world system defined as a "dog eat dog world" that is a cutthroat and ruthless business practice where people are after the "almighty dollar" instead of seeking Almighty God. These unsaved businesspeople are willing to harm one another to succeed. The business world is a competitive environment where "survival of the fittest" is the rationale of acting selfishly to move ahead of others. The phrase "survival of the fittest" was coined in the mid-1800s during the Industrial Revolution by first Herbert Spencer in his book, *Principles of Biology,* but he was adapting his book referencing Charles Darwin's book titled *On the Origin of Species by Means of Natural Selection, or the Preservation of Favoured Races in the Struggle for Life*. Subsequently, Charles Darwin liked the phrase and used it in describing his thesis. Being a caring Believer Business Owner functioning shepherd is contrary to worldly business owners whose ideas are to be tough and ruthless, and in this life their shrewdness and uncaring actions are rewarded financially. Yet, at the end of their lives these ruthless business unbelievers will stand before God at the White Throne Judgment and will be thrown into everlasting punishment in the Lake of Fire (Revelation 20:15). Thus, I simply ask, "Was the acquisition of money all that important compared to seeking first God's Kingdom where you could rule and reigned with Christ throughout eternity? (Revelation 5:10)

Again, Jesus said in Matthew 10: 16, "Behold, I send you forth as sheep in the midst of wolves: be ye therefore wise as serpents, and harmless as doves." There are a lot of immature Believer Business Owners and Believer Business Employees whose souls are not transformed. Believer Business Owners and Believer Business Employees must have the wisdom and discernment to know when someone who calls himself a Christian is trying to sell you something or get you to invest in their business or project by using the serpentine methodologies of lying about the condition of their hearts. It is like a used car salesman who tells you what a great used car that he is trying to convince you to purchase, but then he makes the customer sign that the customer received a Bill of Sale that the auto is sold "As Is," without any warranties expressed or implied.

However, Believer Business Owner functioning pastors must equip and train their Believer Business Employees with the understanding that in the Kingdom of God, honesty, loyalty, stewardship, servanthood, giving, and honoring each other and customers and clients are character prerequisites for God's favor and prosperity (Luke 6:38).

THE BIBLICAL PATTERN FOR BELIEVER BUSINESS FUNCTIONING PASTORS.

In scriptures, God and the Lord Jesus Christ often refer to Himself as a Shepherd of His people. (Genesis 49:24; Psalm 68:7).

God as a Shepherd goes before His flock. (Psalm 68:7). In business, the Believer Business Owner functioning pastor's flock would be both Believer Business Employees and customers or clients.

The Lord as a Shepherd in business leads His flock (Psalm 23:3). Jesus as the Good Shepherd leads both His Believer Business Owners and Believer Business Employees with scholastic teaching and kinesthetic training of how to become and live as mature servant ministers of the customers or clients who also become the flock of the Believer Business functioning ministers.

The Lord as the Shepherd in business leads His flock (Believer Business Owners and Believer Business Employees) to lie down in green pastures and leads them beside the still waters (Psalm 23:2; Jeremiah 50:19; Isaiah 40:11).

God as a Shepherd in business protects His flock with His staff (Psalm 23:4). A mature Shepherd of the flock has the duty to confront the sin and demons in Believers' lives. There are many wolves in the world who will try to take advantage of the innocent flock of sheep.

God as a Shepherd in business whistles to those of the flock going astray (Zechariah 10:8).

God as a Shepherd in business gathers the flock who are dispersed in the land (Isaiah 56:8).

God as a Shepherd in business carries the lambs in His bosom (Isaiah 40:11).

God as a Shepherd in business gently leads those caring for the young (Isaiah 40:11).

Also, Jesus is the Door that the sheep may enter (John 10:9), and He is the Good Shepherd (John 10:11) Who was about His Father's business Who was the Great Shepherd of the sheep.

Jesus came to earth to be about the Father's business (Luke 2:49), and in so doing, to demonstrate the Father's love for His flock. Jesus chose Peter, Andrew, James, John and others who were doing business in the marketplace as His under-shepherds for His *Ekklesia* that He was establishing.

Jesus, as the Pattern for business good shepherds or functioning pastors, established that a good shepherd will lay down His life for God's sheep. (John 10:15).

Jesus, as the Pattern for business good shepherds or functioning pastors, never criticized the flock, but demonstrated the Father's love with true compassion and love for the flock. (Matthew 9:36; Mark 6:34).

Jesus, as the Pattern for business good shepherds or functioning pastors, placed great value on each individual sheep (Luke 15:4).

Jesus commanded Peter, His chief functioning apostle to also shepherd (*basko* - verb) His flock as a sign of *agape* love toward Him. (John 21:15-17). Thus, a sign that a Believer Business Owner loves the Lord is how he or she loves the Believer Business Employees placed under his or her care, mentoring, and maturing.

Jesus constantly looked to "under shepherds" to feed and tend to His sheep in the business (Ephesians 4:11; 1 Peter 5:2).

A Believer Business Owner functioning pastor must be a leader who already has walked the road of obedience as one of the sheep, who has been matured through the daily incremental problem solving interactions in the business (John 10:4). He or she must be an example who has and is obediently walking before the Believer Business Employees in the ways of God.

The Believer Business Owner functioning pastor, as well as the other Ephesians 4:11 Business functioning ministers, should lead by example. The principle is that the farmer must be the first partaker of the fruit (2 Timothy 2:6).

The Believer Business Owner functioning pastor must be filled with the Holy Spirit (John 10:1, 3, 9).

The Believer Business Owner functioning pastor must be the first to study God's word and pray for the business if he wants others to pray.

The Believer Business Owner functioning pastor must be the first to tithe and give if he wants others to tithe and give.

In conclusion, the Believer Business Owner functioning pastor, as with the other Ephesians 4:11 functioning ministers, must exhibit a lifestyle that the sheep can emulate (Hebrews 13:7; 1 Peter 5:2-3; 1 Corinthians 1:1).

The Believer Business Owner functioning pastor must know how and be diligent in feeding and watering the flock (employees and customers and clients) by leading them to green pastures and still waters. (Jeremiah 23:4; Jeremiah 3:15; Ezekiel 34:1-3; Acts 20:28; 1 Peter 5:2-3; Psalm 23).

The Believer Business Owner functioning pastor must provide proper spiritual food and water that will nourish, strengthen and edify God's flock in business. (Genesis 29:7; Psalm 23:2).

The Believer Business Owner functioning pastor therefore must be constantly involved in preparing the food and water, i.e., studying and preparing the word of God in prayer. (Acts 6:4; Jeremiah 10:21). The Believer Business Owner functioning pastor must bring the word of God and prayer first into the business environment and then into the marketplace.

The Believer Business Owner functioning pastor, as with the other Ephesian 4:11 Believer Business Owners functioning ministers, must have "fresh *manna*" from heaven for his or her Believer Business Employees to bring proper mature growth and refreshing for an increase in God's business in ministry. The same old, stale revelations do not bring proper nourishment for Believer Business Employees and customers.

The Believer Business Owner functioning pastor in business must also provide green pastures belonging to others, along with vitamin supplements, which means to lead the flock to other Ephesian 4:11 functioning ministries to expose them to a balanced diet for proper growth (Ephesians 4:13). A Believer Business Owner functioning pastor by herself or himself cannot provide a balanced diet and must allow other Ephesians 4:11 functioning ministers to also participate in spiritual transformation of the souls of the Believer Business Employees.

The Believer Business Owner functioning pastor must also be able to feed all levels of the Believer Business Employees, from the very young to the very mature in the Lord, i.e., sheep at every level of development (Isaiah 40:11, 29; John 16:12).

The Believer Business Owner functioning pastor must develop trusting relationships with the Believer Business Employees like a professor in college trying to remain inspirational while teaching the same subject with the same books year after year; like a conductor of an orchestra trying to make harmony with the many different instruments; like a parent who has six children who have to share three bedrooms and two bathrooms in the home, or a driving instructor who guides his inexperienced driver practicing how to drive a car amongst aggressive other drivers in heavy traffic. A true Believer Business Owner functioning pastor knows his or her sheep, and the sheep trust him or her because they know his or her voice (John 10:27).

The Believer Business Owner functioning pastor must train through scholastic teaching and kinesthetic training the Believer Business Employees by each knowing the names and family members of each other and Believer Business Employees and regular customers or clients (John 10:3). Learning the Bible and training to use those biblical principles and ethical standards requires a trustworthy relationship between the Believer Business Owner Ephesians 4:11 functioning minister and the Believer Business Employee.

Hosea 4: 6 says, "My people are destroyed (Hebrew Strongs H1820 *damah*, meaning brought to silence without saying anything spiritually important or wise) for lack of knowledge (Hebrew Strongs H1820 *da'ath,* meaning an intimate relationship as between a Rabbi and a Talmid, as the Talmid is the Hebrew term for a disciple or student)...." A Talmid's dedication was to be so devoted to his Rabbi that the Talmid would imitate the Rabbi's actions and words to act and think like him. The main difference between imitate and emulate is that imitation is copying Rabbi's specific words and actions, whereas emulation is the acting or speaking to try to equal or excel the Rabbi, not disrespectful, but by being inspired by the Rabbi's achievements and following Rabbi's journey but following the Talmid's unique path inspired by Rabbi.

Paul said we are to be imitators of Christ, who is Believers' ultimate Rabbi.

Several scriptures in the New Testament state that disciples of Christ should be imitators of Jesus. In Ephesians 5:1-2 the functioning apostle Paul instructs Believers to imitate God and walk in *agape* love as Christ *agapao* loved Believers. In Philippians 2:5 the functioning apostle Paul instructs Believers to "Let this mind be in you, which was also in Christ Jesus." Similarly, in 1 Peter 2:21 the functioning apostle Peter encourages Believers to duplicate Christ Jesus' steps because Jesus left Believers an example. Finally, in 1 John 2:6, the functioning apostle John states that a Believer who says he or she abideth in Christ should walk as Jesus walked.

Also, the Believer Business Owner functioning pastor must allow the Believer Business Employees sheep to know him or her, so when the Believer Business Owner functioning pastor speaks, they know his or her voice; they stop talking and listen to what the Believer Business Owner functioning pastor says (John 10:3). Of course, these rules of conduct, motivations, and spiritual conduct and motivations apply to all the Believer Business Owner Ephesians 4:11 functioning ministers.

Paul referring to his great Business Owner functioning Pastor, Jesus, said in Philippians 3:10, "That I may know Him, and the power of His resurrection, and the fellowship of His sufferings, being made conformable unto His death." In like manner, as the Believer Business Owner functioning pastor, it is imperative that you show good impeccable character to your Believer Business Employees, so you can state as Paul said to imitate you as you imitate Christ Jesus. In 1 Corinthians 11:1 the functioning apostle Paul urges Believers to follow him as he, Paul, imitates Christ and follows Him.

The Believer Business Owner functioning pastor especially must let the flock know he or she also is one of God's sheep, himself or herself (Ezekiel 3:15; Philippians 1:28-30). The Believer Business Owner should stay humble and never be haughty or be spiritually egocentric in his or her relationship with Christ Jesus. Every Believer falls way short in comparison of Jesus Who never committed one sin. 1 John 1:8 says, "If we say that we have no sin, we deceive ourselves, and the truth is not in us."

The Believer Business Owner functioning pastor especially must have a true, sincere heart of compassion for the Believer Business Employees and customers or clients.

A Believer Business Owner functioning pastor must be an example in laying down his or her life to protect the Believer Business Employees sheep and to take time to train the Believer Business Employees sheep in biblical economics, morality, and servanthood (John 10:15; 1 John 3:16; Revelations 12:11) and as a shepherd to protect them, make sure their salaries are paid on time, have health insurance, a retirement or an IRA contribution, and sure the business is compliant to all state and federal laws regarding vacations, breaks during the day, lunch time, sick leaves, pregnancy leave, bereavement leaves, maintaining a safe work place, having fair procedures and fair disciplinary actions with found guilty of misbehavior allegations, and so on. Again, I suggest that these principles and terms of employment are put in an "At Will Employment Agreement," which are executed at time of acceptance of employment but before the first day of working. (Just a little free legal advice from this old business attorney.)

Again, the Believer Business Owner functioning pastor must be very loyal to the Believer Business Employees sheep, especially if he or she promises the Believer Business Employees sheep new benefits or bonuses at end of year.

The Believer Business Employees must know their spiritual duties of employment with the Godly Believer Business Owner functioning pastor in that the business is not just a job, but a ministry calling of God.

The Believer Business Employees sheep must know that the Believer Business Owner functioning pastor will lay down his own life's priorities for his Believer Business Employees sheep.

There must be full commitment by the Believer Business Owner functioning pastor to the Believer Business Employees and vice versa. The Believer Business Employees must have a strong work ethic, must show up on time, do the assigned tasks competently and within the time limits envisaged.

The Believer Business Owner functioning pastor must pour out his life and strength for the Believer Business Employees sheep (John 10:11; John 10:13; Ezekiel 34:4).

The Believer Business Owner functioning pastor will stay with the Believer Business Employees sheep during times of their spiritual attack and trouble, and the Believer Business Owner functioning pastor will visit them in their homes if they have a serious illness, pray for them, and pay sick leave to take off the economic stress upon the Believer Business Employee sheep (John 10:12; Jeremiah 23:2).

The Believer Business Owner functioning pastor continuously is watchful for the protection of the Believer Business Employees sheep from abuse of managers, other employees, or customers or clients (Hebrews 13:17). This is all part of providing a safe place to work. On the other hand, abuse is not just discipline when the Believer Business Employee sheep needs to be corrected by a Manager or the Believer Business Employee is consistently engaged in social talking with other employees and not working, has been late to work, from coming back from lunch, or leaving too early without permission.

To be sure, the Believer Business Owner functioning pastor must always place the well-being of the Believer Business Employees sheep above his own life and business ministry.

The Believer Business Owner functioning pastor is always seeking to find the backsliders or prodigal sons (Luke 15:4) and use his or her business as a point of contact for people who have been abused by the world system or are lost in the sins of a decadent world.

The Believer Business Owner functioning pastor watches out for wolves (John 10:12; Acts 20:29). This includes looking at the signs of the times, and the evil that lurks in the fallen world marketplaces.

The Believer Business Owner functioning pastor must apply the loving discipline of the rod, which is used for correcting and protecting along the road of maturation. Discipline must be as a parent lovingly disciplines a child to train the child away from evil (Matthew 18:15-20).

HUMILITY AND SUBMISSION BY THE FUNCTIONING PASTORS IN BUSINESS WHO DO WRONG AND HAVE TO REPENT.

The Believer Business Owner functioning pastor must remain humble, submissive to the Holy Spirit, and have and maintain a teachable soul to continue to grow spiritually. All living things continue to grow, replace used up life, and entertain changes to health to your soul and body. Your born again spirit never is unhealthy because he is absolutely righteous and holy, perfect, and sinless all the time (Ephesians 4:24; Hebrews 12:23; 1 John 3:9)

Jeremiah 2:8 says, "The priests (pastors) did not say, 'Where is the Lord?' And those who handle the law did not know Me; the rulers also transgressed against Me; The prophets prophesied by Baal and walked after things that do not profit." Notice that the spiritual leaders transgressed the law of the Lord and became hypocrites.

The Believer Business Owner functioning pastors must remember they are also Believer Business Employees sheep in their relationship to the Lord (Colossians 3:17, 23-24), and they must maintain a relationship with the Good Shepherd, Jesus, God the Word made flesh, Who is the King of the Kingdom of God. Jesus Christ is the Great Business Employer or all Believers.

The Believer Business Owner functioning pastor should study the word of God, daily, as an example to his or her Believer Business Employees. Acts 6:2-4 says, "Then the twelve summoned the multitude of the disciples and said, 'It is not desirable that we should leave the word of God and serve tables. (3) Therefore brethren, seek out from among you seven men of good reputation, full of the Holy Spirit and wisdom, whom we may appoint over this business; (4) but we will give ourselves continually to prayer and to the ministry of the word.'" The Word of God has answers to business problems and life problems in general that the Believer Business Owner functioning pastors can use to counsel the Believers, so the Believer Business Owner functioning pastors have planning to do, financial decisions to make, have personal responsibilities to handle, and they have to be sure the cash flow is adequate to pay the expenses of the business in ministry. Also, because of the fact the Believer Business Owner has thoroughly committed to make the business ministry, he or she will be the target for government intrusion, from people in the world that believe there is a separation of church and business, that government can shut down the business for a season, there are leases to consider, health insurance policies for all people in the company, and so on that require the Believer Business Owner to make wise decisions for his own family and for each employee. Being a Believer Business Owner is a tough position to be in, as it causes pressure while at the same time making other decisions. Eventually, as did Moses when his father-in-law came to the Israelite encampment when Moses was exhausted acting as Judge of all disputes, so at Jethro's advice delegated every tribe to choose Judges to resolve disputes, and Moses sat has the Supreme Judge on appeal. Thus, eventually, the Believer Business Owner functioning minister learns to delegate tasks for those who have competence and trustworthiness.

Satan knows that if he can smite the Believer Business Owner functioning pastor, the flock or employees will be scattered, and the Romans 12 gift of giving will not be in full operation; and God's children will not continue in the daily grind of maturation. Believer Business Owner functioning pastors are always the special object of satanic attack. The result is that Believer Business Owner functioning pastors need always to be guarded and protected by intercessory prayer by Believer Business Employees, family members, and those in their local *Ekklesia.*

Zechariah 13:7 says, "'Awake, O sword, against My Shepherd, against the Man who is My Companion,' says the Lord of hosts."

Matthew 26:31 says, "Then Jesus said to them, 'All of you will be made to stumble because of Me this night, for it is written: "I will strike the Shepherd, and the sheep of the flock will be scattered."'"

The Believer Business Owner functioning pastor who works only for financial gain can make the altar impure. Since business is a ministry and a place of ministry, the altar can be made impure through bad motives of the leadership in the business, especially the Believer Business Owner functioning pastor. Financial gain cannot be the only or prevailing motivation and reason behind the Believer Business Owner functioning pastor's reason for being in business. The Believer Business Owner functioning pastor must adopt the same goals of God the Father of maturing His children through the daily incremental problem solving stimuli encountered in the business.

1 Peter 5:2 says, "Shepherd the flock of God, which is among you, serving as overseers, not by compulsion, but willingly, not for dishonest gain, but eagerly."

1 Timothy 3:3 says, "Not given to wine, not violent, not greedy for money, but gentle, not quarrelsome, not covetous."

Jesus warned of thieves, robbers, and hirelings. John 10:1 says, "Most assuredly, I say to you, he who does not enter the sheepfold by the door, but climbs up some other way, the same is a thief and a robber."

John 10:9 and 10(a) says, "I am the door. If anyone enters by Me, he will be saved and will go in and out and find pasture. (10) The thief does not come except to steal, and to kill, and to destroy..."

2 Peter 2:3 says, "By covetousness they will exploit you with deceptive words; for a long time their judgment has not been idle, and their destruction does not slumber."

A thief is one who steals through subtle or trickery behavior. A Believer Business Owner functioning pastor must watch out and guard the Believer Business Employees from wolves. A robber is one who steals through violence or the threat thereof. The profit-only business owner in the world is one who works only for the income and profit and has little heart for the Believer Business Employees. John 10:13 says, "The hireling flees because he is a hireling and does not care about the sheep."

Therefore, if work in the business is done only for financial gain, the wrong motive will cause the business not to prosper.

Believer Business Owner functioning pastors should not be in business ministry seeking worldly recognition and power.

Ezekiel 34:4 says, "The weak you have not strengthened, nor have you healed those who were sick, nor bound up the broken, nor brought back what was driven away, nor sought what was lost; but with force and cruelty you have ruled them."

1 Peter 5:3 says, "Nor as being lords over those entrusted to you but being examples to the flock."

Luke 22:24-27 says, "Now there was also a dispute among them, as to which of them should be considered the greatest. (25) And He said to them, 'The kings of the Gentiles exercise lordship over them, and those who exercise authority over them are called benefactors. (26) But not so among you; on the contrary, he who is greatest among you, let him be as the younger, and he who governs as he who serves. (27) For who is greater, he who sits at the table, or he who serves? Is it not he who sits at the table?'"

Some immature Believers crave power, control, and authority to fulfil some ungodly psychological needs. Some of these predators will prey on employees who lack power and are fearful of losing their jobs.

However, a Believer Business Owner functioning pastor is a humble servant, as the other Ephesian 4:11 functioning ministers, who must exemplify a servant's heart. A Believer Business Owner functioning pastor must put the employees first, and the goals of the business will be realized. Even a loving father or mother sometimes must discipline as well as extend favors to his or her children. Yet, in all disciplinary measures there must be *agape* love, and the discipline shall be design of making the Believer Business Employee a better disciple of Christ.

A self-centered immature Believer Business Owner functioning pastor, who is looking only for a position of authority and income, will expect Believer Business Employees to serve and wait hand and foot on him when it should be the other way around. The greatest in the Lord's Kingdom is the chiefest servant (Mark 10:44). When the Believer Business Owner functioning pastor does all word and deed unto the Lord, then he or she will be a servant like the Lord, Who was a ransom and laid down His life for His sheep.

God looks at the condition of the Believer Business Owner functioning pastor's heart and motivation more than the good work completed.

A Believer Business Owner functioning pastor must not overly work or overly drive the Believer Business Employees that causes stress, although overcoming stress does make you stronger. A Believer Business Owner functioning pastor must lead the flock into taking the yoke of the Lord and entering God's rest while working in business. A Believer Business Owner functioning pastor must encourage the Believer Business Employees to work as unto the Lord as obedient servants (1 Corinthians 10:31; Colossians 3:17, 23-24), but to rest and take a Sabbath every week. Remember, the Believer Business Owner functioning pastor in the traditional church warehouse lecture hall paradigm structure must work on his sabbath in the office of the functioning priest.

In Matthew 12:1-8, Jesus was rebuked, along with His disciples by the Pharisees for allegedly working on the Sabbath. His disciples were hungry as young men, so they were seen plucking and eating grain as they walked through a field. The Pharisees stated this was a violation of Sabbath law. Jesus later healed a man with a withered hand on the Sabbath, further provoking the Pharisees to say Jesus violated the Sabbath.

Jesus answered the Pharisees in Matthew 12:3-8 by saying, "But He said unto them, 'Have ye not read what David did, when he was an hungered, and they that were with him; (4) How he entered into the house of God, and did eat the shewbread, which was not lawful for him to eat, neither for them which were with him, but only for the priests? (5) Or have ye not read in the law, how that on the sabbath days the priests in the temple profane the sabbath, and are blameless? (6) But I say unto you, That in this place is one greater than the temple. (7) But if ye had known what this meaneth, I will have mercy, and not sacrifice, ye would not have condemned the guiltless. (8) For the Son of man is Lord even of the sabbath day." In 2 Samuel 6:14-22 King David wearing a linen ephod danced with all his might before the Ark of the Covenant when the Ark of the Lord was brought into Jerusalem. The Israelites shouted and played musical instruments. David was a Shepherd, King, and Priest; and David used his kinesthetic shepherd training and protection of the sheep to kill Goliath. Then, David used kingly authority to enhanced his priestly calling.

Jesus' humanity nature was David's progeny, and Jesus was the Good Shepherd. John 10:11-17 says, "I am the Good shepherd: the good shepherd giveth his life for the sheep. (12) But he that is an hireling, and not the shepherd, whose own the sheep are not, seeth the wolf coming, and leaveth the sheep, and fleeth: and the wolf catcheth them, and scattereth the sheep. (13) The hireling fleeth, because he is an hireling, and careth not for the sheep. (14) I am the good shepherd, and know my sheep, and am known of mine. (15) As the Father knoweth Me, even so know I the Father: and I lay down My life for the sheep. (16) And other sheep I have, which are not of this fold (referring to non-Jews): them also I must bring, and they shall hear My voice; and there shall be one fold (both Christian Jews and Christian Gentiles), and One Shepherd (Jesus with His divine nature and humanity nature). (17) Therefore doth my Father love Me, because I lay down My life, that I might take it again."

Genesis 33:13 says, "And he said unto him, My lord knoweth that the children are tender, and the flocks and herds with young are with me: and if men should overdrive them one day, all the flock will die." Believer Business Employees sheep should not be overdriven but given green pastures and still waters to rest and regain their strength.

What Believer Business Owner functioning pastors call as their Believer Business Employees sheep usually have been working during the week and are tired, but they come with obedience to the warehouse lecture hall building to fulfill their calling and hopefully acquire their spiritual Vocations and spiritual Gifts. The functioning pastors should have a small flock, not try and set up a mega-church where it is impossible to scholastically teach and kinetically train one on one as Jesus did His functioning apostles and disciples. Likewise, how can a small group of Believer Business Owners functioning pastors perform the mandated duties of Ephesians 4:12-13, which again is "For the perfecting of the saints, for the work of the ministry, for the edifying of the body of Christ: (13) till we all come in the unity of the faith, and of the knowledge of the Son of God, unto a perfect man, unto the measure of the stature of the fulness of Christ." Therefore, the small family business is a better place to conduct business as a ministry. In Ephesians 4:13 the word "perfect" in the Greek is *teleios,* which means in Strongs G5046, "*complete* (in various applications of labor, growth, mental and moral character, etc.); neuter *completeness:* - of full age, man, perfect." This is the same word regarding the perfection in our born again spirits, which in Hebrews 12:23 says, ". . . to the spirits of just men made perfect." The Greek for perfect in Hebrews 12:23 is *teleioō,* which in Strongs G5048 means, to *complete*, that is, (literally) *accomplish*, or (figuratively) *consummate* (in character): - consecrate, finish, fulfil, (make) perfect."

Consequently, a Believer Business functioning pastor cannot try to take on more than he or she can handle personally. In a large business, the Believer Business functioning pastor first must teach scholastically and train kinesthetically Believer Business Employee Managers, for the Believer Business Manager then to in turn oversee and scholastically teach and kinesthetically train other Believer Business Employees. My suggestion is that there should not be more than 70 Believer Business Employees in the business as ministry, so the Believer Business Managers are not overly burdened with too many Believer Business Employees. A Believer Business Manager must go to the Believer Business Employee where the fire in the heart is hot. That Believer Business Employee and be trained as a spiritual Manager leader that scholastically teaches and Kinesthetically trains other Believer Business Employees.

If the Believer Business Owner functioning pastor would go to the local fellowship congregation, and recruit Believer Business Employees who seek employment where there is a business ministry teaching and training eight to ten hours a day, five to six days a week where they can be matured in their souls and be activated into business ministry.

Often church growth happens because there is a church split. What I am revealing is that home fellowship members and *Ekklesia* members should be instructed to seek employment with a Believer Business Owner where they can receive scholastic spiritual teaching and kinesthetic spiritual training daily eight to ten hours a day for five to six days a week where they are perfected for the work of the ministry and get paid for such education. Believer Business Employees need to be scholastically taught and kinesthetically trained to look elsewhere to minister outside the warehouse or cathedral auditorium pyramid paradigm structure and not covet the functioning pastor's pulpit.

Likewise, the Believer Business Employees should not covet the Believer Business Owner's business. The Believer Business Employees should decide to start their own business or look for another Believer Business Owner who also sees his or her business as a place of ministry as a partner or shareholder in the business. Then you both can establish business as a ministry that activates Believer Business Employees into ministry to learn biblical economics, have a moral compass, being a servant as the highest stature, having a strong work ethic, learning about cash flow security and management, learning steps to attract and acquire new customers or clients, maintaining constant research and development, thinking long term instead of short term, practicing teleology, learning that debt is enslavement, and having a heart full of *agape* love to give to fulfill the mandates of Matthew 25:35-38. These ideas are what the Believer Business functioning pastors should be practicing and teaching others.

THE BELIEVER BUSINESS OWNERS AND BELIEVER BUSINESS EMPLOYEES IN MINISTRY

Now, God always will keep His obedient Believer Business Owner functioning pastor ahead of the Believer Business Employees in revelation knowledge, wisdom, insight, and lifestyle. The obedient Believer Business Owner functioning pastor will also see the green pastures before the worldly competition does, and he or she will lead the Believer Business Employees where there is good profit for the business to ensure the Believer Business Employees that they will have steady salaries and benefits. Also, the good Believer Business Owner functioning pastor will lead the Believer Business Employees beside the still waters, so they do not go after income streams that will not be prosperous.

The Believer Business Owner functioning pastor must know the speed or intake level which the Believer Business Employees can absorb spiritual scholastic knowledge and biblical economic principles, as the Believer Business Owner cannot take them farther than their maturity level can allow. This requires good business management involving proper delegation and checkups with every task assigned.

Therefore, new illuminations from Scripture must be introduced slowly to ensure the Believer Business Employees are not frustrated, as they will leave the employment, and all the scholastic biblical teaching and kinesthetic training with them. However, new inventions are to be expected as the Believer Business Owner functioning pastor should help the Believer Business Employees to learn new products and new services as the Believer Business Owner functioning pastor assures them that these changes will be easy to understand and put in practice. The Believer Business Owner functioning pastor is the man or woman the Believer Business Employees look to if they are having problems with the work training or if there are relationship problems with other Believer Business

Employees. The Believer Business Owner functioning pastors have the patience to listen to Believer Business Employees' problems. With all the podcast specialists that are available, any new product, any new procedure, any new health insurance plan, or with a new satellite business opening, a podcast can be recorded where the Believer Business Employee can watch them repeatedly to obtain the knowledge needed to sell the new product or service to a new customer.

Most people, including Believers, learn until they get into a habit of work activity or a comfort zone and want to stay there. New Believer Business Employees must be challenged at the time of hiring that new products or services will be added to the business. New Believer Business Employees must consent to learning about these new products or services without complaint as part of their job description? Or the Believer Business Employer can put a paragraph in the "At Will Employment Agreement" which you can show them if there is protest.

THERE ARE PRINCIPLES OF SOWING AND REAPING THAT OPERATE AGAINST DISOBEDIENT BELIEVER BUSINESS OWNER FUNCTIONING PASTORS.

One of the lessons that Galatians 6:7-8 says is that everyone has a right to choose their own choices, but they do not have a right to choose the consequences.

All Believer Business Employees belong to the Lord, not the Believer Business Owner, and as with the other Ephesian 4:11 functioning ministers, the Believer Business Owner functioning pastor is a minister of the Lord in business and must protect and lead the Believer Business Employees.

For example, if the Believer Business Owners decide to create a retirement plan or a profit sharing plan under the requirements of the Internal Revenue Code and regulations, the Believer Business Owner functioning pastor must make sure those savings and contributions are kept secure, earning interest in a safe investment, and never take the money from that account for any business purpose. The Believer Business Owner functioning pastor must stand up strongly against such intrusion if other Believer Business Owners of the Corporation or LLC that try to convince that use of the money being held for the Believer Business Employees. If necessary, the Believer Business Owner functioning pastor might have to retain an attorney to seek an immediate temporary restraining order to stop the potential pilfering what are being held in trust for the Believer Business Employees. Thus, the Board of Directors of the corporation must agree in writing when a retirement plan is chosen to never invade the retirement plan for capital needed or wanted by the corporation. This would be unethical biblical practice, regardless of if it is legal. Also, do not ask the Believer Business Employees to consent to use their retirement deposit for business growth or expenses, as Believer Business Employees sheep are not the ones who are to decide where the green pastures or the still waters are. As the Believer Business Owner functioning pastor, those decisions are your responsibility.

Jeremiah 23:1-2 says, "Woe be unto the (functioning) pastors that destroy and scatter the sheep of My pasture! saith the LORD. (2) Therefore thus saith the LORD God of Israel against the Pastors that feed My people; Ye have scattered My flock, and driven them away, and have not visited them: behold, I will visit upon you the evil of your doings, saith the LORD."

Believer Business Owner functioning pastors and shepherds must realize that the Lord Jesus Christ, as the Good Shepherd, has only one sheep fold, both Jew and Gentile (John 10:11).

Because of this, all Believer Business Owner functioning pastors shall be held accountable in this life and at the Judgment Seat of Christ for what they have done for or against the Believer Business Employee sheep (Hebrews 13:7; Ezekiel 34:10; Jeremiah 23:1-2).

I advise that you put in your "At Will Employment Agreement" that antisemitism in word or deed will be grounds for discipline or termination. Jesus was of the Tribe of Judah through His mother, Mary, and the word Jew really refers to those Israelites of the Tribe of Judah. Also, the names of Joseph's sons were Ephraim and Manasseh. Jacob adopted Joseph's two sons. By adopting Joseph's two sons, Jacob granted them full territorial inheritance rights to obtain two full Tribal ownership shares equal to his other sons, such as Reuben and Simeon, effectively giving Joseph a double portion of his inheritance and ensuring that both Ephraim and Manasseh became the progenitors of two distinct tribes of Israel with the right tribal land ownership. When the spies went into the Promise Land at command of Moses, there were still twelve Tribes with territory land inheritance because the priestly Tribe, Levi, did not receive a territorial land inheritance. The Levi Priestly Tribe were not represented as one of the spies chosen to go to the Promise Land. However, there were still ten Tribes, including Tribes of Ephraim and Manasseh, that had lack of faith and that caused God to make them sojourner in the wilderness for forty years. Once the children of Israel come into the Promise Land at the end of the forty years in the desert. This arrangement reflects God's providence and the fulfillment of His promises to Abraham, Isaac, and Jacob regarding their descendants, where there would be twelve tribal territorial inheritances would be distributed the Promise Land.

John 10:11-17 says, "I am the good shepherd: the good shepherd giveth his life for the sheep. (12) But he that is an hireling, and not the shepherd, whose own the sheep are not, seeth the wolf coming, and leaveth the sheep, and fleeth: and the wolf catcheth them, and scattereth the sheep. (13) The hireling fleeth, because he is an hireling, and careth not for the sheep. (14) I am the good shepherd, and know my *sheep,* and am known of mine. (15) As the Father knoweth me, even so know I the Father: and I lay down my life for the sheep. (16) And other sheep I have, which are not of this fold: them also I must bring, and they shall hear my voice; and there shall be one fold, *and* one shepherd. (17) Therefore doth my Father love me, because I lay down my life, that I might take it again."

John 10:16 reveals that Jesus' sheep fold is both Jews and Gentiles, and both Jews and Gentiles will be the *Ekklesia* and together will be one flock (*Ekklesia*). Jesus as the Messiah and Christ will be and is the One Shepherd, which is the resurrected and ascended Christ Jesus.

GOD IS STRICT ON HIS FUNCTIONING PASTORS OR SHEPHERDS

First, God, as a discipling Father, will take the business away from unfaithful Believer Business functioning pastors if they fail to set up a business ministry where the Believer Business Employees are scholastically taught biblical principles with a moral compass and kinesthetically trained as business servants and functioning ministers while they work at the business eight to ten hours a day, five to six days a week to mature and transformed their souls to be spiritual and no longer carnal. God commands the Believer Business functioning pastors to exhibit *agape* love, grace, mercy, and protection.

Jeremiah 23:1-3 says, "Woe be unto the pastors that destroy and scatter the sheep of my pasture! saith the LORD. (2)Therefore thus saith the LORD God of Israel against the (Believer Business Owner functioning) pastors that feed My people (Business Employees); Ye have scattered My flock (Believer Business Employees), and driven them away, and have not visited them (Believer Business Employees): behold, I will visit upon you the evil of your doings, saith the LORD. (3) 'But I will gather the remnant of My flock (Believer Business Employees) out of all countries where I have driven them, and bring them back to their folds; and they shall be fruitful and increase.'"

Jeremiah 10:21 says, "For the (Believer Business Owner functioning) pastors are become brutish, and have not sought the LORD: therefore they shall not prosper, and all their flocks (Believer Business Employees) shall be scattered."

Second, God, as a discipling Father, if the Believer Business Owner functioning pastor mistreats the Believer Business Employees, then Father God will send the Believer Business Employees to some other Believer Business Owner functioning pastor who is more faithful and expresses *agape* love and continue scholastically teach and kinesthetically train Believer Business Employees to become mature in their spiritual Vocations and spiritual Gifts.

Jeremiah 23:4 says, "And I will set up (Believer Business Owner functioning) shepherds over them (Believer Business Employees) which shall feed them: and they shall fear no more, nor be dismayed, neither shall they be lacking, saith the LORD."

There is a new breed of Believer Business Owner functioning pastors with hearts that want to care for and scholastically teach and kinesthetically train their Believer Business Employees and launch them into their spiritual Vocations and spiritual Gifts to fulfill what God has called them to do. These new Believer Business Owner functioning pastors are willing to shepherd their Believer Business Employees unto the ways of the Lord involving biblical economics, business morality, strong work ethic, servanthood, *agage* love, long term thinking, saving for research and development, maintain cash flow security, and cash flow management.

Third, God will allow the principle of bad stewardship and mistreatment of Believer Business Employees to have its negative result on the businesses where the Believer Business Owner functioning pastors have failed to lead, care, protect, and *agape* love their Believer Business Employees in the ways of the Lord.

Jeremiah 12:10-13 says, "Many (Believer Business Owner functioning) pastors have destroyed My vineyard; they have trodden My portion under foot; they have made My pleasant portion a desolate wilderness. (11) They have made it desolate, and being desolate it mourneth unto Me; the whole land is made desolate, because no man layeth it to heart. (12) The spoilers are come upon all high places through the wilderness: for the sword of the LORD shall devour from the one end of the land even to the other end of the land: no flesh shall have peace. (13) They have sown wheat, but shall reap thorns: they have put themselves to pain, but shall not profit: and they shall be ashamed of your revenues because of the fierce anger of the LORD."

Again, Jeremiah 23:1-5 says, "'Woe be unto the (Believer Business Owner functioning) pastors that destroy and scatter the sheep of my pasture! saith the LORD. (2) Therefore thus saith the LORD God of Israel against the (Believer Business Owner functioning) pastors that feed My people; Ye have scattered my flock (Believer Business Employees), and driven them away, and have not visited them: behold, I will visit upon you the evil of your doings, saith the LORD. (3) And I will gather the remnant of My flock (Believer Business Employees) out of all countries whither I have driven them, and will bring them again to their folds; and they shall be fruitful and increase. (4) And I will set up (Believer Business Owner functioning pastors or) shepherds over them which shall feed them: and they shall fear no more, nor be dismayed, neither shall they be lacking, saith the LORD. (5) Behold, the days come, saith the LORD, that I will raise unto David a righteous Branch, and a King shall reign and prosper, and shall execute judgment and justice in the earth.'"

God is a business Father (Luke 2:49). Shepherding or pastoring the flock of God is being about the Father's business. The Father's flock leaves the warehouse or cathedral lecture hall pyramid paradigm structure after the meetings and goes back home to seek employment with a Believer Business Owner *agape* loving functioning pastor and will bring Kingdom principles, salvation, and servanthood into the business.

Jeremiah 50:6-7 says, "My people hath been lost sheep: their shepherds have caused them to go astray, they have turned them away *on* the mountains: they have gone from mountain to hill, they have forgotten their resting place. (7) All that found them have devoured them: and their adversaries said, 'We offend not, because they have sinned against the LORD, the habitation of justice, even the LORD, the hope of their fathers.'"

These verses can pertain to Believer Business Owner functioning pastors. Ezekiel 34:1-10 says, "And the word of the Lord came to me, saying, (2) 'Son_of man, **prophesy against the shepherds of Israel**, prophesy and say to them, "Thus says the Lord God to the shepherds: 'Woe to the shepherds of Israel who feed themselves! Should not the shepherds feed the flocks? (3) You eat the fat and clothes yourselves with the wool; you slaughter the fatlings, but you do not feed the flock. (4) The weak you have not strengthened, nor have you healed those who were sick, nor bound up the broken, nor brought back what was driven away, nor sought what was lost; but with force and cruelty you have ruled them. (5) So they were scattered because there was no shepherd; and they became food for all the beasts of the field when they were scattered. (6) My sheep wandered through all the mountains, and on every high hill; yes, My flock was scattered over the whole face of the earth, and no one was seeking or searching for them.' (7) "Therefore, you shepherds, hear the word of the Lord: (8) 'As I live,' says the Lord God, 'surely because My flock became a prey, and My flock became food for every beast of the field, because there was no shepherd, nor did My shepherds search for My flock, but the shepherds fed themselves and did not feed My flock'-- (9) Therefore, O shepherds, hear the word of the Lord! (10) "Thus says the Lord God: 'Behold, I am against the shepherds, and I will require My flock at their hand; I will cause them to cease feeding the sheep, and the shepherds shall feed themselves no more; for I will deliver My flock from their mouths, that they may no longer be food for them.'"

The above scripture passages are very strong indeed against those Believer Business Owners functioning shepherds or functioning pastors who fleece their flocks, which are their Believer Business Employees by not paying fair wages and not scholastically teaching them biblical economics and principles and kinesthetically training them with practical applications in all areas of the business, but especially maintaining the vision and purpose of business as a place of ministry. Applying wisdom and knowledge during the workweek is the best way to mature and transform the souls of Believer Business Employees.

A very good teaching that can be applied to scholastically teach and kinesthetically train by Paul in Colossians 3: 12-17, which says, "Put on therefore, as the elect of God, holy and beloved, bowels of mercies, kindness, humbleness of mind, meekness, longsuffering; (13) Forbearing one another, and forgiving one another, if any man have a quarrel against any: even as Christ forgave you, so also do ye. (14) And above all these things put on charity (*agape* love), which is the bond of perfectness. (15) And let the peace of God rule in your hearts, to the which also ye are called in one body; and be ye thankful. (16) Let the word of Christ dwell in you richly in all wisdom; teaching and admonishing one another in psalms and hymns and spiritual songs, singing with grace in your hearts to the Lord. (17) And whatsoever ye do in word or deed, do all in the name of the Lord Jesus, giving thanks to God and the Father by him."

The Believer Business Owner functioning pastors must protect the Believer Business Employees from idol worship, avoiding false soothsayers, witchcraft, and false ideas. Zechariah 10:2-3 says, "For the idols speak delusion; the diviners envision lies and tell false dreams; they comfort in vain. Therefore the people wend their way like sheep; they are in trouble because there is no shepherd. (3) My anger is kindled against the shepherds, and I will punish the goatherds. For the Lord of hosts will visit His flock, the house of Judah, and will make them as His royal horse in the battle."

Although seen as an unworthy profession in an agrarian society, Acts 20:28 says, "Take heed therefore unto yourselves, and to all the flock (Believer Business Employees), over the which the Holy Ghost hath made you (Believer Business Owner functioning pastors) overseers, to feed the church of God, which He hath purchased with His own blood."

The Believer Business Owner functioning pastors' ministry God considers as a very worthy and important ministry. God sees Believer Business Owner functioning pastors caring and guiding His Believer Business Employees sheep, in scholastic teaching and kinesthetically training to be leaders in business, leading others about biblical business principles, finances, giving, work as a holy calling, stewardship of assets and people, *agape* loving, and servanthood.

God is strict on Believer Business Owner functioning pastors especially because they must learn discipleship teaching and training with *agape* love, biblical principles, business ethics, for the spiritual transformation and maturation of the souls of every Believer Business Employee.

CHAPTER ELEVEN

THE BELIEVER BUSINESS OWNER FUNCTIONING TEACHER

BELIEVER BUSINESS OWNERS FUNCTIONING TEACHERS RECEIVE ILLUMINATION BY STUDYING THE BIBLE AND HEARING DIVINE INSPIRATION

Ephesians 4:11, 12 & 16 says in relevant part, "And He gave some as (Believer Business Owner functioning) teachers... (12) for the equipping (spiritual scholastic teaching and kinesthetic training) of the saints (in business) for the work (vocations) of ministry (in business) for the edifying (building up by scholastically teaching sound doctrine and kinesthetically training with *agape* love to produce pure hearts, good consciences, and sincere faith as Believers in business) the Body of Christ (working in business) … (16) from whom the whole body (in business), joined (as mature Believer Business Employee disciples of Christ) and knit together (in *agape* love with sound biblical principles and servanthood) by what every joint supplies (with their spiritual vocations, grace, and measure of gifts), according to the effective working (as Believer Business Owner functioning teacher) by which every part does its share causes growth (in maturing by spiritual transformation of souls through sound teaching) of the body (in business) for the edifying (with freedom in knowing the truth from scholastic teaching and kinesthetic training and studying God's word) of itself in *(agape)* love."

Believer Business Owner functioning teachers are especially needed in these end times to come up against Satan, who uses as his number one weapon in the marketplace of ideas which is confusions, lies, and deceptions. Spiritual discernment along with biblical scriptures that are applied in business as to what is truth and what is false is a life and death decision and a poverty and prosperity reality.

Again, the purpose of all Ephesians 4:11 Believer Business Owner functioning ministers is through biblical scholastic teaching and hands on kinesthetic training and applying in business biblical truths. This purpose is especially true of the Believer Business Owner functioning teachers for the maturation of Believer Business Employees to determine the measure of grace given by Christ Jesus to each Business Believer Employee according to the measure of Christ's gift.

God demonstrates His fullness through His matured Believer Business Employees, especially those who have been matured by scholastic teaching and kinesthetically training while working in business. Until the Believer Business Employees become spiritually soulishly matured, God cannot manifest His fullness through His business functioning ministry to acquire a substantial market share in commerce. This is why God needs glorious (mature) Believer Business Owners and Believer Business Employees without spot or wrinkle.

All Business Believers are given the same Vocations, but each is responsible to submit to God and submit to Ephesians 4:11 Believer Business functioning ministers to allow God the Father to prune away the flesh in the soul (John 15:2), God the Word to wash and sanctify the soul with the *rhema* word (Ephesians 5:26), and God the Holy Spirit to mortify the deeds of the flesh in the soul (Romans 8:13).

Yet, all Believer Business Servants have been given God's grace but there are different measures of each Believer's business spiritual Vocations and spiritual Gifts to those working in business. Again, Ephesians 4:7 says, "But unto every one of us is given grace according to the measure of the gift of Christ."

Grace is given based upon the ministry calling and assignment, but the measure of that gift will vary based upon the will of God. Again, all Believer Business Owners and Believer Business Employees are called with the same Vocations as kings, priests, lords, ambassadors, and Soldiers. However, not all Believers have been called as one of the Ephesians 4:11 Believer Business Owner functioning ministers, but each is given different spiritual Gifts and a measure of grace in the use of those Gifts. Again, 1 Corinthians 12:29-30 says, "Are all apostles? are all prophets? are all teachers? are all workers of miracles? (30) Have all the gifts of healing? do all speak with tongues? do all interpret?"

Similarly, Paul stated in Romans 12:3-8, "For I say, through the grace given unto me, to every man that is among you, not to think of himself more highly than he ought to think; but to think soberly (not drinking of the fallen world's libation), according as God hath dealt to every man the measure of faith. (4) For as we have many members in one body, and all members have not the same office: (5) So we, being many, are one body in Christ, and every one members one of another. (6) Having then gifts differing according to the grace that is given to us, whether prophecy, let us prophesy according to the proportion of faith; (7) Or ministry, let us wait on our ministering: or he that teacheth, on teaching; (8) Or he that exhorteth, on exhortation: he that giveth, let him do it with simplicity; he that ruleth, with diligence; he that sheweth mercy, with cheerfulness."

There should be no division based upon gifts that differ amongst Believer Business Employees. 1 Corinthians 12:25-26 says, "That there should be no schism in the body (of Believer Business Employees); but that the (Business Employees) members should have the same care one for another. (26) And whether one member suffer, all the members suffer with it; or one member be honoured, all the (Business Employee) members rejoice with it."

The whole body of Christ is built upon the foundation laid by the Believer Business Owner functioning apostles and functioning prophets in the workplace as seen in Ephesians 2:20-22, which says, "And are built upon the foundation of the (functioning) apostles and prophets, Jesus Christ Himself being the chief corner stone; (21) In whom all the building fitly framed together groweth [additionally as the doors (functioning evangelists), windows (functioning teachers), roofs (functioning pastors), gifts of healing, givers of donations, gifts of rulership in various areas of society, gifts of mercy, workers of miracles, gift of faith, gift of various tongues, interpretations of tongues, word of wisdom, word of knowledge] unto a Holy Temple in the Lord (22) In whom ye (other Believers who have other gifts) also are builded together for an habitation of God through the Spirit." Properly applied, all Believers have spiritual Gifts, including Believer Business Owner functioning teachers who scholastically teach and kinesthetically train Believer Business Employees through studying Scriptures and hands on kinesthetic tutoring. All Believer Business Owners and Believer Business Employees can only be pure, submitted, humble vessels through which God pours out His fullness by being joined harmoniously together in unity as one spiritual body with diverse spiritual Gifts but with the same spiritual Vocations.

1 Timothy 1:1-5 says, "Paul, an (functioning) apostle of Jesus Christ by the commandment of God our Saviour, and Lord Jesus Christ, which is our hope; (2) Unto Timothy, my own son in the faith: Grace, mercy, and peace, from God our Father and Jesus Christ our Lord. (3) As I besought thee to

abide still at Ephesus, when I went into Macedonia, that thou mightest charge some (functioning teachers) that they teach no other doctrine, (4) Neither give heed to fables and endless genealogies, which minister questions, rather than godly edifying which is in faith: so do. (5) Now the end of the commandment is charity (*agape* love) out of a pure heart, and of a good conscience, and of faith unfeigned."

The goal of the Believer Business Owner functioning teacher is to instill into the Believer Business Employee disciples God's "*agape* love from a pure heart and good conscience and a sincere faith" and to put in practice kingdom principles, faith, hope, and *agape* love.

Therefore, the Believer Business Owner functioning teacher's job is to teach scriptures and teach biblical economics and servanthood to the Believer Business Employees as illuminating truths experienced in the business. Truth builds trust toward the Believer Business Owners functioning teacher and Believer Business Employees because truth about products and services increases goodwill with customers and clients. Truth must be the foundational primary morality in business is very important to change most people think that Business Owners merely will say anything to sell their products or have people retain them for services. Without question, truth in business enhances its reputation, fosters respectful relationships with Believer Business Employees, simplifies decision-making based on biblical information. Therefore, I think every Believer Business Employee shall put their hand on the Bible and then verbally say and afterwards sign a Truth Pledge to operate the business and deal with customers, clients, Believer Business Owners, Managers, and fellow Believer Business Employees with truth, not falsehoods.

The Believer Business Owner functioning teacher has the purpose of transforming carnal souls in Believer Business Employees into spiritual souls, with spiritual truthful thoughts in their minds, spiritual truthful feelings in their emotions, and spiritual truthful beliefs in their hearts, so there are experiences through kinesthetic training. This spiritual transformation of the soul is required for a season when each Believer Business Employee's soul is as a worm that must enter a cocoon to be released at the end of the season to become a spiritual soulish butterfly.

While in the cocoon the carnal Believer Business Employee's worm-like soul is out of sight from other Believer Business Employees, where he or she must be restricted while being transformed into the spiritual soulish butterfly Believer as a servant of God. As the divine Teacher, Jesus taught His apostles, several of which were in business, in Mark 10:44 that the chiefest in ministry is the servant of all. In every Believer, there is a season for their carnal worm-like soul must be transformed from a crawling nature to a spiritually soulish butterfly soaring in the spiritual atmosphere of God's Kingdom.

A worm is similar to a snake, but everybody loves the butterfly into which the worm is transformed. Romans 12:2 says, "And do not be conformed to this world, but be transformed (*metamorphoo*) by the renewing of your mind (Greek-*nous* meaning the whole soul), that you may prove what the Will of God is, that which is good and acceptable and perfect." A Believer Business Owner functioning teacher educates the soul of the Believer Business Employee with God's word and instructs him or her how the purging out the carnal nature in his or her soul by the Godhead that causes the soul to become spiritually transformed and matured.

Jesus' commandment in Matthew 28:20, "…Teaching them to observe all things whatsoever I have commanded you."

OLD TESTAMENT BELIEVER BUSINESS TEACHERS

The Patriarchs in the Old Testament were all men in business. In Hebrew, there were two words used for "teacher" or "to teach."

The Hebrew word, *yarah* means "to flow as water like rain; figurative to 'point out' (as if by pointing the finger), to teach. This Hebrew word is translated in English as "direct, inform, instruct, lay, shoot, shew, teach, trough, rain." (Exodus 4:12, 15; 18:20; 35:34; Deuteronomy 24:8; Psalm 45:4; II Kings 12:2; Hosea 6:3; 10:11; Isaiah 30:20).

The Hebrew word, *lamad* means "to goad, to teach (the rod being an incentive to learn)." The word was translated in English as "diligently instruct, learn, skillful, teach, Teacher, and teaching." (Deuteronomy 5:1, 31:13, 11:19; Psalms 25:4, 5; 119:7, 12, 26, 64, 66, 68, 108; 43:10; 1 Chronicles; 5:18; 25:7; Ezra 7:10; Jeremiah 12:16; 23:33).

THE FUNCTIONING TEACHER MINISTRY IN THE OLD TESTAMENT

Patriarchal Business Owner functioning teachers. Adam, Noah, Abraham, Isaac, Jacob, Moses, and David all had their own businesses, mostly herding animals and taught their families the ways of the Lord and were men of faith and became teachers of God's word to their families and extended families (Genesis 18:18, 19; Hebrews 11:1016; Job 1).

Parental teaching in homes. Deuteronomy 6:7 says, "And you shall teach them diligently to your sons and shall talk of them when you sit in your house and when you walk by the way and when you lie down and when you rise up." The words of the Lord were to be everywhere around the home and as frontlets between their eyes at the lower part of the forehead.

The Books of Proverbs and Ecclesiastes were the instructions of a father and a mother to a son, but much of the wisdom contained therein were about serving and worshiping God, avoiding bad relationships, about the proper use of money, riches, and wealth, and about the conduction of business. According to Jewish scribes, Shimei ben Gera was one of Solomon's teachers. Solomon's Father, David was also a mentor to Solomon, along with his mother, Bathsheba who guided Solomon on how to lead God's people with wisdom.

Fathers and mothers are the first teachers responsible to their children and accountable to the Lord to teach their children the word of God and the wisdom, knowledge, and ways of God.

Teaching in the nation of Israel. The Levitical Priesthood were given the responsibility to teach the tribes of Israel the Law of the Lord and how to conduct themselves in the Temple (Deuteronomy 33:811; 24:8; Malachi 1:19; Ezekiel 44:23; 22:26; Romans 2:20).

Princes, priests, and prophets were also required to teach the people the Laws of the Lord (Ezekiel 22:23-31). The Believer Business Owner functioning prophets were also Believer Business Owner functioning teachers and interpreters of the Law of Moses. (Isaiah 43:27; 42:19; Hosea 12:10).

Scribes and Elders generally taught the Scriptures in the synagogues. Of course, they opposed the carpenter and stonemason, Jesus' teachings because they interpreted Scriptures with the wrong meaning that were based upon their religious traditions, combined with the sins of their elitist pride and unbelief. (Matthew 5:20; 7:29; 12:38; 16:21; 23:134; Luke 11:44, 53; Acts 4:5). These scribes were called Doctors in Luke 2:46, Masters in John 3:10, and Rabbis or Teachers in John 3:2, 3:13. In doing so, the elitist Scribes took away the "key of knowledge" from the people and brought condemnation upon themselves (Luke 11:46-49).

One of the main methods of instruction in Israel was *catechism* classes. The word **"instructed"** in Luke 1:4; Acts 18:25, and Romans 2:18 means orally instructed but not kinesthetic trained. The Greek word used for "instructed" here was *katecheo,* which means "to instruct by asking questions and correcting answers."

THE NEW TESTAMENT FUNCTIONING TEACHER MINISTRY

The Greek words used in the New Testament for functioning "teacher" or "to teach" came from the basic word *didasko.*

The Greek word d*idasko* means "to learn, to teach," and is translated in the verb form as "teach."

The Greek word d*idaktikos* means "instructive" (*didactic*) and is translated "apt to teach."

The Greek word *didaskali"* means "the information, teaching, or doctrine taught."

The Greek word *didaskolos* means "the Believer functioning teacher or instructor." It was translated as "Doctor" 14 times, as "Master" 47 times, as "Teacher" 10 times, and as "Scribe" 67 times.

CHRIST JESUS IS THE MOST LEARNED MASTER, FUNCTIONING RABBI AND TEACHER

The Lord Jesus Christ is the Master functioning Rabbi and Teacher.

Nicodemus recognized Jesus as a functioning Rabbi or Teacher Who had come from God (John 3:2; 3:13).

Jesus spent much time in all Ephesians 4:11 office functioning ministries preaching and teaching as well as healing the people (Matthew 4:25; 5:2; 9:35, 36; 11:1; 21:23; Mark 10:1; Luke 13:10; 20:21).

Jesus fulfilled in a measure the prophetic word of Isaiah 54:13, "All thy children shall be taught of the Lord." Jesus taught everywhere He went (Luke 13:26; 19:4; 21:37; Mark 14:49). He especially taught His disciples (John chapters 13-16). He taught with the anointing of the Holy Spirit (Luke 4:1819).

Jesus also taught with instruction from His divine nature authority, as God the Word, not as an echo of others, as did the Scribes and Pharisees (John 7:29; Matthew 7:28, 29; Mark 1:22).

Jesus also taught what God the Father said to Him to teach (John 7:16; 8:28; 12:48-50).

Jesus' final commission to the *Ekklesia* was to make disciples of all nations, "teaching them to observe all things whatsoever I have commanded you ..." (Matthew 28: 20).

THE EPHESIANS 4:11 BELIEVER BUSINESS OWNER FUNCTIONING TEACHERS

Ephesians 4:10-11 says, "He that descended is the same also that ascended up far above all heavens, that He might fill all things. (11) And He gave some … (Believer Business Owners functioning) teachers."

God hath set in the *Ekklesia*, thirdly, (Believer Business Owner functioning) teachers (1 Corinthians 12:28, 29).

There were certain prophets and teachers at the *Ekklesia* in Antioch (Acts 13: 14; 15:35).

The Believer Business Owner or Manager functioning teacher is to wait on the Holy Spirit to receive the Lord's scriptural teaching or kinesthetic hands-on training lesson (Romans 12:7).

The Believer Business Owner or Manager functioning teacher is to teach faithful men and women in business who can teach others (2 Timothy 2:2). Thus, the Believer Business functioning teachers must multiply themselves by training other Believer Business functioning teachers.

The Believer Business Owner or Manager functioning teacher is an elder, as he or she who teaches the word of God and impart those spiritual principles and must honor the Believer Business Owner or Manager functioning teachers. Galatians 6:6 says, "Let him that is taught in the word communicate unto him that teacheth in all good things."

Paul was a Believer Business Owner functioning teacher and functioning apostle (Acts 18:1; 1 Timothy 2:7; 2 Timothy 1:11).

Apollos was a great functioning teacher of the word (Acts 18:24).

There is a cluster of teaching ministries, such as teaching of children, teaching of women, teaching of Bible classes for all age groups, and as the Ephesians 4:11 functioning teacher.

GUIDELINES FOR THE BELIEVER BUSINESS OWNER AND MANAGER FUNCTIONING TEACHERS

1 John 2:20, 27 says, "But ye have an unction (anointing) from the Holy One, and ye know all things … But the anointing which ye have received of Him abideth in you, and ye need not that any man teach you: but as the same anointing teacheth you of all things, and is truth, and is no lie, and even as it hath taught you, ye shall abide in Him."

The Believer Business Owner or Manager functioning teacher must depend on God the Holy Spirit, as well as the Master Teacher, the Lord Jesus Christ, Whose divine nature is God the Word.

John 14:26 says, "But the Helper, the Holy Spirit, whom the Father will send in My name, He will teach you all things and bring to your remembrance all that I said to you."

A Believer Business Owner or Manager functioning teacher is admonished that "the letter kills but it is the Spirit that gives life" (2 Corinthians 3:6). All Believer Business Owners and Manager functioning teachers must not to be an educated elitist, must be *agapao* loving, kind, merciful, graceful, and tolerant to Believer Business Employee students.

An Ephesians 4:11 Believer Business Owner and Manager functioning teachers speak with divine authority to the Believer Business Employees, as he or she must hear first from the Holy Spirit before teaching so as to impart proper scriptural illumination. Jesus, the Master Teacher, through His divine nature, will manifest His truths through the Believer Business Owner and Manager as functioning teachers with manifested signs of wisdom, knowledge, and power to fulfill the purposes of God in the business ministry.

The pattern to follow is the greatest Business Owner functioning Teacher, Who was and is Jesus. Jesus must be the central figure of every teaching, as He talked about the Kingdom of God and His righteousness which Believers are to seek first daily. The Believer Business Owner and Manager functioning teachers must establish John 14:6 as foundational teaching, which says, "Jesus said to him, 'I am the way, and the truth, and the life; no one comes to the Father, but through Me.'"

John 3:2 says, "The same came to Jesus by night, and said unto him, Rabbi, we know that thou art a teacher come from God: for no man can do these miracles that thou doest, except God be with him.'"

The Believer Business Owner and Manager functioning teachers should be grounded in sound doctrine concerning the ways of conducting business with biblical principles and demanding Believer Business Employees maintain servanthood that matures the Believer Business Employees, along with making of profit for the business and donations given to expand and maintain the local *Ekklesia.*

1 Timothy 6:3-5 says, "If any man teach otherwise, and consent not to wholesome words, even the words of our Lord Jesus Christ, and to the doctrine which is according to godliness; (4) he is proud, knowing nothing, but doting about questions and strifes of words, whereof cometh envy, strife, railings, evil surmisings, (5) Perverse disputings of men of corrupt minds, and destitute of the truth, supposing that gain is godliness: from such withdraw thyself."

The Believer Business Owner and Manager functioning teachers will compare spiritual thoughts with spiritual words. 1 Corinthians 2:12-13 says, "Now we have received, not the spirit of the world, but the Spirit who is from God, that we might know the things freely given to us by God, (13) which things we also speak, not in words taught by human wisdom, but in those taught by the Spirit, combining spiritual thoughts with spiritual words." The Believer Business Owner and Manager functioning teachers must avoid bringing into the business any ideas in the marketplace that do not correspond to biblical truths and absolutes.

Believer Business Employees must be taught God's scriptures as the only written truth, so God's scriptures about biblical wisdom, knowledge, and understanding will not be questioned by the Believer Business Employees. The Believer Business Employee must request God's truths if the Believer Business Employee wants to enjoy freedom from the fallen world and the devil's enticements, along with promotion in the business ministry.

Jesus said in John 8:31-32, "Then said Jesus to those Jews which believed on Him, If ye continue in My word, then are ye My disciples indeed; (32) And ye shall know the truth, and the truth shall make you free."

Similarly, Jesus said in John 8:34-36, "...Verily, verily, I say unto you, 'Whosoever committeth sin is the servant of sin. (35) And the servant abideth not in the house for ever: but the Son abideth ever. (36) If the Son therefore shall make you free, ye shall be free indeed.'"

The Believer Business Owner and Manager functioning teachers must invite and depend upon the Holy Spirit to take the *logos* word he or she teaches and pray that it becomes *rhema* that enters the hearts of the Believer Business Employees (Luke 12:12; John 14:26; 1 John 2:20, 27).

The Believer Business Owner and Manager functioning teachers should have a divine passion for the scriptural *rhema* word and *logos* word that causes him or her to constantly search and study God's *logos* word (Jeremiah 15:16; Matthew 4:4; John 6:63; Romans 10:17, Ephesians 5:26; 1 Timothy 4:13). The Believer Business Owner and Manager functioning teacher should know how to apply the word of God to business, financing, teaching and training disciples, and application to current events, locally, nationally, and internationally as those events effect the business, value of currency, and the products being sold in the marketplace.

The Believer Business Owner and Manager functioning teachers must remain teachable also, as an example for Believer Business Employees and other Believers he or she is in fellowship (Romans 2:21; 1 Corinthians 2:13). The example of a functioning teacher was Apollos, who was a great teacher, but was humble and teachable to learn more from and be corrected by from Priscilla and Aquilla, who also were in a tent-making business with Paul and heard Paul's teachings daily as they made tents together (Acts 18:24-27; 20:19; 1 Peter 5:5; 1 Corinthians 6:12; James 1:21).

The Believer Business Owner and Manager functioning teachers must not specialize in just one area of the word of God and become unbalanced in their teaching but should teach the full counsel of God from the *logos* word of God. Otherwise, the Believer Business Employees are only mature in one area and are left open for deception in other areas.

THE BELIEVER BUSINESS OWNER FUNCTIONING TEACHER SHOULD BE A LIVING EXAMPLE OF WHAT HE/SHE TEACHES.

The Believer Business Owner and Manager functioning teachers must live by precept as to what he or she says (2 Timothy 3:10).

The Believer Business Owner and Manager functioning teachers must live by example as to who he or she is (2 Timothy 3:10).

The Believer Business Owner and Manager functioning teachers must live by conduct as to what he or she does (John 13:12-15; Acts 1:1; Isaiah 2:14).

THE RESTRICTIONS THAT GOVERN THE MINISTRY OF THE BELIEVER BUSINESS OWNER AND MANAGER FUNCTIONING TEACHER

Matthew 5:19 says, "Whoever then annuls one of the least of these commandments, and so teaches others, shall be called least in the kingdom of heaven; but whoever keeps and teaches them, he shall be called great in the kingdom of heaven."

Therefore, the consequences that govern the Believer Business Owner and Manager functioning teachers are: "What you teach, you better live, be, and do as an example to other Believers."

Pharisaism is that the false or just religious teachers say and do not what they teach (Matthew

23:13). Biblical doctrine must be followed by practical application and passing this wisdom, knowledge, and truth to the Believer Business Employees through scholastic teaching and kinesthetic training.

Yet, God is not just an information center; He is the source of life itself. The Believer Business Owner and Manager functioning teachers must seek the *logos* letter becoming the living *rhema* with spirit and life while teaching under the unction and anointing of the Holy Spirit. This is why teaching is so rewarding. The Believer Business Owner and Manager functioning teachers must scholastically teach the fresh relevant truth as imparted to him or her by the Holy Spirit and then kinesthetically train the Believer Business Employees how to apply these truths while working at the business and when they go home.

The Believer Business Owner and Manager functioning teacher must make leaders, who are able to teach other Believer Business Employees as leaders, not just followers. 2 Timothy 2:2 says, "And the things that thou hast heard of me among many witnesses, the same commit thou to faithful men, who shall be able to teach others also." The more the Believer Business Owner and Manager functioning teachers scholastically teach and kinesthetically train the Believer Business Employees how to perform their working tasks without constant oversight, give them the time to do other tasks of planning and analyzing the business health, failures, accomplishments.

The Believer Business Owner and Manager functioning teachers must always be seeking biblical truths because the goal is to activate Believer Business Employees into their spiritual Vocations and spiritual Gifts in business while using biblical economic principles, kingdom mores, *agape* love, grace, faith, and humble servanthood, Hebrews 5:12 says, **"**For though by this time you ought to be teachers**,** you have need again for someone to teach you the elementary principles of the oracles of God, and you have come to need milk and not solid food."

The Believer Business Owner and Manager functioning teachers must operate with divine wisdom, knowledge, and understanding (Exodus 35:34; Isaiah 33:6). Knowledge is the possession of the application of the facts and whether those facts are God's truth. Wisdom is the application of the truth in a practical business manner. Understanding is the interpretation of the biblical truth to be in right standing with the leading of the Holy Spirit and the Lord Jesus Christ, as He is the manifested Truth personified (John 14:6).

The Believer Business Owner and Manager functioning teachers should avoid pride of intellect, for knowledge puffs up**.** 1 Corinthians 8:1-2 says, "Now as touching things offered unto idols, we know that we all have knowledge. Knowledge puffeth up, but charity (*agape* love) edifieth. (2) And if any man think that he knoweth anything, he knoweth nothing yet as he ought to know."

As with all Ephesians 4:11 functioning ministers, the Believer Business Owner and Manager functioning teachers must avoid and shun flattering titles which tend to rob him or her of humility (Matthew 23:8-10).

GREATER JUDGMENT IS ON THE BELIEVER BUSINESS OWNER AND MANAGER FUNCTIONING TEACHERS THAN ON THE HEARERS OF THE TEACHING.

James 3:1 says, "Let not many of you become (Believer Business functioning) teachers, my brethren, knowing that as such you shall incur a stricter judgment."

The discipline of the tongue verses in James 3 concerns everyone but is especially addressed to Believer Business Owner and Manager functioning teachers.

James 3:3-8 reveals the unruly tongue, "Behold, we put bits in the horses' mouths, that they may obey us; and we turn about their whole body. (4) Behold also the ships, which though they be so great, and are driven of fierce winds, yet are they turned about with a very small helm, whithersoever the governor listeth. (5) Even so the tongue is a little member, and boasteth great things. Behold, how great a matter a little fire kindleth! (6) And the tongue is a fire, a world of iniquity: so is the tongue among our members, that it defileth the whole body, and setteth on fire the course of nature; and it is set on fire of hell. (7) For every kind of beasts, and of birds, and of serpents, and of things in the sea, is tamed, and hath been tamed of mankind: (8) But the tongue can no man tame; it is an unruly evil, full of deadly poison."

Just as there are false Believer Business Owners and Managers functioning apostles (2 Corinthians 11: 13), false Believer Business Owners and Managers functioning prophets (Matthew 24:11), false Believer Business Owners and Managers functioning evangelists (Galatians 1:8-9), false Believer Business Owners and Managers pastors (John 10:1-16), so likewise, there are false Believer Business Owners and Managers functioning teachers (2 Peter 2:1).

2 Peter 2:1 says, "But false prophets also arose among the people, just as there will also be false teachers among you, who will secretly introduce destructive heresies, even denying the Master who brought them, bringing swift destruction upon themselves."

2 Timothy 4:3-4 says, "For the time will come when they will not endure sound doctrine; but after their own lusts shall they heap to themselves (false) teachers, having itching ears; (4) And they shall turn away their ears from the truth, and shall be turned unto fables."

Titus 1:10 -11 says, "For there are many insubordinates, both idle talkers and deceivers, especially those of the circumcision, (11) whose mouths must be stopped, who subvert whole households, teaching things which they ought not, for the sake of dishonest gain." If the root motivation for teaching the most popular ideas in a particular season is for financial gain, then this is a wrong motive on the part of the Believer Business Owner or Manager functioning teachers.

The Believer Business Owner and Manager functioning teachers cannot be like the Pharisees and Scribes who become Judaizers or legalizers who corrupted the Gospel of Christ as they deny who He was.

The Believer Business Owner and Manager functioning teachers must not be just the teacher of the world's business traditions as such makes the word of God of no effect (Mark 7:13).

A Believer Business Owner and Manager functioning teacher must not proclaim false doctrines. Examples of false doctrines the Believer Business Owner and Manager functioning teachers must avoid are:

Denying the bodily resurrection of Christ (2 Timothy 2:16-18).

Turning the grace of God into a license to sin (Jude 3, 4; Revelation 2:20).

Those who caused division contrary to sound doctrine (Romans 16:17).

Teaching material prosperity only for greed, avarice, and covetous personal gain (1 Timothy 6:6-19; 2 Peter 2:3; Titus 1:10, 11).

Teaching the doctrine of Balaam (Revelation 2:14).

Teaching the doctrine of the Nicolaitans which is a false elitism and laity system because the truth is that all Believers are functioning ministers (Ephesians 4:12; Revelation 2:6, 15).

Teaching fables as truth (2 Timothy 4:3).

Teaching the doctrines of devils, as forbidding marriage and forbidding eating of meals (1 Timothy 4:15).

Romans 2:20 says, "A (Believer Business Owner or Manager functioning) instructor (*paideutēs*-training by kinesthetic methods) of the foolish, a (Believer Business Owner or Manager functioning) teacher (*didaskalos* – teaching from the *logos* word) of babes, which hast the form of knowledge and of the truth in the law." The Believer Business Owner and Manager functioning teachers has the awesome responsibility to teach the babes and youths who are Believer Business Employees the biblical truths concerning biblical business economics, biblical business principles, biblical business accounting, biblical business budgets, biblical business practices, biblical cash flow management, biblical cash flow security, biblical business plans, biblical business servanthood, and a lifetime of biblical giving from the profits earned.

Therefore, a greater and special responsibility is on the Believer Business Owner and Manager functioning teachers than on other Ephesians 4:11 functioning ministers. During the formative years of growth of a spiritual baby or spiritual youth of Believer Business Employees, God especially wants purity of teaching in that season. Consequently, there is a stricter judgment on Believer Business Owner and Manager functioning teachers, who are the mentors, scholastic teachers, and kinesthetic trainers of Believer Business Employees for the work of the spiritual Vocations and activation of Spiritual Gifts.

CONCLUSION

Almost every movement or revival of the Holy Spirit has shown a concentration of majoring in one area needing change. In this current time, the Holy Spirit wants to activate Believer Business Owner Ephesians 4:11 functioning apostles, prophets, evangelists, pastors, and teachers that scholastically teach and kinesthetically train Believer Business Employees about biblical economics, long term thinking, with *agape* love, grace, faith, mercy, biblical economics, biblical morality, sound work ethic, long term thinking, saving money for unknown expenditures, praying for wisdom, knowledge and understanding, being submissiveness, stay humble, and strive to be the chiefest servant toward others in the business.

BELIEVER BUSINESS OWNERS AND BELIEVER BUSINESS EMPLOYEES MUST ACCEPT THAT THEY WILL EXPERIENCE SUFFERING AND PERSECUTION

Christianity is not just esoteric ideas like those of the Gnostics of old, who espoused the goal of enhancing their humanistic ideologies for self-exaltation, self-aggrandizement, or self-worth in the eyes of others.

Believer Business Owners are not to seek after natural riches but rather spiritual riches. 2 Corinthians 8:9 says, "For ye know the grace of our Lord Jesus Christ, that, though he was rich, yet for your sakes he became poor, that ye through his poverty might be rich." Jesus was not speaking just about monetary riches but rather spiritual riches. This passage highlights Jesus's voluntary sacrifice of natural riches for the spiritual riches His sacrifice gave to Believers.

Where should the Believer Business Owner and Believer Business Employees lay up their treasures? Jesus said in Matthew 6: 19-21, "Lay not up for yourselves treasures upon earth, where moth and rust doth corrupt, and where thieves break through and steal: (20) But lay up for yourselves treasures in heaven, where neither moth nor rust doth corrupt, and where thieves do not break through nor steal: (21) For where your treasure is, there will your heart be also."

The Bible makes it crystal clear that all Believers, including Believer Business Owners and Believer Business Employees will experience suffering and persecution by unsaved people in the fallen world, along with Believers promoting false doctrines, and Satan's doctrines of demons from his realm of darkness. Here are some of the scriptures.

Jesus said in Matthew 5:10-12, "Blessed are they which are persecuted for righteousness' sake: for theirs is the kingdom of heaven. (11) Blessed are ye, when men shall revile you, and persecute you, and shall say all manner of evil against you falsely, for My sake. (12) Rejoice, and be exceeding glad: for great is your (spiritual) reward in heaven: for so persecuted they the prophets which were before you."

Likewise, Jesus said in Matthew 24:9, " Then shall they deliver you up to be afflicted, and shall kill you: and ye shall be hated of all nations for My Name's sake."

Similarly, Jesus said in John 15:18–20, "If the world hate you, ye know that it hated Me before it hated you. (19) If ye were of the world, the world would love his own: but because ye are not of the world, but I have chosen you out of the world, therefore the world hateth you. (20) Remember the word that I said unto you, 'The servant is not greater than his lord. If they have persecuted Me, they will also persecute you; if they have kept My saying, they will keep yours also.'"

Additionally, Jesus said in John 16:33, "These things I have spoken unto you, that in Me ye might have peace. In the world ye shall have tribulation: but be of good cheer; I have overcome the world."

Also, Jesus said in Matthew 16:24-26, ". . . 'If any man will come after Me**, let him deny himself, and take up his cross, and follow Me**. (25) For whosoever will save his life shall lose it: and whosoever will lose his life for my sake shall find it. (26) For what is a man profited, if he shall gain the whole world, and lose his own soul? or what shall a man give in exchange for his soul?" Jesus' admonition to deny oneself and take up one's own cross and follow Jesus is repeated by Him in Matthew 10:38, Mark 8:34, Luke 9:23, and Luke 4:27.

These verses highlight that following Jesus demands self-denial and a commitment to His path of serving others and allowing the Holy Spirit to mortify the deeds of the self-centered flesh's influence in the disciple's soul. Even when it involves personal sacrifice, servanthood requires prioritizing God's Will above the disciple's own desires, security, and Will. To be in humble, submissive, and obedient, Jesus requires every Believer Business Owner and every Believer Business Employee to seek first the Kingdom of God, His righteousness, and to follow the leading of the Holy Spirit.

Paul stated in 2 Timothy 3:10-12, "But thou hast fully known my doctrine, manner of life, purpose, faith, longsuffering, charity, patience, (11) Persecutions, afflictions, which came unto me at Antioch, at Iconium, at Lystra; what persecutions I endured: but out of them all the Lord delivered me. (12) Yea, and all that will live godly in Christ Jesus shall suffer persecution."

Paul stated that Christ made Paul strong when Paul thought about, and entered into the sufferings of Christ in 2 Corinthians 12:10, "Therefore I take pleasure in infirmities, in reproaches, in necessities, in persecutions, in distresses for Christ's sake: for when I am weak, then am I strong." Having the same thought, Paul said in Philippians 3:10-11, "That I may know Him, and the power of His resurrection, and the fellowship of His sufferings, being made conformable unto His death; (11) If by any means I might attain unto the resurrection of the dead."

Paul revealed the challenges that all Believers face when they seek the enjoyment of *zoe* life in 2 Corinthians 4:8–10, which says, "We are troubled on every side, yet not distressed; we are perplexed, but not in despair; (9) Persecuted, but not forsaken; cast down, but not destroyed; (10) Always bearing about in the body the dying of the Lord Jesus, that the (*zoe*) life also of Jesus might be made manifest in our body."

Paul comforted Believers with Romans 8:35-39, "Who shall separate us from the (*agape*) love of Christ? Shall tribulation, or distress, or persecution, or famine, or nakedness, or peril, or sword? (36) As it is written, 'For thy sake we are killed all the day long; we are accounted as sheep for the slaughter.' (37) Nay, in all these things we are more than conquerors through Him that loved us. (38) For I am persuaded, that neither death, nor life, nor angels, nor principalities, nor powers, nor things present, nor things to come, (39) Nor height, nor depth, nor any other creature, shall be able to separate us from the love of God, which is in Christ Jesus our Lord."

THE EKKLESIA NEEDS THE EPHESIANS 4:11 BELIEVER BUSINESS OWNER FUNCTIONING MINISTERS TO ACTIVATE AND MATURE BELIEVER BUSINESS EMPLOYEES

Believer Business Owners are mandated by the Lord (Matthew 28:20) to teach all that He commanded in making disciples, which means to activate and mature the souls of Believer Business Employees during the working hours at the business to find solutions for problems in line with God's Kingdom economics, *agape* love, humility, holiness, righteousness, and morality that are truths in the Bible.

The greatest among Believer Business functioning ministers are the ones who are the greatest or chiefest servants of all (Matthew 23:11; Mark 10:44). This means dealing with *agape* love and grace with fallen unsaved people in the world and taking care of other Believers, plants, animals, fish, birds, and those loving and helping activities listed in Matthew 25: 35-46, which should be the focus as part of the giving of the profits of the business by the Believer Business Owners and Believer Business Employees.

There are many responsible Believers in government, in businesses, and in professions that do not accept that their workplace is where they are to be ministers for the Godhead and the Lord Jesus Christ. This includes policemen arresting criminals, prosecuting lawyers enforcing the law that brings peace and civility, and defense lawyers representing alleged criminals to ensure their Constitutional rights are being protected, doctors taking care of patients, nurses attending patients in hospice care facilities while people are dying, dentists caring for people's teeth cavities, designers making clothes, cooks and waitresses serving food to hungry people in restaurants, maids in hotels cleaning rooms and changing bedding, inventors making new products, factory workers making cars, farmers growing food, dairymen daily feeding and milking milk cows, feeding chickens and collecting and selling eggs, and those caring for all other animals, highway workers building bridges and laying concrete and asphalt on highways, carpenters building homes, plumbers plumbing homes, along with cleaning out sewer drains and septic tanks, counsellors helping alcoholics and the drug addicted, mechanics getting grease on their hands repairing cars, salespeople selling products they do not like, mothers changing diapers, cooking meals, and training up children in the way they should go, teachers teaching children to read, write, spell, add, subtract, multiply, and divide numbers, real estate agents helping owners sell real property when the owners think their homes are worth far more, secretaries typing letters, and morticians and funeral directors with dignity burying the dead.

All necessary products are sold, and services are being offered at the workplace where Believer Business Owners and Believer Business Employees work and earn a living without priests, bishops, pastors, teachers, and reverends activating them and equipping them to be ministers. Yet, Believer Business Owners as Ephesians 4:11 ministers functioning as apostles, prophets, evangelists, pastors and teachers are equipping Believer Business Employees as ministers in training and soul transformation through the daily incremental scholastic teachings and kinesthetically training at workplaces into their spiritual Vocations and spiritual Gifts. The Believer Business Owners Ephesians 4:11 ministers functioning as apostles, prophets, evangelists, pastors and teachers training Believer Business Employees eight to ten hours a day, five to six days a week. The Believer Business Owners Ephesians 4:11 ministers functioning as apostles, prophets, evangelists, pastors and teachers are doing what the church priests, bishops, pastors, teachers, and reverends in their large auditorium warehouse buildings are not doing as mandated by Ephesians 4:12-13 mandates them to do.

God wants all Believer Business Owners and Believer Business Employees to be activated as His functioning ministers in business preaching the gospel of the kingdom and repentance and remission of sins to unbelievers in the world while performing ministers and to be God's kingdom earthly spiritual kings and priests (Revelation 1:6), spiritual lords (1 Timothy 6:15), spiritual ambassadors (2 Corinthians 5:20), and spiritual soldiers (2 Timothy 2:3-4).

BELIEVER BUSINESS OWNERS AND BELIEVER BUSINESS EMPLOYEES ARE NOT TO FOCUS ON ESOTERIC KNOWLEDGE AND INNER ENLIGHTENMENT

Functioning apostle Paul said in 2 Corinthians 11:14, "And no marvel; for Satan himself is transformed into an angel of light." Paul reveals that Satan can appear to be good or righteous to deceive even Believers and lead them away from God's truth revealed in Scriptures. To avoid Satan's trespass and control over Believers' souls, Believers must request of the Holy Spirit to give them the gift with the ability to discern and test the spirits, whether of God or of Satan. Furthermore, Believers must study and be grounded in the teachings of Jesus Christ and the epistles written by various ministers, including but not limited to, the functioning apostolic gifts of Peter, Paul, John, James (Jesus' brother) and others who wrote letters that all became the New Testament word of God in addition to the four gospels of Matthew, Mark, Luke, and John.

When the leaders of the *Ekklesia* decided to choose writings to put in the New Testament to canonize the Bible, it rejected Gnostics, who wanted intellectualism and enlightenment to prevail amongst the elites, more like the Greek Philosophers.

The *Ekklesia* is not a place to focus on esoteric knowledge and inner enlightenment. True Christianity is a lifestyle, a relationship with the Godhead and the Lord Jesus Christ's humanity nature, not just a religion that promotes inner enlightenment apart from an intimate relationship with the Godhead and the Lord Jesus Christ. Believers must accept Jesus, Himself, as the Way, Truth, and Life; and no one comes to Father God except through Jesus Christ (John 14:6). To rescue fallen unsaved people, the ministers must go to the places where fallen people are working and shopping to purchase products at retail centers, fuel service stations, schools, beauty salons, theaters, even fellowships at a Believer's home, and numerous other places. Those are the places where ministers are supposed to go and find unbelievers who need salvation. Jesus traveled everywhere in Israel and Judah to find Jews who needed rescuing, needed healing, needed deliverance, and needed the gospel of the kingdom and gospel of repentance and remission of sins. In those places of *koinōnia* the Holy Spirit is present, and the new Believer experiences God's *zoe* life, goodness, *agape* love, and righteousness, peace, and joy in the Holy Spirit, which are the blessings of living in the Kingdom of God.

All people living must get up every day and contend with the mundane and drudgeries of existence to find food, water, maintain shelter, have proper clothing, go to a store, fix meals, take children to school, and go to work at a factory or an office job eight to ten hours a day, five to six days a week. On Saturday or Sunday Believers attend a warehouse or cathedral auditorium lecture hall pyramid paradigm structure, enjoy participating in praise and worship, and listen to a 45 minute sermon. Afterwards, an offering plate or box in the back to place tithes and offerings, where Believers actually are paying "tuition" for the teaching sermon, support for the church leader and other employees, and pay for expenses for the building. At these meetings, the unsaved may go forward and confess Jesus as Savior and Lord to obtain their eternal salvation, and they are told that they are saved and are going to heaven. The new Believer is told he or she has received a born again spirit and there is no further work required of the new Believer, quoting Ephesians

2:8-9, which is a true statement only for the initial salvation that is a gift and not earned. Yet, after initial salvation they do not read to the new Believer Ephesians 2:10, Philippians 2:12-13, or James 2:14-17 because the new Believer's soul must be transformed (Romans 12:2) through the cleansing work of the Godhead (John 15:2; Ephesians 5:26-27; Romans 8:13) because the soul was not born again. It requires submissive work of the new Believer to allow the Godhead to have permission to transform the new Believer's soulish mind, emotions, and heart where the Believers Will is.

The new Believer may question, "So is this what it is all about after initial salvation? So, my reward is I get to go to heaven when I die? However, what do I do with my sinless born again spirit and sinful soul now here on earth? What is my godly purpose while I am still living? Why do I feel I am missing something? Why does my mind in my soul remember my old, committed sins if I am born again? Why do I not feel saved? Why do I have to pay every week tithes and offerings for salvation that is free and Jesus' sacrificial suffering and death on the Roman cross gave me eternal life? Is there something missing in my walk with the Holy Spirit?"

Yes, what is missing in this questioning new Believer who attends the warehouse or cathedral auditorium lecture hall pyramid paradigm structure is that he or she is not being activated after initial salvation to do the work of ministry or spiritual Vocations as a spiritual king, priest, lord, ambassador, and soldier for the Kingdom of God or activated with their spiritual Gifts.

He or she may think, "Where do I sign up to be taught and be trained to be a minister? Where do I get the money to build a large warehouse or cathedral auditorium lecture hall pyramid paradigm structure like this to minister on stage and preach the gospel like I am seeing and hearing? Is this the pattern for ministry? I must conclude I cannot be a minister because I cannot afford it. I surmise that my life really is not going to change here on earth; I must wait until I die and go to heaven."

BELIEVER BUSINESS OWNERS MUST BE PATIENT

Patience or long suffering is a fruit of the Spirit (Galatians 5:22). The Believer Business Owner functioning teacher must be patient and suffer with spiritually immature Believer Business Employees dealing with temptations, relationships, and soulish problems that need to be resisted, healed, and transformed. Believer Business Employees suffer self-condemnation, inferiority, and rejection because of their history of employment failures, disappointments, addictions, bad financial decisions, failed relationships, and betrayals. They feel they are buried alive with insurmountable problems and insufficiencies and even debt. The Believer Business Owner must work with the premise that most Believer Business Employees have troubled thoughts, hurt emotions, fallen world beliefs, a heart and Will that is nursing hurts as opposed to being servants as God's ministers. These Believer Business Employees often have buried memories that cause self-defeat, depression, and lack of faith and hope.

These Believer Business Employees may not truly understand that God and the Lord Jesus Christ's humanity nature see Believer Business Employees as chosen, worthy, and special. God does not see them buried in their soulish problems but see them as planted now in God's best soil. The Believer Business Employees past sins, failures, and mistakes must be confessed, repented, and released to God and the Lord Jesus Christ for forgiveness. These Believer Business Employees must have their souls transformed by pruning away the flesh in their souls by God the Father (John 15:2), washing away the flesh and sanctifying their souls by the *rhema* word by God the Word (Ephesians

5:26), mortifying the deeds of the flesh in their souls by God the Holy Spirit (Romans 8:13). Yet, the duty of the Believer Business Employees is to submit to produce more spiritual fruit, not get out of the washing before the cycle is done, and entering into the crucifixion of Christ and allow Him to live His life in them instead of the sins of lusts of the flesh, lusts of the eyes, or pride of life (Galatians 2:20; 1 John 2:16).

1 John 2:15-17 says, "Love not the world, neither the things that are in the world. If any man love the world, the love of the Father is not in him. (16) For all that is in the world, the lust of the flesh, and the lust of the eyes, and the pride of life, is not of the Father, but is of the world. (17) And the world passeth away, and the lust thereof: but he that doeth the will of God abideth for ever."

The new spiritual seeds of God's forgiveness, *agape* love, mercy, and grace spring up resurrection life of new beginnings in the hearts of Believer Business Owners and Believer Business Employees. Spiritual growth and transformation of the soul begin with humbling, trusting, and accepting that the God-centered business is their place of spiritual activation, transformation, and growth because of what Christ Jesus has accomplished on the Roman Cross, along with the Godhead cleansing out the carnality and the spiritual transformation of the soul after initial salvation. The reality is that even after initial salvation, and after receiving a born again spirit that is holy, righteous, perfect, and without sin, there still are fractures in the souls of Believer Business Employees that have damaged their personalities and haunt them in their memories that must be healed. Sometimes, the fractures in their souls wrongfully healed differently than God's creative design and must be rebroken and reset, so the Believer Business Employees are not crippled for life. Healing of the soul is as peeling an onion. When you peel the onion, you will cry unless you first immersed the onion in water. According to Revelation 22, the River of Life flows to quinch the thirst of the Tree of Life. Oftentimes, there are people who hurt the Believer Business Employee, and to transform the soul the trespasser must be forgiven to begin healing. The Believer Business Employee must see the trespasser as someone who also needs the Godhead and the Lord Jesus Christ as Savior, as the trespasser did what he did because he was driven by lust of the flesh, lust of the eyes, and pride of life.

There is an interesting parallel between Jesus' assassination and Charlie Kirk's assassination. Jesus died as a young man when He was only 33 years old. Charlie died as a young man when he was only 31 years old. Jesus' functioning apostles when called were twelve, and Peter was the only one married and was around 22-24 years old. John the Beloved was the youngest functioning apostle and was a teenager who was between 14 to 16 years old. When Jesus died at 33 years old, Peter, the oldest, was still a young man between 27 and 28 years old, with John the Beloved who was then around 17 to 19 years old. Charlie Kirk's audience of young people are the GenZ population in the U.S. which are between ages 13 to 28 years old.

After Jesus' death there was a great revival that went out to Judea and Samaria and through the Roman Empire, and the Greek, European, and Asian countries. After Charlie's death as of October 10, 2025, there is estimated between 70,000 to 100,000 new applications to become chapters of Turning Point USA.

Charlie's wife, Erika stated a very important fact, "After Charlie's assassination, we didn't see violence. We didn't see rioting. We didn't see revolution. Instead, we saw what my husband always prayed he would see in this country: We saw revival." Now, there are a lot of young people following Zohran Mamdani, because he's a socialist, and yet we have young people following Charlie Kirk because he was a Christian. So the battle is between Satan and

God right now. We need to make sure that those who believe in our Lord and Savior Jesus Christ are the ones that we lift up in prayer. They are the ones that we want to edify, to bring life abundantly by their testimony, to other young people. Those who are the disciples of and who are voting for Mamdani will be disappointed in what he does because he will fail as a mayor of New York

Believer Business Employees often live with false pretenses, lie a little about their accomplishments, are sometimes very defensive, and have areas of impenetrable hard shells around their souls. The idea of hard protective shells around the souls of the Believer Business Employees make them resistant to counseling and struggle engaging in friendships. The words "protective shell" is a metaphor for a variety of psychological and spiritual problems in their souls. These psychological or spiritual problems can manifest as different defense mechanisms and forms of resistance, especially when the Believer Business Owner attempts to correct the Believer Business Employees. Some Believer Business Employees may sincerely think, emote, and believe that any kind of corrective advice is a threat to their freedom of speech, thoughts, or actions. When a Believer Business Employee feels that the Believer Business Owner's reprimand, advice, or criticism is challenging them and is an attack, or is an attempt to control their thoughts, emotions, beliefs, or behavior, the Believer Business Employee sometimes denies any wrongdoing or failure and thereby resists transformation of their souls.

A history of trauma, betrayal, or abuse can cause Believer Business Employees to develop these impenetrable hard shells as a self-protective measure. Their inability to accept spiritual help is a result of learned distrust and the expectation that others will hurt them.

The Bible speaks about people with a hardened heart. Those described in the Bible that have a hardened heart are those who have a spiritual obstinacy or a stubborn refusal to listen and obey someone in spiritual authority, such as the Believer Business Owner. The Believer Business Employee must submit to the Believer Business scholastic teaching and kinesthetic training using God's words of wisdom, knowledge, and understanding of God's ways of doing business. The hardened heart is where the Believer Business Employees' beliefs are held. The Believer Business Owner must teach truths from the word of God that dispels the false beliefs in the hardened hearts of the Believer Business Employees. This problem mandates the Believer Business Owner to sow new biblically-based truthful beliefs that are opposed to traditions that make void the Commandments of God. Also, the Believer Business Owners must not sow a mixed seed of tares and wheat, although they look alike. The Believer Business Owners should not try to sanctify the world's ways of conducting business by trying to mix it with God's sacred ways of doing business.

In psychology, the resistance to soul transformation and maturation of Believer Business Employees generally is a defense shield to protect themselves from painful emotions like guilt, shame, loneliness, frustrations, unworthiness, inadequacy, hatred, anger, despair, envy, greed, avarice, emptiness, or untrustworthiness. It can also be a subconscious opposition to revealing repressed memories of abuse by people in authority, like a teacher, policeman, judge, or a church leader. Finally, it can stem from history of bad feelings, unbiblical thoughts, or even the past encounters with evil that brought on tremendous anxiety, fear, or even harm.

The resistance to soul transformation and maturation of Believer Business Employees may also be because they have an underlying cynical mindset. These Believer Business Employees use their cynical mindsets as defensive mechanisms to avoid vulnerability and potential disappointment. These cynical mindsets assume the worst in other people, situations, ideas, or lifestyle changes. Cynicism can make the Believer Business Employees resist any procedural changes to feel safe with their spiritual traditions, but this also prevents them from being led by the Holy Spirit and can discourage them from submitting to an *agape* loving Believer Business Owners, which damages their current faith and future hope. The cynics are usually very negative in speech.

Also, the Believer Business Employees can have negative biases, prejudices, stereotypes, dehumanization, hostility, and self-reinforcing negative beliefs of other cultures. Most of the time, these thought patterns are a form of cognitive distortion, irrational thinking, and even family generational mindsets. The immaturities connected with these ridiculous, broad, oversimplification, assumptions about another person based upon their association and affiliation with a particular group or culture is because they ignore each individual uniqueness as God has created everyone different. Categorizing what other people think, emote, or believe based upon the particular group the people belong makes those Believer Business Employees feel the other people pose a potential threat. When Believer Business Employees internalize in their souls these false societal stereotypes and prejudices can make the Believer Business Employees have self-doubt, feelings of worthlessness, and low self-esteem. On the other hand, those who are in the receiving end of the stereotypes and prejudices can develop a stereotypy or prejudice threat toward them. What happens is Believer Business Employees' actions on both sides act fearfully or defensively because of the sin of stereotyping or prejudice as the focus. Stereotyping and prejudice are very harmful in transforming and maturing the souls of Believer Business Employees, so the Believer Business Owner must have strict rules that any stereotyping or prejudice would be grounds for dismissal from employment.

Regardless of whether someone thinks the cause of resistance to transforming and maturing the souls of the Believer Business Employees is psychological, spiritual, or both, it is not wise to use the confrontational approach, or saying "It's my way or the highway." My experience is that the confrontational, aggressive, and direct approaches (that lawyers almost instinctively do) often trigger stronger resistance by the Believer Business Employees. Instead, a respectful and reflective style, like that used in motivational interviewing, can be more effective. In a spiritual context, this might look like a gentle approach focused on humility and compassion rather than condemnation.

BELIEVER BUSINESS OWNERS MUST INSPIRE FAITH AND HOPE

Hebrews 11:1 really means that faith is the substance of the impossible brought by God. Faith is the evidence of our spiritual future which is not yet seen but for which we have hope.

A Believer Business Owner needs to examine the young Believer Business Employees to discover and ascertain the potential God sees and wants to ordain in them that advances, edifies, and releases the spiritual authority and spiritual power within them. The spiritually young Believer Business Employees need to accept the spiritual vision of the business. As they voluntarily accept and press into the business vision, then God's provision meets where and when the vision becomes their goal to build the Kingdom of God through the hearts of those employed in the business. The motivation must be the receiving of *agape* love from God and the Lord Jesus Christ's humanity nature and then giving and receiving that same *agape* love to and from other Believers they encounter in the business.

God then anoints the Believer Business Owner and the Believer Business Employees with the Holy Spirit and with *dunimis* power. Obeying Galatians 2:20 is the goal of their motivation to enter the crucifixion of Christ, from which springs Christ's resurrection life that is shared with other Believers. "I am crucified with Christ: nevertheless, I live; yet not I, but Christ liveth in me: and the life which I now live in the flesh I live by the faith of the Son of God, Who loved me, and gave Himself for me."

The Believer Business Owner and the Believer Business Employees then no longer live but allow Christ to live (through His divine nature) in his or her soul and allow Christ to minister through him or her. Once submission allows Christ (through His divine nature) to live in and through him or her, the Believer Business Owner and the Believer Business Employees live their lives by the faith of the Son of God and experience a strong spiritual life of witnessing Jesus and following the leading of the Holy Spirit to do the impossible and supernatural.

Both the Believer Business Owner and the Believer Business Employees may think in the natural that the ministry vision is too big, too complicated, and may reason the vision requires greatness that neither the Believer Business Owner nor the Believer Business Employees are qualified. Nevertheless, both the Believer Business Owner and the Believer Business Employees by faith, submission, and obedience must accept the mandate of the vision and take individual steps one after another for its ongoing fulfillment. Incrementally the vision will be fulfilled. Then, the Believer Business Owner and the Believer Business Employees will have greater faith that with God all things are possible (Matthew 19:26). Success with the leading, anointing, and power of the Holy Spirit build faith, which raises greater hope that God will do it again. The Believer Business Owner and the Believer Business Employees will experience how to live a crucified life that springs up resurrection life by living in God's Kingdom. Through incremental spiritual success with guidance, anointing, and power of the Holy Spirit continues the spiritual growth and maturation of Believer Business Employees' souls. Then comes the faith in the Believer Business Employees' souls when God speaks for a greater task be done to be accomplished in business. The result is that the Believer Business Owner and the Believer Business Employees will grow their faith because they witness that the impossible becomes possible as a blessing of God. "The things which are impossible with men are possible with God" (Luke 18:27).

Every believer wants to go to heaven, but he or she does not want to die first to get there. Similarly, all Believers say they want to seek first the Kingdom of God and His righteousness, but they do not want to enter the crucifixion of the King who paid the price for Believers' salvation and to establish the Kingdom of God here on earth.

TRUE BELIEVER BUSINESS SERVANTS OF THE LORD MUST BE HUMBLE AND CARING AND HELP PEOPLE WHO ARE HURTING

There are many non-profit secular organizations in society that are doing good work that should be done by the *Ekklesia,* individually and as a fellowship community. It should not be the government using taxpayer money or loans to do these good works.

Many secular non-religious organizations and charities are carrying out work that aligns with the charitable missions historically that were done by Believers in the church, including providing food, shelter, healthcare, education, and support for the vulnerable and marginalized. Indeed, there are some church leaders that are trying to help feed people, where people come to the church building to pick up food, and that is good; but there are many people who do not have transportation to get to the warehouse lecture hall church buildings to pick up the food. They need food brought to them. Yet, some of this activity is still promotion of the church building (wrongfully called the "church") trying to get more people to come there for their needs and regular attendance.

Matthew 25:34-46 says, "Then shall the King say unto them on his right hand, 'Come, ye blessed of My Father, inherit the kingdom prepared for you from the foundation of the world: (35) For I was an hungred, and ye gave me meat: I was thirsty, and ye gave me drink: I was a stranger, and ye took me in: (36) Naked, and ye clothed me: I was sick, and ye visited me: I was in prison, and ye came unto me.' (37) Then shall the righteous answer him, saying, 'Lord, when saw we thee an hungred, and fed thee? or thirsty, and gave thee drink? (38) When saw we thee a stranger, and took thee in? or naked, and clothed thee? (39) Or when saw we thee sick, or in prison, and came unto thee?' (40) And the King shall answer and say unto them, 'Verily I say unto you, Inasmuch as ye have done it unto one of the least of these My brethren, ye have done it unto Me.' (41) Then shall He say also unto them on the left hand, 'Depart from me, ye cursed, into everlasting fire, prepared for the devil and his angels: (42) For I was an hungred, and ye gave me no meat: I was thirsty, and ye gave me no drink: (43) I was a stranger, and ye took me not in: naked, and ye clothed me not: sick, and in prison, and ye visited me not. (44) Then shall they also answer him, saying, Lord, when saw we thee an hungred, or athirst, or a stranger, or naked, or sick, or in prison, and did not minister unto thee? (45) Then shall he answer them, saying, 'Verily I say unto you, Inasmuch as ye did it not to one of the least of these, ye did it not to Me. (46) And these shall go away into everlasting punishment: but the righteous into life eternal.'"

Has the Church for the most part abdicated its responsibility in teaching and training every Believer to feed the hungry, give drink to the thirsty, clothed the naked, visit the sick, and visit those in prison?

To their credit there are Believer functioning ministers living in the cities near the homeless who are providing food daily to feed them hot meals, and these Believer functioning ministers are preaching the gospel of repentance and remission of sins, but they need to also preach the gospel of the Kingdom of God.

There are non-profit secular organizations that fill the void that the church leadership is not doing. So, God allows this, so the needs of homeless are met, but this does not fulfill God's mandate that His Believer adopted children, after receiving salvation by Christ Jesus must take responsibility in doing these acts of kindness.

If secular non-profit organizations are doing wonderful work, then the *Ekklesia* needs to do the same individually by those in fellowship in the *Ekklesia.* Every Believer Business Owner and Believer Business Employee can pick a couple of families to help with delivering food, water, used clothing, and spend time in fellowship without a superior attitude. Also, every *Ekklesia* home fellowship should be taking care of the needs of the families in that home fellowship. "Salvation Army" is a Christian organization of many years, and its local homeless shelters offer temporary housing and support to those experiencing homelessness, fulfilling the *Ekklesia*'s historical work of providing refuge and support.

Non-profit secular organizations like "Feeding America" and local food banks provide food for the hungry, mirroring the *Ekklesia's* historical role in providing for the hungry. Feeding America is a secular national network that partners with over 200 local food banks across the United States, acting as a critical link between food donors and local communities. Businesses like Walmart, Sam's Club, and Whole Foods Market work with Feeding America to donate food that would otherwise go to waste. Companies such as Tyson Foods and General Mills provide significant contributions of food and financial support to Feeding America. Nonprofit foundations such as "Walmart Foundation," along with many other corporations, provide financial contributions and grants to support recipients of Feeding America.

Also, a secular organization called "Doctors Without Borders" and local free health clinics provide medical care to the poor, again which historically was work of the *Ekklesia.* "Doctors Without Borders" is on the ground in over 70 countries, providing urgently needed humanitarian aid in moments of crisis and conflict.

Secular organizations like "Teach For America" and local tutoring programs that teach underprivileged children, fulfilling a historical role that the *Ekklesia* use to provide as after secular school education program to poor communities.

Similarly, the YMCA, Boy Scouts, and Girl Scouts and other boy and girl clubs provide after-school programs, youth development, and community support for children and families, taking over what was the *Ekklesia*'s historical responsibility in helping parents scholastically teaching and kinetically training children to be good citizens.

Believer Business Owners should help donate in *Ekklesia* working in giving away food, providing shelters, providing after school programs with Christian Tutors to help young people, teaching why electronic games, smoking, and drugs can be harmful and addictive. Having Christian platforms in these ministries that focus attention with donating to Believer Medical Doctors would cause the *Ekklesia* help to fulfill its biblical mandates.

The problem comes when secular non-profit organizations are supported by governments and make the government go into debt, and that is not what we want for the U.S. The U.S. is almost 38 Trillion dollars in debt, and the national debt must be paid, not increased. We need to slow down the run-a-way train, without an Engineer, with full throttle wide open going down the tracks. Invariably, there will be a financial crash if the debt making train is not stopped, and the debt start being paid.

Western World countries are paying money to help the needy because their national governments are run with the philosophy of Socialism, and the Catholic Charities and the Salvation Army also depend on government contracts for more than 50% of their needed funding. "Employees and their religious commitments virtually define an agency," says Steven Monsma, a political scientist at Pepperdine University and the author of When Sacred and Secular Mix. Monsma continues, "If a faith-based agency may not limit their hiring to persons of their own faith, the religious nature of that agency would be effectively destroyed." Caution should be followed by faith based, government funded organizations. When government is funding the faith based organization, the government can regulate the religious freedom of the faith based organization; and if there is no compliance, the faith based organization loses its funding.

Most all church leaders confess that the "church" is not the building but people, but in practice they all reference the building as the church; and most all the money donated is for the church building and the church employee who are the paid salaries as employed workers at the church building. It is common to say, "I will meet you at church." When the true *Ekklesia* does ministry, it is called an "outreach." That sounds like legitimate *Ekklesia* activity that is designated outside the warehouse auditorium pyramid structured church. The *Ekklesia* consists of all the Believers in a congregation not the building, so ministry is where the Believer ministers are performing services for people in the community. The *Ekklesia* is to be full of nothing but heartfelt servants who are laying down their lives to help other people, not to bring the people back to a "church building" but for ministers to bring *zoe* life and *agape* life where that person is existing and hurting, not just to down-and-outers but also to up-and-outers. The homeless on the street and the wealthy living in a twenty million dollar home will both lose life eternal without accepting Jesus Christ as Lord and Savior.

Every Believer in the community *Ekklesia* is responsible for feeding the hungry, clothing the naked, visiting the sick, and visiting those in prison, and this is certainly a practical definition of ministries that the Lord wants done, but there is other work that God wants Believers to do?

A good example in the Old Testament of a spiritual leader being led by God to provide a miraculous financial provision for a deceased prophet's widow is in 2 Kings 4:1-7, which memorializes the story of the prophet Elisha and the supernatural increase of a widow's oil. In this passage, Elisha encounters a widow in dire straits who is facing her deceased husband's debt, who was a prophet. Creditors threatened the widow that if she did not pay, her sons would be imprisoned and suffer involuntary servitude until the debt is paid to creditors. The deceased prophet's widow informs Elisha she has nothing of value except a small jar of olive oil. The functioning prophet Elisha instructs her to borrow as many empty large jars as possible from her neighbors. Then he instructs her to go home with her sons, shut the door, and start pouring the oil from her single jar into the large jars, setting each large container jar aside when it is full. Miraculously, the widow's oil continued to flow until all the jars were filled. The widow then sells the oil, pays off all the family's debts, with enough money left over to support herself and her sons.

PROMOTING THE COUNTRY AS GOD'S HOLY NATION

The holy nation of God in every country is where God's Kingdom is. God's owns the whole world, the people, and everything in the world. Psalms 24:1-5 says, "The earth is the LORD'S, and the fulness thereof; the world, and they that dwell therein. (2) For He hath founded it upon the seas, and established it upon the floods. (3) Who shall ascend into the hill of the LORD? or who shall stand in his holy place? (4) He that hath clean hands, and a pure heart; who hath not lifted up his soul unto vanity, nor sworn deceitfully. (5) He shall receive the blessing from the LORD, and righteousness from the God of his salvation."

Although God owns the earth, the world system, the people, and everything in the world, 1 John 5:19 says, "And we know that we are of God, and (but) the whole world lieth in wickedness (devil and his evil realm)." Jesus said in Matthew 6:10, "Thy kingdom come. Thy will be done in earth, as it is in heaven." Jesus commanded in Matthew 6:33, "But seek ye first the kingdom of God, and His righteousness; and all these things (that you need to live) shall be added unto you." So, the devil is ruling the world, and God wants possession back by expanding His holy nation in every country throughout the world with God's Kingdom ministers who are the disciples of Christ Jesus.

Believer Business Owners and Believer Business Employees must not only work to help those in need but also to take back possession to Father God of the earth, the world system, the people, and everything in the world. Those who go into the world system everyday are not the Ephesians 4:11 functioning ministers who have established a warehouse lecture hall church ministry, as they want people, both saved and unsaved to come to their building for salvation and a few hours of fellowship a week with other Believers along with attending special events, such as a safe place to come when the world is celebrating Halloween. Some church ministries do have marriage and alcohol and drug counseling, but they usually charge extra money above the tithe and offerings for those services.

As easily can be seen, one of the best training school venues to equip the Lord's ministers through scholastic teaching and kinesthetic training is in working in a business where the employers are Believer Business Owners, who will mature the souls of Believer Business Employees.

Honoring the manifestation of the presence of the anointing of the Holy Spirit is a foundational prerequisite for miracles of multiplication in business to happen. Otherwise, Psalms 78:41 says, "Yea, they turned back and tempted God, and limited the Holy One of Israel."

Maintaining holiness and liberty by the Believer Business Owner as an example will inspire the Believer Business Employees to do the same. The Believer Business Owners must avoid debt because it affects the blessing of liberty. Proverbs 22:7 says, "The rich ruleth over the poor, and the borrower is servant (slave) to the lender."

Also, never co-sign for the debt of another, as in so doing you become a debtor without getting the loan proceeds for yourself. When you co-sign a debt, you become legally responsible for the entire loan amount, and the lender can pursue you for payments and collection costs if the primary borrower defaults without going after the primary borrower. Proverbs 22:26 says, "Be not thou one of them that strike hands, or of them that are sureties for debts." 2 Corinthians 3:17 says, "Now the Lord is that Spirit: and where the Spirit of the Lord is, there is liberty." Never give a loan to a Believer Business Employee or to a friend because this diminishes your authority as an employer and relationship as a friend. Romans 13:8 says, "Owe no man anything, but to love one another: for he that loveth another hath fulfilled the law."

Matthew 6:12 says, "And forgive us our debts, as we forgive our debtors." Debt can put you in bondage and worse yet can take away the liberty that the Lord has given you. Therefore, spread liberty, not bondage of others. Avoid lending money to other Believers.

Always plan financially with a savings account for expenditures you know are going to happen. For example, if you have a daughter, put aside money in a separate bank account for her wedding expenses. Personally, I usually set aside money to purchase an automobile for cash in the future to avoid the bondage of debt payments every month. Buy a one to two year old car with low mileage, have it inspected, and then you are buying an automobile for cash, having no debt, and you maintain your liberty.

Being debt free is a truth that will support your liberty. If you have credit cards, pay them off every month, or at least every 90 days. Never use a credit card to go out to dinner. Pay cash for your food, fuel, clothing, and entertainment. Always save up cash for Christmas and for birthdays for your spouse, children, and grandchildren. You should not use credit cards to purchase gifts for Christmas or for birthdays. Love is great, but do not go in debtor bondage to show your love

Thus, good stewardship is for Believer Business Owners to set aside in savings accounts money for research and development of new products, for capturing a greater market share, for future expenditures when machines must be replaced, for expansion of a satellite business, for payment of future taxes, and for other expenditures, such as Christmas employee bonuses. In other words, God demands accountability from His Believer Business Owners and Believer Business Employees before He does a financial multiplication miracle. He wants the sudden gain of wealth to be used as a testimony of the goodness of God and that the increase was not by the Believers Business Owner business acumen or experience of earning the money but because like the parables of the Talents and the Minas, God rewards the faithful, not the fearful.

If God delivers you from a lawsuit, heals you from a debilitating disease, or causes you to become a wealthy person, do not think you are allowed to spend the money on your own self-aggrandizement. God has a ministry He wants you to perform, a place He wants you to go, and a particular donation that He wants you to give. Everything that comes to you by anointing or miracle must be honored as they have a sacred quality and a sacred purpose.

Jesus knew that Father God's business every single day is feeding people, animals, birds, and every living creature on earth. Father God's business is taking care of people regarding all their needs. Likewise, a similar compassion must be developed in God's Believer Business Owners and Believer Business Employees.

GOD'S BUSINESS REWARDS ARE ETERNAL, AND THE TREE OF ETERNAL LIFE WILL BE BROUGHT BACK TO THE EARTH IN GOD'S NEW HEAVEN AND NEW EARTH

Revelation 22:1-2 says, "And he shewed me a pure river of water of life, clear as crystal, proceeding out of the throne of God and of the Lamb. (2) In the midst of the street of it, and on either side of the river, was there the tree of life, which bare twelve manner of fruits, and yielded her fruit every month: and the leaves of the tree were for the healing of the nations."

In Revelation 22:1-2 there is mentioned that the water of life flows from the Throne of God, which is the place of authority. Life comes to Believer Business Owners and Believer Business Employees when they accept God's authority and order. God's purpose is to bring life, not death. God hates the chaos in people's lives. This water of life is pure without any bad motives, and this water of life is crystal clear which means there is nothing hidden with God's life abundantly.

When God sends Believer Business Owners and Believer Business Employees His *zoe* life, it is good; whereas, if the devil comes he will give people addictive drugs, alcohol, money, and all kinds of carnality that works to kill, steal, and destroy your life (John 10:10). However for Believer Business Owners and Believer Business Employees in Revelation 22:1-2 there is the Tree of Life. What is the Tree of Life? The word "Tree" here is the Greek word, *xulon*, which means a cut down tree, which represents Jesus' Cross at Calvary. The fig tree that Jesus cursed in Mark 11:12-14 had roots and is the Greek word, *suke*.

The Tree of Life bears twelve spiritual fruits from a tree without natural roots. Jesus' death on the Roman Cross brought eternal life. The Tree of life also has leaves for the healing of the nations (*ethnos*) in the world. Jesus said in Matthew 28:19 to go throughout the world and make disciples of all nations (*ethnos*) in every country. God created all races and loves all races, and God sent His only begotten Son to heal all nations. Therefore, since every Believer is mandated to lead people to the Lord, then it does not matter where we go to make disciples. The chosen people now are all races. The Promise Land is the whole earth, but the center of power of Jesus, and His throne, will be in Jerusalem when He returns with the New Jerusalem City of Believers (Revelation, Chap. 21).

The sides of a river are called banks, and the water of the river flows because of the current. This is where we get our ideas that banks hold our currency. The idea that currency is where we obtain our cash flow, but the banks want the currency cash flow to stay within its boundaries. Thus, God wants the Believer Business Owner to teach and train the Believer Business Employees to maintain order where a current of money flows within the borders of the business and nothing is lost. God does not want His miracles of business wealth to be wasted. He expects the Believer Business

Owner and the Believer Business Employees to feed the hungry, quinch the thirst of those needing water, give clothing to those who are without, use the money for research to heal the sick, and to visit the prisoner and find the innocent to get them released from a bad jury verdict. God expects the Believer Business Owner and the Believer Business Employees to put money in a savings account for the overhead for at least 120 days, set aside money for the employees retirement, save money for research and development, spend money for capturing a market share, and save money for machine replacements if you have machines that wear out. By doing this, the Believer Business Owners are caring for the Believer Business Employees and for God's purposes in expanding the business as a ministry.

1 Peter 2: 9 says, "But ye are a chosen generation, a royal priesthood, an holy nation, a peculiar people; that ye should shew forth the praises of him who hath called you out of darkness into his marvelous light." In God's heart, no Believer is demeaned in the body of Christ. Every Believer is a Royal Priest and belongs to the Holy Nation that God has established in every country. There is no longer just the Children of Israel who are God's chosen. They were chosen to bring forth the Jewish Messiah, the only begotten Son of God, Christ Jesus. The Jewish Messiah, Jesus' humanity nature was a Business Man, as Jesus was a Carpenter and Stonemason, who dealt with the business in the secular world while being about God the Father's business (Luke 2:49).

The whole Christian world of Believers have to honor the Jews for bringing to us the Messiah and Savior of the World to fulfill the Abrahamic and Davidic covenants with God. This is why we Christians in the United States love and support the Jews in Israel. What is unknown is that most Jews believe in a coming Messiah as prophesied in the Old Testament, but they believe that the Messiah will come in the future. Believers know that Jesus Christ is the Jewish Messiah, Who has come once as the Sacrificial Lamb of God, and believe He is coming again to live here in a new heaven and new earth joined together where all Believers will reign with Him throughout eternity over the entire nations here on earth (Revelation 5:10; 11:15; chap. 21).

Here is a small outline of the scholastic teaching that Believer Business Employees must be taught by Believer Business Owners. So, let us look at the foundational process of the creation of the World, mankind's creation as the Bride of Christ, fallen mankind being born again with a new spirit, having their souls transformed, and receiving a new resurrected body when Jesus returns back to earth. These matters are foundational, and every Believer, especially those in business, should be taught these truths and teach them to Believer Business Employees and others.

Salvation has more to do than merely receiving eternal life, although very important. Yet, that is looking up to God, but what is God's interest looking down to earth and seeing unbelievers and Believers. After the initial salvation and receiving a born again spirit (1 Peter 1:23), the ongoing benefits of salvation are transformation of the mind, emotions, and heart where the Will is in the soul (Romans 12:2); and then, when the Lord Jesus Christ returns to earth He brings all those Believers who already died and every Believer still living here on earth will be receiving a new spiritual body (1 Corinthians 15:23, 42-44), to complete the process of becoming the new creature in Christ (2 Corinthians 5:17). Then we are qualified and prepared to rule and reign with Christ throughout eternity (Revelation 5:10)

THE SPIRITUAL AND NATURAL WORLDS' CREATION: Jesus' divine nature, God the Word, and His humanity nature, the only begotten Son of God, participated in the creation of the natural and spiritual worlds. The image (or pattern) that God used to make the entire spiritual and natural universes is Christ Jesus' humanity nature (Hebrews 1:3). Colossians 1: 15-18 says, "Who is the image (Jesus' humanity nature, John 1:14) of the invisible God (God the Father, God the Word, and God the Holy Spirit), the firstborn (Jesus' humanity nature) of every creature: (16) For by Him (Jesus' divine nature, God the Word, John 1:1) were all things created, that are in heaven, and that are in earth, visible and invisible, whether they be thrones, or dominions, or principalities, or powers: all things were created by Him (Jesus' divine nature, God the Word), and for Him (Jesus' humanity nature): (17) And He (Jesus' humanity nature) is before all things, and by Him (Jesus' divine nature, God the Word) all things consist. (18) And He (Jesus' humanity nature) is the head of the body, the church: who is the beginning, the firstborn (Jesus' humanity nature) from the dead; that in all things He (Jesus' humanity nature) might have the preeminence."

MAN'S CREATION AS CHRIST'S BRIDE: Mankind was made in the image and likeness of God, both male and female (Genesis 1:26-27). Believers are not only the betrothed of Christ Jesus' humanity nature but will be the multi-member wife of Christ Jesus' humanity nature as He prepares to return to live in the new heaven and new earth (Revelation 19:7-8; 21:2,9; 22:17). This is why being born again with a new spirit, having the soul spiritually transformed, and receiving a new resurrected body like Jesus is the ultimate purpose of God in dealing in the affairs and experiences of Believers.

BORN AGAIN SPIRIT: Jesus' resurrected humanity nature is the Everlasting Father of our born again spirits (Isaiah 9:6), and Believers are His children (Hebrews 2:13). Believers legally received eternal life (John 3:16), are new creatures in Christ (2 Corinthians 5:17), are born again to see the kingdom of God (John 3:3), and with a new born again spirit from the resurrected humanity nature of Jesus (1 Peter 1:23). Believers' born again spirits are perfect (Hebrews 12:23), are sinless (1 John 3:9), and are holy and righteous (Ephesians 4:24). Believers' born again spirit are joined with Christ Jesus' resurrected humanity nature in fellowship as one spirit (1 Corinthians 6:17). Believers' born again spirits become the Second Man in Christ (1 Corinthians 15:47). Believers are brought into the family of God, are joint heirs with Christ (Romans 8:17), and are adopted children of Father God (Romans 8:15). Believers' born again spirits are seated with Christ Jesus in heavenly places through His omnipresent divine nature, God the Word (Ephesians 2:6).

SPIRITUAL TRANSFORMATION OF THE SOUL: After being born again and thereon receiving a new spirit, the Godhead enters the Believer as the Temple of God (2 Corinthians 6:16). The Godhead starts the ongoing process of spiritually transforming the Believer's mind (thoughts), emotions (feelings), and heart (beliefs) (Romans 12:2). Ephesians 4:22-23 says, "That ye put off concerning the former conversation the old man, which is corrupt according to the deceitful lusts; (23) And be renewed in the spirit of your mind." Ephesians 2:10 says, "For we are his workmanship, created in Christ Jesus unto good works, which God hath before ordained that we should walk in them." Philippians 2:12-13 says, "Wherefore, my beloved, as ye have always obeyed, not as in my presence only, but now much more in my absence, work out your own salvation with fear and trembling. (13) For it is God which worketh in you both to will and to do of His good pleasure. 1 Peter 1:22 says, "Seeing ye have purified your souls in obeying the truth through the Spirit unto unfeigned love of the brethren, see that ye love one another with a pure heart fervently."

The Godhead living inside the Believer as His Temple is not idle but is continuously working in transforming the Believer's soul. God the Father prunes away the flesh in the soul, so the Believer produces more spiritual fruit (John 15:2). God the Word washes and sanctifies by washing with the *rhema* word all the dirty flesh out of the Believer's soul, so that Jesus "...might present to Himself a glorious church, not having spot, or wrinkle, or any such thing; but that it should be holy and without blemish" (Ephesians 5:26-27). Finally, God the Holy Spirit mortifies the deeds of the flesh in the Believer's soul, so that the Believer may have more _zoe_ life (Romans 8:13).

NEW RESURRECTED SPIRITUAL BODY: When Jesus returns in the new heaven and new earth (Revelation 21:1), Believers receive their new resurrected bodies (1 Corinthians 15:23) which is like Jesus' humanity nature body that is incorruptible, powerful, spiritual, glorious, and immortal (1 Corinthians 15:42-44, 54).

BELIEVERS WILL RULE AND REIGN WITH CHRIST. Revelation 5:10 says, "And hast made us unto our God kings and priests: and we shall reign on the earth." 2 Timothy 2:12 says, "If we suffer (in this life), we shall also reign with Him (Christ Jesus): if we deny Him, He also will deny us." 1 Corinthians 6:3 says, " Know ye not that we shall judge angels? How much more things that pertain to this life?" Daniel 7:18, 22 says, "But the saints of the most High shall take the kingdom, and possess the kingdom for ever, even for ever and ever. . . (22) Until the Ancient of days came, and judgment was given to the saints of the most High; and the time came that the saints possessed the kingdom."

These are fundamental truths that Believer Business Owners functioning ministers must scholastically teach and kinesthetically train to Believer Business Employees, so they know biblical truths, how to witness to others, are willing to submit to the Godhead in having their souls transformed, and they are activated with their spiritual Vocations and spiritual Gifts. These truths and practices make disciples, not just converts.

For initial salvation unto becoming born again, Matthew 24:14 says, "And this gospel of the kingdom shall be preached in all the world for a witness unto all nations; and then shall the end come." After Jesus resurrection just before His ascension, He told His apostles and those watching, and said in Luke 24:47, "And that repentance and remission of sins should be preached in His name among all nations, beginning at Jerusalem."

The preaching of repentance and remission of sins unto eternal life is futuristic after a Believer dies. Yet, the preaching of the gospel of the Kingdom of God is here and now on earth (Matthew 6:10,33; 24:14). Jesus' authority in Matthew 28:18 says that He received all authority in heaven and earth because He is King of God's Kingdom and Creation.

Ephesians 1:19-23 says, "And what *is* the exceeding greatness of His (Godhead's) power to us-ward who believe, according to the working of His mighty power, (20) Which He wrought in Christ, when He (Godhead) raised Him (Jesus Christ) from the dead, and set Him (Jesus Christ) at His (Godhead's) own right hand in the heavenly places, (21) Far above all principality, and power, and might, and dominion, and every name that is named, not only in this world, but also in that **which is to come:** (new heaven and new earth Revelation chap. 21) (22) And hath put all things under His (Christ Jesus') feet, and gave Him (Christ Jesus') to be the head over all things to the church (*Ekklesia*), (23) Which is His body (born again Believers), the fulness of Him (Godhead) that filleth all in all."

Since Believers are Jesus' kingdom kings, priests, lords, ambassadors, and soldiers (Daniel 2:37; Revelation 1:6; 1 Timothy 6:15; 2 Corinthians 5:20; 2 Timothy 2:3-4; Revelation 7:14; 19:16), then Believers have been given Jesus' authority as His representatives in a limited way to fulfill Believers' duties of being His witnesses here on earth (Acts 1:8) and making disciples of all nations (Matthew 28:19).

There must be order in the business that is established by the Believer Business Owners before God will pour out His manifold financial blessings, so none of the capital invested or good will is lost. The Believer Business Owners must establish cash flow security and cash flow management. The foundation work is done first in the natural then the spiritual (1 Corinthians 15:46). Once God's purpose and plan is given to the Believer Business Owner, then he or she must be about the business of obtaining the startup capital, forming a corporation or LLC, leasing a place for the business, setting up telephones, ordering products or the ingredients to make products, employing spiritual and competent Believer Business Employees with "at will" written agreements, with paragraphs to protect company secrets and no competition paragraphs, setting up websites, establishing a plan to acquire new customers and clients, taking steps to obtain a market share, hiring a company for payroll preparation, obtaining workers compensation insurance, seeking a liability insurance policy, and numerous other business start-up things to do which an experienced attorney and accountant can advise.

Then the scholastic teaching and kinesthetic training must begin with the Believer Business Employees, regarding topics such as biblical business principles, job promotion based upon humility, competence, work ethic, God's vision importance of servanthood, motivated by *agape* love, long term goals, understanding why continuous research and development are important, having a tight budget, targeting customers and clients, establishing strict rules for a safe workplace, and following all federal, state, and local secular laws governing businesses. Also, start reading with the employees verbally of the Bible daily, having daily prayer, discerning the spiritual maturity of each employee, establishing work assignments, selecting managers, enforcing of a strong work ethic, instituting the rule of no lying, no swearing, no stealing, no harassing and no arguing with other employees, and promoting good moral character.

With the establishment of order and function of the business by the Believer Business Owner, he or she ensures that each Believer Business Employee is cared for without any loss to the business. God's foundational order precedes God's blessing.

Remember, John 3:2 says, "Beloved, I wish above all things that thou mayest prosper and be in health, even as thy soul prospereth." Let the Lord receive all the glory and honor!

BIO OF DR. NOVA DEAN PACK

Dr. Nova Dean Pack was called into ministry as a young boy after his mother died at age 10. He taught Sunday School to other students his age and a little older. While he went to college and law school, he was inactive as a minister. Dr. Pack has been a Christian attorney at law since 1974 with his office currently in Ontario, California. As a lawyer, he specializes in business and estate planning.

Dr. Pack started seeking a stronger relationship with the Lord in 1979. In 1987, he started ministering the word of God in a local church that he attended and as a missionary during short turn around trips into Central America countries.

Dr. Pack was ordained by Dr. Chuck Flynn and Dr. Richard Maiden in 1992, and Dr. Pack's ministry was licensed with the Independent Assemblies of God International, Santa Ana, CA in 1993.

Dr. Pack produced a radio talk show entitled "Business in Ministry" in San Bernardino, Ca., from 1990 to 1993 where he taught business men and women how to make their businesses a place of ministry, with the obligation to activate their employees into ministry. In 1997 through 1998, Dr. Pack produced a daily radio program that aired in Riverside and San Bernardino Counties, California, where his numerous sermons became the subjects of radio broadcasts. He pioneered his own church and ministry for six years from 1993 through 1999 in Redlands, California.

Dr. Pack ministered to business owners as to how to make their businesses a ministry at various churches on Monday nights for one 50 lessons per year at each church. He especially focused on how to activate their employees as ministers. He also went to business owners' places of business to counsel them regarding wise decisions concerning finances, increasing customers, setting up cash flow management and cash flow security, and many other issues.

Dr. Pack is a prolific writer, having published five books to date, including this book. Also, he is an accomplished public minister who teaches under a strong anointing with great wisdom, knowledge, and understanding from the Bible how to practically apply biblical principles to life's issues. Dr. Pack has learned how to bring the dynamic of bringing the intellectual endeavor under the authority and anointing of the Holy Spirit. He has scholastically taught and kinesthetically trained many employees while working in his law office.

Dr. Pack oversees different ministries. He is also the attorney for the Independent Assemblies of God International, Santa Ana, CA, where he also is ordained.

Dr. Pack has traveled to several countries ministering to business owners, foreign governmental officials, bankers, lawyers, judges, and other leaders on how to make Biblical principles a reality in the affairs of business and governmental policies in their countries.

Currently, Dr. Pack has three podcasts, including Biblitarian Ministries, Holy Nation, and Activating Business Ministers that are on youtube.com, Facebook, and other streams.

www.ingramcontent.com/pod-product-compliance
Lightning Source LLC
Chambersburg PA
CBHW080853120626
46553CB00007B/2417
9798218875855